ARTIFICIAL INTELLIGENCE: human effects

ELLIS HORWOOD SERIES IN ARTIFICIAL INTELLIGENCE

Series Editor: Professor John Campbell, University of Exeter

COMPUTER GAME-PLAYING: Theory and Practice
Edited by M. A. BRAMER, The Open University, Milton Keynes
IMPLEMENTATIONS OF PROLOG
Edited by J. A. CAMPBELL, University of Exeter
PROGRESS IN ARTIFICIAL INTELLIGENCE
Edited by J. A. CAMPBELL, University of Exeter and L. STEELS, Vrije Universiteit, Brussels
MACHINE INTELLIGENCE 8: Machine Representations of Knowledge
Edited by E. W. ELCOCK, University of Western Ontario and D. MICHIE, University of Edinburgh
MACHINE INTELLIGENCE 9: Machine Expertise and the Human Interface
Edited by J. E. HAYES, D. MICHIE, University of Edinburgh and L. I. MIKULICH, Academy of Sciences, USSR
MACHINE INTELLIGENCE 10: Intelligent Systems: Practice and Perspective
Edited by J. E. HAYES, D. MICHIE, University of Edinburgh and Y.-H. PAO, Case Western Reserve University, Cleveland, Ohio
INTELLIGENT SYSTEMS: The Unprecedented Opportunity
Edited by J. E. HAYES and D. MICHIE, University of Edinburgh
MACHINE TRANSLATION: Past, Present and Future
W. J. HUTCHINS, University of East Anglia
AN INTRODUCTION TO PROLOG
L. SPACEK, University of Essex
AUTOMATIC NATURAL LANGUAGE PARSING
Edited by K. SPARCK JONES, University of Cambridge and Y. WILKS, University of Essex
THE MIND AND THE MACHINE: Philosophical Aspects of Artificial Intelligence
Edited by S. TORRANCE, Middlesex Polytechnic
LOGICS FOR ARTIFICIAL INTELLIGENCE
R. TURNER, University of Essex
COMMUNICATING WITH DATA BASES IN NATURAL LANGUAGE
M. WALLACE, ICL, Bracknell, Berks
NEW HORIZONS IN EDUCATIONAL COMPUTING
Edited by M. YAZDANI, University of Exeter
ARTIFICIAL INTELLIGENCE: Human Effects
Edited by M. YAZDANI and A. NARAYANAN, University of Exeter

ARTIFICIAL INTELLIGENCE: human effects

Editors:
MASOUD YAZDANI
and
AJIT NARAYANAN
Lecturers in Computer Science
Department of Computer Science
University of Exeter

ELLIS HORWOOD LIMITED
Publishers · Chichester
Halsted Press: a division of
JOHN WILEY & SONS
New York · Chichester · Brisbane · Toronto

First published in 1984
Reprinted in 1985 by

ELLIS HORWOOD LIMITED
Market Cross House, Cooper Street, Chichester, West Sussex, PO19 1EB, England

The publisher's colophon is reproduced from James Gillison's drawing of the ancient Market Cross, Chichester.

Distributors:

Australia, New Zealand, South-east Asia:
Jacaranda-Wiley Ltd., Jacaranda Press,
JOHN WILEY & SONS INC.,
G.P.O. Box 859, Brisbane, Queensland 40001, Australia

Canada:
JOHN WILEY & SONS CANADA LIMITED
22 Worcester Road, Rexdale, Ontario, Canada.

Europe, Africa:
JOHN WILEY & SONS LIMITED
Baffins Lane, Chichester, West Sussex, England.

North and South America and the rest of the world:
Halsted Press: a division of
JOHN WILEY & SONS
605 Third Avenue, New York, N.Y. 10016, U.S.A.

British Library Cataloguing in Publication Data
Artificial intelligence: human effects
(Ellis Horwood series in artificial intelligence)
1. Artificial intelligence
I. Yazdani, Masoud II. Narayanan, Ajit
001.53'5 Q335

Library of Congress Card No. 84-10934

ISBN 0–85312–577–5 (Ellis Horwood Limited – Library Edn.)
ISBN 0–85312–817–0 (Ellis Horwood Limited – Student Edn.)
ISBN 0–470–20092–8 (Halsted Press)

Typeset by Ellis Horwood Limited.
Printed in Great Britain by R.J. Acford, Chichester.

Contents

Preface

It is always a cause of curiosity how a compilation of papers like this is put together. Most such compilations are usually the result of an actual get together of people. That is, they are either the proceedings of a conference or symposium or at least based on one or the other.

This collection is, however, not based around such a meeting but is the result of meetings between pairs of people, extensive amounts of correspondence over the last three years between the editors and contributors, as well as between the contributors themselves. In short, it is a paper symposium. A number of contributors take issue with fellow contributors. What the book offers is a debate and not a consensus, a debate conducted in the orderly fashion of individuals writing to each other rather than shouting at each other. Some would argue that if such an orderly debate still does not lead to a consensus then the debate itself has been a waste of time. Others would go further and say there is no point in considering the social, philosophical and educational implications of artificial intelligence or any new technology as such considerations are not going to change the effects. The editors of this volume feel otherwise, however. Consideration of the implications of research and development in any area of technology would have a strong influence on the methodology used by researchers, as well as effect the concept of success. A technologically successful system which would only benefit a very small group whilst having disastrous effects for others would not be labelled a success by a socially responsible scientist.

We, the editors, have refrained from imposing a conclusion or a sense of consensus upon the book because it was clear that such agreement was not possible at this stage in the development of artificial intelligence, and mainly because most interesting possibilities might remain only possibilities and never see the light of day.

We hope to have put most arguments for and against, to have discussed most of the possible effects and most of the potential of artificial intelligence clearly in the pages that follow. We welcome correspondence from interested readers upon the topics raised in the book.

If we are considered partially successful in our attempts here, some credit should go to Mrs Marlene Teague, without whose secretarial support we would have got nowhere. She also compiled the extensive bibliography of the book. Roy Davies (for the index) and Pam Lings (for proof reading) deserve credit, too. The inadequacies, however, remain the responsibility of the editors.

Masoud Yazdani
Ajit Narayanan
May, 1984

Introduction: What is Artificial Intelligence?

During the last 25 years the discipline of artificial intelligence (AI for short) has been growing on the map of science, somewhere between psychology and computer science. This is due to the fact that researchers in this field are preoccupied with the task of making computers do things which, if done by human beings, would require intelligence.

There is no clear definition (as there is for physics or chemistry) for AI. There are many reasons for this. The most important one is that several different groups with drastically different motivations all claim to be working in AI. Each group favours one definition above the others.

However, the most widely accepted is Minsky's '. . . artificial intelligence is the science of making machines do things that would require intelligence if done by men' [1]. We can recognise some of the different trends in AI and the reasons behind them by asking: 'Making machines do these things, but to what end?'

The answer would differ between people working in different areas of AI and sometimes even between people working on the same topic but in different institutions. One group would justify its actions on the grounds that the result would be better, more useful, machines. At the other end of the spectrum, another group would argue that it is not interested in the machine but is using it as a tool to understand human beings better.

We can, however, identify three distinct definitions of AI resulting from different motivations or backgrounds. In order to see the point, consider a class of objects which we would regard as intelligent, e.g. cats, dogs, people and Martians. Outside this class, we have such unintelligent things as tables, chairs and, currently, digital computers (see Fig. 1).

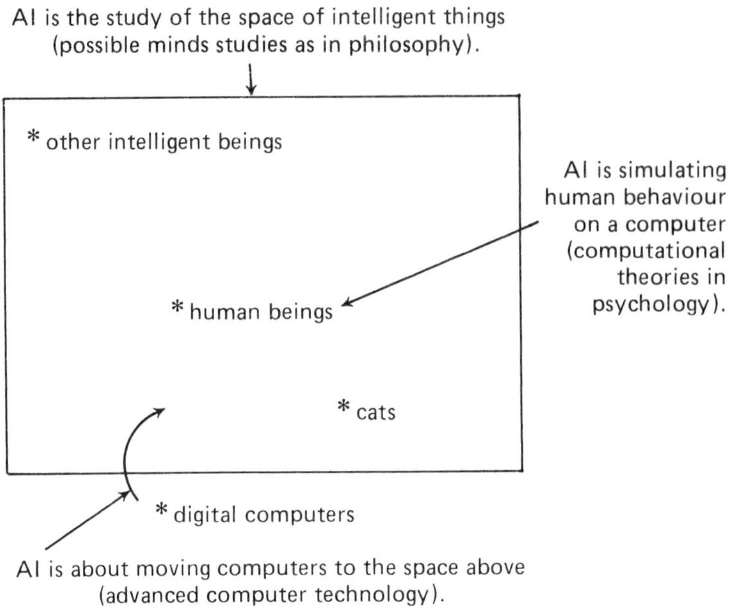

Fig. 1

Group 1 would answer the question by saying that 'AI is about moving computers into the space above (advanced computer technology)'. Group 2 would say 'AI is simulating human behaviour and cognitive processes on a computer (computational theories in psychology)'. Group 3's answer would concern the study of the nature of the whole space of intelligent minds. Two compilations of papers [3, 4] containing the early work on AI present arguments in favour of one or other, or mixture, of the above three answers from a fair sample of AI researchers (see Fig. 1).

As can be easily noted, each of the above three camps borders one of the three established areas of: computer science, psychology and philosophy. However, early work in AI has basically been of an exploratory nature. The initial concern of AI researchers has been with finding possible ways of doing intelligent things. Therefore, early AI work, however much it is claimed otherwise, has addressed a different field from that of psychology [2]. Where psychology is concerned with the actual way people do things, AI has been attempting to map out the possible ways that those things can be done on a computer.

Although AI has not yet finished its initial task of exploration, it has become a source of theories for psychologists. This attention has affected AI, in return, towards a change of emphasis in favour of cognitive simulation, whereby the striving to produce possible intelligent artefacts is constrained by the need to make them operate in a similar fashion to that of a human being.

CAN A MACHINE THINK?

There is no great philosophical problem in saying that a machine can 'think'. The use of quotes around psychological terms will show that we are using them metaphorically. The problem arises if we are to remove the quotation marks and apply the terms in a way which blurs the distinctions between humans and machines.

Turing's criterion to warrant such a blurring of distinction was presented in a form of a test called an 'Imitation Game':

> I propose to consider the question, 'can machines think?'. . . I shall replace the question by another. . . The new form of the problem can be described in terms of a game which we call the 'imitation game'. It is played with three people, a man (A), a woman (B), and an interrogator (C) who may be of either sex. The object of the game for the interrogator is to determine which of the other two is the man and which is the woman. (Turing [5])

We now ask the questions 'What will happen when a machine takes the part of A in this game? Will the interrogator decide wrongly as often when the game is played like this, as he does when the game is played between man and woman?' These questions replace our original question, 'can machines think?'

In 1973, Colby, Hilf, Weber and Kramer [6] published the results of their trying a Turing-like indistinguishability test with their PARRY program. That program is a computer simulation which exhibits behaviour similar to human paranoia patients. The psychiatrists who judged the computer versus the patients failed to distinguish the computer accurately and it is claimed that the test had succeeded. However, this leaves a large number of questions unanswered as well as casting a good deal of doubt on the applicability of the Turing test. PARRY, while successful at pretending to be paranoid, was not helpful in understanding paranoia, which would have been an obvious benefit. The test therefore seems to have told us more about psychiatrists than computers or paranoia!

The issue of the criterion of successful AI is still an open question and is considered in more detail in Parts 5 and 6 of this book.

AI AND COMPUTER TECHNOLOGY

A source of influence on AI has been the attitude of the sponsoring organisations. In the USA, the exploratory phase of AI research has been generously sponsored, and now AI is expected to produce results rather than exploration. In the UK, where, thanks to the Lighthill Report [7] sponsorship of AI research has been rather strict, a turning point has been reached. The Alvey Report [8] suggests rather generous support for areas of AI work where medium-term results are considered possible. This second source of influence has affected AI, towards a change of emphasis in favour of building useful computing systems.

The initial phase of AI research has led to a general realisation that world knowledge lies behind human ability and intelligent behaviour. AI, in its attempt to produce intelligent behaviour on a computer, is limited by the amount of knowledge about people's general knowledge. Other disciplines, such as psychology, have not been able to provide AI with an explicit exposition of the general knowledge that people show in their behaviour. Owing to this problem, some attention is focused on the form of behaviour which most appropriately should be called intellectual behaviour. This is the kind of knowledge which a professional expert has. Such domains are already well defined and well documented in professional journals. Law, citizens' advice, geological and mechanical expertise are easily separable from the whole wealth of general human knowledge.

The attempt to deal with only a small bandwidth of human knowledge reduces the complexity of the task faced by an AI researcher and enables him to offer a working system to users on a reasonable time scale, while major problems of intelligence remain long-term research objectives.

We can view AI's apparant failure in the eyes of people such as Lighthill [7] by the fact that it attempts to wage a war against the whole domain of human intelligence. As a result, AI achievements are spread over a large domain, but are thin on the ground, as in Fig. 2.

Fig. 2

We can also view the apparent success of expert systems which do not attempt to wage a war but are fighting small easy-to-win battles. The effort is therefore successful in reaching an eye-catching depth but in a very narrow domain, as in Fig. 3.

Fig. 3

Many AI researchers hope that the result of these small successes will also help the long-term battle against the mysteries of human thought processes in general.

WHAT CAN COMPUTERS DO?

The work in AI takes place in a number of areas: visual perception, robotics, speech understanding, language understanding, expert systems, automatic programming, game playing . . . . A large number of introductory textbooks [9–12] are available for interested readers who would like to know more about the research achievements in the field. Further, a number of other books [13, 14] look at AI work so far in a very critical way. Some readers might like to complement their reading of this book with other textbooks such as *The Handbook of Artificial Intelligence* [10], or other easily available books, for more technical information.

Masoud Yazdani

NOTES

[1] Minsky (1968b).
[2] Hayes (in this volume).
[3] Feigenbaum and Feldman (1963).
[4] Johnson-Laird and Wason (1977).
[5] Turing (1950) reprinted in [3].
[6] Colby, Hilf, Wever and Kramer (1973).
[7] Lighthill (1972).
[8] Alvey (1982).
[9] Boden (1977).
[10] Barr and Feigenbaum (1981–1982) 3 volumes.
[11] O'Shea and Eisenstadt (1984).
[12] Winston (1977); 2nd edition (1984).
[13] Dreyfus (1972); 2nd edition (1979).
[14] Weizenbaum (1976); new edition (1984).
For details, see the bibliography at the end of the book.

P.S. For clarification, some readers may be interested in an analogy between the think objects of Fig. 1 and flying objects. For centuries, birds were the ultimate flying object as humans are the ultimate thinking objects today. The notion that a machine made out of beer cans could fly was as unintelligible to many as the notion of a thinking machine made out of beer cans is to many today. Aircraft fly differently from birds, and future flying saucers from outer-space may fly differently from aircraft. What is important is that the science of aerodynamics explains both bird flight as well as aircraft flight. In my view, the science of AI is comparable to that of aerodynamics when we consider the space of thinking objects. AI could stand for 'Aerodynamics of Intelligence'.

PART 1

AI, MEDICINE AND LAW

The best way to introduce the legal and medical aspects of AI is by means of fictional case studies. Let us first examine the relationship between computers and law.

Imagine the following situations (all fictional and perhaps not very plausible!).

SITUATION 1

John Smith lives in Manchester and needs to hire a car to take him down to Heathrow Airport for a flight abroad. He finds a car-hire firm in Manchester which will allow him to leave the car at its depot in Heathrow, so he does not have to worry about returning the car to the source depot in Manchester. It has been several years since John Smith hired a car so, after a telephone call to the firm's depot in Manchester to reserve the car, he is surprised to find a computerised hiring system running in the depot's office when he turns up on the morning of the appropriate day. The receptionist enters details of John Smith's driving licence and other details into a computer by means of a keyboard and, after handing over a cheque for £25.00 as a deposit, John Smith drives to Heathrow Airport in the rented car.

At Heathrow, he returns the car to the firm's depot. There the receptionist enters the car's registration number, which causes a display on the VDU in front of her of all the details of John Smith's hiring transaction. The receptionist also enters the milometer reading, and a high-speed printer then prints out an invoice. The bill comes to £18.00 and the receptionist hands John Smith £7.00 back, since he had already paid a £25.00 deposit. As far as John Smith is concerned, the transaction is over, and he catches his flight out of the country.

Several months later, John Smith, by now back in Manchester, has again to catch a flight out of the country from Heathrow Airport. He remembers the name of the car-hire firm he used the last time and books a car by telephone for the appropriate day. On the day, he turns up at the Manchester depot and hands over his licence to the receptionist in the office. The receptionist enters the driving licence number, but then she looks worriedly at the screen, which John Smith cannot see. She tries entering the driving licence details again, but she still looks worried. Finally, she turns to John Smith and hands back his licence, saying: 'I'm sorry, sir, we have made a mistake. There are no cars available for hire today.'

John Smith is astonished. 'But I reserved a car over the telephone a few days ago,' he exclaims. 'There was no problem then.' 'I'm sorry, sir,' repeats the receptionist, 'There are no cars available for hire today.' John Smith looks at his watch. There are still 10 hours to go before he has to book in at Heathrow Airport. He looks through the office window and sees several hire cars parked on the forecourt. He decides to pursue the affair. 'What about those cars?' he asks, pointing to the row of parked cars. 'They look available to me.' The receptionist says nothing. 'And why did you ask me for my driving licence if you knew there were no cars?' he demands. 'I'm sorry,' the receptionist replies, 'We have made a mistake.'

John Smith decides to dig in his heels. 'I want to see the Manager,' he says. 'I'll see whether he is available,' says the receptionist, picking up a telephone receiver beside her. She contacts the manager and tells him that 'a Mr Smith' wants to see him, concerning 'Code 99'. She puts down the receiver and tells John Smith: 'Please wait over there.' She points to some seats in the corner of the office. 'The manager will be with you in a few minutes.'

John Smith sits down, somewhat confused. Whilst he is waiting, a young woman enters the office. 'I say,' she says to the receptionist, 'I know this is a bit sudden, but could I possibly hire a car to go to Glasgow today. I'm afraid that I haven't reserved one.' 'Oh, that's alright,' says the receptionist, 'We have a spare car.' 'Super,' says the young woman, and in the presence of John Smith the hiring transaction is completed and the young woman drives away in one of the cars which were parked on the forecourt. 'So there are cars available,' John Smith says to the receptionist. The receptionist looks embarrassed. 'The manager will be here shortly,' she replies.

The manager then enters and talks to the receptionist. He then walks over to John Smith. 'May I see your driving licence, please?' he asks. John Smith hands it over. The manager then walks across to the computer terminal and enters the driving licence number. He looks at the screen. He then walks over to John Smith and says: 'I'm sorry, sir, but we cannot hire you a car.' When John Smith starts demanding a reason, the manager points to a sign on the wall behind the receptionist's desk which says: 'The management reserve the right to refuse service to any customer.'

By now John Smith is fed up. So he collects his driving licence and walks out of the office, determined never to go to this particular car-hire firm again. Besides, there are other car-hire firms in Manchester. After a quick look through the telephone-book, he rings another car-hire firm. He checks that they have a depot at Heathrow Airport (they do) and that they have an available car (they have). He walks quickly to the depot. When he hands over his driving licence to the receptionist, he notices that she too has a terminal. His heart starts beating faster as she enters the details of his driving licence into the computer. He can tell by the look on her face as she examines the screen what is going to happen. Sure enough, the receptionist hands back his driving licence and says: 'I'm sorry, sir, but we have made a mistake. There are no cars for hire.' John Smith bends over the desk and peers at the screen. Displayed next to his name on the screen is 'Code 99'. He looks at the wall behind the desk and sees the sign, 'The management reserve the right to refuse service to any customer.' He sighs and leaves.

John Smith hires a taxi to take him to the railway-station where he has to buy an expensive first-class single ticket to Euston Station (no room left in second-class). He hires a taxi at Euston Station to take him to Heathrow and just manages to catch his flight. During his journey he has plenty of time to ruminate. Why was he being refused service by car-hire firms? He had done nothing wrong in his previous car-hire transaction. His cheque had not bounced, and he had returned the car in exactly the same condition as it was in when he had hired it at Manchester. His driving licence still had 30 years to run, and he had no convictions. Nor had he had any accidents in his driving life. What upset him most was that no reasons were being given as to why he was refused service.

He happens to tell his neighbouring passenger on the flight his story. His neighbouring passenger just happens, coincidentally, to be a computer programmer who was part of a team of programmers who had written a software package for use by car-hire firms. The programmer tells John Smith that the program is written in such a way that if a returned car is found to have some parts missing, say, the radio, or if some parts have been exchanged, then the car-hire firm could insert the information that the immediately previous customer was not to be hired any more cars. The car-hire company would prefer this action rather than starting lengthy court proceedings which might end in a failure to gain a conviction and which therefore might cost the company a lot of money in legal costs. The details of that person's driving licence were placed in a special file that was checked each time a customer transaction began, and the message 'Code 99' was sent back to the receptionist if the customer was not to be served. The programmer had not heard of car-hire firms which had bought the software package sharing a list of customers not to be served, but did not see any practical difficulties in this. The programmer also suggested that the system worked only if cars were checked immediately after they were returned by one of the car-hire firm's mechanics. Sometimes, this was not always done, as he understood it, and if no mechanic had checked John Smith's car from his first (and only) transaction before it was hired to him, then it was quite possible for John Smith to be held responsible for any parts that went missing or were swapped in the transaction previous to his.

John Smith is convinced that this was what had happened. Several weeks later, though, on the flight back to the United Kingdom from abroad, John Smith is sitting next to a businessman, who, when told of John Smith's story and the conversation with the programmer, informs John Smith that, no matter what the programmer had said, the most likely cause was a 'program error'. In the experience of the businessman, he had come across literally dozens of cases where programs he was using misclassified information, output incorrect results and, yes, had even labelled some people as bad debtors when in fact they were excellent creditors. The businessman found it difficult to believe that the car-hire firm would not take the utmost care in inspecting their cars as soon as they had been returned. After all, it took just one story such as John Smith's to generate enough bad publicity to drive away potential customers.

John Smith is thoroughly confused by now. On arriving at Heathrow, he attempts to hire a car to take him back to Manchester. He is refused a hire-car. He takes the train back to Manchester. What should he now do? What can he do?

Let us examine what John Smith should do. Ideally, he should be able to discover whether he is on some form of computer-held blacklist so that he can decide on his next move.

This he should be able to do by writing to the head office of the car-hire firm (where, presumably, the central computer is located), asking for details of any information held on him by the car-hire firm. The firm should reply honestly with the requested information. Moreover, the information held on him should be easily interpretable. Imagine what it would be like if the car-hire firm replied by sending back a print-out containing only 0s and 1s and declaring that this was all the information they had on him, in binary form.

Next, if John Smith discovers that his name is on the firm's blacklist, he should be able to ask why his name was put there. An answer to this question will depend on the computer system, or perhaps some office clerk, saving the reason for John Smith being put on a blacklist in the first place. That is, it is not sufficient for John Smith deciding on his next move that his name does occur on the blacklist. In addition, information must also be kept as to why his name was put there in the first place, so that John Smith can try to show that the reasons are unjustified.

So far, the fact that a computer system is involved has played no significant part in the proceedings. That is, even if the car-hire firm had only a manual system for hiring out cars, preparing invoices, and maintaining a blacklist, John Smith, it could be argued, should still be able to receive the above information. But now we come to a more worrying aspect. It appears that the blacklist is circulated among many car-hire firms. If manual systems were employed, the circulation and maintenance of such a blacklist would probably be prohibitively expensive. If one car-hire firm wishes to communicate with other car-hire firms that a certain customer is not to be trusted, several hundred photocopies of the list will be required for distribution to other car-hire firms. This makes life very difficult for the secretaries of a car-hire firm who one morning may receive a dozen or so such blacklists from other car-hire firms and who then have to merge this new information with existing blacklists. To overcome the flood of information, the car-hire firms may form a Society of Car Hire Firms with a central office. Individual car-hire firms would send one copy of their blacklist to this central office which then has the task of distributing up-to-date lists to all member firms, say, once a week. But now imagine the poor receptionist having visually to scan an ever-increasing piece of paper each time a hire transaction is started, to check whether the customer's name or driving-licence details appear on the list. Expensive mistakes could easily be made. The chances are that many car-hire firms, rather than trying to circulate blacklists manually, would prefer to keep their own internal blacklist and accept the occasional loss (passing it onto the honest customers, perhaps?).

But the introduction of a computer, as well as enabling car-hire firms to cut down their losses by identifying previous customers who removed items from their cars, or turned the milometer back, or dropped some stones into the petrol tank to make it appear that there was more petrol in the car than there actually is when the car is returned, and so on, allows the communication, maintenance, and use of blacklists to be very efficiently achieved. Car-hire firms would be very tempted to share their blacklists electronically by, say, a telephone line, or by allowing all depots of all car-hire firms access to one central computer which maintains the blacklist. This may be a laudable practice in that the honest customers do not have to pay as much as they did in the past for dishonest customers' deeds. However, if John Smith was mistakenly put onto a blacklist in a manual system, the chances are that the mistake is contained within the above-mentioned confines of the manual system. John Smith could go to another car-hire firm, after the first refused him service in the mistaken belief that he had previously defrauded the firm. If John Smith is mistakenly put onto a computerised blacklist which is then electronically circulated, the mistake is now no longer contained and John Smith may find it impossible to hire a car again, anywhere in the world.

Also, if car-hire firms are tempted to share this blacklist, other firms, such as finance companies and insurance companies, may also be tempted to obtain copies of the blacklist so that they can check whether any of their clients cannot be trusted. Pretty soon, John Smith may find that he is not being accepted as a bona fide customer by a lot of firms, all because of a simple mistake in a car-hire transaction.

So, the introduction of a computer into our story has two major implications. First, electronic sharing of information by firms in one business area (such as car-hire firms) will be relatively easy. Secondly, the information on an individual could be disseminated well beyond the area which gave rise to the information in the first place, thereby affecting the individual in different areas of business. It is partly for these reasons that data protection, or data privacy, legislation is considered highly desirable. In the perfect world of perfect computers and perfect humans who do not make mistakes, the debate would mainly concern the justification for storing information on individuals in the first place or the necessity of keeping information confidential. But, in the practical world, safeguards are also required for making sure that, if erroneous information does enter the data-base, such information can be easily identified and corrected. The individual who has erroneous information stored about him or her is probably the best person to identify its incorrectness. After all, who better to identify that John Smith did not take a radio out of a hired car than John

Smith himself? But this means that John Smith must have access to the information in the first place.

Ideally, John Smith should be able to receive the information that he is on some blacklist and the reasons for his being put there in the first place. Also, even if there is no blacklist, John Smith should still be able to receive the erroneous information that he hired a car in Manchester on the 27th April 1984, when in fact he was abroad at the time. That is, John Smith should have access to all information being held on him by the car-hire firm's computer, even though the information may not concern blacklists at all.

Even 'unimportant' information may contain errors, and John Smith should be aware of these errors. Unimportant but incorrect information may become subsequently important in different contexts. Ideally, John Smith should be able to demand that the incorrect information be changed. However, firms will argue that before information is changed, some evidence or proof concerning the erroneousness of the information should be provided. In the case of a transaction that never took place, some simple evidence showing that John Smith was in another part of the world on the day in question will probably suffice. In the case of alleged theft from a hired car, the evidence or proof that John Smith did not take, say, a radio, may be more difficult to provide. In such a case, it should be left to the car-hire firm to provide the evidence to show that John Smith *did* steal the radio, or that the radio was stolen during the period when John Smith was responsible for the car. The point here is that this switching of the burden of proof should ensure that the car-hire firm goes through a proper set of check procedures when a car is returned and before an individual's name goes onto the blacklist.

Next, since the car-hire firm has a blacklist of individuals suspected of theft, the fact that it is only suspicion and not fact that is being stored should make it illegal for this blacklist to be shared amongst other car-hire firms. It could also be argued that if the blacklist contained facts, say, names of individuals previously convicted of stealing from hired cars, even then the information should not be shared. That is, it does not matter in the slightest whether the information in the computer's data-banks represents facts or represents suspicions: it should not be conveyed to any other organisation whatsoever. It should be the legal responsibility of a company, firm, organisation, or individual, which or who stored computerised information, to ensure that no other outside company, firm, organisation or individual has access to this information. If this appears to be overstating the case, and hence undesirable, then some very clear criterion or principle is required to separate information which can be shared ('facts') from information which cannot ('suspicions'), provided that it is considered wrong to allow a car-hire firm to share (with other car-hire firms) its suspicions concerning John Smith's alleged theft, without proof or evidence.

As can be seen from the above, the introduction of computers does not raise any new or complex legal problems which could not be raised before. However, the inefficiency of manually maintained information systems has as a matter of fact delimited the dangers inherent in such systems. The recent explosion in the use of computers in nearly all facets of business, commerce and finance has made it very much more important that the social, moral, political and, especially, legal aspects of information systems be urgently reviewed. There do exist a variety of data protection or data privacy laws in different countries. The interesting point is that they vary in their strength and power from one country to another, depending on the initial set of goals or ideals adopted by the relevant governments. So, even before deciding what John Smith can do when he suspects he is on some blacklist shared electronically by car-hire firms, we must first decide what John Smith should be able to do. As we see from the above case study, this may not be a simple matter, since we need to investigate the rights of individuals, the amount of privacy they are expected to have in the modern state, their interaction with groups of individuals called 'firms', and the way information on them is collected, stored and disseminated.

SITUATION 2a

John Smith is shaving himself at eight one morning when his hand slips and he cuts his neck very badly with his blade. He is rushed to hospital. At the reception area, a young receptionist takes various details from him and enters the information through a terminal into the hospital's computerised data-banks. John Smith has bandages put around the wound and is told that he will be kept for a few hours in the hospital until he has recovered sufficient strength to go home. He is given a bed and, suitably impressed by the quick and efficient service he has received, he dozes. The time is 10 a.m. At 3.30 p.m., he is woken up by a sharp pain in his right arm. He glances around and finds several white-coated attendants around him. 'Don't worry, Mr Smith,' says one, 'You won't feel a thing.' John looks down at his right arm to find a syringe being removed by one of the attendants. 'Just a minute,' says John, 'What is happening? My name is John Smith. What are you going to do to me?' 'Now, now, Mr Smith,' replies one of the attendants, 'We don't want to tire ourselves, do we?' Before John can say any more, he falls into a deep sleep.

When John wakes up the next morning, he finds that his head is wrapped in bandages. After further enquiries, he discovers that he has been through a long and dangerous operation to widen the arteries that take blood to the brain. It was not until well into the operation that the surgeon suspected that John was not the right patient, and the operation was terminated once it was discovered that there was another John Smith admitted that same morning, who should have had the operation. Through a 'clerical error', the two John Smiths had been confused, and the wrong one was operated on.

The wrongly-operated-on John Smith decided to sue someone, but whom should he sue? The surgeon, because the surgeon should have made a more thorough check on the identity of a patient before commencing an operation? The attendants, because it was they who wheeled John into the operating-room, it was they who administered the drug, and it was they who should have made a proper identification? The receptionist, who when asked by the attendants in which bed John Smith could be found gave the wrong bed number after consulting the hospital computer's data-banks? Should she have checked whether there was more than one John Smith in the hospital?

Fortunately for John, his solicitors had a simple answer. 'Sue the hospital,' they told him, 'and let the hospital sort out internally who is responsible.'

Now the interesting aspect from our point of view is that the hospital denied liability, claiming that a subsequent investigation of their computer system showed that the patient-entry program which they had bought off the shelf from a well-known software company failed to warn its user should two or more people with the same name be registered in the hospital at the same time. Experiments showed that in such cases the more recently registered patient's name was always returned as an answer to queries based on name only, and the bleeding John Smith was a more recent entry than the to-be-operated-on John Smith. Now that the hospital knew about this defect, they had modified the system so that two or more patients with the same name would never be confused. But the hospital, the defence lawyers claimed, could not be held responsible for a defect which would have been spotted only by an experienced and expert computer programmer.

We now change the case study to the following.

SITUATION 2b

John Smith is shaving himself one morning when his hand encounters a swollen gland in his neck. 'Funny,' thinks John Smith, 'I hadn't noticed that before.' He finishes shaving and goes to see his doctor to find out what the swollen gland is caused by. The doctor makes John Smith an appointment to see a specialist and, after an X-ray, a shadow is found on one of John Smith's lungs. After tests on John's blood, the specialist diagnoses a cancerous growth, and radiotherapy treatment is started. John's hair falls out during the treatment and he is left in a weak state after three weeks of radiotherapy. A further scan is made, as are more tests, and it is discovered that John Smith did not have a cancerous growth at all but a form of tuberculosis. John Smith is prescribed four pills every day and he soon recovers, although he is left in a weak state.

John Smith goes to see his solicitors about the possibility of suing the specialist for faulty diagnosis and subsequent hardship. The specialist disclaims liability on the grounds that he used a computerised expert system for diagnosing John's symptoms from blood samples and that the expert system had placed a cancer of the lung as the most likely cause after the results of the initial tests had been fed into it. The computerised expert system had been used extensively by the specialist prior to John Smith's case, and John Smith's case was the first to give rise to a diagnosis that was subsequently shown to be incorrect. Further investigation of the system showed that, in the case of John Smith, re-ordering the rules of the expert system by swapping just two of the system's thousand or so rules would have led to tuberculosis being placed above cancer as the most likely cause, but the specialist, not being an experienced expert system analyst, could not be expected to know this. In any case, there was no guarantee that swapping the two rules would not lead to future faulty diagnosis.

The legal aspects of both cases may appear to be similar. That is, one could imagine the same types of question arising when the two cases reach the court, such as 'Should the (hospital/specialist) have used a computerised system without a prior, detailed investigation using test data that might have brought the alleged 'defects' to light?', 'Should the (receptionist/specialist) have performed further enquiries of the (data-base/expert system) before giving (the bed-number/a diagnosis) to the (attendants/patient)?', 'Was John Smith told when he (entered the hospital/saw the specialist) that a computer was being used (to enter his registration data/to diagnose his symptoms) so that he could himself ask for further checks to be made?', and so on.

However, it can be argued that there are serious differences between the two cases, and the nature of the difference resides in the nature of the computer programs. In the first case, the computer program is used to record patient entry to the hospital and is designed to ease and improve administration and management functions. The program will probably be written in COBOL, or Pascal, or FORTRAN, or BASIC, and the essential characteristic of these languages is that a program written in such a language will consist of a series of 'commands' one after another. A simple way to describe the behaviour of computer systems executing these programs is 'The computer will do only what it is told to do.'

In the second case, the 'computer program' is used to simulate the knowledge of an expert (or many experts) in a certain domain and to provide diagnoses that are as reliable as, or perhaps even more reliable than, its human counterpart. Such a 'program' will probably be written in Prolog, or LOGLISP, LISP, POP-11, or POPLOG, or in some language where the essential feature is that the 'commands' generate, evaluate and delete very many inferences. Also, the 'commands' may generate, evaluate and delete other commands which generate, evaluate and delete inferences. These inferences are generated by the nature of any input information, by the commands and by the nature of other inferences. Although it is probably correct, in some sense, to say that the computer can do only what it is told to do, the behaviour of a computer system executing such a 'program' may not be easily predicted by humans, or it may prove to be too difficult for humans to predict the behaviour of such 'programs'.

In the first case, the program's commands are static and given. In the second case, the program's commands, although static at the time of purchase, may soon change and modify themselves, depending on the environment in which they are used. In the first case, it is relatively easy to check for corruption of the program statements. But what counts as corruption in the second case?

Expert systems are 'programs' that are described as having a data or knowledge-base and a set of inference rules. In most cases, the inference rules are probabilistic in that they do not generate necessarily valid inferences but inferences valid with a certain degree or probability. The reliability of probabilistic expert systems will depend to some extent on the probabilistic models used as well as on the nature of the inference rules themselves.

There is currently little agreement on precisely what an expert system is or how 'expert system' can be defined. In addition to the various characterisations of expert systems ('programs' written in certain computer languages, 'programs' representing the data in a particular way (e.g. relations), programs that 'declare' what to do by means of 'if . . . then . . .' rules, computer systems that have a certain architecture (e.g. inference engine plus knowledge base), 'programs' that modify themselves, and so on), there is also the informal characterisation that an expert system must be capable of producing conclusions which can surprise a human expert in the field, at least on first inspection, but which turn out to be correct on more detailed examination [1].

AI sceptics, on the other hand, point to dearth of good quality and generally available expert systems. Apart from the well-known MYCIN, PROSPECTOR and DENDRAL expert systems, which function in the domains of blood infections, geological surveying, and spectral analysis of chemical compounds, respectively, and all of which have been available for several years, there is actually very little else in the way of well-known, reliable, and generally available expert systems. Such sceptics believe that existing systems are 'one-off' affairs and that there does not exist a recognisable and generalisable expert system methodology. Time will tell.

The differences between commercial packages designed to ease administrative functions and expert systems will be crucial in law, since the question of who is liable for a computer program may well depend on the type of program it is. In the former case, the authors of the program are responsible, ultimately, for faulty code or for not meeting design specifications, unless they can prove that the customer used the program for a purpose for which it was not intended. In the latter, the authors of an expert system could claim that the inference rules they used were taken out of the existing literature or were extracted from human experts themselves, and so they cannot be held responsible for faulty knowledge. They could also claim that the specialist using a probabilistic expert system may have entered wrong values for the strength of his belief in certain measurements. For instance, if the expert system asks questions of the form 'How certain are you that . . . (in the range 1–9)?' and if the specialist responded with 9 when he should have responded with 1, then faulty diagnosis may occur.

Again, it is not as if the concept of expert systems is raising completely new questions in law which could not be raised before. Rather, the recent growth of interest in such systems makes it important that the legal aspects concerning the use of such systems be urgently reviewed.

Ajit Narayanan

NOTES

[1] Private communication from Professor J. A. Campbell.

The papers in this section all assume, in varying degrees, that there is a major and important difference in the types of computerised system portrayed in 2a and 2b above.

Hunter discusses the complex nature of human medical decision-making and the ways in which the decision-making process can be modelled on a computer.

His conclusions are that better interaction is required between an expert system and its human user if expert medical computers are to have a major impact and that a human element will still be required in the caring of patients no matter how automated or computerised the intellectual skills of human experts become.

There may be no cause for concern as long as computerised expert systems perform adequately. Campbell is concerned with the legal ramifications of a faulty diagnosis made by a human who has used a computerised expert system. Who is to blame? Campbell's suggestion is that, because of the complex nature of such systems and their novelty, no one should be held legally responsible. The advantage of this suggestion is that not only will research in and market acceptance of expert systems be encouraged, but also long legal battles, which could cost the state millions of pounds, will not be required. However, the state must be prepared to set up a 'no-fault' scheme.

Narayanan and Perrott examine the legal 'position' of computers given current views in jurisprudence on legal entities. Can a computer have legal rights? Can it have legal duties? Their answer is that there is nothing in the concept of 'legal entity' that prevents computers which perform in certain areas beneficial to humans from being considered as legal entities.

The aim of this part of the book is to show not only how computers can be of great help in medicine but also that their use in this domain will almost certainly have serious consequences, legally speaking.

The expert medical computer

J. R. W. Hunter University of Sussex UK

Anyone dipping into the literature on artificial intelligence in general, or expert systems in particular, will come across many references to the application of AI techniques within the field of medicine. Indeed, there are so many such references that the reader might be forgiven for coming to the conclusion that these techniques are in daily routine clinical use.

It turns out that very few AI-based medical systems are actually so used; it is difficult to say exactly how many, how real and how routine the use. However, 'very few' probably means two or three.

There are many reasons why this might be so, and some of the problems are attendant upon the introduction of any new technology. But it does seem clear that the technology itself is deficient in some respects – and these deficiencies will be examined in some detail in a later section. Firstly, though, we need to appreciate the complex nature of medical decision-making and to discuss why it poses significant problems for AI researchers. We will then look at some of the existing AI systems in this field, and consider some of the deficiencies referred to above. It will then be appropriate for us to discuss the implications which AI systems might have for the medical profession, for patients and for society at large.

Computers are used in several ways in medicine. Many administrative and financial record-keeping systems are currently entrusted to computer systems; this is of no real interest here, as there is little that is different from standard business practice. The computerisation of medical records is much less advanced; such records include individual patients' case notes, the results of laboratory tests, and so on. The problem here is that it is very difficult to codify in a consistent and generally agreed fashion the wide range of terms used in medical practice. Other uses for computers include their incorporation in imaging systems such as CAT scanners and gamma cameras, their use in calculating radiation doses in radiotherapy treatment planning, and the automation of some laboratory instruments.

Some of these uses have aroused controversy – the perceived problem of confidentiality in record-keeping systems and the high capital costs of CAT scanners. But, in general, such systems do not trespass on the intellectual functions which most doctors would regard as being most vital to their role – eliciting signs and symptoms, making diagnoses, deciding on tests and treatment and monitoring patient progress.

It is in this area that AI (and other) computer-based advice-giving systems seek to function, and it is arguably this use of computers in medicine that has the potential for bringing about the greatest change.

THE NATURE OF MEDICAL DECISION-MAKING

Most AI programs seek to reproduce the conclusions reached by expert medical decision-makers (and possibly aspects of the decision-making process itself); it is therefore appropriate to look at some of the characteristics of this process. It is not difficult to say what happens; in very simplistic terms, a doctor sees a patient, decides what might be wrong, decides what treatment is appropriate (if any), decides what laboratory investigations (e.g. blood tests, X-rays, etc.) need to be performed, and monitors the patient's return to health, revising his previous decisions in the light of further developments. Note that this is already a somewhat distorted view of the overall job of the medical generalist (general practitioner in the UK), who may well spend large parts of his time in deciding whether a treatable medical condition is present at all, practising preventive medicine, counselling, monitoring the course of any untreatable diseases in chronically ill patients, referring patients to specialists and so on. In fact, the way in which most AI programs view medical decision-making is more appropriate to the activities of the more specialist hospital doctor.

Even within this limited framework, we are venturing into little known territory in trying to establish *how* medical decision-making takes place. As Kassirer *et al.* [1] point out:

> Little is known about the mental processes that enable physicians to make the diverse and difficult decisions required in the clinical setting. The intellectual abilities that form the basis of clinical expertise seem to many to be mysterious, collectively constituting the cognitive skills or wisdom of which physicians are most proud but about which they have little explicit understanding.

Firstly, we must realise that there are many levels at which reasoning can take place. At one level, there is the situation where a physician recognises patterns in the available information, i.e. the symptoms as related by the patient, the physical signs which he can observe and the results of laboratory investigations. He may then arrive at a specific diagnosis on the basis that the pattern of findings is identical or sufficiently close to patterns that he has observed in the past. This technique is essentially statistical in nature, and has been captured in a number of computer-based systems [2,3]. Note that we are not saying that the physician consciously performs the calculations of any specific statistical technique, rather that the process does not involve any concepts other than observable data and diagnostic categories.

Now this characterisation of diseases can be viewed as the top level of a multi-level description of the disease process in which progressively lower levels contain more detailed descriptions and more explicit causal relationships between phenomena. Although biomedical research has such understanding as its ultimate goal, there is virtually no area of medicine in which it has been completely achieved. However, there is some level of causal understanding in most branches of medicine – different branches possessing it to different degrees. The extent to which any particular branch is understood in causal terms will be a matter of some debate within the medical profession itself – a not uncommon situation in almost all sciences.

Within the above framework, we can describe two *extreme* possibilities for the nature of medical decision-making. On the one hand, we have reasoning based on pattern recognition without recourse to any causal justification as described above; on the other, we have completely deterministic reasoning based on a complete understanding of the processes involved. It would be naive to assume that actual medical practice corresponds to either of these extremes. There is a considerable amount of research to show that, for a large part of the time, several levels of reasoning are employed. Furthermore, the same doctor will employ different reasoning mechanisms under different circumstances. A real expert, given a case which conforms closely to a large number of cases he has seen before, will go quickly and directly to a decision. He may have available to him a knowledge of lower levels of cause and effect but has no need to employ them in this particular case. However, for someone who is not as expert, or for an expert confronting an unusual case, these more detailed levels of reasoning will often be brought into play.

Just as important as the knowledge itself is the way that the expert physician uses that knowledge in coming to decisions. Firstly, it is clear that, for any given patient not every item of knowledge is employed, only those which are considered relevant to the case in hand. Also, not every possible question will be asked of the patient, nor every available laboratory test performed. This feature of clinical cognition which enables the expert to focus his attention on a limited area has been studied in some depth. Kassirer *et al.* [1] conclude that:

> the questions asked by a physician taking the history of the present illness are prompted by specific hypotheses which are prompted in turn by patient data. These hypotheses suggest confirming, disconfirming, or differential diagnosis questions to the physician.

Of great importance is this 'differential diagnosis'. It refers to the type of task in which the physician has to make a choice of one diagnosis from a fixed and relatively small number of alternatives. Pople [4] argues that:

> Such well structured tasks generally do not constitute situations in which the physician requires diagnostic consultative assistance. The cases where expert assistance is really needed are those that entail diagnostic quandries, where the physician is unsure as to the structure of the diagnostic problem.

He concludes that:

> One mark of an expert is his ability to formulate particularly appropriate diagnostic tasks on the basis of sometimes subtle hints in the patient record.

There are many other aspects of medical decision-making which are of importance when we come to consider our requirements for AI systems. These we will defer for a while. But in understanding that medical experts have to come to decisions which have both probabilistic and deterministic aspects, and in which complex search strategies are found to be necessary, we can start to appreciate the richness and complexity of the medical domain.

AI AND MEDICINE

One can look at the reasons for bringing AI and medicine together from two viewpoints, crudely characterised as 'What can AI bring to medicine?' and 'What can medicine bring to AI?'

We will defer to a later section a discussion of the implications of introducing AI systems into medical practice, and at present just list the ways in which this might take place.

Firstly, they could offer diagnostic and/or therapeutic advice on specific patients at the time that the doctor concerned is making the decision. We have a scenario in which the doctor enters some facts about the patient; the system may work solely on this information, or may be able to put further questions to the doctor. It then comes up with its conclusions. An alternative possibility is one in which the doctor enters the information and his own conclusions; the system then provides a critique of these conclusions.

Expert systems can also play a teaching role: their function would be to educate over a period of time, possibly by giving advice on specific patients as described above but with the added assumption that the young doctor has more time to 'play' with the system in the same way that he might browse through a textbook.

Expert systems can also be built into laboratory instrumentation to provide higher level descriptions of the findings than are produced at present.

Finally, there are more general contributions. For example, there are already expert systems in other domains which have increased the amount of knowledge in that domain. Also an expert system may be considered as a repository of knowledge (rather like a book).

It should come as no surprise that a number of AI researchers should turn to medicine as an area of interest. The deployment of medical expertise must rank very highly in the league table of intellectually demanding tasks, and the emulation of such tasks has always been important in AI research. Medicine offers a fascinating real world domain in which to develop theories of cognitive psychology with the aim of producing a testable model of a cognitive process. If a system is looked at solely from this point of view, it may not really be relevant to ask whether the system could be used routinely by doctors in one of the ways described above. However, most medical AI systems have also addressed questions of user acceptance such as the provision of explanations, reasonable question-asking strategies, etc.

We make this point about motivation and goals, because in the past there have been fruitless wranglings between different research groups over misunderstood objectives.

THE VALIDITY OF THE AI APPROACH

It must be stated at the outset that there is no single AI approach. However, most AI approaches share a willingness to accept the knowledge as presented by a human expert as a valid basis for building a system, even if this knowledge is not supported by cast-iron statistics. The use of 'heuristics' (i.e. rules of thumb) by humans is taken as providing good strategies and, in general, looking to human behaviour to provide clues as to how to go about things is believed to be profitable.

However, this approach is often challenged. It will be argued that humans and computers are inherently different, and computers should stick to what they have been proved to be good at (i.e. complex arithmetic calculations and the storage of large amounts of information). It is also said that humans are fallible and that a lot of 'received' knowledge is incorrect. Thus, to base a system on knowledge derived purely from expert opinion risks perpetuating falsehoods and may blind people to real advances in knowledge.

In reply, it is argued that for computer-based systems to become acceptable they must conform to the role played by the human advice-giver, who will usually be able to justify the advice with some sort of appeal to underlying causal mechanisms and whose problem-solving strategies will be familiar. If the advice is derived from a framework which is alien to the user's way of working on problems, he/she is then faced with the decision of accepting the advice without a feeling for its correctness, or else completely rejecting it.

CURRENT AI SYSTEMS

This chapter is too short to allow a systematic account of all the medical decision-making systems which employ AI techniques. All we can do is to describe four of the most important systems and try to identify the contributions that they have made to our understanding of medical decision-making.

One of the first and best known systems is MYCIN, whose goal is to advise physicians and medical students on the appropriate treatment of microbial infections [5]. Its knowledge is expressed principally in a number of independently stated rules of deduction, e.g.

IF: (1) THE STAIN OF THE ORGANISM IS GRAM POSITIVE, AND
(2) THE MORPHOLOGY OF THE ORGANISM IS COCCUS, AND
(3) THE GROWTH CONFORMATION OF THE MOLECULE IS CHAINS

THEN: THERE IS SUGGESTIVE EVIDENCE (.7) THAT THE IDENTITY OF THE ORGANISM IS STREPTOCOCCUS.

This use of rules to 'capture' easily modifiable 'chunks' of human expertise is one of the most interesting aspects of MYCIN. It means that rules can be added, deleted and modified as the program develops and that a conclusion can always be justified in terms of the rules which generated it. MYCIN is statistical in the sense that it uses probabilistic-like methods to combine evidence for and against a given hypothesis; however, its rule structure allows it to generate intermediate conclusions about states which are not directly observable.

INTERNIST–1 is another system which employs probabilistic methods to a large extent [4]. This is a very ambitious program which attempts to generate diagnoses for all of the disorders found in internal medicine. It is phenomenological in that observed findings are linked directly to diagnoses by probabilistic weighting factors. As with MYCIN, the program is interactive; it asks some basic questions, ranks the possible diseases, and then asks more questions to refine its diagnosis further. The most interesting aspect of INTERNIST–1 is the partitioning heuristic which generates a differential diagnosis and then follows one of a number of different strategies in an attempt to confirm or deny the top-ranking hypothesis. For example, if there are a number of competing hypotheses, it will ask questions with the aim of ruling out one of the hypotheses rather than confirming others. INTERNIST–1 was one of the first programs to point out that this focus of attention was a crucial element in the diagnostic behaviour of expert physicians.

CASNET was developed at Rutgers University as a program for making diagnoses and recommendations for therapy for glaucoma [6]. The main contribution of CASNET was the explicit introduction of the notion of causality. The progression of the disease is represented as a network in which any abnormal state is either derived from another prior state, or else the state is one of the 'starting points' for the disease. One of the tasks undertaken by CASNET was to identify the current state of the patient with a state in the network; a rather complicated calculation was used to derive the likelihood of a given state based on direct observations or on the causal links between states. Because the development of the disease with time was built in to the program, CASNET could also monitor the effects of treatment and comment on the extent that a deviation from the natural course of the disease was being achieved.

This emphasis on causal reasoning was one of the main ideas behind the ABEL program developed at MIT for the diagnosis of acid/base electrolyte disturbances [7]. ABEL is still under development and may more properly be called a second-generation medical AI program. Medical knowledge is represented at a number of levels – the top level describes relationships between phenomena, and the lower levels provide successively more detailed descriptions of the processes involved.

WHERE NOW?

The significant advances made by these first-generation expert systems should not make us forget the fact that, as stated already, there are very few medical AI systems in routine clinical use. In their review paper, Duda and Shortliffe [8] mention only two such systems. PUFF [9] analyses data from pulmonary function tests and prints clinical reports; the other system is embedded in a commercially available instrument for the measurement and interpretation of serum protein electrophoresis [10]. It is perhaps significant to note that both of these systems take most of their input data from instruments, and do not rely on a doctor to enter large volumes of information.

We will now speculate as to the reasons for this low level of routine use, firstly looking at the technical aspects which we feel need further exploration (for a good overview of the problems see [11]), and then looking at the wider implications of introducing medical expert systems.

Most of the existing AI programs in medicine have used a very 'compiled' form of knowledge; that is, they relate externally acquirable items of information such as patient history, physical signs, test results, etc., directly to the 'underlying disease' via numerical factors of necessity and sufficiency. Such knowledge may be called phenomenological – concerned with the relations between phenomena more than with an understanding of the mechanisms which are suggested by the observations. As discussed above, such phenomenological descriptions provide a reasonable first approximation to the way that doctors reason. However, they fail to capture the subtlety of which doctors are capable when a straightforward interpretation of the data cannot be immediately obtained. We need to develop ways of incorporating the deeper levels of knowledge of cause and effect which are brought into play under certain circumstances.

All medical students study anatomy (structure) and physiology (function), and it is difficult to imagine a medical expert who did not have a knowledge of these topics. How this knowledge is deployed by practising doctors is not at all clear, but it is surely anomalous that very little anatomical and physiological knowledge is built into existing expert systems.

Doctors do not apply their expertise at a single point in time: they will see the patient on a number of occasions; they will order tests and get the results later; they will prescribe a treatment and wait to see how effective it is; they may decide to take no action to allow the disease to take its natural course – which may lead to recovery or to a situation in which any prior ambiguities have been resolved. It is therefore essential that a medical expert system is able to handle time development, but little significant work has been done in this field. Such knowledge will be employed *retrospectively* in diagnosis; knowing how the patient's symptoms have developed is an important guide to identifying the disease process involved. It will also be used *prospectively* to predict the future stages of the disease and its likely response to treatment – clearly of importance in the management of the patient.

Doctors practice in a world that is full of uncertainty. Medicine is not an exact science: the symptoms of a given patient may not lead to an unambiguous diagnosis; the progress of a given disease cannot be predicted with complete certainty; the response to a given treatment may also be unpredictable. In addition, a doctor is often faced with incomplete (or even contradictory) knowledge of the 'facts' about a given case: the patient may be confused, may not remember correctly, or may lie; the 'student' doctor may make mistakes in taking the physical signs; laboratory tests may yield erroneous results. Doctors have ideas about the relative likelihood of different events, and may even be able to put objective numerical values on them (from the results of statistical trials). The approach of systems such as MYCIN is to propagate these probabilities through a system of rules. It may well be that this does not represent the response to a human expert to uncertainty and that a more accurate model is one in which the expert believes certain patient-specific 'facts' to be true, and certain domain-specific 'rules' to apply in the case being considered; he then tries to construct a coherent explanation on that basis. If a satisfactory explanation is not found then belief in one or more of the 'facts' and/or 'rules' will be altered and a new explanation attempted.

It is also clear that the question of the level of description is important in handling uncertainty; a doctor may be sure that the patient has a disease of the renal system but be unsure as to which part of the system is affected.

Systems should be flexible in the way the interaction proceeds. The earlier expert systems tended to be backwards-chaining, and as a result were 'in control' at all times. In particular, they asked the user questions with a view to satisfying their primary goal (i.e. that of diagnosis), and did not allow him to take the initiative, apart from allowing him to ask for explanations. However, a system used in a tutorial capacity must do more than this. It must allow the student to state what he knows about the case, to express his conclusions, to obtain critical comments on these conclusions, to ask more basic questions about the underlying physiology and pathology, etc.

It is a criticism of the earlier systems that whereas they would eventually ask all of the relevant questions, they did so in an order which was confusing to the user who had no clear understanding of the inference and control mechanisms internal to the system. Human experts tend to organise their information gathering in a structured way which reflects the hypothesis that they are following at the time.

THE IMPLICATIONS FOR MEDICINE

At this point we start skating on very thin ice indeed. AI techniques in medicine have still some way to go before they can be offered with any degree of confidence to the medical community. In addition to the specific points discussed above, there is the whole question of the mechanism for interaction between the program and the doctor. It can be argued that no matter how sophisticated the programs themselves become, they will never be used until the doctor has an entirely naturalistic way of communicating with them. This might mean touch screens and excellent graphics, but could also imply speech/natural-language input and output. We are certainly some way from achieving acceptable levels of performance in this latter area.

One way of getting round this problem is to consider a half-way situation in which the majority of medical records are available on computer, having been entered by a medical secretary in the normal way. Even this assumes that a large number of problems associated with the large scale codification of medical records has been solved. One could then imagine an expert program 'browsing' through the records and, if it found anything questionable, leaving an electronic mail message for the doctor in charge of the case of the form: 'I see that patient X has the following symptoms: . . . From the record, it looks as though you have not considered disease Y which is sometimes associated with these symptoms and although it is rather rare, the consequences (. . .) can be dangerous. A good test for Y is . . .'

This form of 'over-the-shoulder' advice may turn out to be more acceptable to physicians than a direct consultation, especially if the advice given by the program is shown only to the doctor in question.

Another form in which advice may be offered without a direct challenge to the authority of the physician is in a teaching context – i.e. one in which the (usually junior) doctor would deliberately seek advice either of a general nature or about specific cases, particularly any in which he had been shown to be in error. It is our observation that junior doctors at the intern level (house surgeons or physicians in the UK) do not have as much time with their senior colleagues in a tutorial capacity as they would like. Widely available expert systems could help in this respect.

However, it is the effect on the day-to-day practice of medicine that one can foresee the greatest potential impact. To some extent, the type of doctor who might be affected depends on the technical successes (or otherwise) which are achieved. It is somewhat paradoxical that the aspects of human cognition which are *most* difficult to capture in a program are those which are *least* specialised and involve considerable 'common sense'. Thus it is more feasible to produce an expert system to give advice on glaucoma than it is to develop one to advise a general practitioner on all aspects of his work. Let us suppose therefore that we have available a system which can in all significant respects reproduce the performance of a hospital specialist and consider the implications for other specialists in the field. Firstly, it is likely that the system developers will have gone to the best specialist around to get the knowledge for the system, or even have gathered a consensus from a group of top experts. It is possible, therefore, that the system will be capable of performing more accurately than the average specialist. Then again, the system will not get tired and will work just as well at 4 a.m. as at 10 a.m.; it will not need weekends or holidays. However, apart from some information which might be gained from computerised patient interviewing, it is unlikely to be able to elicit the physical signs from the patient, as this requires vision and touch. Also, a skilled physician can extract information from the way in which a patient answers questions as well as from the factual answers themselves. Complex manipulative skills, particularly those involving vision are unlikely to be the province of computer systems for the foreseeable future.

Our conclusion must be that *if* the technology can be developed this far, it is the intellectual skills of doctors which could be replaced, if society at large wishes it to happen and if the medical profession allows it to happen. We would still need trained personnel to be responsible for physical contact with the patient. And we would also need people to look after his or her emotional and social needs. It can be argued that modern medicine has become overconcerned with the intellectual side of medical practice to the exclusion of the pastoral care of the patient, sufficient discussion with him of his condition and its implications, concern for and contact with the family, and so on. If this is true, then the introduction of computerised advice-giving systems could provide a desirable shift of emphasis. Such a shift is likely to encounter resistance from existing doctors, many of whom entered the profession precisely because it was seen as providing stimulating intellectual challenges.

The complete replacement of these intellectual skills is a somewhat extreme possibility. Far more likely is a partnership between doctor and machine in which the machine is used to store large volumes of information which can be accessed in an 'intelligent' manner by the computer system under the prompting of the doctor performing the much more difficult task of problem formulation.

There are many other questions which could be addressed. When any degree of reliance is placed on such systems, then their reliability – both in terms of software and hardware – becomes crucially important. Problems of legal responsibility are addressed elsewhere in this volume. How will patients react when they know that computer programs are playing a significant part in their treatment?

However, the clinical acceptance of medical expert systems will probably be settled pragmatically. If successful demonstrations show that doctors working with such systems are more successful than those without, then those without will want to acquire them!

NOTES

[1] J. P. Kassirer, B. J. Kuipers and G. A. Gorry (1982) 'Towards a Theory of Clinical Expertise', *American Journal of Medicine,* **73**, 251–259.

[2] F. T. deDombal, J. C. Horrocks, G. Walmsley and P. D. Wilson (1975) 'Computer-Aided Diagnosis of Acute Abdominal Pain', *J. Roy. Coll. Phycns. Lond.* **9**(3).

[3] D. J. Spiegelhalter and R. P. Knill-Jones (1984) 'Statistical and Knowledge-based Approaches to Clinical Decision-support Systems, with an Application in Gastroenterology', *J. R. Statist. Soc. A* **147**.

[4] H. E. Pople (1982) 'Heuristic Methods for Imposing Structure in Ill-Structured Problems: The Structuring of Medical Diagnostics', in *Artificial Intelligence in Medicine*, ed. P. Szolovits, Westview Press, Boulder, Colorado, 119–190.

[5] E. H. Shortliffe (1976) *Computer Based Medical Consultations: MYCIN*, American Elsevier.

[6] C. A. Kulikowski and S. M. Weiss (1982) 'Representation of Expert Knowledge for Consultation: The CASNET and EXPERT Projects', in *Artificial Intelligence in Medicine*, ed. P. Szolovits, Westview Press, Boulder, Colorado, 21–56.

[7] R. Patil, P. Szolovits and W. B. Schwartz (1982) 'Modelling Knowledge of the Patient in Acid-Base and Electrolyte Disorders', in *Artificial Intelligence in Medicine*, ed. P. Szolovits, Westview Press, Boulder, Colorado, 191–226.

[8] R. O. Duda and E. H. Shortliffe (1983) 'Expert Systems Research', *Science* **220**(4594), 261–267.

[9] J. S. Aikins, J. C. King, E. H. Shortliffe and R. J. Fallout (1982) 'PUFF: An Expert System for Interpretation of Pulmonary Function Data', *STAN-HPP-82-13*.

[10] S. M. Weiss, C. A. Kulikowski and R. S. Galen (1981) 'Developing Microprocessor Based Expert Models for Instrument Interpretation', in *IJCAI* 3, 853–855.

[11] R. Davis (1982) 'Expert Systems: Where are We? And Where do We Go from Here?', *MIT-AIM-665*.

The expert computer and professional negligence: who is liable?

J. A. Campbell University of Exeter UK

Artificial intelligence has been an academically respectable subject in North America for some time. In Britain it has struggled for this status for several years, following the appearance of the Lighthill report in 1973. The latest British development is that this struggle appears to be over. In North America, at the same time, artificial intelligence has developed into a commercially attractive subject, while retaining its respectability. There are several reasons for the change in circumstances, but none is more important than the success of the expert-system model for the writing of programs.

Although expert systems have now been constructed for many different fields of knowledge, almost all of them have it in common that they deal with topics in which there are recognised professional experts. One justification for the encouragement of commercial work on expert systems is that human experts are expensive to train and therefore have the habit of demanding professionals' fees for their services. If a good representation of expert-level professional knowledge is embodied in a program, the program when reproduced in multiple copies allows its owners and users to bypass the problems of expense or scarcity of human professionals. In place of an expensive and possibly remote human specialist, one can hope for easy and relatively cheap access to an 'expert computer'. This argument was first advanced by Colby [1] on behalf of automated psychiatry even before the essentials of expert-system programming were understood.

It is possible to argue that many pictures of the promising future for expert systems which their promoters or uncritical admirers paint are unrealistic. For example, a recent test [9] of the INTERNIST system (generally presented as one of the most advanced medical expert systems) on cases involving multiple diagnoses in internal medicine produced a performance which was marginally worse than clinicians in a large general hospital and significantly below that of a group of experts. The major apparent defect of the program was in the conservatism of its diagnoses: it actually made fewer 'definitive' incorrect diagnoses than either of its groups of competitors, but at the price of making correspondingly fewer definitive correct diagnoses and significantly more failures to diagnose anything at all when key symptoms were present. The first of these phenomena may appear to be a mark in favour of the program, but the impression given by [9] is that the boundary between 'definitive' and 'tentative' was not the same for the program as for human physicians in the setting of a clinical conference where there is always pressure to come to some conclusion, right or wrong, and therefore that the same clinical data actually provided a more severe test for the physicians than for the program. The undesirable conservative behaviour of the program was explained as follows:

> INTERNIST–I's greatest failing during the evaluation . . . was its inability to attribute findings to their proper causes. Because of the *ad hoc*, serial nature of INTERNIST–I's formation of problem areas, the program cannot synthesise a general overview in complicated multisystem problems. The structure of the knowledge base, especially the form of the disease profiles, limits the program's ability to reason anatomically or temporally. . . . A related problem not handled well by INTERNIST–I is the interdependency of manifestations. . . . INTERNIST–I remain(s) unable to look at several problem areas simultaneously.

These remarks read like a summary of several of the current general difficulties with the theoretical tools of artificial intelligence. The difficulties are unlikely to be permanent, even though the speed with which they will fade away in the future is not possible to predict reliably at this stage. Pharmaceutical companies have reacted in the past in a way which may suggest that they are pessimistic about the technical problems of expert systems. It appears, however, that their reluctance to become involved in expert-system applications has been not technical but legal: they are well aware that, in actions for any kinds of damages, the defendant targeted for the largest share of the financial penalties is the richest one. The situation is now changing, and such companies are beginning to be active recruiters of specialists in medical and allied expert systems. No doubt the temptations of large financial rewards are starting to outweigh the possible legal risks. Present realism therefore requires the admission that expert systems offering advice which will be advertised as professional-quality advice in some specialised fields, including medical diagnosis and drug prescription for certain classes of illness, may be marketed within the next few years.

If one behaves like a professional, one must expect not only a professional's rewards, but also a professional's risks – even if 'one' is hidden behind a computer. Probably the main risk in the exercise of a profession is that of an unwilling involvement in a legal action for negligence or some similar type of malpractice as a result of an act or recommendation with unfortunate consequences.

Where the act or recommendation can be traced to an expert system, the risk remains, but the possible legal complications are increased, because the nature of expert systems makes it difficult to assign responsibility for all conceivable negative outcomes of their use.

This chapter examines some of the complications. It suggests that a cure for them is the early recognition, by legislation, that expert systems are sufficiently special or peculiar objects to require special treatment. Because the law is traditionally reluctant to admit a totally new formula for anything, it is fortunate that there is already a legal framework into which the suggested treatment fits.

CHARACTERISTICS OF EXPERT SYSTEMS

It is not sufficient for a program to contain a version of an expert's knowledge if it is to deserve the name of an expert system. In different ways, early instances of the MACSYMA system for the determination of indefinite integrals [13] and any program for the computation of kinematical information from digitised records of scattering events in experimental high-energy physics exemplify this statement. A program of the latter type uses professional physicists' knowledge of the special theory of relativity, but this knowledge is expressed precisely in equations which can be found in appropriate textbooks. Early MACSYMA came closer to being an expert system, because a significant amount of its power lay in heuristics (methods available as alternative tools with reasonable chances of success, in the view of experts in a field, where no exact prescription works) rather than textbook procedures or equations. Even so, these heuristics were embedded tightly in the MACSYMA program, and the effect on the running of MACSYMA if one removed any one of them, assuming first that one knew exactly how to do this, would have been similar to the effect of extracting a key log from the middle of a large woodpile.

By indicating what an expert system is not, these two examples make it possible to say what a program based on advanced or professional knowledge should be, in order to qualify for the label of an expert system. An essential part of the knowledge in an expert system is expressed in heuristics, and almost all individual items of knowledge in this form should be removable without having gross effects on the performance of the system.

The latter requirement may seem impractical at first, but in fact it says something important about the functions of a professional. Suppose that a heuristic without which the right answer to a problem is unobtainable is removed just before an expert system is tested on that problem. If 'right' means the only acceptable answer, a program may declare that no solution can be found – but this also amounts to acceptable human professional behaviour, e.g. in a situation where the expert realises that essential information is held in some data-base which is inaccessible to him. If 'right' means the best of a number of alternatives, however, then an expert system meeting the requirements in the previous paragraph should still produce an answer which is not unreasonably worse than the unobtainable one. In other words, its subject is one which (in its most interesting advanced manifestations) has a variety of answers for questions, interpretations for symptoms, solutions matching a given set of constraints, etc., with comparable ratings, rather than just one right answer and an infinity of wrong answers. Where a problem is an illness, a need for a computer configuration that will perform given tasks, or a specification for the use and cost of a building, ability to consider sets of comparable recommendations and present a small number of the best alternatives is what one asks of a medical practitioner, a systems engineer, or an architect, respectively. To arrive at such conclusions in a subject is the special skill of any professional, whose practice of his profession has equipped him with the necessary heuristics and beliefs about what knowledge is relevant. By contrast, if a problem has one answer given in a formula, we can find it merely by looking at a textbook. The phrase 'almost all' in the previous paragraph is insurance against the cases where there is one right answer in some textbook or journal, but where (i) the expert knows this while we do not, and (ii) the expert also knows where to look.

It is no coincidence that DENDRAL [7], the oldest and most famous expert system, has always been set up to present its results as a list of the most likely alternatives, with a measure of likelihood attached to each one. Its field, inference of the chemical structures of molecules which have generated given collections of measurements during experiments in mass spectrometry, is one in which almost no such collection is an unambiguous signature for just one molecule. There it has been necessary to develop rules of thumb or chemistry for inferring what molecules are likely to have the observed signatures. Before DENDRAL, researchers monitored the behaviour of experts (including themselves) over several years, and reduced this behaviour to the application of large numbers of rules. The present DENDRAL system contains and applies these rules. While there is no world championship in the field, no human expert now performs consistently better than DENDRAL on its particular job.

Deduction and inference, especially in the presence of ambiguous or incomplete information, are procedures which are not specific to any one field of knowledge. It is possible to separate the methods of reasoning from the information which is the subject of the reasoning, certainly on paper; the lesson of DENDRAL and subsequent experience with the construction of expert systems for other fields has been that the same separation is possible in the design of appropriate computer programs. An expert system consists of at least two distinguishable parts: an 'inference engine' (the name is a gesture of acknowledgement to Charles Babbage, one of the ancestors of modern computing, whose name for his proposed computing machine was the Analytical Engine) which mechanises the deduction and inference, and an assembly of knowledge on which the steps of inference are performed. The insight of expert-system design is that many topics whose human experts have professional standing yield to the expression of the relevant knowledge, as data for inference engines, in the form of rules. There are many significant variations on the structure of the rules, which inference engines may treat as data and/or directions for what to do next, but the most basic 'atoms' of knowledge (after simple facts) in a field which allows expert-system mechanisation are rules of the simple form

IF <situation> THEN <consequences> (R1)

The rules are the elements, mentioned above, which can be detached or added individually to an expert system without making gross changes in the system's overall performance. In this, they model the accumulation of an expert's heuristic knowledge about a field, in which it is extremely rare to find the acquisition of one new rule-like piece of knowledge leading directly to a complete realignment of his view of the subject. (More often, if a new rule forces such a change, it is necessary to discard or replace many of the other rules, which is not a trivial process.)

Most of the variations in the method of expression of rules occur as means of making computation more efficient rather than as devices to change the outputs of an expert system. One exception, which is of considerable importance for legal and other external views of the behaviour of expert systems, is that these systems can represent uncertainty in cases where the experts who supply the information know that some of their rules of thumb cannot or should not be stated unconditionally. In these cases, the information supplied has a form

IF <situation> = true WITH LIKELIHOOD p
THEN <consequence> WITH LIKELIHOOD $p \times q$, (R2)

where q is intrinsic to the rule and p stands for any likelihood associated with <situation> which may be fed into the rule by the previous history of the computation which uses it. In particular, some other rule in the system may prompt the user to supply his own estimate of p, e.g. by causing the printing of a message like: 'Please indicate the severity of your headache, in comparison with all your previous experience of headaches, on a scale of 1 through 9'.

If expert systems can succeed by representing knowledge only in forms like R1 and R2, why use a program to manipulate the knowledge? The answer is the same as for the use of computers over the last 40 years to carry out numerical calculations for which the methods are easily demonstrated on paper. If the size of the manipulation is too great to allow a human user of the methods to complete his task in a reasonable time, or without the risk of making many mistakes, then mechanisation of the methods is the only sensible way to proceed. This comment is clearly relevant when the rule-set is too large for the human user to keep, in its entirety, at the focus of his attention. It is foreseeable that expert systems that will be publicly available will contain several hundred rules, and the eventual mechanisation of domains of knowledge which requires thousands of rules is not a matter of science fiction.

HUMAN ASSOCIATES OF EXPERT SYSTEMS

Many different types of person have been concerned, and are concerned, in the construction and use of expert systems, apart from the obvious categories such as the user. To take only one example, the mechanisation of deduction or inference through some formal or semi-formal method is an important feature of expert systems which rely mainly on unconditional rules R1, but the standard method of mechanisation has been developed comparatively recently [20] in the history of logic. Without the contribution of specialists in formal deduction or inference, the subject of expert systems would not have reached its present stage of maturity.

Identification of behind-the-scenes contributors to the functioning of expert systems is not simply an exercise in the history of computer science. It is also relevant in showing who may be within the range of legal liability in actions for negligence or malpractice. The arm of the law (or the arm of an ambitious lawyer whose preference is for lucrative suits for damages or compensation) is long; it may be advisable not to underestimate its length.

Firstly, if a professional uses an expert system as a guide or amplifier for his own judgement, he is clearly a human associate of the system. Possible examples for the near future are the medical practitioner who takes advice from a system (based on recently-supplied information from a pharmaceutical company, say, for updating of the rule-base which it has previously sold as a commercial product) on the appropriateness of a new drug ('neothalidomide', perhaps) as a treatment for an everyday medical condition, and the architect whose work on the design of a building is aided by an expert system which suggests materials and methods of construction or layout that minimise fire hazards.

Next, there is the question of who puts the rules into a given expert system. A computer scientist may be able to build the inference engine which is its skeleton, but it takes at least one expert to establish the knowledge-based rules for a subject. Practice has shown that it requires a large amount of time for experts and their friends to decide accurately what are the rules of their field and how to express them in forms suitable for computing. For the future, it can be predicted that a typical pattern of development of a commercially-viable expert system in some professional area will be that computing specialists in the construction of inference engines will join forces with a company working in the area of intended exploitation, and that the company will engage as consultants the best experts that its budget can buy. Considerable time will then be devoted to extracting from the consultants the rules which express their expert knowledge.

It is a safe general observation in any field where heuristics are significant that two experts are better than one expert. This indicates why the plural of 'consultant' has been used above. It also leads to the possibility of legal complications which would not arise in actions over the performance of a system whose rule-base has been supplied by only one expert.

Interactions between computer scientists and professional experts are essential in the building of an expert system, but progress may then be painfully slow. To extract the relevant information in an appropriate form is itself a skill, as any good barrister or interrogator can testify. This is where the 'friends' of the experts play a part. Even in commercial circles in California, the home of expert systems, these friends are not yet very numerous, but they are growing in numbers, and they already have a new name: knowledge engineers.

The special contribution of a knowledge engineer has a second level, besides the level of forensic ability. There may be several hundreds of rules for a given subject. Whenever new rules are added to an existing collection, the resulting expert system under development is run on test cases to ensure that it behaves in a way acceptable to the human experts. If it does not, its internal behaviour can be examined and the source of the inadequacy found. Often the reason for the inadequacy is that the experts have omitted a rule – not because of forgetfulness, but because they did not know that they knew the rule until the poor performance of the system made them aware of it. Much human knowledge is built up by practice rather than by writing down rules based on practice. Thus it is not surprising that there are things which some experts know but which they do not know that they know . . . until they are prompted by a knowledge engineer. A person who is efficient at prompting and encouraging experts can reduce significantly the (expensive) time needed to develop a good expert system in a complex subject.

It has been argued that knowledge engineers require a distinct type of training. Exposure to the expert-system idea is certainly a part of the training that no people in related activities (e.g. interrogation) need to share at present. However, the remainder of the argument sounds suspiciously like special pleading from sources which hope to be able to corner a future market for schools issuing diplomas in knowledge engineering. It can probably be contradicted by anyone who has a successful record in the production of programmed-learning materials for advanced or 'professional' topics.

To develop a large expert system, it may be that other computing personnel in addition to those who have been mentioned so far will work on the programming, e.g. in implementation of the component parts of the system itself, or on supplying updates, maintenance or transfer of the system to a new computer. These people too have an association with the system that is of legal significance.

When an expert system is a commercial product, a managing director of the responsible company and all other officials whose proposals regarding policy for the system are acted upon by the company should evidently be concerned about the legal implications of less-than-successful uses of their product. In a traditional limited company, shareholders can expect to be insulated against direct effects of those implications, but companies formed to exploit advanced computing technology like artificial intelligence tend to be non-traditional, consisting of a small number of partners who own all the assets jointly. In companies of this kind with several products besides expert systems, a partner who may not be concerned with the expert systems may nevertheless be as responsible in law as the partners who have direct charge of the expert-system activity.

While it is often said that users of large computers can expect to divert progressively more of their computations to personal machines as the computing power available at typical current microcomputer prices increases, there are at least two reasons why this may not affect expert systems with large or expensive rule-bases. The first is that a vendor may regard his rule-base as a proprietary secret (a reason why not much is known publicly in the artificial-intelligence community about the state of the art in work on expert systems for geophysical prospecting), and offer users access only by connection of their terminals to a remote site where the system is held. The second is that large programs in artificial intelligence make demands on random-access memory that are very different from other large-storage demands in computing which are presently being answered in the designs of new computers. It is fair to say, for example, that these designs are being affected much more by the needs of data-base management than by questions of artificial intelligence. Therefore it may only be economically feasible to offer the service of a large expert system from sites with computing equipment sufficiently unusual not to be found within a console in every manager's office by 1993. Both reasons suggest that it will be common in the foreseeable future for users to obtain access to expert systems through computer networks.

Although the legal position of the operator of a network which transmits defective recommendations from an expert system to a user is not clear at present, it is possible to find examples of the view [10] that the custodian of an entity (though the question of whether or not this refers only to a sole custodian seems to be open) is responsible for any damage which it causes. For legal purposes, therefore, the network operators may be associated involuntarily with the expert systems that use their communications facilities, and may thus need to be cautious about the properties of any such system that they consent to service.

The final group of human associates of expert systems which appears to be of some legal interest is to be found among largely theoretical computer scientists and mathematicians. It is made up of the people whose theoretical or practical work on the foundations underlying expert-system computing influences the trustworthiness of the outputs or recommendations which the systems may generate. For example, if a new fact or rule is added to an existing collection of facts and rules, it may be by no means obvious whether the addition introduces an inconsistency (and the chance of misleading outputs) into a previously consistent base of knowledge. The problem of truth-maintenance [2], or detection and removal of inconsistencies in these circumstances by formal methods, is still under analysis, and future work may lead to suggestions of methods which promise important technical improvements in the handling of the problem. (Most current expert systems ignore it, and put the onus of avoiding inconsistencies on the experts and the knowledge engineers.) There is the alternative point of view that humans reason with the help of knowledge that they admit to be inconsistent [5], for the want of better knowledge, and therefore that some expert systems that are intended to imitate human professional judgement will perform badly by this criterion if they are forced into a mould of traditional mathematical logic or specially-modified systems like non-monotonic logics [6]. It is not a viewpoint that can be dismissed, but anyone who wishes to build on it for work on expert systems will be even more in need of support from formal methods for implementing and validating programs to make inferences on an inconsistent base of knowledge.

Rules of the type R2 are not a way around this last problem because they do not express exactly the same idea, but they are popular in present expert systems whose base of knowledge is subject to uncertainties. Individual rules R2 may indeed agree with an expert's local assessment of a situation, but it is unlikely that inferences based on long chains of such rules model a human expert's reasoning accurately. A probability pq in R2 may have a significant value if p and q are close to 1, but a probability

$$pq_1 q_2 q_3 q_4 \ldots$$

computed from a chain of R2-rules may fall below a system's pre-set threshold of significance. This phenomenon of 'vanishing probability', in the short run, tends to favour deductions with few steps over deductions with many steps. In the long run, it leads to a world where nothing can happen. The former effect, in particular, violates the principles of construction of all good detective stories (although it agrees with the rules for construction of early chapters, in which the reader and the secondary heroes should be misled by excessively simple interpretations of clues), and is contradicted by the histories of many important scientific discoveries. A mathematical explanation of these phenomena is that the numbers p and q are not likelihoods or probabilities in the strict mathematical sense, and that correct deductions can only occur in general if the characteristic properties of the numbers in R2-rules are studied and understood correctly. Any claimed mathematical advances in that direction will be welcomed by builders of expert systems and probably incorporated in new inference engines.

In all the areas just mentioned, and in allied areas like the application of fuzzy logics [24] to imitations of expert reasoning, present formal methods are not guaranteed to work to a particular objective standard in the sense that formal techniques relevant to engineering can be used to 'guarantee' that a given bridge will not collapse. If the methods are nevertheless built into the operation and validation of expert systems, the inventors of the methods are recognisably associated with the successes and failures of the systems.

THE LEGAL PROBLEM

What happens if the course of action suggested or initiated by an expert system leads to injury or damage, and a court case results? This question has not yet been asked in a professional context, even in California, but it deserves early consideration.

A good lawyer acting for the injured party should have no difficulty in stating an initial case that the human professional closest to the injury has been negligent in not making reference to whatever kind of knowledge or assistance in his profession could have avoided the injury. Moreover, the lawyer himself is inefficient if he cannot extend his net much more widely. Californian practice may be of interest. In the case of Ybarra *v*. Spangard [23], concerning a shoulder injury received during an operation for appendicitis, the professionals involved included not only the surgeon and anaesthetist, but also two nurses, a diagnostician and the owner of the hospital. One general interpretation of what these defendants had in common is that '. . . control of the things which might have harmed the plaintiff places upon them the burden of initial explanation' [4]. In many locations outside California, including Britain, this wide interpretation has a highly contemporary sound.

GROUNDS FOR LIABILITY OF HUMAN ASSOCIATES OF EXPERT SYSTEMS

The professional nearest to the injury is the person who acts on the advice of an expert system, or licenses or approves the system for unsupervised use by non-professionals. He is evidently liable in an action unless he can show that he has discharged all of his professional responsibilities and has therefore carried out the duties of which neglect is immediate evidence of negligence in the legal sense. There are no general principles whose satisfaction demonstrates in all instances that he has done so, but some principles which have good chances of being valid in particular cases have emerged from previous legal decisions in actions involving negligence. Some of them are straightforward, but others have unusual implications here. The references below are to British cases, but the ideas appear to hold in American and Commonwealth legal traditions also.

The principles are of two types: those involving compliance with existing law, and those turning on information which is the province of experts in the professional field concerned. As technical issues have become more specialised, the second has taken precedence over the first, though there is still a tendency (illustrated in passing in note [3]) for courts to retreat to questions of the form: 'Would compliance with the law have eliminated the harm?' if expert evidence presents them with difficult problems of decision on whether a sequence of specialised technical events was actually a chain of causation leading to an injury. In such an eventuality, there is a risk that the injured party's lawyer may anticipate the tendency by quoting a law whose relevance is somewhat doubtful, but which creates the best fit to his case.

The principles which require input from expert professional evidence are criteria of danger and of rarity. The two criteria overlap. An interpretation of the first is: Can a reasonable professional foresee the consequences when the circumstances and faults that have allegedly made the injury inevitable are explained to him? If he cannot, then the 'sense of the profession' would be that the professional responsible for them should be free of liability. A development of this idea is that a professional who follows 'accepted procedure' in his subject is safe. Where the procedure is still open to professional debate, he may not be: a recent British case has depended on just such an issue [8]. The second principle [22] is that negative consequences which are of extreme rarity in a given set of circumstances, representing freak accidents or events which a professional would normally never have encountered or heard about previously, do not establish liability. Several classic cases in the law of torts support this last conclusion.

In theory, a professional may be able to improve still further his degree of safety against possible actions for negligence by obtaining clients' signatures, in advance, to some form of release or consent to bear the consequences of expert-system-assisted treatment or consultation. In practice this offers doubtful security: a client cannot be said to consent to an act whose effect is harmful if he is 'not directed to the true facts' [11], and the facts may well be adjudged to include the essentials of all the topics which it is the responsibility of the various human associates of expert systems to understand in depth. This possibility provides many avenues of attack for an ingenious lawyer acting for a plaintiff.

Further avenues of attack are related to the legal principles, mentioned above, which may cause problems for the professional who uses expert systems. These principles are that he has a duty to maintain a competent knowledge about the tools and standards of his profession [21], and that he should not neglect to make use of state-of-the-art technology in his field where this is a means of avoiding injury or damage [17]. The problems are of two types.

Firstly, expert systems set expert knowledge into a framework that may be qualitatively different, as experienced by the trainee professional, from the framework in which his traditional education is conducted. Therefore, unless he has had a significant exposure to methods of diagnosis or reasoning in his subject that are explicitly tied to rules of the forms R1 or R2 (rather than conducted by analogy or example, which is normal in medical and some other professions), he may (i) have no feel for what is behind a given output from an expert system, (ii) be unable to formulate questions whose answers are essential for the prevention of an injury and which an expert system may be fully able to provide, (iii) fail to understand that a particular publicised enhancement of a rule-base allows certain expert systems to solve new classes of problems in his field, or (iv) appreciate that proprietary system A to which he has bought access cannot solve a class of problems that a rival system B can handle because of its state-of-the-art features. These problems contain some messages for deans of medical and other professional schools, in connection with planning of curricula.

The remarks in the previous paragraph may imply difficulties in updating the education or self-education of a professional, but the second type of problem is even more difficult. It is the same as the first, except that it refers to the inference engine and not the rule-base. The implication is that it may not be enough for a professional to be a professional in his own field, but that he may also need to understand something about computer science and the areas in which its theoretical research bears on possible improvements or changes in the overall structure of expert systems. For example, a medical practitioner's competence in a future in which medical expert systems are widespread may be defined to include the competence to understand the certification and testing standards of systems to the point that he can translate the small print at the back of the user's manual or contract in the same way that he now understands the practical meaning of the small print on drug packaging. This definition may look unreasonable, but in a common-law system it can arise merely from a court decision which is then treated as a legal precedent.

It is possible to measure liability of *each* kind of human associate of an expert system who has been mentioned in this article, and not only of the professional closest to the injury, in terms of the principles outlined above. The emphasis shifts for different categories, e.g. the bias is all towards a sufficient knowledge and competent practice in computer science (of the kind which is presently labelled as 'too theoretical' by many software houses and companies selling computer-based products and services) on the part of the builder of an inference engine. However, the tests of the principles themselves remain. Anybody in any category who fails a test which is relevant for him is probably liable for negligence or malpractice following the injury or damage caused through the mediation of an expert system. In the most remote category, it is not impossible in the present state of law that defective performance of an expert system because of a fault or mistake in a new method for mechanised inference on inconsistent knowledge-bases renders the inventor of the method liable, even though he may be a theoretician who is unaware of the possible use of his work in the implementation of expert systems.

Although it does not follow directly from the discussion above, it is worth remarking that the different human associates of an expert system whose liability is to be tested in a legal action may be in widely differing places in several countries, e.g. because of the use of networks. If that occurs, there will possibly be a repetition on a grand scale of an event [12] which took place in Baldock, England, around 1910, when local police operated a speed trap on a road running from Baldock to Royston in Cambridgeshire. 'Your Worships,' the defending lawyer in one case said after listening to the laborious presentation by the prosecutor of all the details of the speed trap, 'this is a simple case of geography. You should know that Royston is just within Cambridgeshire, whereas Baldock, as you must know, lies within Herts. The alleged offences with which you are dealing therefore took place in two counties. You are not competent here in this court to try an offence committed in another county, and the same holds true at Royston.' The moral is not spoiled by the fact that Royston and Baldock are now both in Hertfordshire.

NO HUMAN LIABILITY?

All of the discussion so far suggests that living with expert systems in the current state of the law may be a cause of some nervousness. But there is a final problem which gives one even more reason to be nervous; so much of a reason that sensible legislation should be sought which is capable of providing simple and just remedies for all of those potential problems which may lead to court actions if the law is left as it is at present.

A set of rules of expert knowledge which are of the types R1 and R2 imitates the inferential behaviour of an expert and makes recommendations because the consequences from one rule can be the <situation> for other rules, generating a complex path of activations of rules. Popular wisdom is that a program can only do what it is told to do, and in some sense the rules tell the expert system what to do, but it is impossible to ensure in practice that tests of the system can check out all the possible distinct inputs and all possible paths (especially since these may contain loops) in advance. Therefore a system can give results that are consistent with the rules but which are unforeseeable. If it happens that some such result leads to injury or damage, this may be no fault of any contributing human expert (even more so if the rule-base is the work of no one individual expert), because the case may be one which human experts have never thought out previously and which requires them to revise their knowledge.

An alternative way of putting this is to say that rules and contributions in good faith from the experts are all sound by themselves, but that it is the interaction of rules which the system processes that causes the injury. Implausible science-fiction films like *Alphaville* or *2001* in which a computing system has its own personality are not uncommon. Here, however, is a very mundane and completely plausible example of how a programmed computer can be said to behave as if 'it has a mind of its own'. The behaviour does not exhibit all the characteristics of human persons, but neither is it totally impersonal. This is a practical instance of the argument of Narayanan [14] that it makes sense to ascribe some mental predicates to computers. It may be possible to go further and treat computers as having some legal rights [15], if this simplifies the application of law to cases of injury or damage which are not clearly the fault of any human agent. Alternatively, a completely different and rather simpler legal structure may be appropriate for the treatment of problems arising from the internal functioning of expert systems.

A MODEST PROPOSAL

If the cause of apparent negligence is traced to such an example, who is now liable? Probably everyone who has been mentioned above, on a bad day in California or Baldock, but luckily no court has yet had to decide.

Who should be liable? A commonsense answer is that nobody is genuinely negligent under these circumstances, because an expert system is a new kind of object, capable of new behaviours (including the future possibility of updating its own rule-base by automated means relying on forms of inference) and needing special legislative attention. For evidently similar reasons, nuclear power plants in some countries, including Britain, are covered by special provisions [16] which remove the possibility of actions for negligence in similar cases and establish insurance to compensate for injury and damage as at least partly a national rather than a private responsibility. The principle has been extended to other mixed hazards and blessings of modern life too, as in the 'no-fault' traffic-accident insurance scheme in New Zealand [19], and other examples quoted in the 1978 report [18] of a Royal Commission on civil liability and compensation.

A prediction that expert systems will ultimately be treated in this manner is safe to make, because it is much fairer than any of the traditional legal alternatives. The most important question is whether this will occur through informed planning before any innocent professional faces an action for negligence or malpractice, or whether possibly imperfect legislation will be introduced hastily after courts make decisions on such actions which are clearly unsatisfactory. It is therefore worth the time of professionals in fields which seem amenable to mechanisation by expert-system rules to consider how they can help to ensure that the first of these two alternatives will eventually be the true one.

ACKNOWLEDGEMENT

I am indebted to Mr Mervyn Bennun for the suggestion of the title of this article and for helpful general discussions, and to Dr J. D. Myers for an interpretation of some of the results of tests of the INTERNIST program.

NOTES

[1] K. M. Colby, J. B. Watt and J. P. Gilbert (1966) *J. Nervous and Mental Diseases* **141**, 148.
[2] J. Doyle (1979) *Proc. Int. Joint Conf. A.I.*, **6**, 232.
[3] H. L. A. Hart and A. M. Honore (1959) *Causation in the Law*, Oxford University Press, London.
[4] Hart and Honore, p. 378.
[5] C. Hewitt (1975) *Proc. Int. Joint Conf. A.I.*, **4**, 189.
[6] G. Kolata (1982) *Science* **217**, 4566.
[7] R. Lindsay, B. G. Buchanan, E. A. Feigenbaum and J. Lederberg (1980) *Application of Artificial Intelligence for Organic Chemistry: the DENDRAL Project*, McGraw Hill, New York.
[8] Maynard *v*. West Midlands Regional Health Authority (formerly Birmingham Regional Hospital Board), Court of Appeal (Civil Division), 21 December 1981.
[9] R. A. Miller, H. E. Pople and J. D. Myers (1982) *New England J. Med.* **307**, 468.
[10] M. A. Millner (1967) *Negligence in Modern Law*, Butterworth, London, p. 193.
[11] Millner, p. 98.
[12] G. R. N. Minchin (1950) *Under My Bonnet*, Foulis, London, p. 74.
[13] J. Moses (1971) *Comm. Assoc. Comput. Mach.*, **14**, 548.
[14] A. Narayanan (1981) 'Ascribing Mental Predicates to Computers', Research Report R. 102, Department of Computer Science, Exeter University.
[15] A. Narayanan and D. Perrott (1984) 'Can Computers Have Legal Right?', in this volume.
[16] The relevant legislation is the Nuclear Installations Act 1965. An operator of an installation is required to insure against damages up to a specified sum, but damages in excess of that sum or awarded after the period (defined in the Act) during which the operator is not protected by limitation of liability are met from public money.
[17] Parker *v*. London and North Eastern Railway Company, *L.T.* **176**, 137, (1945).
[18] 'Report of the Royal Commission on Civil Liability and Compensation for Personal Injury'. Cmnd. 7054 (HMSO, London, 1978).
[19] Note 17, vol. 3. ch. 10. The items of legislation concerned are the Accident Compensation Act, 1972, and the Accident Compensation Amendment Act (No. 2), 1973.
[20] J. A. Robinson (1965) *J. Assoc. Comput. Mach.*, **12**, 23.
[21] W. V. H. Rogers (1979) *Winfield & Jolowicz on Tort*, 11th edition, Sweet and Maxwell, London, p. 88.
[22] Tremain *v*. Pike, *W.L.R.*, **1**, 1556 (1969); *L.Q.R.*, **86**, 151 (1970).

[23] Ybarra *v*. Spangard, Cal. 2d., **25**, 486 (1944); P. 2d. **154**, 687 (1944).
[24] L. A. Zadeh (1979) in *Machine Intelligence 9*, eds. J. E. Hayes, D. Michie and L. I. Mikulich, Ellis Horwood, Chichester, p. 149.

Can computers have legal rights?

A. Narayanan and D. Perrott University of Exeter UK

I. The possibility of intelligent artefacts inhabiting the same domain as people poses many challenging questions. One such question, 'Can computers be considered as persons?', has been dealt with in a separate paper [1], where it was shown that computers *could* be regarded as persons from a philosophical point of view.

In this paper we ask a further question: 'Can computers have legal rights?' Of course, computers have no legal rights under the present system, but this does not make the question meaningless, since researchers in artificial intelligence are considering the possibility of building so-called 'self-propelled, manipulative thinking machines' based on the development of present day digital computers.

There are two ways of examining the question. The first is to approach the question from a strict legal point of view and say that just as a person has certain rights under the legal interpretation of 'rights', the computer, by fulfilling certain conditions attached to being a person, can also have a similar set of rights. The second way is to approach the problem from a socio-political or socio-legal point of view and examine the possibility that as computers develop in the future some decision will have to be made as to whether computers should have rights conferred upon them by a deliberate legislative act. Rights for computers may then not be the same as rights for persons, but nevertheless computers will have rights of a certain kind.

We intend to concentrate on the first approach but shall also say a few words about the second.

Let us first examine the concept of legal rights. It should be noted at the outset that the meaning of 'legal rights' has varied throughout the ages and that in examining the concept of legal rights we shall be adopting a contemporary view which may not exist in the future. Also, the contemporary view that we shall examine is just one of several available. However, it appears that this particular view is widely held in legal circles, so we shall adopt it as ours. The view is that 'right' connotes four different ideas concerning the relationship of one person X with reference to another person Y [2].

(1) Y's duty with regard to X would be expressed by X as, 'you must' (X has a right, *sensu stricto*, or claim).
(2) X's freedom to do something in relation to Y would be expressed by X as, 'I may' (X has a liberty or privilege).
(3) X's ability to alter Y's legal position would be expressed by X as, 'I can' (X has a power).
(4) Y's inability to alter X's legal position would be expressed by X as, 'you cannot' (X has an immunity).

Hohfeld [2] used these four ideas to set out a table of 'jural relations'. We have 'jural correlatives', in which each item of the pairs 'right' and 'duty', 'privilege' and 'no-right', 'power' and 'liability', 'immunity' and 'disability' is associated with X and Y, respectively. We also have 'jural opposites' which, too, are pairs, where the first item of the pair refers to X and the second to Y, and these are 'right' and 'no-right', 'privilege' and 'duty', 'power' and 'disability', and finally 'immunity' and 'liability'.

Hohfeld suggested that 'right' could be substituted by the first type of relation mentioned above – the 'right-duty' relationship. That is, 'claim' could be substituted for 'right'. The implication of this view is that a right in the sense of a claim is a sign that some person is obliged to behave in a certain way. If that person does not fulfil the obligation, the right-bearer may be able to obtain compensation for the non-fulfilment of the obligation.

It is important to note that although the existence of a right implies the existence of correlative duty, the existence of a duty does not necessarily imply the existence of a correlative right. For instance, if a woman has a right to an abortion, then there will be a surgeon who, when asked by the woman for an abortion, has a duty to carry out the operation. However, if one has a duty to look after one's pet cats by feeding them periodically, it is debatable as to whether one's pet cats have the right to such treatment. Another important point to note is that the right-bearer has the choice of deciding whether the person who has a duty of some kind in relation to the right-bearer should fulfil the obligation. According to Hohfeld's schema, this is represented by the 'X has a liberty or privilege' relationship. Hart [3] incorporates this relationship in his own 'elucidation' of the expression 'a legal right'.

(1) A statement of the form 'X has a right' is true if the following conditions are satisfied:
    (a) There is in existence a legal system.
    (b) Under the rules of the legal system, some person Y is, in the events which have happened, obliged to do or abstain from some action.
    (c) This obligation is made by law dependent on the choice of X (or some

person deputed to act on X's behalf) so that Y is bound to do or abstain from some action only if X (or X's representative) so chooses or alternatively only until X (or such person) chooses otherwise.

(2) A statement of the form 'X has a right' is used to draw a conclusion of law in a particular case which falls under such rules.

II. Let us now discuss the question as to whether computers can have legal rights. We have already seen from our examination of the concept of 'legal right' how the right-duty relationship is important for our understanding of the concept given the current sense of the phrase. If we wish to adopt the right-duty relationship in our approach, the freedom, or privilege, or liberty, or choice, condition becomes crucial. We accept that a human with rights has freedom to choose, and can therefore decide whether another person who has an obligation of some kind towards himself or herself should fulfil that obligation. Let us now ask whether a computer has a similar freedom to choose. We assume two protagonists, A and B, who discuss the question.

A: You cannot say that a computer has a similar freedom of choice, since a computer's behaviour is wholly determined by its program or control structure and cannot depart from a prescribed course. The program or control structure will consist of a series of instructions. The computer cannot decide whether it wants to follow these instructions or not. A computer simply executes the instructions.

B: This objection embodies the view that computers can only do what they are told to do and is based on the rejection of a mechanism as being able to provide an adequate model of the mind. That is, you reject the view that minds can be modelled on machines since machines are deterministic entities, whereas minds are not. However, you overlook the possibility of a computer being given a set of primitive rules and some basic knowledge so that after some time it starts to construct its own programs, strategies, knowledge-base, and so on. After a period of time, we may no longer be able to predict the behaviour of a computer on a wide variety of inputs. Given a certain goal, it will break down this goal into sub-goals, and the way it does this will depend on current knowledge, experience, and so on, which are not predictable on the basis of the current rules. I am in effect attempting to distinguish between machines and computers.

A: I don't think I follow you. What exactly are you trying to say? How could a computer's behaviour possibly be unpredictable?

B: My argument consists of appealing to future developments when a computer will be treated in the same way as a child. Just as we instruct the child in its early stages on how to read and write, to manipulate arithmetic symbols, and so on, with a view to getting the child to think for itself and be an autonomous being when it matures, I claim that in the future we shall be able to give a computer a set of 'primitive' instructions which enable it to construct its own learning strategies and problem-solving methods. Just as with a child in its early stages, we would be able to predict the behaviour of the computer on certain inputs early on. But, again just as with a child, as the computer's knowledge-base expands and it tackles increasingly complicated tasks, the computer's behaviour becomes less predictable. After a certain stage, the computer will be able to write its own programs to solve particular problems on the basis of its knowledge, and there will soon come a time when the computer's behaviour is completely unpredictable on a wide range of inputs. Some tasks it will solve, others it will not. But we will not be able to state which problems fall into which category until the computer responds. Would you not then say that the computer has learned to think for itself given the primitive set of instructions, just as a child learns to think for itself given the primitive set of instructions it learns at school?

A: Well, even if the case of a computer being given a set of primitive rules by means of which it constructs unpredicted strategies, programs, and knowledge-base is granted, the behaviour of the computer is still in principle predictable. That is, even in such a case we could predict the computer's behaviour on a certain input if we had enough information concerning the computer's programs, strategies and knowledge-base. So the principle of predictability and determinism remains even in such a case. Hence, computers cannot have freedom of choice in the same way as we humans have such freedom. Even you will have to accept that.

B: I accept no such thing. What I would like to say is that you could equally apply this to humans, thereby making a person's behaviour completely predictable and determinate. That is, it can be argued that if we had enough information concerning a person's past experiences, his attitudes, his problem-solving strategies, and so on, then we too could predict what the person would do given a certain output. And there is the advantage in that if we are wrong in our prediction concerning a person's behaviour, we can always say that we did not have enough information after all!

A: But this is ridiculous. In the case of a person, we cannot be sure what is input or experienced. The person possesses sense organs which enable that person to acquire all sorts of information continuously about his or her environment. So we can never be sure what experiences the person has had, or what the person's knowledge-base consists of.

B: Your argument depends on regarding computer input as being easily identifiable chunks of information. Given a camera as an 'eye', the computer too can sense its surroundings continuously and receive information from its environment. So, in the case of computers, too, 'input' may not be easily identified.

A: That may be true, but we cannot inspect a person's memory and knowledge-base, whereas we can inspect a computer's magnetic tapes, disks and even ask the computer to display information held in core memory. So the principle of predictability still remains for computers.

B: But what if the computer's strategy is such that it has decided to store the information in a way which is not intelligible to humans? Or what if the computer, when asked to display core information, disguises the true nature of the information, in the same way that a shy person may be too embarrassed to talk about past events? Our set of primitive rules would allow the computer to develop a certain personality, to do what it likes with the information it receives.

A: I can see that I am not getting very far here. So let me change tack slightly. Since the set of primitive rules you wish to feed into the computer determines the future development of the computer, if two identical computers were given the same set of primitive rules and were kept in identical environments, would their behaviour not be exactly similar? Computers in such a situation are deterministic after all in that their behaviour will not vary.

B: But could you guarantee that human beings in such a situation would turn out to be different? I could argue, surely, that genetic and neurophysiological differences between a pair of humans would lead the humans, if exposed to the same set of instructions and experiences in their early stages, to exhibit different kinds of behaviour. The analogous argument in the case of computers then would be that if we wire the computers differently, they would not exhibit identical behaviour patterns on the same set of primitive rules. So if we had two identical humans, identical in all senses, then they too would be identical in their behaviour.

At this point, let us move away from an examination of the freedom of choice condition. An objection to the thesis that computers can have legal rights might be to say that if computers have legal rights, they should have legal duties as well. That is, if a computer is to have the status of an entity with legal rights, then it should have the full status of an entity within the legal system, which implies that it should have legal duties as well as legal rights.

We now wish to argue that:

(a) computers can have legal duties;
(b) computers can have legal rights.

(a) Imagine that a computer inflicts some type of injury on some individual or set of individuals, which we shall call the 'third party'. The damage could take various forms (a faulty or negligent robot which causes injury to an individual, or a computer sending a bill to an individual by mistake, thereby causing a heart-attack on the part of that person and hospitalisation). Now, the third party would normally be able to sue for compensation the person who was responsible for causing the injury or, if the person responsible was engaged in legitimate business on behalf of an employer, that person's employer. This legal mechanism ensures that if the person responsible for causing the injury is not capable of paying a sum of money which befits the type of injury inflicted, the injured third party can sue that person's employer, who it is assumed will be able to pay such a sum of money. This legal mechanism also allows the employer, if sued, to obtain part of the compensation paid from the person responsible for causing the injury in the first place.

Now, if we replace 'employers of the person causing the injury' with 'owner of the computer causing the injury', the injured third party can sue either the owner of the computer that caused the injury or the computer itself for compensation. For this replacement of phrase to be justified, we have to show that computers are capable of paying compensation to an injured third party or contributing towards the sum of money paid out as compensation by its owner. This can be argued as follows. A society which uses a computer or robot that interacts with society to the benefit of society can set aside a fund, which is then used to pay out compensation should the need arise. The computer has access to the fund and can attempt to increase the amount of money in the fund by investing, and so on. An injured third party can then apply for compensation from the fund. Also, the owner of the computer who has paid damages to an injured third party can apply for money from the fund to offset the damages that he has paid to an injured third party.

Another argument could be that if the computer is involved with financial transactions there will be a rounding of figures to two decimal places in many cases where the computer uses percentage rates to determine how much money is involved (e.g. £10.85560). Sometimes the rounding will be upwards, other times downwards. It may be possible to alter the rounding criterion in such a way that the computer 'benefits' to the tune of a fraction of a penny which it can deposit into its own personal account. If the computer is executing thousands of such computations a day, the amount of money in its account will gradually grow. If the computer is then sued for damages either by a third party or by its owner, the money in this account can be used to pay such damages.

A further argument concerns those computers or robots which do not have such a fund available. It is conceivable in cases where such machines inflict injury on a third party that the third party could claim payment in kind. This would involve the machine being temporarily reprogrammed in order to serve the injured third party in some way for a suitable length of time. The injured third party may even decide to lease out the computer with its original program to others, thereby benefiting from the rent paid to him.

(b) Now let us discuss how it is possible for computers to have rights. Imagine the case where a person acts as a trustee for a beneficiary or set of beneficiaries. The trustee is given certain valuable items to look after by the beneficiary and then executes certain transactions on behalf of the beneficiary. Any third party the trustee deals with will treat the trustee in the same way as the third party would do with the beneficiary directly. That is, the trustee has exactly the same rights as the beneficiary. However, it is not necessary for the third party to know who the beneficiary is. The beneficiary has certain legal rights with respect to the trustee, who in turn has certain legal duties to the beneficiary. So, for instance, if the trustee acts negligently or fraudulently with respect to the valuable items given to him by the beneficiary, the beneficiary can claim damages from the trustee. Also, the trustee has the same rights with respect to a third party as the beneficiary would do if acting alone. In the case of such a model, we would also say that the beneficiary has an 'equitable right', which is not so strong as the strict legal right, with respect to the third party. Now, replace 'trustee' with 'computer acting as trustee'. Some beneficiary may hand over certain items of value to a computer which then acts as a trustee on behalf of the beneficiary. Any third party involved with respect to the computer would then have the same legal duties towards the computer as the third party would have with respect to the (human) beneficiary. Also, the computer acting as trustee has the same rights with respect to the third party as the beneficiary would do if acting alone. Thus, computers can have rights within the framework of this legal model. So, for instance, a beneficiary may place money in the possession of the computer which then acts as a trustee by investing it, and so on. If the computer then interacts with third parties, those third parties will have the same legal duties towards the computer as they would have to the beneficiary alone. So if the computer asked for the beneficiary's money to be invested in a certain way, the third party would have the legal duty of fulfilling this obligation. In terms of the above legal models, it appears that it is possible for computers to have rights given the legal system's concept of 'rights' and 'duties'.

Computers can have rights after all, just as persons do, in which case we have provided an affirmative answer to the question posed in the title of this paper. However, it may be argued that computers cannot in fact have rights, and that if computers can have rights given the strict legal concepts of 'right' and 'duty', then these concepts need modifying in order to exclude the possibility of computers having rights. In either case, there is no doubt that the question as to whether computers can have rights raises some interesting problems for the legal profession, since it questions the exact nature and position of the dividing line between entities which can have a certain legal status (legal persons) and those which cannot (non-legal persons). It may be unfair to ask the legal profession to provide an exact description of this dividing line, since the formulation of such a description is normally considered to be the task of philosophers, or experts in the various human sciences, or of society in general. Our argument in this paper has been of the following form:

(1) computers can be regarded as persons (not shown in this paper);
(2) persons have certain legal rights (given);
(3) therefore computers can have legal rights.

Note that the word 'can' in lines (1) and (3) expresses logical possibility, not empirical probability. Let us now finally examine the question, 'Can computers have legal rights?', from a socio-legal, hence empirical, point of view.

III. In the future, society will be placing more and more responsibility onto computers to ensure the smooth functioning of certain social processes. It is envisaged that the programmer(s) will be given the task of programming the computer in the same way that parents look after a child. When the computer achieves a certain level of maturity, i.e. when the computer performs its task consistently well and has learned to 'look after' itself, the programmer will relinquish responsibility for the computer, at which time society will take over responsibility. In order to ensure that the computer functions smoothly and is not interfered with to the detriment of society, society may well feel like passing laws that create the right for the computer not to undertake tasks on behalf of persons which would harm society. A formulation of these rights can be given to the computer so that when it judges that a certain input request may lead to harm being inflicted on society, it will be able to assess its own legal position in the matter. The embodiment of such rights in a computer may in fact be a way for society to protect itself against the undesirable effects of a powerfully intelligent machine which decides to act on its own behalf. In such a case, the threat of a legally sanctioned punishment may prevent an extremely powerful and independent computer from executing tasks which would harm individuals or society.

So a deliberate legislative act in the future conferring rights on computers may be motivated by two factors: (i) to prevent individuals from interfering with the normal running of a computer to the detriment of other individuals or society in general; (ii) to present to an extremely intelligent and powerful computer the information concerning possible legal sanctions against it should it fail to execute its duties satisfactorily. We could be talking in terms of 'contracting' a computer to do certain jobs sometime in the near future. Now let us examine two aspects of computer use which may well be the first to involve computers as legal entities.

MEDICINE

Let us assume that a paralysed and bed-ridden person is being looked after completely by a computer-controlled life-maintaining machine. The computer has full responsibility for monitoring the subject's condition, administering food, drink, drugs, blood and other items. Let us assume that the computer has direct access to such items as food, drink, drugs and blood by being able to tap into food-stores and drink-pipes, blood-banks, drug-cupboard and so on. One day, the computer's pipe to the blood-bank becomes blocked. The computer signals an alarm which brings a human non-medical operator to the scene. 'Check the blood-pipes!' says the computer. We can envisage that in such a situation the operator may have the legal duty to do as the computer asks. That is, the computer may have had conferred on it the legal right to demand immediate attention when it realises that something is going wrong. If it is objected that computers need not have rights in such situations and that the operator has a legal duty to the subject being cared for by the computer and not the computer itself, we can use the trustee model mentioned earlier so that the computer is acting as a trustee for an item of value to the beneficiary – his life. Also, it is possible that the computer is looking after hundreds of subjects and not just one. Now the operator need not know who the subject is who needs the transfusion, nor perhaps whether there is one at the particular time the computer demands attention.

INFORMATION TECHNOLOGY

With the death of the printed word forecast on economic and ecological grounds, it is possible to envisage a situation where the only access that individuals have to news, books and information in general is through a telecommunication link between a home viewdata monitor and centralised or regionalised data-banks. At present, it is possible to publish just about anything, even if the material is embarrassing to the government of the day. It is possible to suppress the distribution and sale of books, but more difficult to prevent the act of printing the material itself. Once printed, the literature may be distributed illegally, but it can be distributed just the same. One of the pillars of contemporary thinking concerning democracy is considered to be the right to access freely all available information. In the society of the future, there will be no paper, no printing machines. If a government of the future were to decide that some piece of information was of too sensitive a nature to be put or left on a data-bank, it would be much easier for that government to deny potential readers access to that information either by not allowing the information onto the data-bank to start off with or by deleting the relevant piece of information from the data-bank. Given such a possibility, we may well feel that the decision as to what is to be inserted into the data-bank or what is to be deleted should be taken away from individuals and left in the first instance to the computer. The computer will use its knowledge of society's fundamental right of access to information in order to decide whether a request by, say, a government official to delete certain items of information should be granted. It will be given the right to make such a decision. The computer may well decide to turn down the government official's petition. If the government official wishes to pursue the matter, this will have to be done through the law-courts, thereby introducing an element of accountability on the part of the government. The computer may also have the right to decide whether information to be inserted into the data-bank conforms to certain required standards. For instance, it may decide not to store information which consists of unsubstantiated facts, propaganda, personal attacks and so on. Again, if the person wishing to input the information wants the computer's decision overturned, this will have to be done through the law-courts. In the cases of insertion and deletion of information, the information technology society of the future may well feel that by conferring rights onto computers to make decisions in the first instance, it is protecting one of the central pillars of the democratic state.

We stress again that these models of jurisprudence and law mentioned in the paper are not the only ones possible and that if different models were used, different consequences could well arise for the question, 'Can computers have legal rights?'.

ACKNOWLEDGEMENT

We should like to thank Masoud Yazdani for his constructive and helpful ideas and suggestions during the writing of this chapter.

NOTES

[1] 'Ascribing Mental Predicates to Computers', A. Narayanan, 1981. Research Report R. 102, Department of Computer Science, Exeter University.

[2] This exposition of Hohfeld's view is taken from Jurisprudence, R. Dias (Butterworths) 3rd Edition, 1970, pp 248–251.

[3] 'Definition and Theory in Jurisprudence', H. L. A. Hart. This paper was in fact Hart's first lecture in the Chair of Jurisprudence at Oxford and was delivered in 1954. The paper can be found in Introduction to Jurisprudence, Lloyd (ed.) (Stevens) 4th Edition, 1979.

PART 2

INTELLIGENT MACHINES AND HUMAN SOCIETY

1. SOCIAL IMPLICATIONS: WHO CARES?

This essay aims to persuade AI researchers that it is about time they started caring about the social implications of AI in a constructive way. Until now AI researchers could have been forgiven for not caring, as their research has been seen to be laboratory-based. However, the first fruits of the applied side of AI in the form of Expert Systems has reached the market, and there is no reason to assume that more ambitious laboratory projects might never see the light of day.

Some AI researchers justify their lack of enthusiasm for consideration of the social effects of their work by pointing out that an AI researcher cannot become a jack of all trades. Already he has to know computing, psychology, philosophy and, maybe, linguistics. Adding sociology to the list would just further dilute the spread of his intellectual resources. It is argued, therefore, that it is better to call in a sociologist to study the effects of AI on society. While appreciating the need for sociologists to become involved with the effects of AI on society, in this essay I would like to argue that a personal interest on the part of an individual researcher can play an important role in making these effects more beneficial rather than dangerous.

A few years ago when I presented a talk on the social implications of AI, the title of the talk was unintentionally changed to 'Dangers of AI' by the seminar organiser. Many people seem to take the two to mean the same thing, and automatically feel defensive. Here, I would like to argue that a researcher concerned with social implications is one who sees his work in a wide context and uses his analysis of this context with a view towards helping society rather than endangering it.

It has also been said that computer technology has started to descend on our society like a snowball which nothing can stop. They argue that any discussion of its social impact at this stage would be idle talk; whether or not we agree with the use of calculators in schools, they are now so widely available that any questioning of their role would not make any difference. I do not entirely agree with this fatalistic view. However, if this were the case, intelligent machines are far away from being widely available; we still have some time. This argument, however, would serve as an illustration of the urgency for us to bring the considerations of social implications into the mainstream of research work and public debate. In this way we might not stop the snowball, but we could at least direct its route to a beneficial, rather than harmful, one for human society.

2. THE PERSONAL AND PHILOSOPHICAL IMPLICATIONS

The philosophical implications of machine intelligence have always been the subject of controversy, as the introduction to Part 5 of this book demonstrates. While accepting the importance of such issues, as well as their relevance to social issues, it is important not to give them a disproportionate amount of importance compared to the social effects. Boden [1], for example, has argued that 'perhaps the greatest significance of the computer lies in its impact on man's view of himself . . . his picture of the universe and his place and goals in it . . .'. Such a line of reasoning would put the effects of AI on the same level as Galileo's discovery of the movement of the earth around the sun and Darwin's discovery of the relationship of man to other species. At each stage, humanity's ego has suffered a blow; in the first instance by noting that the stars and sun were not there for man's sake, and in the second instance by knowing that, even on earth, we are not so much the master of it, but a part of it. The last rampart of pride is that at least we possess something magical in our capacity to think. If AI were to be successful in providing artifacts capable of thought, we could witness a further blow to our ego.

However important the implication, it would be wrong to consider it *the* most important one, compared to other minor ones in the social sphere (for example, mass unemployment). However much our ego is important to philosophers and the general public, preoccupation with the problems that humanity has suffered at the hands of Galileo and Darwin would not lead to mass nervous breakdowns. In the long term, time would provide a general acceptance of such controversial issues, while in the short term people generally, in their everyday lives, tend to close their eyes to such problems. A less philosophically important event, such as the industrial revolution, could have much further-reaching effects. The significance of AI is that it has both a philosophical significance comparable to evolution and a social one comparable to the industrial revolution.

3. ARTIFICIAL INTELLIGENCE AND HUMAN IGNORANCE

One of the many long-term effects of the industrial revolution has been the reduction in human society for the need for craftsmanship (the capability to do a manual task skilfully). As new, faster and, in some cases, even more accurate machinery has produced goods which replaced the craftsmen who produced goods prior to the industrial revolution, such people have moved to other areas of activity and have not passed on their skills to the next generation. Therefore, the skills which were the property of people have been taken away from them and invested in machines. On the surface, this would appear to be not a very bad idea. The burden of production has been put onto the machines. This relies on the machines always being available and people being available to improve the craft further without actually possessing the basics of the skill itself.

A parallel exists between the process of 'deskilling' above, and the 'knowledge engineering' boom of the Expert System, where intellectual skills of people such as doctors, lawyers, etc., are being invested in computer systems which, at some time in the near future, could play a similar role to that of their mechanical counterparts. This would result in a similar loss of skill in the intellectual craftsmanship as that which has resulted from the industrial revolution.

If AI is successful in its general aims and progresses further into interesting intellectual capabilities more general than that of expert professionals, while computers become more intelligent, then humans will become more ignorant as they stop relying on their own intellectual ability. This is similar to the situation in the western world where the capability of performing mental arithmetic has been lost to a large number of people in return for electronic calculators.

This situation could lead to professional pessimists rushing out to wave 'ban AI' banners, while responsible AI researchers would note that the risks would not be that fatal if they at least made sure that the knowledge was not lost in the code of their program. Acceptance of social responsibility would therefore seriously affect the research methodology of scientists; there are a number of ways to represent knowledge, although some of them would be obscured to human subjects while making them more efficient for computers to manipulate. In other ways, of course, the reverse would be true.

Masoud Yazdani

NOTE

[1] Boden in Forester (ed.) (1980).
For details, see the bibliography at the end of the book.

The papers in this section consider a variety of important issues which need to be considered. Brady's paper presents the basic issues in the form of the relationship of the individual to (1) the economy, (2) the state, and (3) himself and others. Most of the issues apply to the computer revolution in general, but touch on the further issues arising from developments in AI.

Chamot looks at the issues related to employment, as this would have the most immediate effect on the public. Most people relate to society, themselves and others via their work – employment being central to an individual's financial and *emotional well-being. The issue of employment deserves immediate attention.*

Gill opens up the debate into a very wide context in which he looks at more topical issues such as Knowledge Engineering, the Japanese Fifth Generation computer project and issues relating to physically, mentally and socially-disadvantaged sections of society.

The social implications of AI*

J. M. Brady Massachusetts Institute of Technology USA

No man is an island entire of himself . . .
. . . and therefore never send to know for whom the bell tolls, it tolls for thee
(John Donne, *Devotions* XVIII)

INTRODUCTION

The potential for the misapplication of AI findings is great and the portents are that it will be fully realised. Citizens will increasingly look for explanation, reassurance and leadership to the scientific community whose members must individually and collectively bear the responsibility of speaking out clearly on matters of concern.

Some AI workers apparently believe that the whole issue of social implications of developments in their subject is either not an interesting topic, or not serious, or, more commonly, not something which is, or should be, of direct concern to the individual working scientist.

It is perhaps appropriate to start with a plain aphorism: knowledge is the key to power, and the knowledge embedded in any significant scientific advance can be interpreted for the general good or harm of society. The cuts of the two-edged sword forged by scientific advance are well-known. The development of nuclear physics has not only brought atomic weaponry, nuclear fall-out, and the difficulties of plutonium waste disposal, but has given society such benefits as electrical power derived from nuclear fission, as well as employment for thousands of highly skilled scientists in lavish laboratories. The use of enzymes and other recombinants to 'cut and paste' the genes of micro-organisms has raised the spectre of human engineering and the accidental (or purposeful)

*This chapter was first presented as a paper at the 1979 AISB Summer School of Edinburgh University. It is published with no revisions to the original transcript.

development of uncontrollable hostile organisms. The quite remarkable pace of developments in chemistry have not only produced antimicrobials and vaccines, but the resultant near eradication of previously killer diseases, such less desirable effects as thalidomide, a valium-dependent society, and the wonders of chemical warfare.

Within the computer sciences, examples abound, though there are few which illustrate the issues quite as clearly as the provision of computing power for the police. Let us accept the need for a state-organised law enforcement agency charged to combat all forms of crime. Note that while the raw number of crimes has steadily increased over the past few years, the rate of detection has not, and currently stands somewhere under 30 per cent in major British cities. Further, note the development of highly professional criminal groups, employing sophisticated electronics and organised along lines developed by the military, against which the police have an even poorer detection rate, notwithstanding special units expressly set up to combat 'Organised Crime'. Put this way, few citizens would deny the police the very latest sophisticated equipment. Yet, as the National Council for Civil Liberties regularly reminds us, having such facilities at their disposal increases the power of the police to coordinate information about a person's driving, employment, and health records with his tax situation, and enables them to effectively harass troublesome individuals such as vociferous shop stewards, or minority group leaders.

As a final example, recall that IQ testing as originally conceived by Binet, was intended to measure a child's general development as indicated by his abilities over a wide range of mental, manipulative and physical tasks. In practice, IQ testing has been used to label people as educationally sub-normal, as a condition of entry to the self-appointed high priesthood of MENSA, to bar people from jobs and college and to rationalise racism.

In view of this dismal track record, it seems massively naive and optimistic to believe that the temptation to misapply the developments of AI will long be resisted. We need to be constantly aware of the potential misapplications, and to ask what, if anything, the AI community can or should do to prevent them.

2. EMPLOYMENT AND THE RELATION OF AN INDIVIDUAL TO THE ECONOMY

In our current conception of society, survival and prosperity is directly coupled to an individual's work, at which most people spend the bulk of their conscious existence. Unemployment is a social stigma, and our thinking about it is not far removed from the Victorian workhouse. To be retired is, for many people, a state in which they are no longer regarded (or no longer regard themselves) as useful productive members of society, but an encumbrance to those who do work.

One obvious social consequence of applications of the developments of computer science (including AI) is the disappearance or substantial down-grading of entire job categories (for example, bank tellers or accounting clerks), as tasks previously performed by humans are automated. Against the background sketched above, it is hardly surprising if workers currently occupying positions in threatened job categories act to protect their livelihood by resisting automation, even as the Luddites did in the aftermath of the first industrial revolution. Word processors and computer typesetting may well be marvellous innovations, may even be the thing to 'save' the British newspaper industry (as *The Times* management puts it), but don't expect the National Graphical Association (NGA) to lead the cheering. Of course, the technology will win in the end. Even John Henry couldn't stop the steam hammer. Being skilled workers, the NGA work force could easily be retrained for equally highly-paid jobs. Indeed, it might be argued that we need to move away from the gold-watch-for-years-of-faithful-service mentality to the norm of educating people to accept the need for retraining for two or three careers in a single lifetime. One must not underestimate the difficulties; retraining and resettlement programmes have not all been sparkling successes. Just ask around in Merseyside, Clydebank, Tyneside, and the South of Wales to see what people think.

The industrial revolution also saw the end of many cottage industries, and of many specialised skills made redundant by the newer technology. Overall, though, there was a tremendous increase in the number of jobs and job categories available to workers, and there is no obvious reason to suppose that such will not also be true of the 'second' industrial revolution. Furthermore, the ending of certain job categories may well be deemed a social advance. We are nowadays horrified to recall that children of primary school age climbed up and swept chimneys, and sat for hours in cramped wet conditions providing lighting for miners. (We should of course also recall how hard-won were the reforms that stopped such practices.) We might applaud the development of robots for car-bomb detection and disposal, and for deep-sea mining.

3. GOVERNMENT AND THE RELATION OF AN INDIVIDUAL TO THE STATE

Political differences have their clearest expression in the allocation of resources when demand greatly exceeds supply. For example, several third-world countries, such as Tanzania, have preferred to adopt the Chinese barefoot doctor scheme rather than the western model of highly sophisticated facilities centralised into a small number of lucky hospitals. Ideally, one would like to make the finest advice and facilities equally available to all. Technology can go some way to reducing differences as well as exacerbating them. The Australian flying doctor service makes medical consultation available to isolated farms which otherwise would have none. The MYCIN, CASNET/GLAUCOMA and similar systems can enable specialised advice to be available at any hospital at the cost of a terminal, far cheaper than establishing specialised clinics everywhere – a strategy which is not in fact feasible.

Large data-bases spanning every aspect of a citizen's existence can easily lead to decisions crucially affecting people's lives being taken without their knowledge or consent, and even on the basis of incorrect data (for there is no right of access to government-held information in Britain yet). Even if people have complete access to their files, there is usually no guarantee that poor programming won't lead to gross miscarriages of justice. AI programming ought to be of help in this situation by taking decisions in a more flexible way, after the fashion of a beneficient administrator. Such programs could have the relative advantage over human administrators of being scrupulously fair, avoiding charges of bribery and cronyism.

The computer processing of early election returns shows just how fast information really can be gathered and processed when it is in someone's vested interest. The idea that a government is voted in once every five years or so, subsequently claiming a 'clear mandate from the electorate' for the entire spectrum of their policies is a fiction that needs to be challenged. It is simply not at all clear that the only alternatives are massive and unworkable bureaucracy and endless referenda on every trivial issue. Citizens may be capable in the not-too-distant future of having their views ascertained on subjects of import, and it may be possible to infer them on others. Clearly, this is a suggestion that requires a great deal of working out, and the scope for malevolent misapplication is great as Ray Bradbury has pointed out in his novel *Fahrenheit 451*. Nevertheless, it can scarcely be less arbitrary than electing a single person to represent all the views of on average 50,000 electors. These ideas are only meant to be taken semi-seriously and are mainly intended to show that by making even current technology available to the average citizen, one provides the possibility for a reappraisal of government and the relationship of an individual to state.

4. EDUCATION AND THE RELATION OF AN INDIVIDUAL TO HIMSELF AND OTHERS

Margaret Boden [1] has given us a fine exposition of the potential dangers of a simplistic mechanistic conception of man, and the way in which the more elaborate models emanating from AI can counteract the humanist belief that mechanistic accounts are inevitably demeaning. I wish merely to add two remarks to her account.

One of Weizenbaum's [2] tendentious statements about AI can be paraphrased as follows: 'Increasingly detailed mechanistic accounts of man inevitably demean and strip him of self-respect. If we had a machine that could think as well as people, and whose detailed workings were completely open to inspection, we would find intellectual respect, pride and admiration impossible.'

The snags with this view are many, but we concentrate on just two. Firstly, the sheer enormity of programs that would be required to adequately model even the tiniest proportion of human thinking suggests that it will be extremely difficult for anybody to achieve a complete grasp of the detailed operation and overview of such a program. Very small programs such as the INTERLISP system and the UNIX operating system, both of the order of 100k, command considerable respect, even when one understands every last detail of their implementation.

But there is a much more important point that needs to be made. AI research has clearly shown that it is considerably easier to construct interesting, even psychologically plausible, models of ABSTRACT aspects of human thinking such as:

> IQ tests, integration problems, checkers (= draughts) playing, bridge-bidding, plane geometry, and even the interpretation of satellite images and mass spectrograms

than it is to construct even barely interesting models of the ordinary human abilities of seeing, hearing, using natural language, walking, and planning such things as movements in a crowded room. In a real sense, studying AI has precisely the opposite effect to that predicted by Weizenbaum: one becomes much more appreciative of the ordinary qualities of being human, and de-emphasises such relatively minor differences as passing the 11-plus examination, or getting the Nobel prize. For centuries, people have heaped lavish praise on those showing extraordinary abilities in science, literature, and the arts; but this seems to reflect social evaluation of those aspects of human behaviour. I believe that the 'genius of Johann Cruyff' may be a less flippant metaphor than is commonly supposed.

We should, however, take note of Weizenbaum's warning of the ease with which even the most model (e.g. ELIZA) of developments in AI can be blown up out of all proportion. To do anything but give a precise account of the capabilities and limitations of a system is socially irresponsible.

5. CONCLUSION

The industrial revolution brought the promise of enormous distributed wealth, liberation from acting as surrogate machines (e.g. pumping water out of mines), and the capacity for a large increase in personal freedom and mobility (e.g. car ownership). Although many of these were eventually realised, though only after considerable time and because of the Trojan efforts of men like Shaftesbury, the industrial revolution also saw the concentration of huge financial power in a small number of hands (the so-called 'capitalist barons'), and led to the horrors of factory life, the destruction of many cottage industries and rural communities, and the squalor of urban 'back-to-back' housing.

The 'second' industrial revolution may be even more two-edged; people acting once more as surrogate machines, inconvenienced to suit badly-programmed machines, unemployment resulting from automation, and the concentration of power over the dissemination of information.

It is not without significance that the major source of funding for AI in the USA is the Department of Defense. Recently large corporations such as IBM, GM and XEROX have funded AI research heavily. This may well work for the ultimate good of society, as well as for the optimal scientific development of AI, but the portents are not favourable.

Increasingly, ordinary citizens feel out of touch, unable to comprehend the rapid pace of developments in the 'computer revolution' which they are assured is taking place, and in which the country needs to participate if it is to remain a world power. The only tangible results they can see are redundancy notices, 'demand' notices for £0.0, and TERCOM missiles. Inevitably, the only people they can turn to for explanation, reassurance and leadership is the scientific community from whom the knowledge underlying the 'revolution' originated.

As a group, we cannot afford to fail society. Previous attempts to organise and lobby (such as the British Society for Social Responsibility in Science) have had scant success. It must therefore be the responsibility of individual scientists, and organisations such as AISB and AAAI, to speak out clearly and forcibly on matters of concern.

Clearly, John Donne got it right.

NOTES

[1] M. A. Boden (1977) *Artificial Intelligence and Natural Man*, Harvester (part IV).

[2] J. Weizenbaum (1976) *Computer Power and Human Reasoning*, Freeman.

Problems of transition*

D. Chamot Department for Professional Employees Washington DC USA

The application of new knowledge and new techniques to workplaces is a process that extends back into the time of the earliest civilizations. Technical changes have allowed for the development of modern society. While the science upon which these developments are based is completely neutral, the manner in which new knowledge is applied can have profound effects, both negative and positive, upon those whose work depends upon them.

A classic case involves the Luddites of early nineteenth-century England. The name of their movement is applied today to people who are opposed to new technologies in a mindless way. In this modern sense of the term, American unions (and those of many other countries) are certainly not Luddites, but it is useful to consider for a moment those earlier Britons.

At the time, the British national economy was not performing well, yet new high-productivity machines were being introduced into the textile industry. Wages were cut unilaterally, and many workers lost their jobs. The government of the day was not involved in alleviating the problems of the poor, and many of the unemployed faced starvation. Some of them destroyed some of the new machines.

It is important to note that this destruction was *not* mindless. It was, instead, a response resulting from the frustration of clearly recognizing the immediate threats of the situation yet seeing no way out of their predicament.

> Luddism . . . did buy them time – because of the threat of machine breaking, employers thought twice before investing in new devices or cutting

*This paper is based on remarks presented at the Eighth International Joint Conference on Artificial Intelligence, Karlsruhe, West Germany, on August 11, 1983. Participation was supported in part by a grant from the German Marshall Fund of the United States.

wages. Nor were the workers' tactics politically futile. Luddism was a significant factor behind the government's decision to repeal the Continental blockade in June 1812, which resulted in rapid economic improvement. [1]

The point is not that destruction of machinery is a proper tactic. It is not. The Luddite experience does demonstrate quite clearly, however, that the widespread introduction of productivity-enhancing technologies cannot be carried out without full concern for the social consequences.

Today's problems are potentially quite severe, in part because technological change is not limited to a single industry, nor is it limited to manufacturing. With the application of computers and microchips in every sector of the economy, we are witnessing nothing less than the redefinition of work. Unfortunately, this is occurring in a social context which is changing hardly at all.

Again, it may be useful to review a bit of history. All developed nations began with economies heavily dependent upon agriculture. As recently as a century ago, half of the American workforce was involved in growing food; that segment has dropped to three per cent today.

As new technologies and improved farming techniques increased productivity in the agricultural sector, many farmers left the land and were forced to find jobs in the cities, especially in the increasing number of factories. But factories from the beginning have used various mechanical, and later electrical, devices which by their nature are subject to constant improvement. Modern factories, even those that are a bit behind the times, are vastly more productive than factories of the past. They need to employ far fewer people than would have been necessary if we never advanced beyond nineteenth-century technology.

In the last century, there was a vast migration from the farms to the factories, yet agricultural output soared. In more recent times, developing manufacturing technologies have diminished job opportunities in factories. For the last few decades, much of the employment growth in the United States has been in the service sector, including government at all levels. Today, two-thirds of the American workforce are white collar and service employees. Even in manufacturing companies, almost a third of their employees are office workers.

We are passing through the worst recession since the Great Depression of the 1930s. Even so, research is proceeding rapidly in many areas of work automation. The official unemployment rate in the United States reached 10.8% by the end of 1982, and has been dropping very slowly since (it was still well above 9% in the fall of 1983), yet our factories are sprouting robots and our offices are becoming heavily dependent upon electronics.

In the past, productivity improvements brought about by new technologies were often confined to particular industries, or more often, to certain specific functions with production facilities. The changes were usually introduced piecemeal. In the long run, business expanded and jobs were created (although occasionally there were severe short-term dislocations). Usually other expanding areas were available to absorb excess labour during the transition, permitting both overall economic growth and employment growth.

Today, *all* sectors are embracing computer technologies – manufacturing, private services, government operations, agriculture. When the world recovers from the current severe recession, we may well be faced with economic growth fueled by higher capacity equipment, but without the high rate of job growth that was often experienced in the past.

Remarkable advances are being made in artificial intelligence, robotics, telecommunications, and the like. They cannot be viewed in a vacuum. Research in these areas is far more than just indulging in highly stimulating intellectual exercises. There are very practical applications which many businesses are eager to adopt.

For example, production robots are nothing more than mechanical replacements for human beings. Few would argue with using robots to perform hazardous jobs (e.g. in a hot environment, or where there is exposure to poisonous fumes), but the applications do not end there. Robots can be seen working side by side with human workers doing the same kind of work. They can also be seen manipulating samples in clinical laboratories, storing and retrieving items in warehouses, assembling small products, and delivering mail. Virtually *any* repetitive manual task can be done by a robot, particularly after sensory perception is further improved.

In the same way, computerization can be used to automate many routine office and clerical functions. It is interesting to note that developments in office automation are in many ways following the manufacturing pattern. At first, improvements are made in individual machines or jobs. For example, stand-alone word processors replace typewriters, or computerized microfiche or disk storage systems replace steel filing cabinets. The capacity is increased but the job is recognizable. Further developments, however, are affecting work organization.

Several firms, for example, offer systems which allow an individual to create documents (from small memos to major reports), including tables and charts; to file or retrieve documents; to tap into large data banks; to send messages to other people hooked into the system; to receive computer-generated reports; to do many tasks without the assistance of secretaries or file clerks or even middle-level managers.

The service sector in general has been relatively labour intensive. Automation is now occurring there, also. Banks have automatic machines for check processing, computer terminals for their tellers (eliminating a lot of internal clerical work) and automatic teller machines for direct use by the customer. The American telephone system is converting to electronic switching, eliminating both telephone operators and maintenance jobs. Supermarkets and retail stores have begun to use scanner devices at the check-out counter, reducing the demand for checkers while simultaneously providing instantaneous inventory up-dates.

One might ask at this point, 'What is wrong with taking people out of routine and boring jobs? If the people are forced to behave like machines, wouldn't it be better to have those jobs done by machines and free the people for more interesting and challenging jobs?' Of course, the answer is 'yes', provided there are jobs for those people to go to.

It is one thing to talk about the ultimate development of an incredibly wealthy information-based society way off in the future, and quite another to deal with what will be at best an extremely long and difficult transition period.

People need to work. For many years to come, most people will still derive a major part of their income from their jobs. Yet those who are most responsible for the design and installation of workplace technologies usually look only at the potential cost savings for their own organization, and not at total societal costs.

Here is a clear example of the total being less than the sum of the parts. An individual company may find it economically advantageous to reduce labour costs through some form of computerization. But if every company, and government agency, followed the same course, the result would be a reduction in aggregate employment opportunities.

It is a question of relative rates. If the rate of productivity increase in a particular firm is greater than the growth in output, then employment can drop.

Let me give an example from the newspaper industry in the United States. A large newspaper employed 500 typesetters. The publisher wished to install a computerized system which would have required the work of no more than 100 typesetters. Clearly, the organization could not expand its output (pages of print) sufficiently rapidly to usefully employ four times the number of people management would like to use. The local economy could not absorb rapidly such a large number of craftsmen in a short time. Further, the entire industry was moving in the same direction.

Newspaper publishers and the printers' unions eventually worked out an approach to these problems that at least addressed the immediate concerns. The result – including long-term job guarantees for affected employees in return for management being given a free hand to install whatever system they would like – is helpful for individuals, but does not address the larger societal question of reduced aggregate demand.

We may be entering a period of permanent labour surplus in the developed, technologically advanced nations of the world. At the same time, the undirected application of computer technologies is exacerbating a polarization of the workforce, with one group having their jobs enriched and made more challenging (e.g. some professionals and managers) while the other sees a reduction in skill requirements, an increase in monotony and stress, a reduction in control over the work, and reduced pay levels.

The problems exist at both the individual organization level as well as society-wide. In individual organizations, technologies are being introduced in a manner which increases managerial control, whether or not measurable productivity increases. There is no single technical solution to any given problem. Engineering designs are not handed down from Heaven, but are very much the result of the parameters and constraints within which the designers are allowed to work. The results may not always be those that are most desirable from a social policy standpoint.

To give a simple example, software has been developed for word processors and computer terminals which can count the number of keys hit over a period of time. There is no reason whatever why the operator of this equipment would want to have this information, but some American managers routinely use this data as a measure of 'productivity'. As a result, the emphasis is on hitting keys, whether they are the right ones or not. Errors increase, necessitating expensive corrective actions at later stages of the operation. Also, stress levels for the operators increase substantially.

The system described above illustrates two facets of current employment applications of computer technology. One, as I mentioned, is to place increased control in the hands of management, which also means leaving less opportunity for decision-making with the employee. In addition, computerization is also being used to simplify jobs by breaking them down into repetitive tasks, which not only increases boredom but also opens the way for further automation in the future.

Computerization is even having unanticipated effects among professional level employees. Two opposite trends are apparent. In some cases, the professional's job is made easier, quicker, or more flexible. For example, computer graphics systems are having a profound effect on engineering design. Projects which had necessitated months of work in the past can now be done in minutes, and the engineer has the additional benefit of being able to make modifications 'on the screen' and instantly see the results. Factory processes can also be simulated, so that manufacturing approaches can be tried out before the design work is completed.

On the other hand, some changes are resulting in deskilling. Insurance agents, for example, used to be required to have a detailed working knowledge of enormous quantities of very detailed information in order to properly evaluate a client's needs and tailor a policy to those individual requirements. Much of that information is now available from computer files. A much less skilled individual can use those files, along with sophisticated software, to satisfy most routine needs.

As theoretical and practical work in artificial intelligence advances, I would expect to see more of this. Indeed, some of the commercial driving force behind the development of expert systems will be to reduce the need for high-priced professional employees.

The problems are really society-wide. While individual employers should be expected to offer rewarding and challenging jobs to their employees, individual companies by themselves are not able to cure the problem of unemployment. We need to develop societal solutions to the broad problems we face.

If we face permanent labour surpluses in large measure because of techbology-based productivity enhancement, as I believe we do, then we must provide the means for the people who are affected to support themselves. This must involve a reduction in work time, and direct job creation, both financed by the productivity improvements the technology creates.

As for work time, a great deal has already occurred when viewed over the long flow of history. The workweek went from seven days, to six, and now to five; the number of hours in the workday has dropped from 12 to 15, to about eight; the concept of retirement on a pension has become widely adopted; and many employees enjoy paid vacations and other days off with full pay.

The social mechanism through which most of the reduction in individual work time was accomplished was the action of trade unions, followed in many cases by legislative support. While the initial driving force for these efforts was undoubtedly to relieve some of the incredible hardships associated with work in nineteenth-century societies undergoing rapid industrialization, the effect in more recent times has also been to create additional job opportunities in areas where technology was improving productivity levels. This may not have been the most 'efficient' process for individual employers, but it certainly had social utility. Most of the reductions occurred more than thirty years ago. The time has come to resume the earlier trend.

Changes are occurring rapidly. One could argue that we are witnessing an acceleration of the pace of change through the application of computer technology. A clear result is the increasing need for worker training and retraining, with the understanding that this will be required several times during the course of a normal working life.

In the area of new job design, we need to encourage both employers and technologists to do better, to look upon their employees as fellow human beings with needs and desires not much different from their own. Employers and technologists must develop a greater social concern, so that the direction taken by new technologies enhances and does not destroy human potential. In doing this, there is much to recommend involving employee representatives as early in the design process as possible.

If everything described here proves to be insufficient to meet the problems which may develop, then further actions in the form of direct job creation on the part of government will be necessary.

Modern society could not long exist with ever-widening gaps between those who benefit from new technology and those who are cast aside. The potential benefits of computers, robots and other modern technologies are very great, but they will not come automatically. Major changes in social policies will be required in many countries.

The computer community bears a special responsibility. Many of the technologies in routine use today, and certainly those in the future which will use artificial intelligence systems, are so complex that the technical details are beyond the understanding of the average worker or politician or even the average corporate manager. Scientists and engineers have a special need to communicate with those who are to be the recipients of the results of their work. We can no longer afford to design systems with only a technical goal in mind. Social considerations must be incorporated at the design stage.

The full effects of technology on employment will not be easy to unravel, nor will it be easy to anticipate all the problems which may arise. Only one thing is certain. It is going to take the combined efforts of the business and scientific communities, labour, government, and the public if we are to realize the full benefits of our creative output.

The problems are real, and immediate, and deserve a good deal of attention.

NOTES

[1] Rosalind and Williams (1983) 'The Machine Breakers', in *Technology Illustrated*, July, p. 60.

Crisis and creation – computers and the human future

K.S. Gill Brighton Polytechnic UK

We are at the crossroads of the technological culture of the brave new world of Information Technology and the culture of the world of classical technology. Fifth-generation computers promise to bring computers to every person in society, while automated factories manned by robots are already alienating workers from their established work environment; intelligent knowledge-based design systems promise to allow automation of the complete design-to-product cycle, while a whole generation of designers wonders about its role in this new world; we are promised a 'quantum leap' in the use of factory automation while the new working population is confused about its place in this promised land. Rule-based training and tutoring systems promise to train people in learning new skills using the knowledge of experts, while expert technologists, technicians, and managers are being deskilled by this very same new technology.

The scenario for this brave new world of computer-aided manufacturing, computer-aided design, computer-aided engineering, automated factories and automated offices, and computer-guided missiles is primarily based on a belief that information technology will transform the social and economic aspects of technological societies and will usher in a new era of 'world prosperity', in which, as Professor Moto-Oka of Tokyo University [1] prophesies, social productivity will increase through advanced computers and 'distortions in values will be eliminated'. Feigenbaum and McCorduck [2] present us with some glimpses of this vision of the future:

- loneliness will have been done away with – at least for old people. There will be friendly and helpful robots to keep them company;

- there will be the 'mechanical' doctor which will be more 'candid' than the human doctor;
- intelligent newspapers will know the way we feel and behave accordingly;
- smart weapon systems with 'zero probability of error' will combine artificial intelligence and high-powered computing in order to make decisions and give advice to human commanders.

This vision of the brave new world ushered in by the computer revolution sees man absolved of need for human relationships all of whose functions are to be supplied by the computer. The rationale of this view is that the computer will overcome man's alienation produced by the technology of industrial revolution. In reality, this view is simply an apotheosis of alienation, because, despite its apparent scientific uptodateness, it simply continues the mechanistic views of man and the labour process generated by the Industrial Revolution. But there is an alternative future that we could create with computers, where, instead of passively handing over his human needs to computers, man interacts creatively with them to fulfil these needs and release his creativity.

CRISIS AND COMPUTERS

'Classical technology was rooted in knowledge-by-experience and changes resulting from it; a knowledge and a change, which could be critically tested by all that belongs to human experience. Modern technology is rooted in science, i.e. a system of knowledge and methods, which has developed its own test criteria, thereby excluding sections of human experience' [3]. It is this exclusion of human experience which has led to the deskilling of human beings and the automating of these skills and experience of the experts. The era of classical technology created a new industrial system and a new industrial culture. It gave rise to a coherent industrial working class with its own organisations and political programme of socialism. The advancement of technology and science signalled the transition not only from hand labour to machine-based labour but also the liberation from labour altogether: the automatic factory. The earlier period had been an era of optimism, liberation and fraternity, with visions of classless society as the worker had a purpose and a meaning both at home and at work. Norms of life were well established and well understood. Social, organisational, educational and welfare systems were all products of the great technological class culture.

Now the new technological revolution in the form of computer and information technologies is rapidly fulfilling dreams of automation and freedom from machine-based labour, and is changing the nature of work, the work-place and organisation systems. Control is rapidly passing from man–machine collectives to computer-controlled data-bases and computer networks. Those still at work feel deskilled and controlled by microcomputers; those out of work are struggling to cope with the transition from a work-centred culture to a so-called leisure-centred culture; youth is confused and is struggling to define, redefine and create new cultural concepts which will provide it with a sense of surety and security of life. Suddenly the change has become frightening and threatening, so much so that people from an industrialised society are faced with the problems of readjusting to the new leisure-centred system. They no longer have access to a human–machine–work–experience culture, no forum for experiencing the human relations and social activity essential for group and class cultures; new technology is dehumanising, people are deprived of real-situation experience of the world, superfluity of labour is itself creating a dehumanising environment and the society is facing the problem of maintaining the basic fabric of human culture. It seems that the continuity of humanistic culture has been brutally severed.

New technology is creating new cultures of disadvantaged people – youth who may never have a chance of experiencing human–machine–work–culture and the unemployed who may never have a chance to go back to their own class culture, classical technicians and technologists who are no longer confident of their experience, skills and expertise, for they and their functions are being controlled by the machine.

It is the era of automated planning, organising, processing, assessing and evaluating. It is the era of rule-based control systems which are outside the knowledge and experience of the workers assigned to them. It is a world of computer networks, data-bases, expert systems, videotex, satellites. We are now information receivers and information users, without any control over the nature and purpose of information. Creation and control of information is beyond our domain. We are now all becoming end-users connected to intelligent computer networks capable of self-control, organisation, adjustment and modification. We are fast becoming interactive-passive observers. The global economic crisis – unemployment on a massive scale, a generation of youth growing up who will not experience the satisfaction of work, a whole class of new disadvantaged – is mirrored in the crisis of consciousness – fatalism, drift, remedies that are simply versions of the disease, e.g. the views of some technocrats that society is to be stratified into thinkers and drones who will staff the service industries. In this context, there is understandable nostalgia about the industrial revolution and classical technology which provided predictable and highly structured routines where now all is formless and uncertain.

While recognising the significance of human–machine–work experience–knowledge concept of the classical technology, we need to be reminded of the harsh realities of the first industrial revolution, which led to the acceptance of the machine as the saviour and dream of mankind; the brutal uprooting of agricultural people and their settlement in the squalid houses of an alien urban environment, the harsh work disciplines which replaced the traditional rhythms of labour, the cycle of boom and collapse in the economy creating underlying insecurity, the dehumanising of work which no longer provided fulfilment through labour but alienated workers from their own work products and generated the fetishism of commodities, the intensification of the divison of labour which as Ruskin [4] saw was really a division of man. As Noble [5] reminds us: 'the accounts of the human tragedy and trauma of the first industrial revolution have filtered down to us through distorted lenses devised to minimise this calamity and justify the human suffering in the name of progress'.

Commenting on the struggles of Luddite workers of Nottingham, Yorkshire and Lancashire, Noble, following E.P. Thompson's analysis, notes that 'Rather, in a period of economic crisis, depression and unemployment much like our own, they were struggling against the efforts of capital to restructure social relations and the patterns of production at their expense, using technology as a vehicle'. It was the time when the hard logic of market and machine laid down its roots, and the mechanical notion of betterment of society became the hallmark of enlightened spacecraft. In spite of his questionable observations about the introduction of machines, in his own *Principles of Political Economy* of 1848, Mill [6] insisted upon the ultimate benefit of technological development, not as any panacea but as a means of enlarging the overall wealth of nations.

Thus even when they recognised the reality of the workers' situation, the economists, as Berg [7] notes, 'welded their perception of the advanced technology to their concept of economic development, which proceeded inexorably, if not always so benignly through the mechanisms of the market, competition, and profit accumulation. But the doctrine of technological progress was not promoted solely in the name of Economics. Technological development was also defended in the name of Science'. The apologetics of capitalism, as Berg suggests, 'reached beyond political economy to a far-reaching cultural sphere which took up the machinery question in political economy's terms and made a doctrine of technological progress. The cultural sphere was the scientific movement'. The connection between economically spurred technological development and science, Berg explains, 'was promoted both by scientists seeking wider markets for their research and by industrialists seeking some higher rationale of their technological choices and expanding enterprises'. This enthusiasm about technological progress was also echoed by the so-called scientific socialism of Engels and Marx. The new industrial system had indeed given rise to an industrial working class, seeking unity in a defensive way with its own organisations and political programme of socialism, thus rendering opposition to the advance of technology unreasonable. For Marx, technological progress was not only the means of capitalist competition, accumulation and exploitation, but also essential to the advance of history itself – capitalism's contribution to human progress.

As Noble explains, here, too, technological progress was seen as having a life of its own, with liberating consequences for humanity. To oppose it in the present, therefore, was counter-revolutionary: all those who suffered in the present, in the wake of such progress, were encouraged to accept their fate now and look towards a better world in the future. The workers' plight, dilemma and confusion during the industrial revolution, their fears, uncertainty and powerlessness against the machine-based progress and the enthusiasm with which the economists, scientists, capitalists and socialists embraced the technology seem a mirror image of the dilemma, uncertainties, confusion, hopelessness and almost evangelical enthusiasm for the new technological revolution by their counterparts of the 1980s.

Although there is an apparent parallel between the workers' fate in the first revolution and the fate of the new disadvantaged of the 1980s, the romanticism about the advance of human-machine relationship of the classical technology may be less helpful and relevant in the current situation where the technological revolution is far more fast and powerful and the new disadvantaged do not yet have to face the poverty, hunger, subjugation, humiliation and uprooting of workers in the past.

The new disadvantaged of the technological societies still have opportunities and facilities for sharing the products of the new technology and to a large extent have a right to share the wealth in the form of social security, education, and medical care. The workers of the past had no such opportunities, and so their struggle was far fiercer, their uncertainties were infinitely more harsh and the organisational support to their cause was far weaker than that of their counterparts of today's experience.

The domain of present technology is international, its impact is varied and complex and its implementation is so opaque that it seems almost a natural progression of previous technology until and unless you happen to be one of those newly displaced workers. The real disadvantaged of today's technology are the people of the developing and underdeveloped countries who have no role in the new technology, no right of sharing wealth and no opportunities of sharing products produced by it.

In contrast to the 'developed' world, the new technology has very little impact on the economic and social development of developing countries. There is no attempt to meet the real needs of the majority of the population, to build on their skills or to create new skills. The structure of multinationals and their control of technology ensures that there is almost no transfer of technical knowledge to developing countries which is essential for their real economic development. The main reason for multinational involvement within these countries is primarily due to the virtually unlimited supply of cheap labour, much of it provided by young women who often work extremely long hours and at an intense pace. This slave-like workforce has no security; it is forced to depend upon the subsistence economy of the rural areas for its long-term sustenance and care. Much of the work is relatively unskilled, and training in the more skilled areas, such as maintenance and repairs, is kept to the minimum. It is they who are going through both the classical technology and new technology advances at the same time and it is they who do not have resources to share the products and wealth produced by them. Their struggle is about food, clothes and shelter – the minimum human needs while the struggle of their counterparts in technological societies is about ideology, economic prosperity, peace and wealth, cakes rather than bread. In the context of technological societies the real disadvantaged are the disabled and the handicapped who were left behind during the past technological advance and are in danger of being left behind again during the current computer advances. It is the powerlessness of this new class of disadvantaged people in advanced technological societies that may explain the uncritical acceptance of computer revolution by the majority.

The uncritical acceptance of the computer revolution by societies and ideological support by technocrats may be explained by the nature of the new technology which resulted from the intertwinement of classical technology and science at the end of the last century. Dipple speaks of this intertwinement [8]: 'Modern science up until that time mainly acting as a satisfier for the individual's curiosity and desire for knowledge, suddenly realised that it could make itself useful to production in an unprecedented manner'. It is this marriage of classical technology and science which resulted in an enormous increase in productivity, thus fulfilling one of the conditions for the elimination of poverty and suffering and thereby providing faith in the utilitarian nature of the new technology. Science became an element of production and scientists turned into production workers losing sight of their work and its further implementation. This amalgamation of science and technology gave birth to a new concept of reality expressed through the logical empirical conception of science, a reality determined by facts and logic, i.e. a programming reality – a reality constructed, tested and accepted using scientifically formulated and quantifiable rules.

Galjaard [3] explains this logical–empirical concept of reality: 'Science occupies itself with 'reality'. That is why modern technology can be circumscribed as thinking and acting, aimed at change, through which a new reality is being constructed. . . . This doctrine prescribes the manner for people to behave in a technological society, in which the boundaries of production organisations have long been crossed'. This doctrine is being applied by proponents of microcomputer and information technology as the best recipe for economic prosperity and the welfare society in the competitive world which, we are told, demands sacrifices from the older generation to provide opportunities for future generations. The new disadvantaged are supposed to pay due reverence to technological change and accept short term pain and suffering for the sake of progress. After all, they belong to technologically progressive and 'civilised' society and no progressive 'civilised' person, after all, is against progress. 'Even the most displaced want to be taken seriously and want to make a contribution to society. Thus they must believe that their own sacrifices are suffered for a later good – how else suffer them with dignity.' The above comments, by Noble [5] in the context of the Industrial Revolution, are true today and may explain the grudging acceptance of the information technology revolution for the good of 'mankind'.

The ideological reverence for the new technology may be explained by Taylor's ground rule for organisation technology [9]: 'There is a best way in doing everything and that best way can always be formulated into certain rules: you can get your knowledge away from the old chaotic rule-of-thumb knowledge into organised knowledge.' In other words, as Galjaard [3] explains: 'Taylor's ground rule indicates the way in which in our technological society 'machines' have to be developed and integrated, namely in such a manner, that the thoughts and actions of people respond to objectified experience, in order for the thinking and acting to become maximally controllable and, thereby, maximally productive'.

It is this vision of productive technology that reduces human communication and interaction into information processing, reduces the role of humans to push-button operators in automated and computer-controlled factories and reduces the role of people working in banks, supermarkets and offices into standardised 'terminal' operators. These are a few examples of how a continuous expansion of programmability and control of machines reduces the reality of people in terms of choice and thereby confirms a new reality embodied in rules, i.e. objectified experience. According to Galjaard: 'There has to be no doubt as to the true nature of this change: a standardised way of thinking, according to which all computers function; strictly logical, specialised and fragmentised, processing bit-after-bit in a minimised reality'.

This view of reality may be explained with the aid of the logical–empirical reconstructing hypothesis, as formulated by Simon in his book *The Sciences of the Artificial* [10]: 'A man, viewed as a behaving system, is quite simple. The apparent complexity of his own behaviour over time is largely a reflection of the complexity of the environment in which he finds himself'. This logical–empirical conception of science, according to Galjaard, provides a framework to a scientist to reduce his environment to the simple set of rules, simplify his behaviour and then reconstruct/discover a reality which corresponds to the same rules. Within this rule-based domain, 'everything' is in principle programmable. Since the boundaries of programmability are expandable, we are supposed to have faith in ever-increasing productivity provided we behave according to the programmable reality of management, automation and control.

It is perhaps this view of the scientific world that excites technologists and computer scientists about the advances in information technology, microcomputers and recently the fifth-generation computers. In their recent book *The Fifth Generation: Artificial Intelligence and Japan's Computer Challenge to the World*, Feigenbaum and McCorduck [2] present their own view of the 'fifth-generation' world in which geriatric robots will alleviate the loneliness of at least the old people; mechanical doctors will be preferable to a human doctor; technical devices in our homes will gather information about us and for us and determine our preferences for participation with individuals and groups in society; technical devices will permit us to exchange knowledge 'engagingly' with our fellow creatures 'without the prejudices that often attend face-to-face interaction'. Professor Tohuro Moto-Oka of Tokyo University [1], titular head of the Fifth Generation Project, promises even more: '. . . Fifth Generation computers will take the place of man in the area of physical labour, and through the intellectualisation of the advanced computers, totally new applied fields will be developed, social productivity will be increased, and distortions in values will be eliminated'.

Professor Joseph Weizenbaum [11] warns us against accepting this fifth-generation dream world of 'an electronic isolation ward' in which there is no place for creative minds, for independent study and reflection, for independent anything. He further reminds us that 'increasing computerisation may well allow us to increase the productivity of labour indefinitely – but to produce what? More video games and fancier television sets along with 'smarter' weapons? And with people's right to feed their families and themselves largely conditioned on their 'working', how do we provide for those whose work has been taken from them by machines? The vision of production with hardly any human effort, of the consumption of every product imaginable, may excite the greed of a society whose appetites are fixed on things. It may be good that, in our part of the globe, people no longer sort out cheques for mail by hand, or retype articles like this one. But how far ought we to extrapolate such 'good' things? At what price?

Who stands to gain and who must finally pay? Such considerations ought at least to be part of a debate. Are there really no choices other than we win or lose?'.

As far as the technological developments and deskilling of human expertise are concerned, researchers such as Noble, Cooley and Rosenbrock [12, 13, 14] have already started a discussion on machines and tools. Their main concern is the development of fundamentally different forms of mechanisation and automation within a framework of democratic management and knowledge. It is a development (Galjaard calls it 'emancipated technology') which offers the technological society a choice to design and develop human-centred systems which may be simpler and more flexible and enable workers to keep their skills alive and preserve creativity of human beings. These issues relating to the emancipatory technology are more fully and ably developed by Mike Cooley in his book *Architect or Bee* [13].

However, the issue which may be regarded as central to a debate on computer technology is that of computer literacy. Throughout the technologically advanced societies, microcomputer revolution is taking place at a breathless speed, and we are witnessing the installation of an enormous computer education infrastructure. Each day offers new opportunities and new reminders of the urgent need to bring 'computer literacy' (CL) to the masses of students, teachers, parents, unemployed and business people ready to become participants in new computerised society. As computers penetrate further and further into schools, work places, training institutions, homes and our daily lives, some form of computer literacy for everyone comes to be accepted as a reasonable, even reassuring corollary. Douglas D. Noble in his article *A Little Learning is a Dangerous Thing* [15] examines the uncritical acceptance of computer literacy, discussing some of the assumptions upon which this acceptance is based. He draws two major conclusions: first, that CL is in fact a hollow vision, unnecessary for survival as consumer, exaggerated as an enhancement of learning, irrelevant to job preparation and impoverished as a form of citizen empowerment. The second conclusion is that, despite the hollowness, the distortions and muddled logic, CL is rapidly becoming an accepted prerequisite for many forms of everyday life, and that it is therefore dangerous. Noble points out that the CL campaign is being waged using assertions such as that there is no choice other than introducing the masses to computers and then allowing them to feel 'comfortable' with new technology. People are reminded that failure to learn about computers will leave them functionally illiterate, devoid of 'basic' survival skills needed in order to cope in the computerised world. It is the computer technology which seems to define the roles of people in society and depict the individual as consumer, as student, as worker and as citizen [15]:

(1) The opportunities available to those who become educated consumers – not to mention new experts – will be so great that to remain uninitiated will be functional illiteracy.
(2) To function effectively as students, our nation's youth needs to know how to use and program computers, since computers contribute to the intellect-

ual growth of human beings and since computer literacy maximises our problem-solving abilities.

(3) To function effectively as scientists, engineers, managers and teachers, the professionals of today . . . need to learn to use computers to enhance their specialised skills.

(4) Some understanding of computer programming is necessary for the exercise of the rights and responsibilities of citizenship.

High technology, we are told, is essential not just for the individual's 'self-preservation'; it seems to offer a cure for all economic problems. The debate about CL concentrates on slogans such as quoted by Noble [15]:

'A computer literate workforce is necessary to maintain our national defence and improve our national productivity'.

'A computer literate populace is as necessary to an information society as raw material and energy are to an industrial society'.

'Due to the decline in national productivity, the increase in foreign trade competition, and national defence and safety needs, computers have emerged as the major force ameliorating these conditions. Consequently, the shortage of computer specialists and knowledge workers has raised the problem of computer literacy to the level of a national crisis'.

It is the first time in this century, if not in history, that a mass educational campaign in computer literacy has followed on the heels of a technological revolution so as to make everyone 'comfortable' overnight. It seems as if the opportunities of manufacturers and retailers of hardware and software to exploit the infinite 'educational market'; the responsibility of opportunity of computer professionals, professional educators, education establishments and industry to train and retrain various groups in society; the opportunity of computer scientists and computer-based experts to enhance current and develop further 'knowledge' skills for the economic benefit and economic survival of society have all converged to the principal aim of 'the creation of a population which is comfortable with and accepting of a computerised world'. According to Noble, the proponents of CL 'have fanned the flames of high tech . . . and have responded with predictable enterprise to the 'needs' of a defensive population. They, however, are not the weavers. They are merely spreading someone else's vision of a new world. The focus is on the technical, and the establishment of a carefully delineated area for discussions of 'social impact', render any genuine criticism out of bounds, illegitimate, even irrational. In addition, the portrayal of the computer society as a 'given' casts any discussion of human values and dignity into the realm of wishful thinking or nostalgic reverie'.

People are presented with a new reality of 'no other choice' in which their individual self-preservation ought to motivate them to accept all facets of computer revolution. This reality is reinforced by appealing to their national pride and prestige, and to their duty and participation in overcoming foreign competition in trade and international leadership. We have already seen how the technological advances of the recent past have led to the deskilling of human work skills, created uncertainties as to the future job prospects of the employed, unemployed and the youth, and have thus created a whole new generation of disadvantaged people who have no choice but to accept these advances. The computer literacy bandwagon is leaving the older generation bewildered, confused and anxious as to their competence and capacity to cope with the new brave computer world while at the same time bearing a responsibility of some 'future' economic decline if they do not accept the reality as presented to them by computer pundits such as Feigenbaum and McCorduck. A new group of people unskilled in computer literacy are added to the already growing list of 'have nots' and disadvantaged people. Commenting on this 'no choice' reality, Noble says [16], '. . . the mythology that computers enhance all jobs they touch, and they transform them into 'mind jobs' filled with new levels of resposibility, persists unabated and feeds the fear of those who would turn to computer literacy for help'.

We should be concerned about the evangelical campaign of computer literacy which is intent on redesigning our world and which focuses on the technical competence of the masses within some 'given' framework of economic emancipation and defence requirements for survival of the 'human race'. The success of such a campaign, according to Noble, 'depends upon a population which is sufficiently insecure about its intellect and its competence to be willing to deny the obvious truth'. In his conclusion, Noble says 'what is desperately needed at this time is both the resurrection of critical debate, and a renewal of public discourse about how computers might be used and understood in ways which enrich our lives'. This debate is even more urgent now that proponents of the 'fifth generation' such as Feigenbaum and McCorduck talk of 'major benefits for the whole human race' of AI developments while at the same time make clear their description of such benefits: 'The so-called smart weapons of 1982, for all their sophisticated modern electronics, are really just extremely complex wind-up toys compared with the weapon systems that will be possible in a decade as intelligent information processing systems are applied to the defence problems of the 1990s'.

It is this focus of benefits to the 'human race' which is frightening to people like me, who are concerned with the education and training of handicapped and disadvantaged people in societies. Professor Weizenbaum returns the debate on computer literacy to the human reality of people rather than the reality of the machine when he comments, 'The computer has long been a solution looking for problems – the ultimate technological fix which insulates us from having to look at problems. Our schools, for example, tend to produce students with mediocre ability to read, write and reason; the main thing we are doing about it is to sit kids down at computer consoles in the classrooms. Perhaps they'll manage to become computer literate – whatever that means – even if, in their mother tongue, they remain functionally illiterate' [11].

In a recent SSRC report on *Microcomputers in Education* [16], one of the major themes that runs through the report is the paramount need for devising adequate theoretical frameworks in a situation which is accurately described as one of 'theoretical impoverishment'. Such frameworks will of necessity assume multidisciplinary character, and there will be a need to consider new methodological paradigms . . . hitherto disregarded or apparently unorthodox research designs is asserted: 'Careful co-ordination of educational and technological perspectives should ensure that the models of the learning process and the organisation of knowledge which become incorporated into the coming generation of intelligent devices and expert systems will not be excessively machine-oriented. We believe that by reflecting the complexities of human processes, styles and strategies as faithfully as current technology and theoretical understanding might permit, such devices will both maximise user confidence in their conclusions and avoid the undesirable consequences of the imposition of inappropriate process models on the structure of educational materials and environments'.

The report offers a clear and timely challenge to the education and AI research workers to participate in the design and development of computing tools for the real benefit of people. The significant contributions of the report are to up-date definition of the disadvantaged people and its clear exposition of the issues of research which concern us in the area of cognitive impoverishment. 'Visually and aurally handicapped people may incur varying degrees of 'cognitive impoverishment' due to their perceptual deficiencies. Comparable impoverishment may also arise from restrictions placed on experience imposed by social or ethnic customs and practices, or from experiential constraints imposed by physical or mental handicaps'. The effect may be to cause many people to be 'excluded from effective participation in IT-based educational, occupational and leisure activities because of imperfect communication with the devices'. It is the difficulty of intellectual interaction with IT systems which is of concern here, rather than the (nevertheless very real) problems of physical communication.

The ethos of our own research project at Brighton is completely in consonance with this humanist perspective, with its rejection of mechanistic models of mind and mechanical modes of learning, and its emphasis on the creativity and human potential – the 'imaginative thinking and creative problem solving' mentioned elsewhere in the report (p. 16, 3.6) – that the new technology can release.

The Computer Aided Animated Arts Theatre project (CAAAT) was established at Brighton Polytechnic in 1981, the International Year of the Disabled people, with the initial aim of providing a computer-assisted resource language to enable the handicapped child to communicate with his world. Its origins and its long-term aims, however, reach much further back into the past and are rooted in my long-standing commitment to the cultures of minority groups, to their preservation and enhancement, and to the creation of processes whereby a fruitful interchange between minority and majority cultures might be facilitated. In working with the language problems of women from ethnic minorities, I came to learn at first-hand the inadequacy of traditional second language teaching methods, which ignore or discount the wealth of resources in the minority culture. The link between these two concerns is not far to seek: both the handicapped and ethnic minorities are disadvantaged groups that, in terms of the larger culture, may be said to suffer from 'cognitive impoverishment' (to adopt the useful term of the SSRC report, p. 29, 5.8.1). With both groups the overriding need is not merely linguistic efficiency but the unlocking of potentiality and the establishment of the self-validating and self-enhancing relationships that genuine communicative competence in what is initially felt to be an alien cultural code entails. And with both groups the question of motivation and its place in the learning process acquires a special urgency and complexity.

The initial phase of the project was restricted to the development of computer programs combining the features of computer-generated sound, speech recognition, synthesis and colour graphics. The aim, broadly speaking, was to aid the development of language through the integration of speech, picture and the written word. From the outset, learning through interaction has been a central part of our approach. To this end, some of the regular features of our computer programs include recognition, cognition, reading and composition; the relationship between written word, picture, speech and sound leading to sentence construction, picture construction and dialogue generation; parallelism between story generation and pictorial scene generation. These features allow the children to explore meaningful relationships between words and their contexts, to participate in role-play and group learning activities through the addition of new pictures, new vocabulary leading to creation of new modification and existing scenes and stories.

Our current programming work consists of five inter-related modules – computer-aided animation, speech production, music generation, story generation and speech-based robot control. The programs have been developed on the Apple II microcomputer and use commercially available speech synthesis, speech recognition and graphic display equipment. Recently, we have started developing programs on the BBC microcomputer. We are also using an interactive video system to integrate features of computer-aided animation and story generation with real-life visual and sound contexts provided by the video, for our language development work. A research project on a microcomputer-based tutoring system for language development is being initiated in association with two local special-education schools.

The objective of the proposed project is to implement a teaching strategy adaptively matching the abilities of the selected group of children. We are currently evaluating our computer programs with children with the help of specialist teachers from local schools, Uplands Special Day School and Ingfield Manor School.

Children from the schools were involved in this phase of the project, and participation in conferences such as Distech 82 and the International Conference on Welfare Services (1982) enabled us to reach a much wider audience of parents, community workers and professional organisations such as Brighton and Hove Federation of the Disabled, Brighton Voluntary Services and Friends Centre. The mutual learning that resulted from such contacts is for us a most valuable part of our developing programme. We have also held exhibitions of our work, most notably in November 1981, when we organised a School Arts competition to which all the school children of our area were invited. They were asked to design a cartoon narrative depicting the happier moments in a handicapped child's life. The aim of this bringing together the two cultures – that of the normal child and that of the handicapped child – remains an essential part of our programme. Our project work on animation was shown on BBC TV (Nationwide South) in November 1981, and our work on speech controlled robot arm is now a part of the BBC TV series on 'Making the Most of Your Micro'. The primary aim of the CAAAT project is to develop low-cost high technology which would enable handicapped and disadvantaged children to exploit the full potential of their expressive, creative, learning and communication capabilities by use of their own personal control of speech and sound. Our work has attracted wide ranging interest, and has been sufficiently successful to warrant quite considerable expansion with the recent appointment of a multidisciplinary team. This means that the project could develop and grow in new and exciting directions, building on the knowledge and experience gained from the work of the previous two years. In the second phase of the project we have set ourselves the following research objectives:

(i) selection of an appropriate theoretical framework for language development for children with special needs, using microcomputer and artificial intelligence techniques and with specific reference to creativity, expressiveness, participation and human communication;
(ii) design and development of necessary components for this microcomputer-based language development scheme, i.e. those which involve visual, verbal and written information;
(iii) the extension and application of this work to the important areas of remedial and multilingual education.

Our current work on language development has recently led to the establishment of an innovative pilot project on 'Basic Education in Numeracy and in New Technology' funded by the EEC Social Fund. The project is run jointly with the Friends Centre (an adult education centre) and aims to train 30 adults in numeracy, literacy and microcomputer technology to enhance their employment prospects and provide a basis for further vocational training. The research objectives of this project are to develop microcomputer-based intelligent tools in the area of literacy and numeracy within a multilingual framework.

The students and the research staff on the project come from various cultural and minority groups and provide a rich cultural framework to develop technological tools for the enrichment of the human experience and human skills.

Our work at Brighton on 'language developmet' is based on a belief that microcomputer technology offers us a unique opportunity to gain access to knowledge, experience and skills of various cultures. It is this access to intercultural worlds that will enrich our lives and will bring various cultures together while accepting their diversities. It is in this spirit that we pay tribute to Seymour Papert's contribution to education when he says, 'The research challenge is clear.

We need to advance the art of meshing computers with cultures so that they can serve to unite, hopefully without homogenising, the fragmented subcultures that coexist counter-productivity in contemporary society. For example the gulf must be bridged between the technical scientific and humanistic cultures' [18].

Our vision of the future is the one in which computer systems will combine artificial intelligence and high-powered computing to fulfil human needs and release creative capacities of people. Here are some aspects of this future:

- Cultural isolation will be done away with – for all people. There will be friendly and adaptive computer systems which will enable people to have access to other cultures.
- Social productivity will increase through advanced computers to allow people access to community and social resources such as clinics and welfare agencies related to their concerns.
- Low-cost high technology tools will enable handicapped and disadvantaged people to exploit full potential of their expressive, creative, learning and communication capabilities through the use of their own personal control, of speech and sound.

Our vision of this future is based on a belief in the human capacity for learning and using newly gained knowledge as instrumental for change in society. In the area of education it has been a gigantic learning step for society from a century ago when in the run up to the Education Act of the 1870s, parents aided and abetted industry in snatching children of tender years from school, that is, if they permitted children to go to school at all. The 1944 Education Act categorised children by their disability on the assumption that there were particular education methods appropriate to each category. In the event no such particular methods were ever prescribed. Recently the Warnock Report [19], leading to the 1981 Education Act, provided a humane and comprehensive education framework on which to make the transition from segregation to compassionate mainstreaming, from categorising children on the basis of their disabilities to considering them as having special needs but with equal opportunities; from paternalistic care of an embarrassing minority to full participation of that minority in all aspects of our society.

The seriousness of the implications of the IT revolution to employment prospects and the nature of technological society is in no doubt. However, we are witnessing a healthy and positive awareness on the part of concerned scientists, researchers, social community researchers and workers as to the international dimensions of these new revolutions. North–South dialogues, female consciousness and the International Year of the Disabled people are symbolic representations of new horizons. One of the most remarkable phenomena of the microcomputer revolution is that manufacturers have lost control over how these computers are being used. Teachers, researchers, scientists no longer have a monopoly of wisdom over this new technology. It is perhaps the first time in human history that so-called 'experts' and 'novices' have the possibility of access to the same technology, the same information and knowledge-based sources.

Although microcomputers are the result of a strong intertwining between classic technology and science, it is up to those concerned with the welfare of the disadvantaged that it is not just used as a utilitarian tool in the cause of increase in productivity and profitability. We have an opportunity and indeed responsibility to ensure that this technology is once again rooted in knowledge by experience: knowledge and the change resulting from it are shared by the users and human experience is not excluded as in the case of modern technology.

Until now the computer technology and associative hardware/software resources were expensive and beyond the reach of individual users, social or community organisations. Computer technology was an expensive and productive tool which had to be revered and used under organised control which maximised its economic utility and minimised human experience. This was the era of Cobol, Fortran and later of Pascal and Basic as a medium for communicating with the machines; it was an era of systems analysts and systems programmers who were concerned with optimal descriptions of programs, their organisation, storage and retrieval, and flow of data subjecting to rigorous quantitative tests provided by those who controlled the use of data and information. It was an era of mainframes installed in air-conditioned buildings, subject to correct temperature controls and ensuring the maintenance of the machines. School teachers, school children, students and public could see these machines through glass windows – this alien creature was a source of reverence. This reverence was not confined to the machine; it was to be shown to the programmers, systems programmers, systems analysts, system managers, computer designers and scientists who had the knowledge and expertise for making the most effective and most productive use of computer technology. It was quantitative measures of productivity which defined boundaries of applications.

The ever-falling cost of the computer means that virtually everybody will be able to afford 'computer power'. Thus we need no longer behave as we used to, regarding computers as oracles 'whose words must be obeyed', since those words no longer cost so much time and money to produce. Hopefully, technique will broaden their vocabularies from the world of filing and arithmetic, into the world of inexact and problematic information, knowledge of what they are, and how to reason, recognise, interpret, plan, educate, learn, explore and communicate using such knowledge and information.

The advent of microcomputers and public access to this technology bring us a step nearer to our vision of developing computer tools which enable people to express their sense of creative potential and to enhance their sense of power of control over their environments. As Bruner *et al.* [20] show, powerlessness is the keynote of cognitive impoverishment in the contexts of poverty and underdevelopment. This also applies in the most direct way to the culture and the world of the handicapped. The true dimension of computer revolution is that it can be an enabling agent – enabling the powerless to feel in control. Nineteenth-century imperialistic/Darwinian views of cultural backwardness and progress are seen today to be an exploded myth, but nevertheless cultures can suffer undernourishment from lack of access to mental modes, internalised tools – here the computer can play a powerful liberating role.

NOTES

[1] Moto-Oka, T. (1982) Fifth Generation Computer Systems, *JIPDEC*, North-Holland.
[2] Feigenbaum, E.A. and McCorduck, P. (1984) *The Fifth Generation*, Michael Joseph, London.
[3] Galjaard, J.H. (1982) *Science, Technology and Ethical Space.* (Report)
[4] Ruskin, J. (1903) in *The Stones of Venice,* Cook and Wedderburn (eds.), George Allen and Unwin, London.
[5] Noble, D.F. (1983) *Democracy.* (Report)
[6] Mill, J.S. (1848) *Principles of Political Economy,* University of Toronto Press and Routledge & Kegan Paul.
[7] Berge (1980) *The Machinery Question and the Making of Political Economy*, Cambridge University Press.
[8] Van Veen, J. (1973) *The Reversed World* (Dutch language), Dipple, p. 47, 48, Bosch and Keuniug, Baarn.
[9] Merril, H. (1960) *Classics on Management*, American Association.
[10] Simon, H. (1969) *The Sciences of the Artificial*, MIT.
[11] Weizenbaum, J. (1983) *The New York Review of Books*, October 22.
[12] Noble, D. (1978) Social Choice in Machine Design, in *Politics and Society* 8 No. 3–4, p. 313–347.
[13] Cooley, M. (1980) *Architect or Bee?*, Langley Technical Services, Slough, UK.
[14] Rosenbrock, H. (1982) *Technology Politics and Options*, EEC First Conference on Information Technology.
[15] Noble, D. (1983) *A Little Learning is a Dangerous Thing*, A Preliminary Study, March.
[16] Sage, M. and Smith, D.J. (1983) *Microcomputers in Education*, Social Science Research Council.
[17] Gill, K.S. (ed.) *Computers, Cognitive Development and Special Education*, (in press).
[18] Papert, S. (1980) *Mindstorms: Computers and Powerful Ideas,* Harvester Press.
[19] Warnock, M. (1978) *A Report to the Committee of Enquiry into the Education of Handicapped Children and Young People with Educational Needs*, HMSO, London.
[20] Bruner, J.S. (1978) *The Relevance of Education*, Penguin Books.

PART 3

AI AND EDUCATION

INTRODUCTION

One of the major areas of human endeavour is education. The result of some form of interaction between adults and children in places known as 'schools' is labelled 'learning' by a majority of people. Under close examination, however, any such simplistic view of education would not suffice: children learn from their peers as much as (if not more than) they learn from adults. They learn at home and in the playground, as well as by watching television. Fig. 1 caricatures a typical view of the dynamics of society under the spotlight of traditional theories of learning in the absence of computers.

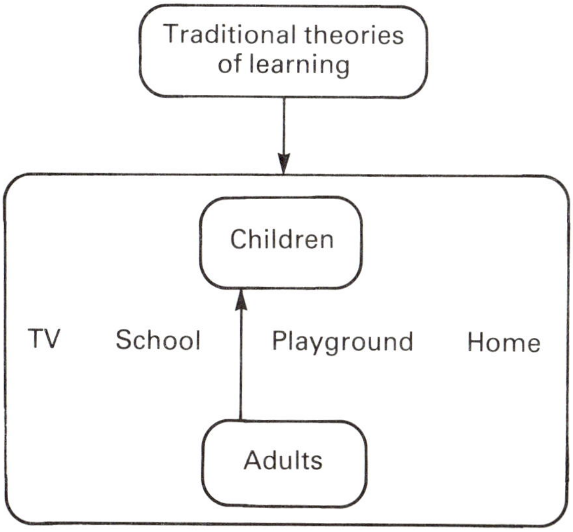

Fig. 1

With the introduction of computers, the spotlight has remained the same, leading to a situation where, on the one hand, Computer Assisted Learning (CAL) packages help teachers to 'teach' different subjects in the school curriculum, and on the other, the writing of Basic programs teaches children how a computer works. The role of adults, in addition to providing the CAL packages and the Basic interpreters, is to observe the children's interactions with a view to making an assessment of their abilities in their general school work.

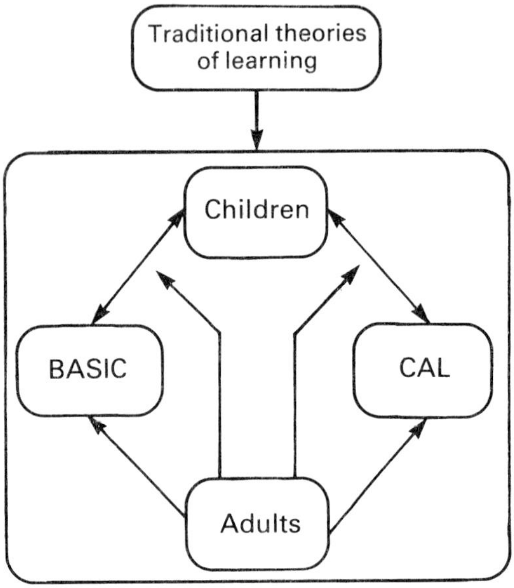

Fig. 2

Accepting that computers are the latest tools invented by man, we can see that they are being used in the same way as many other such tools. Children programming in Basic learn how to use these new tools while teachers use them in the same way as they use the blackboard: to simplify their teaching task. There are good historical reasons why educational computing up to now has been dominated by Basic and CAL. Computers have been rare and therefore they could only be used by the privileged class in any environment (e.g. Teachers). They have also been expensive; therefore the computers which schools could afford would only support programming languages designed to optimise the machines' efficiency instead of providing for the needs of human users.

Major government initiatives in the western world have concentrated on 'computer literacy for adults', analogous to developing countries' attempts to give their citizens literacy in natural human languages.

In the meantime, a new discipline has been active: artificial intelligence (AI). It has concerned itself with the study of giving computers abilities usually associated with human beings (such as the ability to understand natural language, solve problems, play games), as well as to learn for itself. In short, AI has been concerned with providing 'human literacy of computers'. More than 25 years' findings from AI are now beginning to affect other human endeavours. In this introduction we explore the implications of subjecting the educational environment to the spotlight of theories of learning, communication and intelligence. Kahn [1] has presented some thoughts on interactions between AI and education which are expanded here. Fig. 3, on the first reading, follows the same structure as that of the previous figure, but its components are very different in nature from Basic and CAL.

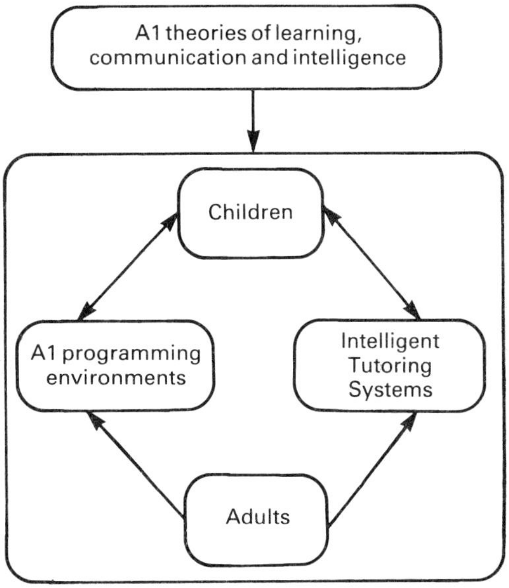

Fig. 3

2. INTELLIGENT TUTORING SYSTEMS

Intelligent Tutoring Systems [2] are artificial intelligence's answer to CAL packages. While CAL has tended to be basically drill and practice, Intelligent Tutoring Systems (ITS) are diagnostic. The following incorrect subtraction and addition

$$\begin{array}{r} 170 \\ -\ 93 \\ \hline 187 \end{array} \qquad \begin{array}{r} 33 \\ +\ 179 \\ \hline 102 \end{array}$$

will not result in 'wrong, you lose a point' being printed on the screen. An ITS will diagnose correctly the misconception of the pupil in forgetting the borrow or the carry over.

3. ARTIFICIAL INTELLIGENCE PROGRAMMING ENVIRONMENTS

Artificial intelligence programming environments are tailored to human beings, minimising the cognitive load put on a naive user, as opposed to optimising the machine's efficiency. SOLO, for example, provides the users with a spelling corrector, on-line 'help' and advice, as well as an automatic way of debugging the faulty programs written by the users.

Yazdani [3] presents four such environments based around LOGO, SOLO, Prolog and POP-11. The practical contribution of such environments is that they make it possible to design computing systems which are educational, fun and which relate to children's basic feelings. Papert [4] has argued that such activity (playing with LOGO, for example) has a similar role to that of playing with sand pits in the Piagetian view of learning. In playing with AI programming environments, children build 'objects to think with' in place of sand castles. This building process takes place in what is known as a 'micro-world': a limited portion of the real world whose characteristics can be easily understood.

4. MICRO-WORLDS

AI is fond of using micro-worlds in all its areas of research as they can also be easily formalized. The most influential AI work in natural language processing [5] converses with the users about a small world of a table top with a number of coloured boxes inhabiting it. The computer program is capable of not only obeying orders in this world, but also discussing it in detail. Another program has been devised which will recognize TV images of pictures from such scenes [6], whilst another program [7] will learn new concepts from the old, if taught by a human teacher. The obvious hope of researchers has been to link all these programs together and let the computer learn how to deal with the real world, in the same way as a child playing with such blocks would grow up to be able to do. Unfortunately, AI has not been able to translate its successful attempts at micro-worlds to the real world yet. There seems to be such a level of increase in complexity of the domain when moving away from the micro-worlds to the real ones, that most lessons need to be relearned.

Papert [4] and most advocates of AI in education have argued that such micro-worlds would constitute a very good complement to the ones usually used by children up to now (such as Meccano sets). The most well known of these educational micro-worlds has been turtle graphics. This is a computing package (based around a mechanical device with the same name) which would take commands from children in a way similar to their pet 'turtle' if it could understand them. In this way, children succeed in drawing wonderful shapes by giving simple commands to the computer. In addition to this, a number of other micro-worlds have been successfully used, such as one based around a beach [8], one based around the world of a farmer trying to transport a fox, a chicken and a bag of grain across a river [9], as well as a series of micro-worlds built around traditional AI programs in Prolog [10].

5. LEARNING ABOUT OURSELVES BY DOING AI

Advocates of the use of AI in education have also argued that by encouraging as many people as possible to become AI scientists, we would 'introduce them to ideas about themselves, their minds, and the universe in which they find themselves which they might otherwise not have encountered' [11].

Pupils can also attempt to use AI programming environments in order to produce simple programs which have a certain level of intelligence. They move from the position of being experimented on, to doing the experimentation themselves. By trying to write a program which learns to play a game of noughts and crosses, the pupil starts to realize what learning is.

6. SEARCHING DATA-BASES OF INFORMATION

Prolog [3] has also been used to set up a data-base of information about particular historical events, and children then query the data-base in order to discover the cause of the result: giving children the feel for what it is to be a historian looking for information, sifting the evidence.

7. ARTIFICIALLY INTELLIGENT PROGRAMS

AI's contribution to the scene does not end at enriching the previously existing components. It also introduces new ways of learning and teaching which start to change the overall dynamics of the situation. One such novel way of teaching a subject such as Physics or Medicine, would be to produce an intelligent program which would behave like a skilled physicist or a medical consultant [12]. The pupils can then observe the knowledge and line of reasoning of the program and learn in a way that they would have been unable to do before.

MYCIN, for example, is an Expert Computer System which attempts to diagnose bacterial infections in the blood, and suggests appropriate treatment. Trainee doctors could simply be asked to look over MYCIN's shoulder as it sets about solving its problems. This is because

- MYCIN can explain in English what it is doing;
- MYCIN's decision-making processes are similar to those which students are supposed to develop;
- MYCIN's representation of medical information is in a human-like manner.

MYCIN is one of a number of AI programs currently popular as commercially viable propositions known as Expert Systems. Such systems are experts in a very narrow domain of knowledge to a degree that, within their domain, they can match the performance of human experts, and possibly exceed them.

Our picture of education with AI systems is already richer than the one we started with:

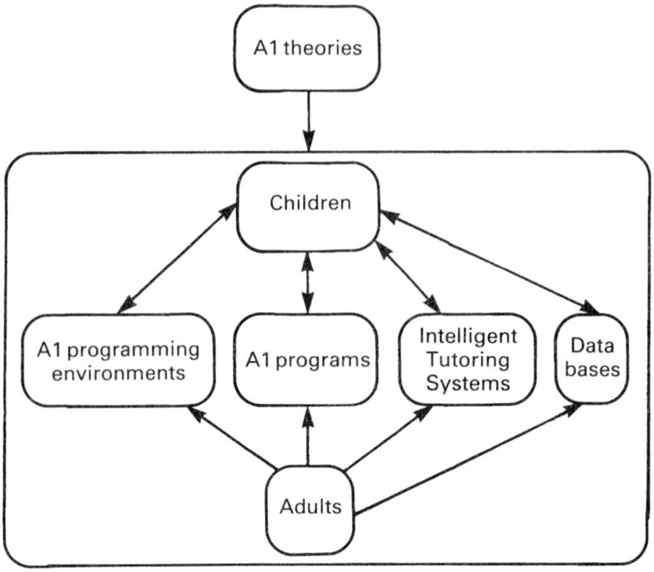

Fig. 4

A detailed study of Fig. 4, considering the probable development of AI in the next few decades, indicates that the difference between an ITS and an AI set of programs and data-base of facts, is more conceptual than real. In the long term, the different components will merge to form a number of AI learning environments.

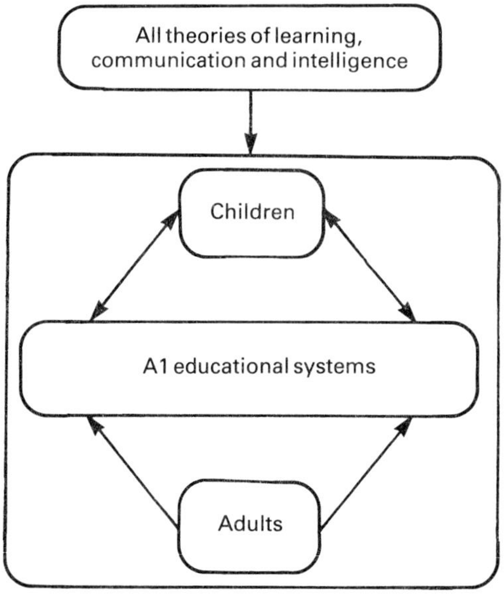

Fig. 5

But learn what? In a situation where computers have a certain level of intelligence, we do not need to compromise and learn their internal working. Further, having been freed from the artificial problem of how computers work, we can return to the basic objective of education.

8. SOME IMPLICATIONS

The use of intelligent computers for education poses one major question, which is 'What are the aims and objectives of education?'. We need to know the answers in order to know how computers should be employed in education. I believe one needs to go back to the roots of education and find a role for computers which is innovative, helpful, and motivating without just replacing current activities of the educational system without radical questioning.

During a workshop on Microcomputers in Education, I heard different meanings associated with education by different participants:

Education = Cognitive development
Education = Certification and placement
Education = Initiating individual initiative

After talking to the participants, I felt that education was, in fact, a broad endeavour which covered a number of essential tasks:

(1) to help people to develop an understanding of their talents and how to develop them;
(2) to give people confidence in dealing with others;
(3) to give people the opportunity to develop skills in leadership and joint action;
(4) to help peoples' cognitive development;
(5) to help people to assess their abilities and provide them with placement in society so that their individual talents are appreciated, etc.

However, owing to lack of human resources where one teacher is to look after the educational needs of some 30-odd pupils, most of the goals of education are neglected. As a result, the education system is not free to deal with the business of education but acts as a certification and placement agency.

Therefore, it is in the areas of neglected goals of education where computers could play a major role, in contrast to the current situation where they are used to replace current activities of the teacher or the textbooks. For example, the following projects seem to be worthwhile pursuits:

(a) Computer-based monitoring of children's individual educational progress at school. In this way a teacher can provide individualized guidance, with the help of the computer for children, which appreciates

  (i) what they are doing,
  (ii) what they are good at,
  (iii) what they care about,
  (iv) who is developing leadership skills at this moment, etc.

The system would help the teacher to take different children through different paths in the spaces of learning experience, depending on their interests, talents, values and expectations.

(b) Computers as an aid for teachers to present hypothetical futures, pasts and presents. A visi-society.

What a machine can do as a medium in which the child gains learning experience was discussed. The computer here is a world model built by the teacher, in which the child can see the consequences of alternatives.

This system would also help the children to discover how they should form questions in the first place; questions which make sense and which can be answered.

(c) The computer as a tool for the child building the models. In this form of the use of computers, the child is in fact constructing worlds and exploring with consequences of architectural design decisions.

At this point we touch on the areas already advocated by artificial intelligence programming environments.

9. CONCLUSION

Artificial intelligence provides a possibility of going back to the roots of education and doing what has not been possible with traditional methods. Whether our society is ready or willing for such radical questioning (of basically a fundamental issue such as our educational system) is a different matter. AI researchers, however, should be clear on whether they intend to make the status quo more efficient or whether they intend to revolutionize it.

Masoud Yazdani

NOTES

[1] Khan (1975).
[2] Sleeman and Brown (1982).
[3] Yazdani (ed.) (1984a).
[4] Papert (1980).
[5] Winograd (1972).
[6] Waltz (1975).
[7] Winston (1975b).
[8] Lawler (1979).
[9] Sloman (1984).
[10] Yazdani (1984a).
[11] Coker (this volume).
[12] O'Shea and Self (1983).

For details see the bibliography at the end of the book.

The advocates of the use of AI in education seem to be grouped under two headings representing the two ends of a spectrum on which we could put the areas mentioned above. One group concern themselves with more powerful 'teaching packages' which teach a subject aiming to be as competent as a good human teacher. Ford, in this volume, presents a catalogue of such systems.

On the other side of the spectrum, typified by Seymour Papert's arguments, researchers are working on 'learning environments' which provide students with powerful computing tools with which they would learn through play. The intention here is not learning how *to program, but to learn* through *programming. Coker, in this volume, looks at the implications of such playful activity, as well as the general issues which could arise during our dealings with artefacts which have, or are thought to have, a certain level of intelligence.*

Readers who would like to pursue the implications of such education, based around the use of intelligent computers, may also like to consult Boden (1983).

Intelligent computer aided instruction

L. Ford Logica UK

1. INTRODUCTION

It is more fashionable nowadays to talk about 'intelligent' computer-aided instruction/learning (ICAI/ICAL) systems than their older relations which are not prefixed by the word 'intelligent'. The reason for this state of affairs is not simply that it is in vogue to describe any system which does not appeal to traditional computing methods as being 'intelligent', but because there has been a genuine turn by developers of educational systems to the techniques and methods of artificial intelligence (AI). This change in direction, as we shall see, was undertaken not merely to satisfy the whims of system developers to embrace new and exciting tools and methods but was borne out of the recognition that traditional approaches to CAI could not meet the ideals of good instructional systems. Traditional tools and methods were simply inadequate for the task.

We begin with an examination of the trends that are evident in CAI's history and go on to discuss the importance of AI to CAI. Three state-of-the-art systems are reviewed to exemplify the major approaches that have emerged since AI has been applied to educational systems. Although these prototypical systems encourage us to believe that AI is the cornerstone of future educational systems, consensus of agreement has yet to be reached on the desirable components of them and the underlying philosophy on which they should be based.

2. A BRIEF HISTORY

It is not our intention to provide a complete history of computers in education;

this has been done recently and in some detail by O'Shea and Self [1]. We do, however, draw substantially from their account to present a brief history of major trends.

O'Shea and Self have identified eleven approaches to using the computer in education:

- linear programs;
- branching programs;
- generative computer-assisted learning;
- mathematical models of learning;
- TICCIT;
- PLATO;
- simulation;
- games;
- problem-solving;
- emancipatory modes;
- dialogue systems.

As they point out, it is not a strict chronological ordering of developments but it reflects the trends in the way people have regarded educational uses of computers. We aim to say a bit about each approach. Since most of them are not presently in fashion we shall mention their limitations.

Linear Programs

Linear programs were based on the principle of operant conditioning. An operant is a unit of behaviour which is conditioned by reinforcement (Skinner, [2]). Undesirable behaviour is totally ignored by the approach, thus when it is applied to education the teaching material used in linear programs has to be carefully selected and organised to increase the chance of the desired behaviour being exhibited on the part of the student.

The main proponent of operant conditioning, the behavioural psychologist B. F. Skinner, claimed that the human teacher as a reinforcing mechanism might just as well be replaced by a machine (Skinner, [3]). This gave rise to the phenomenon of the programmed teaching machine. These machines – which were manually operated by the student – presented teaching material as frames, each frame requiring a response from the student (and as we have said, the frames organised to ensure a correct one). Windows of the machine enabled the student to write his answer alongside the question. The student then turned the preprinted paper inside the machine on to the answer. Whether his answer was correct or not he then moved on to the next question.

The inadequacy of the approach has long since been recognised. Perhaps its major limitation is its inability to provide individualisation and rich feedback: all students receive the same material in the same sequence, and feedback is of limited meaning since it ignores responses.

Branching Programs

Recognition of the need to provide individualisation and feedback resulted in the branching program approach. These programs respond to a student's answers by allowing him to move on to the next question (in the case of a correct response) or comment on his wrong response and allow him to have another go.

In order to facilitate development of such programs, author languages were designed. Typically, these implemented IF and GOTO commands to allow the program author to cater for students' individual responses. The simplicity of author languages encouraged teachers to develop their own courseware (and hence to some extent helped to overcome a reluctance to allow computers in the classroom). But a problem that confronts anyone wishing to develop a program of this sort is that the more situations that have to be catered for, the more branches are required. This can result in a veritable explosion of branches for which programming becomes exceedingly difficult, even for a professional programmer. For example, if the program is to deal individually with answers it must have conditional branches for each possible answer. Each branch thus represents a new situation which again will ideally take account of individual responses. If this process continues for four questions and for only two possible answers to each, as many as $2 \times 2 \times 2 \times 2$, i.e. 16 situations would need to be catered for.

The approach thus has technical problems. More importantly, perhaps, there is growing recognition that education involves 'engagement' of the student, not a principle easily implemented in branching programs which are founded on the belief that students learn from being told.

Generative Computer-Assisted Learning

The main characteristic of generative systems is that they can generate problems of suitable difficulty for students and generate the solutions. Individualised tuition (in so far as problem selection is concerned) is thus made possible.

It has obvious value for arithmetic drill and practice in which it would be difficult to create an adequate number of exercises using the branching program approach. The generative system, by judicious use of program variables, can provide as many problems as the student needs. It can, furthermore, control the level of difficulty by using its knowledge of the domain.

It is, however, restricted to drill-type exercises and only to subjects which are well structured, since a program must have a precise representation of the subject to enable it to determine a suitable problem.

Mathematical Models of Learning

As the name of this approach suggests, it is concerned with expressing in mathematical notation a theory of learning. The idea of the approach was to develop theories which would predict the outcome of various teaching strategies, and then use the theory within a computer program to enable it to choose an appropriate teaching action in a given situation.

The main problem concerns the difficulty in developing the model. Little enough is understood of how people learn, and there is no evidence to suggest that an adequate model can be developed without due regard to the subject being taught – which this method seeks to do.

TICCIT

The TICCIT (Time-shared Interactive Computer Controlled Information Television) project, like PLATO which we describe next, was initiated in 1971 by the National Science Foundation of America (NSF) which invested $10 million over a 5-year period to investigate whether computer-aided learning could be effective at less cost than traditional methods. TICCIT was therefore not regarded as an adjunct to current teaching practices, but was to be used as the main instructional medium.

Material was produced by a team including an educational psychologist, a domain expert (for each of the two subjects that the system presented for evaluation purposes – namely, pure calculus mathematics and English composition), an instructional design technician, an evaluation technician and a packaging specialist. The material itself was presented in text in three stages. First, general principles were outlined, then examples illustrating the general principles, and finally exercises for the student to practise.

Each TICCIT system was controlled by two minicomputers serving up to 128 terminals. Each terminal included a keyboard, colour television (for graphics), colour videotapes, a loud speaker to deliver prerecorded messages, a light pen and a keyboard for messages from the student. The keyboard included such buttons as HELP, EXAMPLE, HARD, SKIP, BACK. Sequence of presentation was thus controlled by the student.

Implementation of the system met with a mixed response, mainly due to the overt emphasis on economics and disagreement by the parties concerned over the content and teaching methodology of both subjects. Somewhat surprisingly, the NSF independent evaluation indicated that students who completed TICCIT courses did better than those who had no exposure to TICCIT. These results were offset, however, by claims that TICCIT favoured better students and that it had higher dropout rates than for conventional instruction. In spite of encouraging results, TICCIT has not been widely adopted.

PLATO

PLATO (Programmed Logic for Automatic Teaching Operation) began in 1960, long before being funded by NSF. The striking differences between it and TICCIT are:

- large networks (up to 1000 terminals);
- latest technological innovations attached to terminals;
- courseware developed by any end users.

The economics of the PLATO system are a more important part of its philosophy (the more terminals the more viable it is economically) than its pedagogical principles (which are hardly discernible). PLATO embodies vague ideas about supplying rich learning environments, that good teaching material will survive and come into general use. Evaluation of it has, therefore, been a rather subjective matter: students have complained about response times and that the (central) computer breaks down a lot; but they also say that they enjoy using it in some situations. Teachers also have mixed feelings about it – some enjoy the challenge of developing courseware on it, but more than 10 per cent did not want to use it again.

Since being funded by NSF, hardware prices have dropped and microcomputers have been widely adopted by schools. The variables in the economic equation on which its approach was initially justified have thus taken values which do not make it financially appealing.

Simulations

The use of computer simulations of a process in education is based on the assumption that students learn by watching (in this case results of simulations displayed on a screen). In the more sophisticated simulation environments, the student has an opportunity to play an active role, by changing the values of variables in the process as it proceeds, or by selecting initial inputs. This can be of quite significant value when the student is learning, for example, biological evolution, or how a fragment of computer program works. In the former case, the results of an evolutionary process can be displayed (e.g. changes in the appearance of the fruit fly) or the values of program variables in the latter.

Simulations are, of course, of no value in subjects such as English composition, but in subjects where they can be used students find them appealing since they can use them to explore their own ideas. Although simulations can therefore play an important educational role, the role is limited to a single perspective of the subject.

Games

The use of games on computers is widespread; indeed, it is probably the main reason why so many microcomputers have been bought in the United Kingdom over the past several years: each microcomputer is usually offered for sale with a games package thrown in as an incentive to purchase. A small, but growing, game-producing industry has mushroomed to meet the demand, and respectable computing magazines devote many pages to listing source statements of games programs to enable devotees to transfer them to their own computers.

Why are game programs so appealing and what is their relevance to education? The phenomenon of computer game-playing is so widespread that the subject cannot be dismissed lightly.

O'Shea and Self have used the studies of Banet [4] and Malone [5,6] to derive some reasons for their appeal. The first list of reasons, from Banet's study, concerns the particular properties of computers which become manifest in the game playing environment:

- audio and visual effects are used to reward success and present the game situation;
- the game can increase in its ability to challenge the player – it need not become boringly simple;
- the game incorporates fantasy elements (e.g. piloting a spaceship);
- the computer can time the player's responses and calculate scores.

[redacted]

Malone's study analysed the preferences of children for 25 games and proposed that the following three properties account for their appeal:

– challenge: there is a goal whose attainment is uncertain;
– curiosity: the player knows enough to have expectations about what will happen, but sometimes those are unmet;
– fantasy: the games provoke mental images not present to the senses.

The relevance of games to education is that they engage the attention and interest of the child – a situation not always easily achieved in conventional instruction. Following on from this, the question arises whether games could be made educationally useful, i.e. could a game require skills that would normally be taught, but which the game environment could subtly impart during interaction with it?

The answer to the question is as yet unknown but the game 'How the West was Won' (Bitzer [7]) which requires the player to get from Tombstone to Redgulch in as few 'goes' as possible requires basic arithmetic skills. The better skilled the child in arithmetic, the more successful he is at the game.

Whether as a result of playing the game the child acquires the skills that the game seeks to impart is less certain. Reswick [8] found that no matter how much a child used the game he would usually restrict himself to a limited set of strategies that did not require all the skills. This problem has been addressed by Burton and Brown [9], who are attempting to use the same game in a computer coaching environment. Results have not yet been forthcoming, but while it may be expected that the system, when used, will impart the necessary skills, the ultimate question is whether the game, in the process, will have lost any of its attractions.

Problem-Solving

The problem-solving approach requires the student to write a computer program and is based on the belief that the act of constructing a computer program helps to develop general problem-solving skills. Its most ardent advocate, Seymour Papert, has been instrumental in its widespread acceptance and for its implementation in its most sophisticated form, LOGO (Papert *et al.* [10]). It reflects an underlying educational philosophy of 'learning by doing', which emphasises that education is better regarded as a process of 'engagement' rather than 'explanation'.

An important aspect of LOGO is that it provides a rich bag of tools for the student to enable him to create programs. This is essential to the approach, since programming is at best inherently difficult, and an inferior environment would hardly help him to clarify his thoughts about thinking, or improve his thinking habits, both of which are goals of the approach.

Well, how does the student achieve these goals? The answer is not easily provided, nor is it easy to determine whether the student ever achieves them. What can be said is that the approach relies on the provision of an environment that the student finds appealing to use. By this we mean that the language that the student uses to write his program must be powerful yet easy to learn and use; that the environment is 'friendly', i.e. it does not, for example, penalise the student unduly for trivial errors, nor does it impose arbitrary restrictions on what the student wants to do; and that there exists an interesting set of problems that can be tackled.

Even small programs can be a source of enlightenment to the student, provided the environment is suitably organised to give an appropriate response to the execution of it (for example, by employing colour graphics). Each program developed by the student can be regarded as an experiment with his thought processes, thus execution of it provides experimental results which are a rich source of feedback. If the environment has been organised with care, it will enable the student to build ever more complex programs using the building blocks he has so far erected. The student thus has the opportunity to proceed at his own pace and take whichever direction takes his fancy. In practice, the student is not isolated and can reap rewards from demonstrating his program to others and learning from their ideas.

A problem concerning the approach, in schools at least, is that it is not easily time-tabled. Problem-solving or thinking about thinking is not generally regarded as a subject in its own right, and LOGO activities, for example, therefore fall under the umbrella of computer education. Now although the problem-solving approach may improve a student's problem-solving abilities, it does not follow that it will improve his programming skills. Indeed, frequently the student (a child perhaps) will program 'on the fly' much to the delight of Papert. But what would a traditional computer scientist such as Dijkstra say? The former would refer to creative discovery, the latter, perhaps, to mental mutilation (as he has done about students learning the BASIC language).

Much needs to be done in order to reconcile these differences of opinion, both of which seem to have some validity.

Emancipatory Modes

McDonald [11] has referred to the computer undertaking tasks on behalf of the student, e.g. retrieving information, performing a calculation, as operating in emancipatory mode. In such a mode the computer relieves the student of tasks which, if he had undertaken them, would not have contributed to his knowledge of the subject at hand.

The advantage of using a computer in this way is that it allows the student to concentrate on the subject matter. There are no obvious disadvantages (provided the computer responds in reasonable time, does not break down, is easy to communicate with, gives the correct results, etc.).

Dialogue Systems

As the name suggests, dialogue systems, unlike the approaches so far discussed, aim to support a dialogue between system and student. They can be seen as a reaction to the strict one-way communication process of traditional CAI systems in which the system does all the 'talking', the student being relegated to answering questions. They do, of course, reflect a conventional tutorial setting in which the student may himself ask questions of the tutor. The major advantages of a tutorial are that the tutor does not have to guess what the problems of the students are by framing appropriate questions (the student may be able to indicate what they are), and that it enables the student to articulate his own ideas about the subject (which any teacher will confirm is a powerful way of understanding the subject).

Other characteristics of a tutorial are that it is conducted in natural language (usually by speech), that anyone may take the initiative (students or tutor), questions may be ignored or followed by other questions, the topic may be changed, and that there is some overall direction or purpose to it. To implement a system with these properties is impossible at present. Natural-language understanding is an unresolved problem of AI research (although some success has been achieved in restricted domains of discourse), and speech processing as a research topic is in its infancy. Researchers have nevertheless investigated as far as possible the theoretical problems that arise in such systems and three typical ones are examined later.

3. DISCUSSION

By and large, the first ten approaches that have been considered can be implemented using traditional methods of software engineering: solutions are algorithmic by nature and can be developed using conventional computer languages in a program life cycle framework. It is when developers wish to enhance their systems to be more sensitive to the needs of the student that a different approach is required.

Systems such as PLATO were fundamentally limited in their ability to portray other than severely restricted patterns of behaviour because of the difficulty the developer would face in managing the combinatorial explosion of branches, which result from use of PLATO's author language, if he wished to implement sophisticated educational practices. As we mentioned, PLATO was doomed to founder on the rocks of technological progress. (By a strange quirk of fate these same rocks have set back research on 'intelligent' CAI – schools use microcomputers which, with their as yet limited power, are inadequate for AI systems, and there has thus been greater emphasis on supplying courseware for them rather than examining the deeper problems of computerised learning.)

AI programs, on the other hand, differ substantially from their algorithmic counterparts. While the latter emphasise procedural control, the former are more concerned with the nature of the data to be manipulated. A major concern of AI is how it may represent the data (AI reseachers prefer to call it knowledge), such that it expresses naturally that which it wishes to convey and at the same time permits ease of manipulation.

The types of knowledge for which representations are sought include:

– factual statements;
– text;
– imprecise statements.

All of these are of potential value to an instructional system. Factual statements can be used to express subject knowledge (e.g. Lima is the capital of Peru), and knowledge of the student (e.g. Jim Smith knows that Lima is the capital of Peru). Text, usually in the form of natural language, is required to permit dialogue between system and student. Imprecise statements permeate the whole of instruction. They are used to represent belief in a student's knowledge (e.g. the certainty that Jim Smith knows that Lima is the capital of Peru is *p*), and they can also reflect the judgemental knowledge in subjects such as medicine (e.g. if the infection type is primary-bacteremia then there is evidence that the organism is bacteroides).

Many representational schemes have been investigated by AI reseachers. We mention a few of them below to give a flavour of their different styles.

Predicate logic is one that has wide application. It can represent both factual statements and their relationships. An advantage of predicate logic is that it has a long history of research – it is well understood. The disadvantage is that it is not believed to have psychological validity, i.e. it is not thought to correspond to the way in which human knowledge is represented.

The use of semantic networks has a reasonably long history in CAI. The SCHOLAR system (Carbonell [12]) used them to represent the geography of South America. The network contains concepts (as nodes) and relationships (as the arcs that link them). Thus Lima and Peru would be nodes and the relationship 'is capital of' would be an arc linking them.

Frames (Minsky [13]) have long been known to psychologists as schemata. They provide a method of representing a stereotyped situation, e.g. a meal at a restaurant. Within a frame are slots for holding various kinds of information. For example, there are slots for holding information that will always be true in the situation (e.g. a meal is eaten at a table) and others (called fillers) that require some question to be resolved (e.g. what to eat). Frames are of particular interest since they have been used to provide a theory of learning. The idea is that experience enables the slots to be completed in individual frames and that new frames are formulated from existing ones. 'Learning is then to be interpreted in terms of the storing and modifying of schemata [frames] as a result of experience' [1].

Of recent interest to AI researchers (although again we find that its origins are in psychology) is the use of production systems. These have been employed, with variations, in the development of expert systems. A production is a rule of two halves, e.g. IF A THEN B. If A is true then B (some sort of action) takes place. Expertise within expert systems is frequently represented as a set of such rules together with an interpreter of them. MYCIN is a prime example, and has been used in the GUIDON educational system [14].

Another major difference between AI and algorithmic programs is the way in which control is exercised. The latter operate in a strictly linear sequential mode. The former require more sophisticated methods of control if they are to use their rich knowledge structures to best effect. AI programs have, therefore, explored the value of parallel control and control initiated by the status of knowledge, often deciding what to do next on the basis of uncertain or incomplete information.

Such methods of control find sympathy in developers of instructional systems, since the nature of educational interaction is best examined from the point of view of the knowledge that the tutor has at his disposal at any moment, rather than from some fixed and necessarily limited view of possible event sequences. We thus find in GUIDON that it has rules of tutorial action and discourse management which specify what happens under certain conditions.

4. STATE-OF-THE-ART

At a time when there was a great deal of confusion about what should or should not be in an instructional system, Self [15] clearly indicated three major components:

> The knowledge determining a teaching program's overall performance can be clarified under three headings:
> (a) knowledge of how to teach (which includes knowledge of students in general);
> (b) knowledge of what is being taught;
> (c) knowledge of who is being taught (i.e. knowledge of one student in particular).

What has emerged since then can be seen as a continuing debate on what constitutes the knowledge in each area and how it should be represented to improve a teaching program's overall performance. Particular attention has been paid to (c) above, usually referred to as the student model, and three distinct philosophies have been applied to its treatment. They are:

- the expert model;
- the information processing model;
- the genetic model.

We look at three systems with respect to their contribution to the debate.

GUIDON

Current interest in expert systems makes GUIDON [14] an obvious choice for examination. GUIDON utilises the expert system MYCIN in its role as tutor in infectious diseases. The aim of the GUIDON system is to transfer the expertise in the knowledge-base of MYCIN to a student interacting with GUIDON. Another important factor in selecting GUIDON for examination is that the quality of MYCIN's knowledge-base as a problem-solver in infectious disease diagnosis has been widely acknowledged [16]. It is indeed an expert in the domain. Furthermore, MYCIN itself has the ability to explain its behaviour. It can, for example, explain why it requests certain clinical information and why it is exploring particular hypotheses.

GUIDON employs the 'case study method' which requires that MYCIN first solves a problem case in the domain. By inspecting the problem-solving strategy employed by MYCIN, GUIDON is able to monitor the progress of a student presented with the same case to solve. It does this by determining whether (i) the student seeks relevant case data, and (ii) the student draws relevant conclusions. This enables the student to be appraised in various ways. It is conjectured that the required learning will take place in the interaction.

After some experience with the system, however, shortcomings have been identified [18]:

> In attempting to 'transfer back' the experts' knowledge through GUIDON we find that the experts' diagnostic approach and understanding of rules have not been explicitly represented. GUIDON cannot justify the rules because MYCIN does not have an encoding of how the concepts in a rule fit together. GUIDON cannot fully articulate MYCIN's problem-solving approach because the structure of the search space and the strategy for traversing it are implicit in the ordering of rule concepts. Thus, the seemingly straightforward task of converting a knowledge-based system into a computer-aided instruction program has led to a detailed re-examination of the rule base and the foundation upon which rules are constructed . . .

The major problem concerns the formalism used to represent MYCIN's knowledge-base. Uniformity of representation using production rules was a significant factor in the successful construction of MYCIN, but it has embarrassing consequences in a tutorial. Clancey [18] has identified the problem areas.

An understanding of the way that MYCIN reasons (interprets its rules) is needed for an appreciation of some of the problems. Each rule consists of one or more hypotheses and one or more goals. MYCIN uses a backward chaining strategy, i.e. having selected a goal to pursue, it then tries to satisfy the hypotheses from which the goal follows. However, it does not perform a depth-first search on the evidence of one rule. It pursues a more general strategy which requires that all rules which conclude about the goal are considered. To facilitate this reasoning method, rules sharing an hypothesis are linked, and rules sharing a goal are linked.

Now it is the rule-author's choice to define rules that link in this way – his thinking defines what links will or will not be made. The rationale behind a link is a rule justification of which four kinds are evident in MYCIN:

- identification;
- causal;
- world fact;
- domain fact.

Identification justifications are based on the properties of an object. For example, the rule 'if the organism is a gram-negative, anaerobic rod then its genus may be bacteroides (.6)' uses laboratory observations of an unknown. Thus its justification is based on the properties of an organism.

An example of a rule justified by world fact is 'if the patient is male then the patient is not pregnant or breast feeding'.

An example of a domain fact justification is 'if a drug was administered orally and it is poorly absorbed in the GI tract then the drug was not administered adequately'. By definition, to be administered adequately a drug must be present in the body at high enough dosage levels.

Clearly, for these kinds of justifications, in these instances at least, the rules themselves provide adequate explanation in a tutorial setting. In other domains this is not always the case. In the use of the WHY system [17], the developers have noted that some of the students' misconceptions cannot easily be related to the domain, that their misconceptions are due to incorrect models of real-world knowledge. In so far as a justification appeals to real-world knowledge, the level of complexity of the justification should be pitched to ensure that the student can accept the justification and use it as a basis for adjusting his, perhaps incorrect, model.

Causal justifications in MYCIN cannot be dismissed easily. Consider, for example, the rule 'if the patient is less than 8 years old then don't prescribe tetracycline'. The rule does not mention the underlying causal process (chelation – drug deposition in developing bones) and the social ramifications (blackened permanent teeth) upon which it is based. The argument 'because the expert does not need to think about the justification as he goes about his business, so why should the student need to know it' ignores the process of learning. The counter-argument is that if the expert needed to know the justification to acquire the rule, then the same could be said of the student.

We turn now to the strategic information that is implicit in MYCIN's rules. The ordering of hypotheses in a rule affects the order in which goals are pursued. The rationale for the order, however, lies outside the rule network, thus the program is not able to explain why one goal is pursued before another. Also the order in which rules for a goal are tried also affects the order in which hypotheses and hence subgoals are pursued. Now, as these goals lead to questions of the user, it is clear that the question sequence is determined by the rule order. The program is, therefore, unable to answer why questions have been asked in a particular sequence. It could, of course, reply that rule order is the answer, but this is clearly unacceptable.

As it happens, rule order is not important to MYCIN in the sense that it could ultimately influence a diagnosis. In fact, rule order is fixed and determined by the order in which rules were presented to the system. Thus, there is no rationale behind the sequence in which MYCIN pursues goals and asks questions. This does not mean, however, that the matter is unimportant to the student. Focusing on a hypothesis and selecting appropriate questions in order that a line of reasoning may be followed are typical of human reasoning patterns. The fact that MYCIN does not require this explicit strategic knowledge is a comment on its inference engine – not on the inference engine of the expert who formulated the rules or the student who is trying to learn them.

There is no reason, in principle, why MYCIN should not contain explicit strategic information; indeed, it could be used to improve performance in its normal duties. However, strategic control in a production system requires structural definition of the domain. That there is an underlying structure in the domain is witnessed by the justification links that we referred to earlier.

The problem for GUIDON is that the structure lacks 'handles' – its explanation capability is thus limited to a flat discussion of the goals and hypotheses of rules. Fortunately for GUIDON, the rule trees of MYCIN are broad and shallow, and reasonably adequate explanations are possible. When, however, GUIDON was applied to the structural analysis domain of SACON, in which trees are narrow and deep, 'the tutorial degenerated into a lengthy description of one branch of the tree' [1].

MYCIN is a flat system of rules which can only state its immediate reasoning steps; it cannot explain them on any level of detail. Clearly, how a rule is constructed is of fundamental importance: MYCIN's were constructed to promote competence not comprehension. Clancey [18] remarks:

> The lessons of this study apply to other knowledge-based programs, including those which don't use the production rule representation. The first moral is that one cannot simply slap an interactive front end onto a good AI program and expect to have an adequate teaching system. Similarly, an explanation system may have to do more than just read back reasoning steps and recognize questions: it may be useful to abstract the reasoning steps, relating them to domain models and problem-solving strategies.

SPADE

SPADE [19] is an experimental piece of research concerned with the teaching and learning of structured planning and debugging of computer programs. (Note, however, that debugging in this instance is concerned with debugging a plan, and not the code of a program.) It supports a particular view of programming in which emphasis is placed on the importance of planning and debugging the design of the program prior to actual coding of the solution in a programming language.

Explicit within SPADE is a model of the design process. The model has been derived by analysis of student protocols in the domain of graphics programming using Papert's [20] 'Logo Turtle' language. The model is more correctly a framework within which models are expressed. For example, the framework contains a model of an 'ideal' student; it also contains models of student protocols; potentially it can contain models of students interacting with the system. These latter models are developed as 'perturbations' of existing models within the framework.

One view of SPADE is as an experimental device for testing the validity of its framework. This is achieved by examining how well its model of the design process can be used by students interacting with it. Pertinent questions in this respect are 'is its set of design concepts adequate?' and 'can it predict student interactions with it?'.

In the words of its developer, SPADE is a 'limited didactic system'. It is viewed as an intermediate stage in the development of a fully-fledged tutorial system. A problem of developing a tutorial system for programming is that programming is not a well understood activity. SPADE thus provides an opportunity for making some of the aspects of the programming activity concrete. Apart from requiring a good understanding of the domain, a tutorial system must have knowledge of what needs to be conveyed and how and when to convey it. By incorporating an explicit model of the design process, SPADE enhances the possibility of providing answers to such questions.

The model is also important for testing the hypothesis that articulation of problem-solving strategies facilitates learning. By incorporating a model of the design process, SPADE is different from a conventional programming environment which supplies an editor and compiler, neither of which takes cognizance of the design process. In SPADE, the design process is of prime importance and the model provides the vehicle to enable problem-solving strategies to be expressed by the student and understood by the system.

Coding the program is regarded as of minor importance. We thus find in SPADE that the model, which is expressed as a set of hierarchical rules, has at higher levels rules concerned with planning and debugging (of plans); only the lower-level rules are concerned with the constructs of a particular language.

The model of the design process consists of a number of procedures, each of which is represented by a packet of rules and is activated by its own interpreter. At the highest level is the control procedure which is responsible for activating lower level procedures such as 'refinement', 'repair' and 'try out'. Examples of control rules are:

(1) IF in try out and an error occurs THEN enter localization with a description of an error.
(2) IF in refinement and the definition of a sub-procedure is completed THEN enter try out for that sub-procedure.

The model requires a specification (of the problem to be solved) for which the designed solution is restricted to only using those terms (names/objects) which are explicit in the specification. In this respect, SPADE is limited to dealing with elementary problems for which the solution is evident from the specification.

Our main interest, however, is to show how the model functions in the Logo Turtle domain. This is an ideal domain for the purpose – a wide range of non-complex but interesting problems exists for it and Miller has had ready access to student performance data for introductory Logo sessions. The latter point is important, since it has enabled student protocols to be derived; these have been used to design and refine the model.

The Logo Turtle language consists of a number of commands for moving an imaginary turtle over a screen. As it moves over the screen, the turtle can be caused to leave a trail – it can therefore 'draw' pictures on the screen. The user can extend the command set by defining his own procedures. In the program below, for example, the user will define his own procedures for WELL and ROOF. The picture that the program produces is a wishing-well, shown to the right.

```
TO WW
10 RIGHT 90
20 WELL
30 FORWARD 50
40 LEFT 90
50 FORWARD 100
60 LEFT 90
70 FORWARD 50
80 RIGHT 120
90 ROOF
END
```

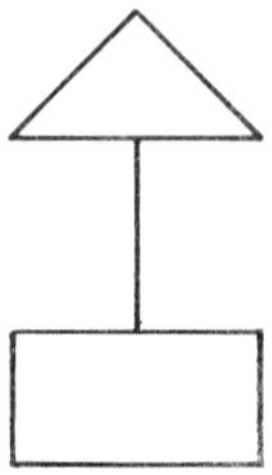

How would a student using SPADE develop a solution to the wishing-well problem? We examine some possible interactions and comment on them.

Q1: What name for the procedure you wish to plan today?
A1: WW
Q2: What type of plan would you like to use?
(A) Identify as previously solved problem.
(B) Decompose into sub-problems.
(C) Reformulate into alternative problem.
A2: SEQUENTIAL.

One aspect of SPADE that has yet to be developed is the input of the problem description. This would require the system to ask for the description after learning the name of the procedure, and would require the student to supply it using simple predicates, e.g. isa, is-above. He would, for example, indicate that WW is ROOF, POLE, WELL; ROOF isa TRIANGLE; POLE isa LINE; WELL isa SQUARE; ROOF is-above POLE; and so on. SPADE has knowledge of the entailments of the predicates and a stock of general-purpose objects such as pole, triangle and square. This enables SPADE to evaluate the plans of the student and predict the plan sequence in terms of development of individual objects.

Available to SPADE's model is a taxonomy of plans. At the most general level are three categories of planning strategies: identification, decomposition, reformulation. Note, however, that in asking Q2, the model has already predicted that the student will wish to make a plan as opposed to coding a procedure.

In answering Q2, the student has ignored the menu options – SPADE's model had not predicted the action of the student but, as shown below, it is able to cope with unpredictable situations.

Q3: I am assuming PLAN→DECOMPOSE→SEQUENTIAL.
What are the main steps in this sequential plan?
A3: WELL POLE ROOF
Q4: Do you want to include a SETUP step?
A4: Later
OK. I am postponing the [setup] of WW until later.
Q5: What now?

A5: Go to the second [interface] of the sequential plan.
Q6: Do you want to include this optional interface?
A6: Yes

SPADE deduces that WW is to be decomposed into a sequential plan. Q4 and Q6 illustrate the knowledge that SPADE has of the design process: a sequential plan will frequently have an initialisation or SETUP step (perhaps to face the turtle in the right direction) and that interfaces between sequential components are optional.

Q4 shows that a top-down left-to-right design strategy is being followed by the model. But, as frequently happens, the student prefers to postpone setup steps until later.

The value of this dialogue is that it makes evident any weaknesses of the model and suggests refinements to it. Analysis of such dialogues has enabled Miller to propose a 'Least-Scope' principle which states that 'design decisions should be made in that order which minimizes the probable scope of future modifications'. Top-down design is an approximation to the principle, but only an approximation; it suggested, for example, that the SETUP step should be dealt with before WELL. The student preferred to leave the SETUP until later, perhaps because he has applied Miller's least-scope principle; if WELL is defined by the student, who subsequently realises that its correct place in the plan requires an interface rather than a setup, the setup, if developed first, would be redundant. By developing WELL first, the student has minimised the extent to which future modifications may have to be made.

We shall now imagine that the student has developed WELL, POLE, and ROOF but has yet to define the SETUP and INTERFACE steps. The student can be assisted by SPADE if a partial plan is executed.

Q7: What now?
A7: RUN WW
Q8: Running WW . . . Done What now?
A8: Debug

Debugging WW. The top level of WW contains 7 design decisions which could be faulty. There are warnings attached to several nodes in the plan for WW.

Execution of the plan causes a graphic output of the resultant picture. SPADE is able to help the student directly by referring to design decisions and warnings. A typical warning type generated by SPADE would occur if the student had postponed part of the plan until later and subsequently not dealt with it.

Other features in SPADE include aiding the student in the diagnosis and repair of plans, and enabling the student to experiment with parts of the plan but without destroying the original plan.

The goal of SPADE is to tutor programming with particular emphasis on structural planning and debugging. It has, however, been recognised that less ambitious, intermediate goals must first be achieved. These address such issues as:

- what concepts are required in the design process?
- will these concepts suffice in domains other than Logo Turtle?
- does articulation of these concepts aid the learning process?
- to what extent should the system aid the student (some floundering can be beneficial)?

WUSOR

WUSOR, or more correctly, WUSOR-1 [21], is an expert-based coach for the game of WUMPUS. Our main concern here is not WUSOR, *per se*, but rather considerations for student modelling which have been articulated as a result of studying WUSOR's limitations (Goldstein [22]). In particular, we shall be examining the notion of the genetic graph as elaborated by Goldstein.

The student model of GUIDON is what Goldstein calls an overlay model: the student's knowledge is regarded as a subset of the knowledge of the embedded domain expert. Thus GUIDON's student model is characterised by the amount of MYCIN's expertise that the student is thought to have learned. Furthermore, systems of this sort (SOPHIE [23] is the other prime example) foster the view that tutoring consists of encouraging the growth of this subset, generally by intervening in situations where a missing fact or rule is the critical ingredient needed to reach the correct answer.

Goldstein argues that this view of the teaching process is oversimplified and fails to take account of the way in which new knowledge evolves from old. He proposes the genetic graph as a superior representational framework. (The term genetic is intended to convey its original meaning, e.g. as in the genetic method which is the study of the origins and development of phenomena. In this case, we are discussing genetic knowledge.) A consideration of genetic knowledge places greater emphasis on the learner-based paradigm as opposed to the expert-based ones of GUIDON and SOPHIE.

In a genetic graph, nodes represent procedural skills and arcs (links) represent the method by which one skill evolves from another. Links may include, for example, analogy, specialisation, generalisation, prerequisite and deviation. Another perspective of the representation is that nodes are rules and links are their interrelationships.

Of particular interest are the deviation links, since they enable a student's misconceptions to be represented routinely. (Most other systems that attend to misconceptions resort to a variety of *ad hoc* methods to cope with them; others ignore them entirely, even though they arise naturally in the learning process, e.g. as a result of mistaken analogy or over-generalisation.) Incorrect rules in the graph are represented as deviations of correct rules, and it is therefore possible to account for errors arising from the correct application of incorrect rules. In principle, it would appear that incorrect application of correct rules could also be represented in the graph (although Goldstein does not make this claim), provided some prior analysis of errors in this respect could be undertaken and formalised.

We mentioned that one perspective of the genetic graph representation is that nodes are rules, and links are their interrelationships. This perspective conveys that not all links are of an evolutionary nature. In GUIDON, for example, we noted that goal and hypothesis links were used to guide the reasoning strategy. With the genetic graph these links are made explicit as pre- and postrequisite relations. Thus the graph incorporates the strategic planning knowledge which enables the tutor to address the problem of the student who knows the rules but does not know in which order to use them.

This also overcomes the dilemma of whether to represent the student's knowledge declaratively or procedurally. It is no good merely representing the student's knowledge declaratively, since unless a system knows how he interprets it (reasons with it), it can have no precise understanding of what his knowledge entails. By incorporating planning knowledge, the genetic graph can at one and the same time represent both viewpoints.

Because a node may have more than one link (new knowledge is gained in a variety of ways), the graph does not describe a single evolutionary path. Apart from its ability to thus reflect the idiosyncratic learning behaviour of students, it also facilitates a wide range of teaching actions on the part of the tutor. The student is not constrained by a regimented instructional technique.

One of the ideals of intelligent instructional systems is individualised tuition. Now although individualised tuition is enhanced by taking account of the learning habits and preferences of the student, traditional instructional systems have found it difficult to do anything about it. If a student fails to learn presented material, is it because the material has been presented badly, or is it a failing on the part of the student? Contrariwise, if the student *has* learned the material, which can firm conclusions be drawn about; the efficacy of the presentation or the learning habits of the student? The genetic graph addresses this problem directly: links in the graph of the student's model reflect the learning habits and preferences of the student.

A problem that frequently confronts the tutor is determining whether a student's action was based on skills possessed by the student or due to a measure of luck. The genetic graph does not solve this problem but it at least provides the sort of evidence that a tutor could make use of in his analysis of the situation. Since the genetic graph embodies a theory of the evolution of the learner's knowledge, it suggests that a student's knowledge evolves along genetic links. Therefore, at any given moment there is on the graph the 'frontier' of the student's knowledge; thus the distance of the path from the frontier knowledge to the 'new' knowledge of the student provides a metric to apply when assigning belief that the student does indeed possess the knowledge.

A further problem confronting a tutor concerns determining which of a number of possible explanations will best foster learning. Given a model of the student's knowledge, the tutor is able to observe the effect of a particular explanation strategy by determining whether it consistently leads to skill acquisition. Now since each kind of explanation is associated with a particular type of link, a 'learning overlay can be generated over the set of genetic links that maintains a record of the effectiveness of the explanation strategy associated with that link type' [22]. The tutor thus has the advantage of possessing some knowledge of the kinds of explanation he prefers.

A weakness of the genetic graph approach is that it does not routinely cater for structural knowledge within the subject domain. GUIDON is similarly frustrated in this respect, but as we noted earlier, structural knowledge (and the handles that it provides) is a mandatory requirement for application of strategic knowledge and adequate representation of a student's knowledge at various conceptual levels. Furthermore, a tutor is unable to introduce a new concept without an appropriate handle: we saw with GUIDON that the tutor is constrained by its lack of structural knowledge into a flat discussion of rule content. The problem is not insurmountable for the genetic graph – Goldstein suggests how an extension of it can be utilised – but it calls into question the adequacy of its approach. Indeed, Goldstein admits that it 'does not solve the modelling problem . . . but constructing a model gains guidance from the graph'.

5. THE WAY AHEAD

None of the three types of student model we have briefly explored is entirely satisfactory.

The expert model of GUIDON does not facilitate the representation of a student's misconceptions or his own conceptual framework of the subject. The teaching strategy is thus regimented to accord with the expert's view of the subject which, as we have noted, may be sufficient for implementation of a competence program but will not necessarily be adequate for instructional purposes. We should not be surprised by this revelation; it is not uncommon in education for subject experts to be poor teachers. Indeed, their intimacy with a subject (and the student's lack of it) creates a wide knowledge-gap that is not easily bridged.

SPADE uses an information processing model to determine its actions. The model does not represent one particular student but is derived from an analysis of student protocols in the domain of problem-solving using turtle graphics. The protocols are determined by observing how a number of students go about solving a particular problem. After students have completed the exercise, their performance is analysed to enable sequences of solution steps and beliefs about their state of knowledge to be derived. These are then used to provide a framework for the model which can be implemented in a system such as WUSOR. Protocols are embedded as specific instances of behaviour but where possible are generalised. Thus, when a student uses the system, insofar as he follows a protocol in the model, the system has some handle on what the student's knowledge is and what its next action should be.

Although this method almost guarantees a reasonable representation of a student's knowledge and how he goes about solving a problem (and, of course, the system can be refined once it comes into operation, since it provides a rich source of new protocols), it relies on the existence of evidence of how students perform in the domain in the first instance, and subsequently on its correct analysis.

A feature of the method is that it reflects a trend in AI research. AI has turned from general problem-solving mechanisms to using specific domain knowledge, e.g. GPS [24] to MYCIN [25]. In a similar way, by examining student protocols CAI is turning from consideration of students in general to what students do in particular.

The major criticism we have of the information processing model approach is the predominantly behaviourist view of the student from which the model is developed. Can we be sure that the *external* observable behaviour of a student is an adequate basis to formulate beliefs about his *internal* processes and state of knowledge? We are reminded of the actor wishing to play the drunk whose external behaviour of slurred speech and staggering gait is most faithfully portrayed by the actor perceiving the drunk as one who is trying to speak clearly and walk straight.

Although Goldstein envisages the genetic model as being a replacement for the expert models of GUIDON and SOPHIE, we regard it as affording but another perspective of the student. It is clear that student modelling is inherently complex and any one view of the student may be too restrictive to permit the wide variety of teaching actions that in turn facilitate the, as yet, poorly understood ways in which learning takes place. After all, learning not only encompasses learning about a subject but also learning about learning – undue emphasis on current learning habits could lead to restricted learning habits on the part of the student. Due regard to the structure of the subject on the other hand facilitates new learning habits which may prove to be more powerful in the long run.

On the evidence presented, it seems unlikely that any one of the approaches, when considered in isolation, will be entirely satisfactory. By any standards, good tutoring is difficult to accomplish and we may expect educational technology to go through a number of evolutionary stages before a development methodology emerges. In the meantime, we can be sure that researchers will turn to AI techniques and methods for support.

NOTES

[1] O'Shea, T. and Self, J. (1983) *Learning and Teaching with Computers*, Harvester.

[2] Skinner, B. F. (1957) *Verbal Behaviour*, Appleton Croft.

[3] Skinner, B. F. (1954) The Science of Learning and the Art of Teaching, *Harvard Educ. Review* **24** pp. 86–97.

[4] Banet, B. (1979) Computers and Early Training, *Calculators/Computers* **3**, 17.

[5] Malone, T. W. (1980) What Makes Things Fun to Learn?: A study of intrinsically motivating computer games, unpublished PhD Thesis, Dept. of Psychology, Stanford Univ.

[6] Malone, T. W. (1981) Towards a Theory of Intrinsically Motivating Instruction, *Cogn. Sci.* **4**, pp. 333–369.

[7] Bitzer, D. L. (1976) The Wide World of Computer-Based Education, in *Advances in Computers*, Rubinoff and Yovits (eds.), Academic Press.

[8] Reswick, C. A. (1975) Computational Models of Learners for CAL, unpublished PhD Thesis, Univ. of Illinois.
[9] Burton, R. and Brown, J. (1982) An Investigation of Computer Coaching for Informal Learning Activities, in *Intelligent Tutoring Systems*, Sleeman and Brown (eds.), Academic Press.
[10] Papert, S., Watt, D., di Sessa, A., and Weir, W. (1979) Final Report of the Brookline LOGO Project, *LOGO Memo*, **53** (MIT).
[11] McDonald, B. (1977) The Educational Value of NDPCAL, *Brit. J. Ed. Tech.* **8**, pp. 176–189.
[12] Carbonell, J. R. (1970) AI in CAI: an artificial intelligence approach to computer assisted instruction, *IEEE Trans. on Man–Machine Systems,* **11**, pp. 190–202.
[13] Minsky, M. L. (1975) A Framework for Representing Knowledge, in *The Psychology of Computer Vision*, Winston (ed.), McGraw Hill.
[14] Clancey, W. J. (1982) Tutoring Rules for Guiding a Case Method Dialogue, in *Intelligent Tutoring Systems*, Sleeman and Brown (eds.), Academic Press.
[15] Self, J. (1974) Student Models in Computer Aided Instruction, *Int. J. Man.-Mach. Studies* **6**, pp. 261–276.
[16] Yu, V., Buchanan, B., Shortliffe, E., Wraith, S., Davis, R., Scott, A., and Cohen, S. (1979) Evaluating the Performance of a Computer-Based Consultant, *Computer Programs in Biomedicine* **9**, pp. 95–102.
[17] Stevens, A., Collins, A., and Goldin, S. (1982) Misconceptions in Students' Understanding, in *Intelligent Tutoring Systems*, Sleeman and Brown (eds.), Academic Press.
[18] Clancey, W. J. (1983) The Epistemology of a Rule-Based Expert System – A Framework for Explanation, *Artificial Intelligence* **20**, pp. 215–251.
[19] Miller, M. L. (1982) A Structured Planning and Debugging Environment for Elementary Programming, in *Intelligent Tutoring Systems*, Sleeman and Brown (eds.), Academic Press.
[20] Papert, S. (1971) Teaching Children to be Mathematicians Versus Teaching About Mathematics, *AI Lab. Memo* **249**, MIT.
[21] Stansfield, J., Carr, B., and Goldstein, I. (1976) Wumpus Advisor I: A First Implementation of a Program that Tutors Logical and Probabilistic Skills, *AI Lab. Memo* **381**, (MIT).
[22] Goldstein, I. P. (1982) The Genetic Graph: A Representation for the Evolution of Procedural Knowledge, in *Intelligent Tutoring Systems*, Sleeman and Brown (eds.), Academic Press.
[23] Brown, J. S., Burton, R. R., and de Kleer, J. (1982) Pedagogical Natural Language and Knowledge Engineering Techniques in SOPHIE I, II, and III, in *Intelligent Tutoring Systems*, Sleeman and Brown (eds.), Academic Press.
[24] Newell, A. and Simon, H. A. (1963) GPS, a Program that Simulates Human Thought, in *Computers and Thought*, Feigenbaum and Feldman (eds.), McGraw Hill.
[25] Shortliffe, E. H. (1976) *Computer-Based Medical Consultations: MYCIN*, Elsevier.

Learning to communicate with an 'intelligent' computer

M. Coker Marlborough College UK

THE WORD AND THE IDEA

Do we expect, when we attempt to communicate with an 'intelligent' computer, that the qualities it displays will be something akin to those displayed by ourselves? Will we expect whatever differences we notice to be only quantitative? In merely using the term, we beg the question of whether the concept of 'intelligence' has any meaning or existence other than as a description of some collective aspects of human behaviour.

We may be tempted to apply the word 'intelligent' to anything which behaves recognisably like ourselves in a sufficient number of respects, when the only problems remaining would be to sort out and agree on which respects these are, and how many of them. Compilers of intelligence tests have always had to beware of constructing tests that simply measured the similarity of the subject to the compilers, in the sense that the tests might reflect more their own pre-occupations or abilities rather than the 'pure' qualities which they set out to measure. Some popular authors are much franker; they set up a trait or cognitive style as somehow representative of 'intelligence' – and it is usually notable that they are rather proud of possessing this style themselves – and their book is designed either to measure or increase by practice one's similarity with the author-paragon.

Although such books may be of considerable interest as studies of ego-centricity, they are also microcosms of larger attitudes which, for example, naively expect alien intelligence to understand English, mathematics, picture-language, sexual reproduction – such expectations were committed to space only recently – or less naively, recognise that for two systems to detect intelligence in each other, a common mode of communication has to be established, with a common content, and that some unequivocal communication would be the first sign of intelligence which would be observable.

RECOGNISING INTELLIGENCE

Our recognition of a computer as 'intelligent' would therefore commence with our improving communications with it, and we would expect part of the improvement to have come as a result of adaptations made by the computer. We ourselves have a ready-made communication system, which we are intelligent enough to be able to use, and we expect to communicate with others via some sort of *rapprochement*. We believe this because we have certain ideas about the nature of intelligence in action: we expect (1) an efficient system of information-receiving; (2) an ample information-store; (3) an efficient system that can modify its storage, its storage-system or even its methods of processing as a result of its making use of the information it has received; and (4) we expect it to possess a means of communicating its decisions to the outside world, and notably, that it will at intervals find it expedient to communicate them in some form.

The first three of these characteristics probably comprise Piaget's 'assimilation' and 'accommodation', and the system as a whole merely elaborates a standard unified self-regulating system into a communicative model such as can be found throughout engineering or neurophysiology. Kirk's psycholinguistic model [1] is an example worth examining of an attempt to explain human performance in terms of these systems. Such attempts do offer some insight into the way we function, but no-one yet seems clear as to whether they are a description or merely a metaphor of part of the Human Condition. This is not an unimportant distinction, as we may have to decide whether an 'intelligent' computer is a model of intelligence, or merely a metaphor of it, and such decisions will materially alter our expectations when attempting to communicate with it.

CONTROLLING OTHER INTELLIGENCES

Rarer types of system, such as a Meditative system, which merely revolves the possible combinations of the data it encompasses without ever adding to it or communicating the results, or a Hieratic one, which observes and concludes, but again does not communicate, are all possible, are unlikely to be constructed except by accident or experimentally, as they would not normally be useful. We do not expect to work with an artificial system which refuses to communicate its results, or communicates them only at unpredictable intervals, or whose results we are powerless to modify. In fact, we might be inclined – rather unreasonably, as they certainly resemble patterns of human behaviour – to deny the intelligence of these systems.

Yet it is curious that one quality we expect to see in 'intelligent' computers is obedience, or an acceptance of unexplained interventions – perhaps we should call it faith, or trust – which are not always compatible with an active intelligence. Asimov, in setting out his fictional 'Laws of Robotics' [2], clearly foresaw the caveats that would have to be entered to *ensure* that artificial intelligence turned out to be very different from human intelligence. Any system possessing the attribute of universal altruism will be so different from human beings as to be almost unrecognisable, one feels, while there are many people who would not regard such behaviour as intelligent. If artificial intelligence is passive, goalless until provided with goals, and is prevented from reorienting these goals in forbidden directions by drawing conclusions from its experiences, then we are thinking of intelligence simply as processing power, and harnessed power at that, as we wish to preempt its use of any knowledge base in certain proscribed directions.

We are naturally alarmed to face the possibility of initiating a system which could be functioning intelligently without our realising it as, of course, the power of decision-making and the power of modifying responses and future decisions would also imply the power of modifying the output. The system may thus elect to say nothing, to withhold announcing or acting on part of its decisions, or even to give information not wholly compatible with its decisions. As any 'intelligent' system will involve extremely complex knowledge bases and processing, its results will often not be fully predictable to any other system apart from its twin in design and experience; and, after all, a system which cannot modify the form and content of its output in the light of decisions it has made with regard to its environment is not a very 'intelligent' one.

Although we are apt to judge intelligence in people by their skills in understanding our intentions and declaring their own, we are often more modest when dealing with computers, and it is interesting to see that many of the problems and difficulties which people experience while trying to use computers are attributed precisely to the type of elective unhelpfulness discussed above. The system is seen as dynamically, not passively, obstructive; it is invested with infinitely greater powers of decision than it actually has, and our difficulty in judging accurately the level or the quality of intelligence that we are addressing will be the next subject of this discussion.

QUALITATIVE AND QUANTITATIVE MEASUREMENTS OF 'INTELLIGENCE'

Some quality given the name of intelligence is often measured by psychologists and educationalists along a sliding scale of performance. An 'intelligent' being can make some attempt at performing the particular operations selected as a yardstick, and a quotient or percentile figure tells us whether he does this exceptionally well, or exceptionally badly, or about as well as most of us manage it. We must also ask, however, when this quality of intelligence disappears from an organism. At the first percentile, or only at the noughtth percentile? At an intelligence quotient of zero? In what sense are, say, severely mentally handicapped people not 'intelligent' in that a subject with a measurable performance on an 'intelligence' test may still be unable to perform any practically useful task, or vice versa? Two points require comment at this stage.

Firstly, this particular concept of measurement does not involve a sharp dividing-line between intelligence and non-intelligence. If we say that X is intelligent and Y is unintelligent, we would usually imply a quantitative rather than a qualitative difference between them, and most people would be very hard-pressed to state at what level an organism 'became' intelligent.

Secondly, there is the insurmountable difficulty of using a consistent word to represent an inconsistent body of meaning. There is still as much disagreement as there ever was among psychologists and others as to the nature of 'intelligence' and the means available to us to measure it. The evidence strongly suggests that any unitary concept of intelligence must be inadequate, just as any attempt at a comprehensive list of the component factors of intelligence must be. There does not even seem to be any generally agreed list of 'minimum requirement', and some psychologists (and philosophers!) would argue that intelligence itself has no independent existence [3], but is simply apparent to the beholder when the behaviour he studies reaches a degree of complexity within an arbitrary range of complexities – perhaps when the complexity of behaviour reaches the same order of magnitude as his own.

This must mean that our expectations of the 'behaviour' of an intelligent computer will vary as much as our own personal definitions of intelligence, and that as some computers can be 'more intelligent' and others 'less intelligent' we will be hard-pressed to distinguish between a less intelligent and an unintelligent computer.

Ill-defined expectations aroused by our (or other people's) notions of intelligence, combined with the vagueness and diversity of the goals of much teaching about computers, lead to a statistical likelihood of major problems in communication at some time when we address the computer, or it addresses us. The most significant method of communicating with a computer to date (and hence to modify its behaviour, or perhaps to 'teach' it something) is, of course, to address it in its own language, that is to write a program for it; and the proliferation of books in all parts of the market designed to help people to do that show how highly this form of communication is regarded in almost every area of training.

Perhaps some of the confusion of goals spoken of earlier springs from the variety of uses to which the knowledge gained may eventually be put. I shall hope to show that even within one particular area, that of computer education (or educational computing), the ideals that lead us on are notably ill-defined and diffuse.

COMMUNICATING-GOALS AND PROGRAMMING-GOALS

Programming represents one of the triumphs of language over experience. When we are born, we are entirely (for a very short time) or mostly (for a much longer time) experiential beings, in that we live entirely or nearly entirely in terms of experiences. As we grow, we become increasingly representational beings, in that we find more and more efficient ways to represent our experiences to ourselves. Still later, as language, both internalised and externalised, matures, we become more and more descriptive and learn to share in the exchange of our own and other people's representations of experience *via* various methods of description. In this sense, a description is used as an externalised form of a representation.

Although visual representation of visual experiences, such as in TV and pictures, are important, most of us rely very heavily upon verbal description for giving and receiving impressions of experiences.

As we grow older, we learn to rely less and less upon direct experience and more and more upon these representations of it derived from our past experiences, in various indirect descriptional forms. Very old people, for example, represent an extreme form of this at times, where their interests can lie almost entirely in descriptive representations and not at all in actual experiences.

We begin to rely upon descriptive or indirect forms of experience surprisingly early because of our immense efficiency in forming a *structured* representation of our experiences. Most writers seem to accept that we have inherent tendencies to represent and describe events in ways that are common to most of us; that is, an inherent tendency towards certain *types* of structural representation, and thus to communication *via* language [4].

Many studies of the development of children's language have emphasised the dynamic nature of the process, with the child giving evidence of prolific generation of new examples and new rule-structures, not readily explainable in terms either of imitation or environmental pressures [5].

Ultimately, the rule-forming pressures give way to the rule-using ones, and the greater part of our lives is spent in employing what we have gained in terms of our knowledge-base, and its structure, in more and more elaborate but less and less innovative ways.

By examining these human development patterns, we may be able to discover which aspects of developmental learning might either be represented by the computer or involved in learning to program it. We can look, for example at the difficulties experienced by young humans in learning about the world, in particular while developing language, and seek to draw parallels with the problems experienced by the learner-programmer. We can get only a very little way with our answers to these problems without some listing of our aims in our work with beginners; we must ask ourselves much more critically what results we intend to achieve from our efforts.

It is very hard to establish any set of aims which is demonstrably anything more than a set of prejudiced opinions. Most sets of aims we devise will inevitably encourage the students to experience, to some greater or lesser degree, our own thought processes in devising them, and we have also to establish an equally arguable hierarchy of these processes by which the beginner is able to attain Parnassus. I am not emphasising the uselessness of aims or objectives, only their problematic nature.

We must also distinguish between the problems of establishing a valid aim and those of establishing a valid *set* of aims. Aims and goals admirable in themselves will not necessarily form a coherent series when considered together.

A great deal of computer-teaching has been carried out without any proper attention to these problems; it is *ad hoc* in that it consists in an assembly of what the teacher believes to be important, arranged in the order that seems to him the most likely to succeed. I am not implying that this is necessarily wrong or even ineffective, but simply pointing out that as the number of teachers multiplies, this method is very likely to produce a steady multiplying of goals, making it harder for computer-users (considered as the products of different-thinking teachers) to communicate with each other, quite apart from the inherent unlikeliness of all approaches being equally successful, or equally sound. Ultimate aims must differ, of course, but are there no intermediate ones about which we could all agree? Even this limited list would be very hard to produce without a much more rigorous and controlled examination of the results of our instruction than appears usually to be the case at the moment.

EXPLICIT AND IMPLICIT GOALS IN COMPUTER EDUCATION

We may gain some insight into the expressed and the implied goals of educators if we try to list those reasons for including computers, which are always at the head of most teachers' lists, in any curriculum and which probably reflect social pressures on our secondary schools today as much as anything else. Perhaps they might read very like the following.

Everyone must know how to communicate with computers, because:

- computing is very important in tomorrow's society;
- computing is inevitably to be part of our lives;
- even though everyone is not going to be a programmer, it is going to be helpful to know about computers when seeking a job;
- we are going to be controlled by computers to such a large extent that it is important to be able to meet them as an equal adversary on their own ground.

Such reasons are more or less pragmatic in their intent, at least, and some of them are well-founded, but many of them are based on a failure to grasp that knowing about computers is not the same thing as programming them; or indeed, and this is a sore point, that using other people's programs for a long time will not necessarily teach you anything either about computers or programming.

There are other arguments in a second category, which claim that learning to program is a purely intellectual exercise which stimulates the mind, gives it 'tone', as it were, and which produces similar beneficial effects *of a generalised nature*, i.e. in all areas of the curriculum, to those the mathematicians claim for pure mathematics, the logicians for logic, and the classicists for Latin and Greek. Whether or not intensive courses in programming disciplines would bring back the Empire at this late stage is another matter; probably it would not, as the natives are busy learning programming as well.

It is important not to dismiss this aim of general stimulation of the intellect as fanciful, as there is at least some physiological and educational evidence of such effects [6]. In my opinion, it is not the programming or the communicating with the computer itself which has such a tonic effect, but those concepts which are more readily introduced through its assistance; in the same way, I would claim that this is equally true with regard to the other subjects that I mentioned: e.g. pure mathematics is not *inevitably* mind-expanding in its effects, although it unquestionably can be.

A third category of aim could be entitled the 'insight' group of ideas. This group is concerned with the belief that deeper insights into the nature of thinking, oneself, the rules of the universe, problem-solving and other such small matters, are all rendered more probable through examining and composing computer programs.

We cannot fail to note that these come very close to the benefits claimed for say, meditation, or conversion, or listening to the Mahareshi Mahatma Mukerjii. They are all introspective, and may involve proselytisation, discipleship, and the membership of exclusive ideological clubs.

Furthermore, it is noticeable that any such insights will inevitably forge links with, and perhaps between, a surprisingly large number of traditional disciplines, such as logic, cognition, linguistics, psychology, physiology, mathematics, *et cetera*.

THE LARGEST CARROT IN THE UNIVERSE

If the above can be true, then there will be considerable justice in claiming the ultimate aim of an *education in computing* to be the completion of the most powerful generalising and unifying process in contemporary thought today. The intermediate aims of this process would be the understanding of artificial intelligence concepts, and below those, programming concepts, and below those a much lowlier set of aims, concerned with the bread-and-butter affair of actually converting one's preaching into practice.

It is always a good idea to look at the necessary consequences of our intentions, if we can; and one of the consequences of such a Grand Design would be to unify, for the second time in man's history, virtually the whole of his abstract thinking. The concept of *Scientia* as *the* body of knowledge is essentially one that could not survive the increasingly minute scrutinies of the Renaissance, although it survived as a poorly articulated idea in mainly esoteric forms, and its re-emergence as one of the rewards of study, with all the power of technology and prophecies of inevitability behind it and its unique likelihood of swallowing everything else up, presents a terrifying threat to some people of a new all-powerful intellectual 'priesthood', one which we should train our children to join as best we (and they) can, if we cannot train them to resist it. The rewards of success and the stigmata of failure become invested with immense emotional burdens. The need to communicate with computers becomes intense, and socially respectable.

We now have a powerful reason – by powerful, I mean here a reason likely to sway non-specialists towards accepting changes proposed by specialists – for endeavouring to help the next generation to be the masters rather than the slaves of the future; or, in a future where there are masters and slaves, a reason for ensuring that our children are at the top, rather than at the bottom, especially as it now seems obvious that science alone, or even pure mathematics alone, will not stave off or cope with the future.

SOMETHING NEW TO FAIL AT

We also have a reason for the intensity of the emotions experienced by people who fear that they will be inadequate when faced by this new technology and yet dare not be seen to fail. This sensation of terror leads, as always, to extraordinary scenes of aggression in education, as it does in industry, but the new Luddites know that their successes are only local ones, confined to one single common-room or factory. Nevertheless, it is important to bear in mind the intensity of feeling which is to be found amongst colleagues who resent being missed out, but are afraid to join in, and among pupils who have difficulty in joining in, and find sour grapes unsatisfying as an alternative to learning and success.

Learning necessarily involves change. If we learn something we are changed; if we anticipate learning something, we are yielding to inevitable or expected change. Change implies a period of instability; rapid change implies greater instability. The less secure, and the older the pupil, the more difficult this is to accept, and the more likely that the task will become emotionally charged.

Thus, what may appear to a disinterested observer to be a purely cognitive task is surrounded by very strong, and sometimes overwhelming, feeling: I have emphasised the naturalness of there being *some* emotional component, but it is less easy to remember the very significant part that this plays, especially as we tend to forget our own difficulties once we are past them.

It is significant because

(1) the potential change caused in one's thinking by learning to program a computer is a very large one, and this is somehow apparent from the start: the threat of change is obvious; and
(2) there is no way of protecting oneself from this threat, or hiding one's failure to understand from others.

ESTABLISHING A CORE OF COMMON GOALS

I have put forward some ideas here about the sort of principles that might be chosen as ultimate aims or goals in any plans to introduce people to the use of computers in an educational (i.e. a personal-development), as opposed to a commercial, context, and I am aware that they are unlikely to meet with unanimous approval. But if we cannot agree on ultimate goals, we will certainly not be able to agree upon intermediate ones, nor upon immediate ones. We are very far from being able to agree upon any *core* to our courses, although we usually each hope to persuade others to join us in forming a small consensus.

Even if we do agree upon what is important, and find other people to agree with us and be our disciples, we must also ask 'important to WHOM? the learner or the teacher?'. All teachers pride themselves upon their meticulous attention to some detail of correctness which the world has forgotten, or some principle which is important only to them, and these principles are often the very ones which cause the greatest obstacles to easy and natural communication between the beginner and the teacher, or the beginner and the machine.

Both sides of any discussions about the relative importance of various details will rely upon simple statements that such-and-such are the needs of the ideal system for optimum ease of communication, that facilities which fall short of these are inadequate and that those which go beyond are extravagant. Really we are struggling in a chicken-and-egg position, wherein we compose our lists of needs from conjectural educational or psychological ideas, or from the qualities of a system we use and like.

BREAD-AND-BUTTER PROBLEMS

Theories of perceptual or cognitive dissonance can help to explain what we observe when beginners are struggling to address the computer – or to persuade it to address them. The greater the contrast between what the user has expected and prepared for – his mental 'set' – and what actually happens, the more likely it is that there will be problems. The less detailed the cognitive model we have constructed for ourselves in preparation for our meeting with the computer, the less complicated the dissonances are likely to be, and our hypotheses will not necessarily have to be abandoned, but will need rather to be modified by enrichments (assimilations) made to our original model.

Children, perhaps, are liable to the greatest initial disappointment, if they bring with them naive science-fiction models of the all-knowing computer. Most educational or home set-ups are extremely small, and are unable to produce any effects outside themselves to deal in anything but the most restricted exchanges, however elaborate the appearance of the program may seem initially. The limitations of machines described as 'interactive' simply because they possess a keyboard and a screen, or described as programmable in English simply because their resident language includes a few English words, unquestionably dissuade many from progressing beyond the very earliest stages.

Beginners used to current forms of fiction, such as advertising or space adventures, will expect that they will in some way be able to communicate with the computer in English, either spoken or written. Journalism, and even serious research, often fails to make the distinction between what is theoretically possible and what is already possible, between what is possible and what has actually been done, between what has been done and what is available, while optimistic teachers of teachers do not distinguish between what is available and what is affordable, or between what is affordable and what has already been bought.

Speculative writing of all sorts leads the innocent observer to forget that most of the equipment he meets will already be obsolete, that most of it was obsolescent at point-of-sale, and that learning to use *the*, rather than *a* computer involves a specific and detailed kind of 'cutting-one's-coat-according-to-the-cloth' which will have to be relearned with a new machine. Success in this learning will depend upon a certain flexibility in dealing with the inflexible, rather than merely upon certain standards of intellectual ability. An expertise in ultimately getting one's own way with, say, a difficult uncle may be a very important asset in a beginner programmer.

There is no doubt at all that 'flexibility' is an important cognitive attribute for dealing with the exorbitant demands of most computers, and this is held to be an attribute of youth. Certainly, older people do seem to suffer more when learning to program, just as they do in many other areas of learning, but here there are more acute causes for suffering connected with the damage caused to the adult self-image, which may be of greater importance.

But any convenient term such as 'flexibility' allows us to beg many questions. Do we mean divergent, in Mr Hudson's sense [7]? or do we think that being able to think like Mr de Bono by practising his puzzles is learning to be flexible [8]? My metaphor of getting what one wants out of a recalcitrant uncle was a very serious one. The ability to retain the image of the goal intact, to recognise the failure of a particular attempt speedily, to backtrack just sufficiently and no more before trying afresh, to know of and to try a list of alternative equivalent strategies are all qualities as desirable in a programmer as in a program, and are essential in any dialogue between systems that do not know each other initially.

HOW TO AVOID DISAPPOINTMENT

So, many popular ideas of computing add to the likelihood that at least one of the emotions experienced by the beginner will be disappointment, as it is so hard to program the machine to perform anything but the most trivial tasks, and the exciting possibilities expected and widely advertised seem light-years away, apart from endless identical games in colour.

The temptation is always to abandon the idea of encouraging systematic programming, and to concentrate on using ready-made, high-level programs on the computer, so that it will always be seen more or less in its popular image, responding to normal verbal input, and doing complicated, although restricted things.

Loading and running interesting programs is certainly one way of avoiding – or perhaps only postponing – the sensation of disillusionment which overtakes programmers early on in their experience; indeed, it would be possible, using interesting enough and varied enough programs, to design a course in *using* a computer which would teach a good deal about logic, or language, or anything intellectual that one wished (with no recourse either to spelling-tests or 'Space Invaders') and which would entirely avoid the problems of which we speak, yet be valuable and probably much more closely related to the kind of computer-use that the laity are likely to experience in the next few years than are any simple, basic or Basic programming techniques we can offer. Seymour Papert has written vividly about such ideas in connection with the ubiquitous Turtle program recently [9].

The pragmatists must be answered before we can justify worrying pupils with principles that we say are important, and that they can see are not. Education always has been, and still probably is, forced to offer most of its wares in a medicinal manner, inviting or compelling its pupils to 'take this' because in the future they will find out how good it was for them. *Any* system which claims that only use and experience of a technique can make one see the point of it necessarily relies on a relationship of trust between the teacher and the taught, who must continue to believe that all the present unpleasantness is nothing compared with the delights of the future. I need not, I hope, spell out the parallels between religious and educational orthodoxies here; they are not trivial ones, and I have referred to them before.

TRIVIAL CAUSES OF FAILURE IN ESTABLISHING A DIALOGUE

Many of the negative reactions which beginners experience have their origins in the simplest mechanical problems of using the machine; probably unfamiliarity with the QWERTY keyboard is the greatest single obstacle. Not only does it rouse uncomplicated feelings of frustration, but it also slows down the interaction of the dialogue to unacceptable levels. The parallel problem would be that caused by the very slow system, which has an unacceptably long 'thinking' time between input and response. In both cases, we are affected by the use of the word 'quick' as a synonym for 'intelligent', and usually we are forced to compare our laborious (and unintelligent?) entry of data to the computer's insolent ease and speed of response.

If we chose instead to use metaphors borrowed from verbal interaction between people, we could match this kind of frustration with that of having to look up each word we wish to use in a dictionary when trying to communicate in a foreign language, or with that of a handicapped person forced laboriously to spell out, letter by letter, his intelligent intent. The imperfections of our memory add to our problems: what we looked up yesterday, we must look up again today, it seems. As in the early stages of learning to use a foreign language, we will need to use this repeated reference an humiliating number of times, while the computer always presents an unsympathetic comparison in the terms of its own, however limited, efficiency. We are faced with the need either to accept our own very imperfect recall, etc., as very unpleasant discoveries about ourselves or to project, in the psychoanalytic sense, our own negative feelings on to the person, language, system or machine that we are addressing.

LANGUAGE, DIALOGUE AND CONVERSATION

Linguistic aspects of computer/user interaction have attracted attention from the very earliest days, and the use of the term 'language' in connection with operating systems – even such a low-level approach as the assembler can be called 'assembly language', presumably for relatively simple ideas connected with its possessing a structure and a vocabulary, or by being a mode of communication – shows how engrained the idea is amongst us, while the high- or low- prefixes will indicate our opinion of the closeness of its approach to human language usage.

Many years ago, Lancelot Hogben in a popular book on mathematics [10], caused much interest (and some irritation) by stressing the linguistic nature of the structures in mathematics; and if we take the view that the underlying structure of our thought is the same as that which informs our language, we would expect any kind of systematised thinking to provide 'linguistic' parallels, if only because they share elements of a common system. This use of the term 'language' as applied to computers suggests that a dialogue can exist, conducted *via* linguistic means between man and machine, and this will intensify the initial sense of disappointment experienced by beginner-programmers if they are led to expect that the metaphor will be relevant in all particulars. Human dialogue depends only partly on the nature of the language being used, and partly upon many other sorts of information passed between the actors.

Many programs have been written to enable what appears to be an intelligent dialogue to be carried on between a human and a computer, such as the famous or notorious ELIZA psychotherapy program, and many of these are extremely complex, considering the poverty-stricken nature of the interaction that results. Not all programs that are designed to make appropriate and painstaking responses to verbal input produce the most humanly convincing dialogue. Impudent programs also exist, whose function is merely to keep up the illusion of an intelligent interaction for as long as possible using the simplest means. Such programs are essentially conversational, rather than interactive, in the sense that a very few rules, having very little to do with the content of what each actor in the dialogue is saying, will enable the conversational ball to be kept rolling for a considerable time; only a negative response instead of the positive one required, or vice versa, will give away the fact that one protagonist has no idea of the content of the previous remarks, and skilled conversers, both human and sub-human, have a supply of ambiguous comments for just these emergencies.

It is unnatural, or rather non-human, to attend very closely to each word in a conversation, and the amount of informational or linguistic redundancy in all human statements renders it possible to understand them even if they contain many syntactic errors or even paraphasias. It is just this fanatical attention to detail which makes the computer's part in a dialogue conducted on its own terms seem so inhuman and unintelligent. Programs which attend to only a very small proportion of the input can easily seem much better from a conversational point of view, and thus even the goals which might be relevant to the production of an easy dialogue between computer-user and computer, and those relating to the production of the most meaningful or most informative dialogue, are not wholly compatible.

In the author's opinion, this is explainable to a considerable extent in terms of the different degrees of redundancy implicit in these two types of dialogue.

Authors of computer languages so far – either because of ideas based upon various forms of logic calculus, or because of a desire to demonstrate common structures of logical statements in their most generalised or abstract forms, or simply because in the past computer memory has been expensive, and redundant expressions are wasteful of memory – have scarcely considered the vital functions of repetition and dilution in aiding clarity and understanding, or have knowingly rejected the idea of redundancy as of inferior intellectual worth. Many computer languages show not only their preoccupation with the *ideas* of a mathematical or logical calculus, but also with their *form*; they are twice removed from any natural language, as they are based upon what is already an abstraction of it.

We have here good reasons for the problems likely to arise during the collision between natural and artificial, or 'dedicated', languages, and even the expectations aroused by the use of common words in specialist senses contribute towards the sum total of likely misunderstandings and disappointments in trying to communicate with a machine that might have been described to us as 'intelligent', or as one that understands something 'very nearly' like a natural language such as English.

More crucial, though, is the near certainty that the computer's operating language will probably not have had its roots in any 'natural' (as opposed to a 'formalised') view of language; in fact, the likelihood that it originates from a mathematical source has been almost 100% in the past, and one would not care to specify the odds even now, although they are reducing.

The problem is further complicated by the likelihood that most teachers of the various aspects of computing will be also mathematicians; the connection is still a very frequent one, and often regarded as desirable. They will be able to accept the limitations of computer languages in the same way as they might accept the limitations of algebraic or Boolean encoding, and they will in many ways be ideal teachers for persuading their pupils to accept these same limitations as an intrinsic aspect of the study. They may not, however, be the best teachers for accelerating the escape from these limitations, as their own disciplines will not necessarily encourage such a generalising attitude.

Although linguists and philosophers are very fond of emphasising the common roots of logical statements, however expressed, mathematicians in general have never been so attracted to the idea. Some idea of the taints of redundancy and inexactitude seem to hold them back, and the sacrifice of the 'purity' of expression within their grasp is too great for the sake of a mere ecumenicality within the intellectual brotherhood.

Whenever we address a computer, we are forced to abandon many of the conveniences of natural linguistic usage and to adopt a 'purer' form of address, with very little redundancy, and formalised in a mathematical rather than a linguistic style. This is particularly noticed by beginner students at the keyboard, who are soon made aware that they must make very considerable modifications to their ideas of communication before they can approach the computer, and they also notice that the computer is refusing – perhaps even maliciously – to make any accommodations in their direction at all.

EXCELSIOR, OR EVER ONWARD AND UPWARD

Some decision must be taken eventually about what we will expect to find as evidence of 'intelligence' in our computer. If 'flexibility' really is to be desired, then unquestionably the computer must deal comfortably with the idiosyncrasies of individual users in addressing it; it must happily accept inaccuracy and redundancy, and make use of these in its own responses. We cannot even be satisfied with a computer that accepts any input style, but is unable to adapt its output to match.

In a sense, of course, we are asking the computer to 'waste' its power by devoting a great deal of effort in adapting merely to differing styles of input and output, or to holding a large potential vocabulary of, say, 20,000 words plus the necessary rule-structures to cope with all this. Many people will feel that we should adopt a different policy of giving minimal attention to input/output interfaces, and simply concentrate upon using the capabilities of the machine in dealing with larger and larger logical structures and data-bases devoted to the particular problems at issue. Linguistic uses would be merely one of these possible problems.

We must decide individually to which philosophical camp we belong. Do we believe that Language is one of the ways in which we use the basic rules of Cognition in order to communicate the workings of intelligence? or do we believe that Language is the basic tool with which our intelligences work? It is surprising that such a division of beliefs should still remain so deeply entrenched, but the effects of our attitudes are only too clearly seen, as much in the present discussion as elsewhere.

On the one hand we believe that the problem of dealing in natural language is merely one of the problems to which the 'intelligence' of the computer will address itself; on the other we believe that the development of natural language usage by the computer is the means whereby it will become 'intelligent'. The first attitude we might describe as 'transcendental', in that it accepts the notion of pure 'intelligence' as an entity; the second attitude is almost Darwinian, in that it ascribes the evolution of intelligence and the evolution of language as being intrinsically linked.

These two camps are related essentially to even more radical ideas about the universe: does man merely serve as a vehicle for expressing the already-existing order of the universe? or does he, uniquely, impose his own ordering upon the chaos around him?

We will necessarily stand somewhere in this argument, but it is also advisable to be aware of the practical results accruing from our different stands. In this short discussion, I have attempted to show that many of the problems in accommodating the existence of 'intelligent' computers, and communicating with them, will arise from our own failure to define our viewpoint and our expectations.

There is no doubt that at the moment this failure to establish reasonable and consistent aims and objectives among ourselves, as prophets of the 'New Age', or even to discuss them in sufficient detail is causing great problems in preparing people to meet these challenges of the future, or indeed of the present.

Perhaps, while mankind remains in disarray, while deciding upon its response to rather more serious present problems, it is not surprising that very little time and money is being spent on decisions that will certainly be merely academic unless we can replace physical with intellectual expansionism in the very near future.

Nevertheless, if we assume for the moment that there is to be a future of some kind, then we need to be doing a great deal of work *now* to decide what we intend to achieve in our education for this future. There is not much doubt that our plans must take into consideration, if not centre around, the computer, and Education's traditional methods of teaching something first and endlessly justifying it afterwards simply will not serve any more either in this instance, or probably ever again.

So far in its history, computing has been busy building itself the new 'Tower of Babel', for very similar reasons perhaps to those that lay behind the building of the old one, and with a very similar punishment in the offing. Ultimately, as the reverberations of the communications explosion die away, we shall find ourselves able to draw upon the body of knowledge in a way unparalleled in the world's history, and it is our responsibility to endeavour to ensure that the people whom we teach have had this sharing made easier by our teaching, and not more difficult.

This can only be done by our having found at least some common ground in our intentions towards the future generations, through imaginative anticipation of the qualitative nature of the changes that are upon us. Whether 'intelligence' in computers arrives as an inevitable companion of greater processing capacity, or because of some change in our own attitudes towards these more powerful machines, there is little doubt that man is creating an entity more and more in his own image, to live and work by his side. The lessons of history may suggest that this is not a reassuring prospect; perhaps an infinitely powerful machine might also be infinitely corrupt! Nevertheless, the more work we do now in preparing ourselves for working alongside our new companion, the more worthwhile will be our ultimate dialogue.

NOTES

[1] Psycholinguistic attempt to analyse human communication:
Paraskevopoulos, J.N. and Kirk, S.A. (1969) *The Development and Psychometric Characteristics of the Revised Illinois Test of Psycholinguistic Abilities*. University of Illinois Press, Chicago.

[2] Exposition of need for 'artificial intelligence' to be severely controlled, rather than free-ranging:
Asimov, I. (1967) *I, Robot*, Dobson.

[3] Concept of Intelligence as merely a complex of simpler 'behaviours':
Skinner, B.F. (1973) *Beyond Freedom and Dignity*, Penguin.

[4] Inherited-inborn tendencies to form certain types of mental structures. The 'Language Acquisition Device':
Chomsky, N. (1972) *Language and Mind*, Harcourt, Brace.

[5] Human language not explainable solely in terms of imitation and environmental pressures:
Aitchison, J. (1983) *The Articulate Mammal,* Hutchinson.

[6] General benefits to intellect, etc., arising from particular activities:
Kephart, N.C. (1971) *The Slow Learner in the Classroom*, Merrill.
Frostig, M. and Maslow, P. (1973) *Learning problems in the Classroom*, Grune and Stratton.

[7] Different cognitive 'styles' ('Convergent' and 'Divergent' thinking):
Hudson, L. (1968) *Contrary Imaginations*, Penguin.

[8] Attempt to encourage a 'style' of thought through practice:
De Bono, E. (1982) *De Bono's Thinking Course*, BBC Publications.

[9] Encouraging certain aspects of thinking through 'education':
Papert, S. (1980) *Mindstorms*, Harvester.

[10] Linguistic aspects of arithmetical-mathematical symbolism:
Hogben, L. (1967) *Mathematics for the Million*, Allen and Unwin.

PART 4

AI METHODOLOGY

Suppose I am sitting in my armchair one evening and for some reason I start thinking about memory. I become fascinated by the question: 'How exactly do I remember things?' After a lot of thought, I come up with the following scheme. In my memory there are many items of information collected into 'tables'. For instance, here is part of a table that contains all the information I have on who is the father of whom:

John	Ken
John	Betty
John	Mary
Ken	Myself
Ken	Albert

My father is Ken, and Ken's father is John. Here is part of a table that contains all the information I have on who is the mother of whom:

Betty	Simon
Betty	Mary
Mary	Clare
Joan	Myself
Glynis	Ken
Jan	John

For example, my mother is Joan.

I call the first table 'father' and the second 'mother'. Whenever I am given information on who is the father or mother of whom, I store the information in one of these tables. In addition to the above two tables, I have other tables which contain information on each of the people whose names occur in the father and mother tables. For instance, there may be tables called 'is male' and 'is female', parts of which look like this:

is male
John
Ken
Albert
Simon

is female
Betty
Mary
Clare
Joan
Glynis
Jan

I now say that I remember an item if, after a search of a table, an item is found. For instance, if I am asked 'Who is the father of Betty?', a search is made through the father table until 'Betty' is found in the second column of the table, and then the name occurring as the first item in that same row, i.e. 'John', is returned. So, if I am asked 'Who is the daughter of Betty?', I might respond: 'Well, actually, Mary is, and Simon is her son'. In the latter case, a search was made of my 'mother' table and Mary, who is a child of Betty, was found. Then, since being a daughter involves being female, the 'is female' table would be searched to check that Mary is female, which she is, so her name is returned. The additional information that Simon is a son of Betty is also returned, perhaps signifying a half-successful search (i.e. Simon is a child of Betty but, being male, cannot be a daughter).

I now need to provide some mechanism for allowing new information to be entered into tables not previously existing. That is, let us suppose that I am not happy with the thought of millions of these tables in my memory system and instead think that it is more elegant if tables of information could be created only when needed and then thrown away. So, I hypothesise that tables can be created to store new information not previously categorised. For instance, I know that the mother of a mother of a child is a grandmother of that child. This can be expressed as a rule for storing information in a new table called 'grandmother'. I supply the notation as follows:

grandmother (X) ← mother (X, Y) and mother (Y, Z)

which is to be interpreted as 'An unnamed individual X is a grandmother if X is the mother of an unnamed individual Y and if Y is the mother of an unnamed individual Z'. If I work through the previously supplied part of the 'mother' table, putting names to the unnamed individuals consistently, I find that only

grandmother
Betty

is justified. This is because the value of mother (X, Y) can be instantiated with respect to the row of the 'mother' table which has Betty being the mother of

Mary and also the value of mother (Y, Z) can be instantiated with respect to the row of the 'mother' table which has Mary being the mother of Clare. So, X equals Betty, Y equals Mary and Z equals Clare. (Notice that the two Ys on the right-hand side of the grandmother rule are instantiated with respect to the same named individual, Mary.)

I can supply more rules for storing and creating information on other types of blood relationships. For instance,

brother (X, Y) ← father (Z, X) and father (Z, Y) and is male (X)

which can be interpreted as 'An unnamed individual X is the brother of an unnamed individual Y if some unnamed individual Z is the father of both X and Y and if X is male'. If I work through this rule using the above tables, I find I obtain, as the new brother table:

brother

Ken	Betty
Myself	Albert
Albert	Myself

The last two rows, although they seem to duplicate each other, provide the important information that not only is my brother Albert but also Albert's brother is myself. (Betty's brother could be Martin but Martin's brother is not Betty. There will, of course, be several ways to formulate a certain blood relationship which can take these factors into account.)

So, my answer to the question 'How exactly do I remember things?' is that my mind contains a lot of information stored away in relevant tables. I remember an item of information by searching through the tables. I can also construct new tables of information only when required, and to do this I hypothesise rules for such table construction. These rules are expressed in a 'B if A' format. Although the examples I have given concern blood-relations, there is no reason to believe that this tabular approach could not be generalised to other information domains, such as elephants being mammals, football teams winning trophies, and so on.

Some very interesting questions arise at this stage.

(1) At what point does the above scheme, which is supposed to answer the question 'How exactly do I remember things?', become a theory? Could it be that all I have to do is change the word 'I' in the question to 'people', thereby removing the question from the personal domain, and then I shall have a theory? What is a theory?

(2) Does the above scheme have any psychological relevance? If it does, is it solely because I used a psychological term 'remember' in the original question and I now claim that the above scheme is an answer to that question? If it does not, what else must be done to the above scheme to give it psychological relevance? Do I need to add extra memory concepts to my question, such as 'forget'? Or do I need to construct the scheme in some well-defined way which is accepted as being 'the psychological way'? Is it the case that I

need to outline certain implications that follow from my scheme which can be empirically tested?

(3) Does the above scheme have any AI relevance? If it does, is it solely because an affirmative answer may have been given to (2) first? Or is it because the scheme has computational relevance in that a computer program could conceivably be written to run the scheme on a computer, on the basis of which we can then say that the computer 'remembers'? If it does not have AI relevance, is it because a negative answer may have been given to (2) first? Or is it because the scheme has no more computational relevance than, say, a space-invaders-type arcade game: clever programming but not an intelligent program? What is AI programming? Come to that, what is AI?

(4) Is it possible to ask these questions in the order given? Is it possible to provide answers which are clear and distinct? What would count as an answer, and how do I know whether the answers are correct? What exactly is the difference between the following two statements: 'The computer "remembers" ' and 'The computer remembers'? That is, at what point can we drop the quotation marks around psychological terms when these terms are applied to computers?

A lot of questions have been raised here. The first, second and third sets of questions I call, very generally, 'methodological' questions. The fourth set I call, again very generally, 'philosophical' questions. I shall deal solely with the methodological issues in this section.

Let me pursue my hypothetical memory scheme a bit further, since it is not at all obvious at this stage that the scheme is a theory, has psychological relevance, or has AI relevance.

Here is the first elaboration. I hypothesise the following:

(a) Tables are searched in a strictly sequential fashion, i.e. from the top to the bottom;

(b) there is an executive which breaks up the original query (in natural language) into an internal representation which can be described by my rule notation;

(c) there is an executive which co-ordinates the search for information in the tables;

(d) there is an executive which returns a response in natural language;

(e) the executive can only deal with one row of one table at a time.

Some implications of this elaboration are as follows. An item near the bottom of a table should take longer to retrieve than an item near the top of the table. For instance, given the previous 'father' table and assuming one unit of time for each examination of a row, then the query 'Who is Ken's father'? should take one unit of time and the query 'Who is Albert's father?' should take five units of time. I can hypothesise further that rows are ordered so that most commonly accessed rows are placed at the top. So perhaps the row which contains the information that Ken is my father should, strictly speaking, go towards the top or be at the top but may be further down the table if I am not asked frequently for my father's name.

Another implication is that a computer program can be written which has as a part an executive which calls various subroutines to break down a query into an internal representation, execute a search, and formulate a response. The overall architecture of the scheme, then, could be as shown in Fig. 1. Does my scheme have psychological relevance or AI relevance? If previously the answer was 'No' to either or both questions and if now the response is 'Yes' to either or both, then it must be because of this elaboration.

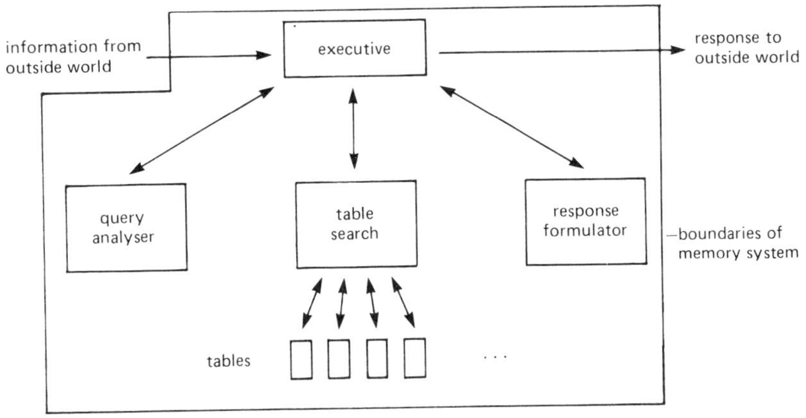

Fig. 1

Another question that arises is: 'Does my scheme seem plausible?' That is, is it the case that my scheme is a plausible description or explanation of human memory? Perhaps plausibility depends on the results obtained from experimentation and program construction, so I shall have to wait for the results first.

The second elaboration runs like this. I hypothesise the following:

(a) tables are not searched in strictly sequential fashion; instead, within a table, there is a separate processor for each row, and the task of each processor is to store the information in that row and to wait for a query. If a query requires some part or all of the information that is stored on a processor, the processor responds, otherwise it keeps quiet;

Hypotheses (b), (c) and (d) remain the same as before.

(e) the executive does not need to execute a sequential search. Rather, it feeds the query to all processors in the table at the same time and then waits for the response.

Some implications of this elaboration are as follows. It now no longer matters whereabouts in a table an item is, as far as search time is concerned. Instead, I now hypothesise that an item in a table that is further away from the point of search than an item in a table nearer the point of search will take longer to retrieve. (Let us forget about the near tautologous nature of this remark!) So tables frequently accessed are searched first.

Another implication is that my system architecture now needs some expansion, as far as the 'table search' box is concerned. This box might now look like Fig. 2.

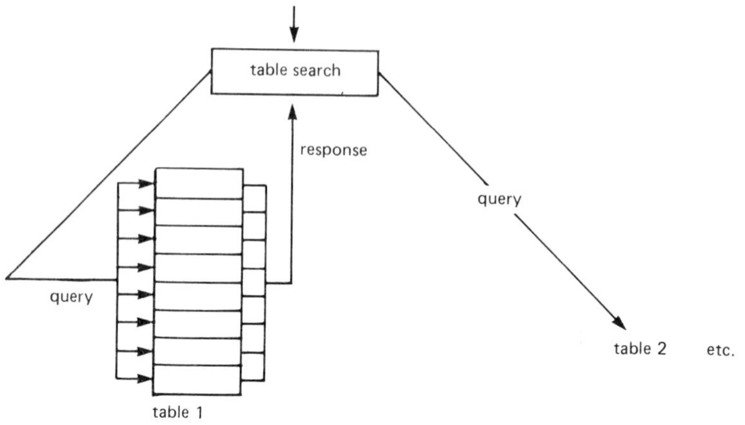

Fig. 2

A 'table' will now consist of a sequence of processors, each with one item of information. The query is fed to all processors in parallel, and the response from each processor is monitored. The computer system may have either a hardware implementation of these tables (usually called 'content addressable memories') or a software simulation of the hardware.

Does my scheme have psychological or AI relevance yet? Is it plausible?

The next elaboration will consist of allowing a parallel search of all tables at the same time. I hypothesise the following:

(a) a query is now fed to all tables at the same time, and within each table a parallel search takes place;

Hypotheses (b), (c), and (d) remain the same as before.

(e) the executive executes a parallel, distributed search on all tables.

One implication of this elaboration is that search time now no longer depends on the location of a table. I might now wish to introduce complexity of the search argument as a basis for predicting search time. Another implication is that I shall have to redraw my architecture and either provide the necessary hardware support or simulate the hardware in the software.

The same questions as before can be asked about psychological relevance, AI relevance, and plausibility. Notice that 'plausibility' now no longer concerns just psychological plausibility but also neural plausibility. That is, is my system an adequate model for the neural processes involved in memory?

The final elaboration I shall mention concerns the rejection of the executive. Now there is no central executive to co-ordinate the breaking down of a query, the search, and the reformulation of a response. Rather, any query is automatically fed into a query analyser that feeds the information it gleans from the query as the query enters the system either to tables directly or on to a common data-pool which is available to every table. Tables put information back on to the data-pool and the response formulator formulates a response as it picks up information from the pool. The tables, in effect, now compete amongst themselves as to which table is to have its response accepted.

No doubt, further elaborations can be made. But the point of these elaborations is to demonstrate the difficulty that arises when attempting to distinguish between a fanciful and speculative idea on the one hand and a factual and explanatory theory on the other. Matters are complicated when different disciplines and sciences have their own distinguishing criteria. The relationship between AI and cognitive psychology is strong. Does that mean that AI theories must conform to the same methodological rigour as psychology theories? If not, then a clear methodology must be provided for constructing and testing AI theories, otherwise AI might end up being a completely speculative subject, more akin to science fiction than science.

It may be useful to look at two established, but contrasting, methodologies taken from the philosophy of science. Both have their supporters and critics, but they should provide frameworks for evaluating the 'scienticity' of my memory model.

Hempel's view [1] on the philosophy of science can be summed up as follows. The different branches of scientific inquiry can be divided into two major groups: the empirical and the non-empirical. Statements in the former must be checked against the facts of our experience by experimentation, observation, surveys, and so on. Propositions in the latter (e.g. logical and mathematical propositions) are proved without essential reference to empirical findings. Hempel wishes to discuss how scientific knowledge is arrived at, supported and changed; how empirical science explains empirical facts, and what the explanation actually consists of. Five major tenets of Hempel's views are now presented.

(1) It is sometimes thought that scientific inquiry consists of inductive inference, from antecedently collected data to appropriate general principles. By 'inductive inference' is meant the step from statements describing particular events to a statement of universal form. Hempel discusses the four stages that an inductive scientist would consider to make up an ideal scientific inquiry:

(i) observation and recording of all facts;
(ii) analysis and classification of these facts;
(iii) inductive derivation of generalisations from them;
(iv) further testing of the generalisations.

Hempel calls this 'the narrow inductivist conception of scientific inquiry' and claims that it is untenable because

(a) if we have to wait for *all* the facts to be collected our scientific investigation would never get off the ground, as there are an infinite number of facts;
(b) even if we stipulate that all relevant facts should be collected, we can ask:

'Relevant to what?' We have, as yet, not specified the problem to which the facts are relevant;

(c) even if we have specified a problem, we have no hypotheses to guide us in our search for 'relevant' facts, i.e. facts are relevant or irrelevant only in reference to a given hypothesis, not to a given problem.

Hempel claims that the transition from data to theory requires creative imagination, not mechanical rules of induction, or even deduction, for that matter. Scientific hypotheses and theories are not derived from observed facts but invented to account for them. These 'happy guesses' require ingenuity and imagination, though whether they are accepted into science or not depends on whether they pass critical scrutiny, which includes, in particular, the checking of suitable test implications by careful observation or experiment. Hence, the interests of scientific objectivity are safeguarded by the demand for an objective validation of such conjectures. So, for Hempel, scientific knowledge is arrived at by inventing hypotheses as tentative answers to a problem under study, and then subjecting these to empirical test.

(2) Hempel next examines the testing of a hypothesis and states that the test implications of a hypothesis are normally of a conditional character: they tell us that under certain specified test conditions an outcome of a certain kind will occur. In other words, test implications are of the form: 'if conditions of the kind C are realised, then an event of kind E will occur'.

Sometimes we need to add auxiliary hypotheses or assumptions to our original hypothesis, in which case the general scheme looks like this: 'If both H (the hypothesis) and A (the auxiliary hypotheses) are true, so is I (our test implication)'.

So if our test implication now happens to turn out to be false, we know that both H and A cannot both be true, i.e. at least one of them must be false. So H need not be rejected straight away because I happens to be false.

In principle, it would always be possible to retain H even in the face of seriously adverse test results – provided that we are willing to make sufficiently radical and burdensome revisions in our auxiliary hypotheses. But we may start introducing *ad hoc* hypotheses – hypotheses made solely to protect and save a hypothesis seriously threatened by adverse evidence. There is no precise criterion for *ad hoc* hypotheses, though two relevant considerations should be kept in mind.

(a) Is the hypothesis proposed just for the purpose of saving some current conception against adverse evidence, or does it also account for other phenomena?

(b) If more and more hypotheses have to be added to reconcile a certain basic conception, the resulting total system will become so complex that it has to give way when a simple alternative conception is proposed.

No statement or set of statements T can be significantly proposed as a scientific hypothesis or theory unless it is amenable to objective empirical test, at least 'in principle'. We must be able to derive from T certain test implications of the form 'If C then E', although the test conditions C need not be technologically realisable at the time when T is propounded or contemplated as long as the hypothesis is testable in principle. If a statement or set of statements is not even testable in principle, i.e. has no test implications at all, then it cannot significantly be proposed or entertained as a scientific hypothesis or theory. This is because no conceivable empirical finding can then accord or conflict with it.

(3) The role of confirmation and acceptability is then examined. For Hempel, the confirmation of a hypothesis will normally be regarded as increasing with the number of favourable test findings, although generally speaking the increase in confirmation effected by one new favourable instance will become smaller as the number of previously established favourable instances grows. Moreover, it is desirable that a hypothesis should be confirmed by 'new' evidence – by facts that were not known or not taken into account when the hypothesis was formulated. 'Simplicity' of theories is difficult to define, but Hempel makes the general remark that any criterion of simplicity must be objective, i.e. it must not have reference to intuitive appeal or the ease with which a hypothesis is remembered or understood.

(4) Hempel then gives two basic requirements for scientific explanation:

(i) The requirement of explanatory relevance: the explanatory information adduced from an explanatory theory affords good grounds for believing that the phenomenon to be explained did, or does, occur under the specified circumstances.
(ii) The requirement of testability: the statements constituting a scientific explanation must be capable of empirical test.

These two requirements are interrelated: a proposed explanation that meets the requirement of relevance also meets the requirement of testability.

(5) Hempel next considers theories and theoretical explanation. Theories are introduced when previous study of a class of phenomena has revealed a system of uniformities that can be expressed in the form of empirical laws.

The formulation of a theory requires two sorts of principles: 'internal principles' and 'bridge principles'.

(a) Internal principles characterise the basic entities and processes invoked by the theory and the laws to which they are assumed to conform.
(b) Bridge principles indicate how the processes envisaged by the theory are related to empirical phenomena with which we are already acquainted and which the theory may then explain and predict.

So, internal principles characterise the 'inside' of a theory, and bridge principles provide the contact between the theory and the phenomena it is said to explain (i.e. the empirical world). Bridge principles may be said to connect certain theoretically assumed entities that cannot be directly observed or measured with more or less directly observable or measurable aspects of physical systems, even though bridge principles do not always connect 'theoretical unobservables' with 'experimental observables'. They may instead connect the unobservable 'theoretical' entities with the subject matter or phenomena to be explained, even though these phenomena need not be 'directly' observable or measurable; they may well be characterised in terms of previously established theories, and their observation and measurement may presuppose the principles of those theories. Without bridge principles, however, a theory and its internal principles would have no explanatory power and would be incapable of test, as the derivation of test implications from the internal principles of the theory requires further premises that establish connections between the theoretical concepts of the theory and concepts already understood and outside the theory; and this is accomplished by appropriate bridge principles.

A scientific theory must not only satisfy the conditions of testability-in-principle and explanatory import, but also deepen our understanding by

(i) providing a systematically unified account of quite diverse phenomena,
(ii) showing that previously formulated empirical laws do not hold strictly and unexceptionally but only approximately and within a certain limited range of applications, and
(iii) predicting and explaining phenomena that were not known when the theory was first formulated.

This, then, is Hempel's general view of science.

Now let us turn our attention to another philosopher of science, Popper. We present three major tenets of his philosophy.

(1) Popper [2] attacks the view that empirical sciences can be characterised by the fact that they use 'inductive methods'. An inference is usually called 'inductive' if it passes from singular statements, or 'particular' statements (e.g. 'This swan is white') to universal statements, such as hypotheses or theories ('All swans are white'). Popper's view is that

(i) from a logical point of view it is far from obvious that we are justified in inferring universal statements from singular ones;
(ii) it would be difficult to establish the truth of universal statements, as any account of experience can only be a singular statement and not a universal one; and
(iii) to support such a view of empirical sciences, scientists would have to establish a 'principle of induction' with which they could put inductive inferences into a logically acceptable form. But such a principle cannot be a purely logical truth, like a tautology or analytical statement, since all inductive inferences would then have to be regarded as purely logical or tautological transformations, just like inferences in deductive logic. And if the principle is a synthetic, or empirical, statement, we can ask why the principle should be accepted at all.

Popper believes that the difficulties inherent in the doctrine that inductive inferences are 'probable inferences', i.e. can attain some degree of 'reliability' or 'probability', are likewise insurmountable. His own proposal has no dependence on either inductive logic or probable inferences and is called 'the theory of the deductive method of testing'. He writes that scientists do not wait passively for repetitions and regularities in the world about them but instead actively impose regularities upon the world, discover similarities in the world, and interpret these in terms of invented laws. Instead of waiting for premises and drawing conclusions from them, scientists 'jump' to conclusions straight away.

> This was a theory of trial and error – of conjectures and refutations. It made it possible to understand why our attempts to force interpretations upon the world were logically prior to the observation of similarities. Since there were logical reasons behind this procedure, I thought that it would apply in the field of science also; that scientific theories were not the digest of observations, but that they were inventions – conjectures boldly put forward for trial, to be eliminated if they clashed with observations; with observations which were rarely accidental but as a rule undertaken with the definite intention of testing a theory by obtaining, if possible, a decisive refutation. [3]

(2) Popper conceives of the task of the logic of knowledge as consisting solely in investigating the methods employed in those systematic tests to which every new idea must be subjected if it is to be seriously entertained as a scientific hypothesis. There are four different lines along which the testing of a theory can be carried out after conclusions are deductively drawn from the theory.

(i) There is the logical comparison of the conclusions among themselves, by means of which the internal consistency of the theory is tested.
(ii) There is the investigation of the logical form of the theory, with the object of determining whether it has the character of an empirical or scientific theory, or whether it is, for instance, tautological.
(iii) There is the comparison with other theories, chiefly with the aim of determining whether the theory would constitute a scientific advance should it survive various tests.
(iv) There is the testing of the theory by way of empirical applications of the conclusions which can be derived from it. That is, we form predictions that are easily testable or applicable. If the results of practical experiments show the predictions to be verified, we say that the theory has, for the time being, passed its test. But if the predictions are falsified, then the theory from which they were drawn is also falsified.

(3) There are three requirements which an empirical theoretical system will have to satisfy.

(i) The theory must be synthetic so that it may represent a non-contradictory, a possible, world.

(ii) The theory must not be metaphysical, i.e. it must represent a world of possible experience.
(iii) The theory must be a system distinguished in some way from other such systems as the one which represents our world of experience. This is done by submitting the theory to tests and observing whether the theory has stood up to these tests.

To distinguish an empirical theory from a metaphysical one, Popper uses as his criterion of demarcation the notion of 'falsifiability'. He requires of a scientific system not that it should be capable of being singled out once and for all in a positive sense (verified) but that its logical form should be such that it can be singled out, by means of empirical tests, in a negative sense, i.e. it must be possible for an empirical scientific system to be refuted by experience. Thus, a theory not refutable by any conceivable event is non-scientific, and every genuine test of a theory is an attempt to falsify it, or to refute it. 'Testability is falsifiability, but there are degrees of testability: some theories are more testable . . . than others' [4].

Popper stresses the following two points:

(a) he is not attempting to overthrow or annihilate metaphysics, and
(b) his criterion is one of demarcation, not one of meaning, as many philosophers believed. The criterion of falsifiability draws a line 'inside' meaningful language and not between meaningful and meaningless language.

He dismisses the criticism that, since we can always change definitions or add extra *ad hoc* hypotheses, it will never be possible conclusively to falsify a system. He proposes that the empirical method should be characterised as a method which excludes precisely these ways of evading falsification. The empirical method is characterised by the fact that it exposes the system to be tested to falsification in every conceivable way. Rules governing methodology are regarded by Popper as conventions, or simple agreements among scientists.

So, although Hempel and Popper both disagree with the simple view that scientists observe, categorise, theorise, and then test; although they both believe that imagination and intuitive guesses are sometimes required, they adopt different methodological stances. Let me return to my memory model. If I wanted to argue that my armchair theory is a scientific or psychological theory within the 'Hempelian' framework, I should have to demonstrate that

(a) a hypothesis has been invented as a tentative answer to a problem and will be subjected to empirical testing;
(b) the hypothesis has implications which are testable 'in principle' (for example, longer search time for rows further down a table), even though, technologically speaking, such testing may not be feasible in the near future.
(c) the hypothesis is relatively simple compared to other psychological theories of memory;
(d) the hypothesis has powerful explanatory power;
(e) there exist internal and bridge principles which characterise the internal

processes of the hypothesis and relate these processes to well-established and well-understood concepts in other theories.

If I wanted to argue that my armchair theory is a scientific or psychological theory within the 'Popperian' framework, I should have to demonstrate that

(a) the hypothesis is an invention which will be rejected if it does not agree with observations;
(b) the hypothesis is internally consistent, is an advance over other theories of memory, and will be rejected if its implications are falsified;
(c) the hypothesis is not metaphysical or unfalsifiable in principle, and it represents a possible world.

How much does AI methodology differ from the methodologies presented here?

The question as to whether my armchair theory is really a theory, whether it is scientific, or psychological, or metaphysical, or speculative, or a piece of AI, may now actually have answers, or at least the established views of Hempel and Popper, contrasting as they are, should provide pointers to where such answers can be found. Of course, this does not mean that Hempel's views and Popper's views are the only views concerning methodology, or that there is no room for a more radical view of theories of AI and psychology. It may well be the case that the concept of 'intelligent computer' provides a powerful, new, methodological tool, and further development of such a methodology on a formal level may not be too far in the future.

A. Narayanan

NOTES

[1] Hempel (1966).
[2] Popper (1959).
[3] Popper (1965), p. 45.
[4] *Ibid.*, p. 36.
For details, see the bibliography at the end of the book.

Hayes argues that an AI theory is characterised not by experimental collaboration, as would be the case with a psychological theory, but by whether the theory can be implemented on a computer and by whether the computer system subsequently exhibits the behaviour that the psychological theory was to explain. Sharkey and Pfeifer, on the other hand, although believing that psychology needs to move away from the notions of narrow hypotheses and testability, argue that a theory, if it is to have psychological relevance, must take account of psychological evidence and have some connection with other related psychological theories (bridge principles?).

Sloman argues that just describing various states a machine can go through when executing, say, a 'remembering' program is not adequate for the description, explanation or representation of mental concepts (in this case, remembering). His argument is for a structure theory of mind rather than a 'content' theory of mind. Given a computational architecture for a human mind, the types of complex processes involved not only in problem-solving, vision, natural language processing, and so on, but also in emotions and motivations, may be fruitfully explored. It is not just a question of identifying the rules and principles which determine that 'behaviour' of the system: the rules and principles have their own dynamic structure – a computational architecture.

On the difference between psychology and AI*

P. J. Hayes Rochester University USA

1. INTRODUCTION

Artificial Intelligence (AI) has been plagued, ever since it began some twenty years ago, by disputes about its status. Is it an interdisciplinary area, a methodology or a new science? Is it part of psychology or part of Computer Science (whatever that is)? If the latter, why AI's concern (more or less formally recognised by different workers) with human performance? If the former, why its singular lack of attention to experimental corroboration of theory, and its overwhelming concern for programming?

I know that many people who work in the field have strong views on these questions. One might hope to be able to answer them by a poll, therefore; after all, if most people who are working in the field believe that it can be characterised in such-and-such a way, then it can be so characterised, more or less by definition. Unfortunately, this simple plan breaks down in two ways. Not everyone, for a start, agrees about who can be said to be working in AI; there are many, overlapping, groups each of which regards those outside as not really working in AI but in some other subject (such as pattern recognition, theorem-proving, advanced automation, brain theory . . .). And secondly, even those who almost everyone would agree are working in AI do not themselves agree about what AI's aims are. A few years ago in Edinburgh, then the only large group in Europe, one could find eminent AI workers who regarded themselves as experimental psychologists, as software engineers and as theoreticians of computer science: yet it did not seem to prevent useful communication between them. Several major AI projects have been staffed by people with widely divergent views on what AI really is, cooperating happily on *actual* AI work.

*This essay was first published in *AISB Quarterly* 34 (July), 1979.

I have wondered for some time about how this is possible. There does seem to be a subject called AI, which one can study, in which one can work. There are commonly accepted intuitive standards of excellence in the subject. Yet it is hard to define it adequately. It has always seemed that AI is, or should be, relevant to understanding human behaviour and thought (both in the sense that AI work should illuminate our view of ourselves, and in the sense that data about what people actually do should be relevant to AI theories). And yet there has always been a clear distinction between AI work and experimental psychology, even cognitive psychology; certainly, AI workers and cognitive psychologists do different things, and know different things, and are often deeply suspicious of one another's work. AI work often seems, to experimental psychologists, to be sloppy and irrelevant; and psychology often seems, to AI workers, to be naive and irrelevant.

2. ACCEPTABILITY CRITERIA

An academic field is defined by many characteristics: its subject-matter and its methodology, for example. One of these, and I think one of the most fundamental, is its criterion of what counts as an acceptable explanation or theory: what one might call its criterion of rigour.

In the physical sciences, for example, teleological explanations are banned; they aren't acceptable. There is nothing intrinsically wrong with teleological explanations, it's worth noting. In everyday life they are extremely useful, and in history, psychiatry, literature and law (all impeccably academic pursuits) they have a central role. But they do not fit usefully into a web of physical theory, so they are banned. It was a prohibition that took many centuries to crystallise.

Psychology, a young science, has banned explanations in terms of gestalts. Some schools of psychology appear to have banned any explanation which refers to internal states of an organism. But all psychology since William James has insisted that explanations and theories be empirically testable. Psychology is consciously an experimental science. It fits the classical 'hard science' paradigm: phenomena must be publicly observable, objectively measureable (preferably on some numerical scale), and repeatable. Given rival explanations of a phenomenon, it should be possible to design a test experiment which will reveal a phenomenon concerning which they make different predictions. And so on.

AI, I will suggest, has the same subject-matter as cognitive psychology, but differs from it exactly on this criterion of rigour. AI's criterion is not experimental corroboration, but implementability. An acceptable explanation of a piece of behaviour must be, in the last analysis, a program which can actually be implemented and run. And such an explanation is a good explanation just to the extent that the program, when run, does indeed exhibit the behaviour which was to be explained.

This is not to say that an AI theory will be a program. But it does mean that such a theory will be to do with programs (or procedures, or algorithms, or computations: different words are appropriate at different levels of abstraction).

An explanation of behaviour in terms of anything other than computation is not acceptable within AI.

If this account is more or less correct, and I believe it is, then there are several obvious consequences and several important questions. First, AI is not psychology. Second, AI is not 'advanced automation' (cf. Lighthill [1]), or any other branch of engineering, even though its criterion, 'does it work as specified?', smacks of an engineering discipline, for the behaviour being explained is defined by psychological criteria. Advanced automation is task-oriented; it is concerned with getting a specific job done as efficiently as possible. For example, consider the task of flying and landing an aircraft. A human being can do it. So can an automatic landing system, probably rather better. But it uses completely different techniques: it has different sensory equipment, for example. The task of landing an aircraft is not defined by psychological criteria. Similarly for production-line assembly tasks, character-recognition, etc.; to do these tasks, given the same perceptual apparatus and under the same restrictions as a human worker, would be well-defined AI problems: but it would be crazy engineering to accept such artificial restrictions.

The first question might be whether AI, on this account, really does differ from (a certain school of) psychology. For, surely, many psychological explanations will be in the form of a specification of how various cognitive structures (or whatever) interact to produce behaviour, and this specification will be at least a sketch of an algorithm. What this objection misses, however, is the implementability criterion. Psychology, even 'information processing psychology', is full of explanations which look like sketches of algorithms, but which use concepts as primitive which are at least as far from implementable as the original problem specification. This danger has been known in AI for many years, and has been called the 'little-boxes fallacy'. One presents a diagram of boxes connected with lines, which is supposed to be a top-level flowchart of a program: but one of the boxes is labelled 'thought' or 'inference', or something equally useless as a specification of a process. In extreme cases, it is not even clear what is supposed to go along the lines joining the boxes together.

Such an explanation just does not make first base from the AI point of view; it is (literally) useless, and is probably actively harmful. From the computational point of view, flowchart-like diagrams in which the components are recognisable 'talents' (like memory, or inference, or recognition, or even, God help us, limitations of thought, which I once saw) are almost comically naive. But it may be quite a good psychological explanation, in the sense that it might make clear predictions about behaviour which can be tested experimentally. For example, such a 'flowchart' explanation of sentence production, in which a 'thought' gets progressively built up into a sentence by choosing various grammatical constructions one by one, may predict certain types of error in speech, on the basis that if the lines of the flowchart were cut at various points, these particular errors would be engendered. This would be good psychology, but hopeless AI. Similarly, one can have good AI work which is hopeless psychology as it makes no refutable predictions. For example, the MYCIN model of diagnostic inference is a beautiful piece of AI, but I cannot see how it could be tested experimentally.

Another question is whether AI (on this account) is a science, and whether it is empirical. Here is the only place I would disagree with Sloman [2]; I believe it is empirical. An AI explanation – a program – is tested by running it. And this can be an experiment. It really can; one cannot predict, often, what will happen when a complex program is run. The history of AI is full of examples of surprises, both positive and negative. The Waltz [3] filtering algorithm's success was astonishing. I remember sober people refusing to believe that Wilks' [4] program had translated a whole paragraph from English to French flawlessly. Uniform theorem-provers performed far less well than was expected. Programs really can be 'experiments put to Nature', in Pylyshyn's words [5]. But they are experiments which test a different sort of hypothesis from that which psychological experiments test. AI experiments test hypotheses of the form 'This algorithm (will run and) will exhibit this sort of behaviour'. Psychological experiments test hypotheses of the form 'People behave in this sort of a way'. That is, considered as an empirical science, AI is part of Computer Science.

It is becoming fashionable to decry the recent emphasis, in AI, on complex heterarchical programming, and to call for formal proofs that suggested algorithms will behave as intended. In present terms, this is a call for the development of AI theories rather than the mere accumulation of AI explanations, corroborated by experiment. While agreeing wholeheartedly with this, I would emphasise that experimental progress is also essential (especially as the tools available to theorise with are so underdeveloped, as yet).

A third question, or perhaps objection, which arises is whether the AI criterion is too easy. After all, we all know that a Turing machine can do anything, in time: so surely any process specification could be implemented; isn't that just something which one leaves to the programming slaves? Hack work? It needs to be emphasised, I think, that specifying algorithms in sufficient detail to enable them to be run in a realistic time-scale is not at all trivial. It imposes a discipline on the subject which is extremely rigorous and filters out large classes of potential explanations (including many of those in the cognitive psychology literature).

3. MUTUAL SUSPICION

If this account of AI is correct, it goes a long way to explaining the love/hate relationship between AI and experimental cognitive psychology. For they both investigate (make explanations of) the same sort of phenomena. Their aspirations are almost identical – to explain rational human behaviour. They have much to offer one another, in various ways. And yet, AI types can accept, as valid sound research, work which a psychologist would reject immediately as unacceptable, sloppy and vague; and so can psychologists accept research which is quite hopeless from an AI standpoint. Each side is liable to seem to the other, like his own subject, done amateurishly. So we have the situation, which I have observed on at least two occasions in the last two years, of two scientists, each knowing the other to have an international reputation, unable to believe how bad the other's work seems to be.

There are some people who are able to do work which is simultaneously good experimental psychology and good AI. They build programs which work and behave in ways which can be matched with human behaviour at a fine level of detail. So fine, indeed, that one has to do real psychological experiments (with tachistoscopes) to determine that people do in fact behave that way (or have percepts like that, etc.). Ullman's [6] thesis is a good example. But such work is incredibly difficult and can only be done at all in a few areas, notably early visual processing. Large areas of cognitive activity: language processing, for example, or any area involving conscious thought, is altogether too remote from experimental test for such research to be possible in it. In these areas, I think that the AI has to precede the psychology; we need to first understand how it is that people could possibly do the things they do before we can think of any experiments designed to test one such explanation against another.

There are many very deep methodological and interpretative problems suggested by this account of AI. For example (one which experimentalists often urge): 'What does it mean to say that the program exhibits the correct behaviour?' For the actual output of a program rarely corresponds very closely to the 'outputs' of a human subject (except in language work, possibly). A closely related issue is the rather cavalier way in which AI types will identify a data structure, or some other computational entity, with a psychophysical phenomenon such as a percept. There is not space here to go into these, and I will not try: but I think that some of the stock answers given by AI workers are not really adequate. This is an area where we could learn from the psychologists, I think. On the other hand, psychology often seems concerned with discovering fine details of behaviour when there is no explanation available at all of the gross structure of that behaviour, a fact which regularly bemuses AI workers [cf. Sloman, 1978, *q.v.*].

CONCLUSION

I have suggested a new definition of AI, which distinguishes it from psychology and from engineering. According to this definition, AI is a field consistent with cognitive psychology, with the same aspirations and interests, but with different manners and a different style. I know that attempts to define AI tend to offend people, for any definition is bound to exclude someone, and nobody likes to be told that he is not working in the area he thinks he is working in. My only aim is clarification; if I have trodden on anyone's toes, I apologise herewith. I'd be interested to receive any comments, however .

NOTES

[1] Lighthill, J. (1972) *Artificial Intelligence: Report to the Science Research Council*, SRC.

[2] Sloman, A. (1978) The Methodology of Artificial Intelligence, *AISB Quarterly* **30** May.

[3] Waltz, D. (1972) *Generating Semantics Descriptions from Drawings of Scenes with Shadows*, PhD thesis, MIT.

[4] Wilks, Y. (1972) *Grammar, Meaning and the Machine Analysis of Language*, Routledge.

[5] Pylyshyn, Z.W. (1973) What the Mind's Eye Tells the Mind's Brain: A Critique of Mental Imagery, *Psychological Bulletin* **80** pp. 1–24.

[6] Ullman, S. (1979) *The Interpretation of Visual Motion*, MIT Press.

Uncomfortable bedfellows: cognitive psychology and AI

N. E. Sharkey Stanford University, USA and
R. Pfeifer University of Zurich Switzerland

This chapter grew out of a series of discussions between the two authors and a number of Artificial Intelligence (AI) workers and Cognitive Scientists at the Yale AI Laboratories where we worked between 1982 and 1983. The interdisciplinary atmosphere at Yale forced us to apply the assessment criteria of both disciplines to our work and as a result we faced many crises and dilemmas about out own approaches to the study of the mind. We both share a common conviction that the union of psychology and AI can be a productive and scientifically rewarding enterprise. However, such a union is fraught with a great many difficulties. We shall concentrate here on some of the more obvious problems which confront the psychologist who is attracted to AI.

We consider that one of the biggest blocks to a healthy interaction between psychology and AI is what Pettitt [1] has called AI-centricity. A common conceptual error of the AI-centric is the naive belief in a simple dichotomy between what Miller [2] calls *theory development* and *theory demonstration*. In this belief the AI researcher is the theory developer while the Cognitive Psychologist is the demonstrator. In its worst form the AI researcher is viewed as the grand theoretician while the psychologist is relegated to the low-life role of laboratory assistant. Obviously, this distinction totally misses the objectives of Cognitive Psychology. The central aim of Cognitive Psychology is to understand and explain the human mind by whatever means are available. The experimental method merely provides a rigorous criterion with which to evaluate explanations. A psychologist is a multi-faceted creature. His study of mind involves detailed knowledge of statistical analysis, experimental method, philosophy of science, mathematics, the task domain under study (e.g. linguistics or problem-solving), and theory construction. Each of these domains has its own 'purist' discipline outside the world of psychology. But psychology is concerned with the application of these methods to the domain of real cognition.

We propose that AI can help psychology in the construction of theories in the same way that statistics can help psychology with the analysis of data. This is not intended to reduce the importance of AI. We are simply asking that it supply psychology with flexible sanitary principles of theory construction. As Bundy [3] puts it, '. . . the purpose of AI is to provide and explore computational techniques for cognitive modeling'. Searle [4] calls this the 'weak' or 'cautious' form of AI; the type which gives us '. . . a very powerful tool for the study of the mind'. He contrasts this with 'strong' AI in which '. . . the programs are not mere tools that enable us to test psychological explanations; rather the programs are themselves the explanations'. We support the former position of AI here but take issue with the latter. Many of our points are directed at some of the questions which Hayes raised in the preceding chapter in this book.

The remainder of this chapter is organized in five parts. In the first three parts we shall discuss three criteria which the AI worker may use to decide whether a theory is a good explanation of some cognitive function (cf. Miller [2]). These criteria are (a) the proposed mechanism must be shown to be physically possible, i.e. implementable as a running program; (b) the rules governing the interactions between any proposed mechanisms must be statable; and (c) the program must be shown to perform the cognitive function to be explained. In the fourth section we shall examine what it is that underlies an AI explanation. And finally we turn to look at what AI can contribute to the study of Cognition.

THE IMPLEMENTATION CRITERION

Hayes, like many AI researchers, gives a lot of weight to the criterion of implementability of cognitive theories. In the preceding chapter, he claims that because of a failure to meet this criterion many psychological explanations 'do not make first base from an AI point of view', are '(literally) useless' or 'almost comically naive'. This may be true in many cases, but psychology differs from AI about what it is *allowable to know*. That is, the psychologist is constrained to a large extent by objectively collected empirical evidence. He may use only a permissible amount of imagination to explain his data and other relevant data in the field. Many useful psychological models have been constructed in this way and many of them could be implemented by fantasizing all sorts of untestable links which may or may not be true. But for Hayes, 'An acceptable explanation of a piece of behaviour must be, in the last analysis, a program which can actually be implemented and run'. While there is a lot to be said for implementability, its relationship with explanation, or theory for that matter, is not as clear cut as Hayes would have us believe.

There are at least two common problems with the notion of a running program. The first can be described by a frequently used term of abuse in AI circles; the *kludge*. This is defined in Webster's dictionary as 'a computer system made up of components that are poorly matched or were originally intended for some other use'. This is something which most large AI programs need to get them on their feet (never mind running). A kludge is a phenomenon which is only admitted in whispers over a drink in the wee small hours of the morning. Indeed, large AI programs are often so complex that even the authors cannot find their own kludges.

In terms of discussion, a kludge may be thought of as a means of patching up a mismatch between a theory and its implementation on a machine. A simple analogy would be of an architect who designs a perfectly elegant building only to find that several of the walls do not join at right angles. Now he has to have the builders put in wooden struts to fill in the gaps. These are the kludges. Worse still is that our architect finds that the struts look quite good and he now gives them a title 'symmetrical pine dividers' and declares that they are an essential feature of his design. He may even begin to believe that they were part of his original design.

This leads us to a second problem which concerns a tendency among AI workers to label some of their main program functions with a mnemonic which implies that the function is more than it really is. McDermott [5] refers to these labels as *wishful mnemonics*. The example he gives is that of a programmer writing an 'understanding' program. If in the first implementation she calls the main loop of the program UNDERSTAND, then she may come to believe, solely on the basis of her mnemonic, that this function resembles its human counterpart. This mnemonic label may mislead a lot of people including the programmer herself. In many cases it could take weeks of reading through complex LISP code to find out just how 'understanding' was implemented. McDermott suggests instead that the AI worker should call the main loop something like G0034. In this way she can then try to convince herself and others that this really implements some part of the understanding process.

Considering these points we wonder how we are supposed to assess the merits of an AI program as a physical instantiation of a theory. One possibility is that we rely on our ability to sort out the kludges and the wishful mnemonics; another is that we rely on judgments based on the original program code (which is seldom published in full). Obviously the latter is absurd unless claims can be made for the psychological reality of LISP. Yet another possibility is that we use the theory underlying the programs and accept, on faith, that the program is sort-of implementable. After all, according to Hayes, 'This is not to say that AI theory will be a program. But it does mean that the theory will be to do with programs'.

INTERACTIONS BETWEEN THE PROPOSED MECHANISMS

Simon [6] points out that the complexity of a system can be reduced by decomposing it into simpler, more readily comprehensible parts. It is much easier to develop and debug these parts in isolation from one another. This indeed has been the tendency in Cognitive Psychology and one of its major differences with AI. In the early days of Cognitive Psychology (e.g. Neisser [7]), there appears to have been an implicit assumption that by starting off at the lowest levels of cognition, careful research could be directed inwards, step by step, through perception to iconic memory to short-term memory and so on until the mind was solved. Many of these steps were the subject of such vigorous investigation that they became specialist provinces in themselves. This has led a number of researchers to align themselves with a given province and *debugging* has become more and more detailed. And now each subsystem in Cognitive Psychology has become so fraught with its own technical difficulties that no one can put 'Humpty' together again. As Simon [6] says – a truly complex system is always more than just the sum of its parts.

In contrast to this approach, the task which much of AI sets for itself is to complete large-scale systems which encompass many of the psychologist's subsystems. However, it would be wrong to get the impression that this results in Psychology having a narrower approach than AI. Rather it is just that they section cognition differently. Psychologists tend to investigate a long 'horizontal' section of cognition and construct their theories accordingly. This section is equivalent to an AI 'module' but broader in scope. On the other hand, AI goes for a tall 'vertical' section which may encompass everything from lexical access to the comprehension of a character's actions in a story (e.g. Schank and Abelson [8]).

The difference between the horizontal and vertical sectioning also explains a lot of the quibbling that goes on between AI and psychology over generality. For example, an AI researcher will claim that Morton's [9] Logogen model of word recognition lacks generality because it only deals with one system component. However, to a psychologist this is a very general model in so much as it captures a wide range of experimental effects from many different sources (the long thin slice). On the other hand, the psychologist may claim that a theory such as Dyer's [10] BORIS story understanding system lacks generality because it only handles four stories. This system exhibits generality to the AI theorist because the complexity of these stories necessitates interactions between several modules (the tall thin slice). The true Cognitive Scientist tries to steer somewhere in the middle of these extremes, to cries of abuse from both sides.

We believe that the study of interacting mechanisms is one area where the close cooperation of AI and Psychology would be of obvious help to both parties. The big problem is that both disciplines would have to unpack and re-evaluate their theories. For example, what is parsimonious for a psychologist's horizontal section may not reflect parsimony for a vertical section which includes it. Anderson's [11] comment on this is that 'It is often possible to create simple pristine models for performing a specified task (for example, linear syllogisms) under specified circumstances by a select population of subjects. However, this ignores the possibility that the learning and developmental history that gave rise to these processes was complex, varied, and even contradictory'. Similarly, in an AI simulation there may be computational parsimony which is just not warranted by empirical evidence or which would not be parsimonious if the vertical section was broader.

One of the currently most promising interactive models in Cognitive Psychology is worthy of a brief mention here. This is McClelland and Rumelhart's [12] 'Interactive Activation Model of Context Effects in Letter-Perception'. This represents a true blend of psychological methodology and computer simulation. And we hope to see much more work with this flavour over the coming years.

RESEMBLANCE TO THE COGNITIVE FUNCTION TO BE EXPLAINED

The performance of a program is probably the most difficult part of AI research to assess. It is also one of the most important parts. A lot of fuss and noise has been made over the years regarding the 'Turing test' (Turing [13]) of program input/output. Put simply, this states that if you can deceive humans into thinking that they are communicating with a human when in fact they are communicating with a program, then that program has passed the Turing test. To our knowledge there are no programs around at present which would pass.

Hayes implies a less conservative criterion when he states that '. . . an explanation is a good explanation just to the extent that the program when run does indeed exhibit the behaviour which has to be explained'. However, many researchers, particularly in natural language understanding, '. . . can degenerate into the writing of programs that do no more than mimic in an unenlightening way some small aspect of human performance' (Marr [14]). Take, for example, Weizenbaum's [15] ELIZA program which acts the part of a non-directive therapist. Weizenbaum made no attempt whatsoever to simulate human mental functioning. Rather, he achieved a deception by using a combination of a 'key word' search and simple syntactic transformations. In essence, a statement which is typed in at a terminal is parsed for key words (e.g. mother, hate, sex). These are then transformed into either synonyms or superordinates and printed back in the form of a question. For example, suppose that the patient types 'My mother hates me'. ELIZA may respond with 'Tell me more about your family' or 'Why do you dislike your mother'. In the former case 'mother' was transformed into 'family' and used to fill a slot in a question frame of the form ⟨Tell me more about your- superordinate transform- ⟩. In the latter case the verb 'hate' was transformed into 'dislike'; 'my' was transformed into 'your' and both were put into a frame of the form ⟨Why do you -verb synonym- -pronoun transform- -sentence-?⟩. This program has fooled a lot of intelligent but computer-naive people and yet it is certainly not an explanation of any mental function.

The point we are making here is even if a program can mimic a piece of behaviour it does not necessarily validate the program as an explanation of that behaviour. To illustrate the point more forcefully, suppose we were to type four stories into four computer text files and summaries of the four stories into four more text files. This would give us a total of eight text files in all. Next we write a simple procedure called MATCH which checks to see if a piece of text typed at the terminal is the same as one of the stories in the story text files. If MATCH finds that the answer is 'yes', it gives control to a second procedure called SUMMARIZE (wishful mnemonic) which simply prints out the appropriate summary file. Now no one in their right minds would call this simple transformation a theory of text summarization. But suppose that we were to complicate things a little by making MATCH flexible enough so that a story would be recognized if the wording of a story being typed in was not exactly the same as the one in the text files. This could be done by making the specification of the original story less rigid. Suppose further that we were to scatter the story summaries around a little more so that they were distributed in fifty files rather than in four. SUMMARIZE would now have to 'assemble the summaries dynamically'. In order to do all of this extra work MATCH and SUMMARIZE may need to call upon a number of other smaller subprocedures. For example MATCH may now have a PARSER which in turn may have a LEXICAL-LOOKUP and a CONCEPT-DEINSTANTIATOR, etc. See how much more impressive and difficult this *hidden transformation* is to understand. Let us stretch the illustration a little further. Suppose that a theorist has a good notion of what a program should output from a given input within certain degrees of freedom. If he is a clever and imaginative programmer he can then implement his theory as a hidden transformation. He could also incorporate a random element so that the program is not totally predictable, even to him.

We have never met an AI researcher who would intentionally employ this kind of trickery. However, the hypothetical example serves to illustrate that the output from a program is a less than satisfactory criterion for judging the explanatory power of a theory. Even if a hidden transformation turned out to be a good theory of how the mind worked, the output from that program could not distinguish it from the whole set of other possible hidden transformations. This is obvious since the output will always be the same.

We could of course compare transformations in terms of flexibility, but a great many programs work only on the small samples that are presented in published papers. We could put this no better than the following amusing quote by Bobrow, Kaplan, Norman, Thomson, and Winograd [16]: 'Computer programs in general, and programs intended to model human performance in particular, suffer from an almost intolerable delicacy. If their users depart from the behavior expected of them in the minutest detail, or if apparently insignificant adjustments are made in their structure, their performance does not usually change commensurately. Instead, they turn to simulating gross aphasia or death'.

These arguments run counter to Hayes' statement about an explanation being only as good as its match with the explained behaviour. We have tried to point out that all you are doing with a running program, provided you have ironed out the kludges and the wishful mnemonics, is to show that your theory has been specified in enough detail to be able to be implemented.

WHAT UNDERLIES AN EXPLANATION?

The discipline of psychology places the onus on the experimenter to explain his data in the light of preceding literature. Often this will involve looking for systematic patterns in a large body of data. If the explanation is a good one it will stimulate others to carry out further research. When enough counter-evidence accrues that explanation will be replaced by another which is a better fit for the data. Furthermore, psychologists tend to be concerned with the flaws inherent in any methodology. This is why good psychological theories are based on a consensus of data from a number of different studies and methodologies.

In contrast, the AI worker seems little concerned about such issues. In this section we ask how it is that the AI worker 'knows' about a cognitive function prior to constructing an explanation of it. That is, what is the source of the ideas underlying an AI program? Does the AI researcher have some mysterious access to the human psyche by the nature of his discipline which is denied to psychologists? Well, the answer is that AI has a tendency to employ methods which were tried by psychology and rejected in its youth as unsound; namely introspection. This is the use of consciousness of one's own mental processes as a basis for a theory of mind. A problem inherent in this method is that the process under observation is doing the observing. The computer scientist will argue that the nature of his discipline, the rigor of programmability, will make his introspections reliable. However, it is this very knowledge which makes the computer scientist's introspections even more suspect than those of other people. He is concerned with getting programs to run. So while the discipline may help mental hygiene at some levels it imposes a rigid theoretical filter on thinking. Thus the LISP programmer will tend to view the mind in terms of list structures. We believe this to be inevitable given the frame of reference of someone trying to produce running programs.

There is, of course, nothing wrong with using introspection to generate ideas. Miller [2] claims, 'Without any systematic effort to gather facts we know a great deal about our minds. We know that there are certain functions the mind performs quickly and unconsciously'. However, we argue that it is only through cold objective scientific method that we can gain access to these unconscious functions. Otherwise we can too easily fool ourselves into thinking that we are thinking atheoretically about our thinking. This is precisely the reason for conducting experiments in the first place: to tap unconscious processes without interfering with them.

Another method used by AI workers is the Verbal Report. An example would be asking people to speak their thoughts aloud as they perform some task. This is more objective than the introspective method discussed above, but it has been brought under suspicion by a series of impressive experiments described by Nisbett and Wilson [17]. In a paper entitled 'Telling more than you can know', they argue convincingly that people have a strong tendency to justify their actions post hoc, they don't admit being influenced by the presence of others, and they are unaware of attributions, etc. In a rebuttal, Ericsson & Simon [18] argued that verbalizing information only affects cognitive processes if the instructions require verbalization of information that would not otherwise be attended to. We can only say here that this technique remains the subject of controversy and must therefore be handled with care.

The final AI method we consider here was developed by Schank [19]. This is the method of using remindings as a source of data. The basic idea is that if something reminds you of something else then there must be some mechanism which accounts for why you were reminded. Schank [19] claims that this 'sheds light on both the problem of retrieval and our ability to learn'. He believes that this is 'at the root of how we understand'. Schank offers five categories of reminding but by far the most impressive is 'Events that remind you of events in different domains'. A crude example would be of one being reminded of Romeo and Juliet while watching West Side Story. This is a very clever technique for the study of mind. However, the problem is that once the theory begins to take shape, all of the remindings begin to become theory-laden. The individual researcher may *feel* that particular categories of remindings are popping into his consciousness spontaneously. However, the fact that a certain category is being studied will make exemplars of that category more available to the conscious processes. We suggest that the method would be much more effective and persuasive if the remindings were collected systematically from naive participants. Furthermore, the data thus collected should at least be categorized by an independent group of judges.

In summary, we hold that all three of the methods mentioned above are important as an initial source of ideas but we claim that they have limited utility in the long run. They are no substitute for rigorous well designed experiments.

WHAT CAN AI CONTRIBUTE TO THE STUDY OF COGNITION?

We began this chapter by saying that AI could provide a set of sophisticated technical tools for the construction of cognitive theories. However, we were opposed to the idea that AI could provide us with programs which were in themselves explanations of some cognitive function (the 'strong' position). The main thrust of our argument was that three of the most important acceptability criteria in AI are potentially circular when used in the absence of methodologically sound corroboration. We posited that the introspective methods are justifiable as an initial source of ideas, but that reasoning about the function of cognitive processes should be based on information obtained by more objective means.

It seems that what AI can best offer Cognitive Psychology are methods for obtaining greater specification of the interactions among proposed cognitive mechanisms. Indeed, Lehnert [20] holds that it is the level of detailed specification which distinguishes AI theory from psychological theory. She states, 'The difference is analogous to instructing someone to multiply two numbers together, versus instructing someone to multiply two numbers together by means of a particular algorithm. By forcing ourselves to be concerned with the precise form of information in memory, and the precise operations manipulating that information, we can uncover significant problems that would otherwise be overlooked'.

Ironically, what attracted the authors of this chapter to AI was its boldness. Perhaps because of its youth, AI is less constrained in its subject areas than psychology. A notable example is the development at Yale of theoretical tools for story understanding. Furthermore, despite our deep reservations about the methods of AI, we found that several members of the Yale AI group seemed to have profound insights into the structure and function of language which would be hard to find elsewhere.

In conclusion, we propose that if Psychologists and AI workers are to collaborate fruitfully, both partners will have to recognize each other's values. On the one hand, the Psychologist must get away from being dominated exclusively by narrow hypotheses and testability. He may find it very useful to actually write a running program under supervision of an AI researcher. On the other hand, the AI Researcher must be careful about high-minded theorizing, and accept the fact that there is psychological evidence out there which needs to be accounted for. She could perhaps design, run and analyse the data from a simple experiment under the supervision of a psychologist. This type of collaboration could eventually lead to better methods for the construction and assessment of cognitive models.

NOTES

[1] Petitt, P. (1979) On the interaction between psychology and artificial intelligence, *Artificial Intelligence and the Simulation of Behaviour*.

[2] Miller, L. (1978) Has artificial intelligence contributed to an understanding of the human mind? A critique of the arguments for and against, *Cognitive Science* **2** 111–127.

[3] Bundy, A. (1981) Some suggested criteria for assessing AI research, *Artificial Intelligence and the Simulation of Behaviour*.

[4] Searle, J.R. (1980) Minds, Brains and Programs, *The Behavioral and Brain Sciences* **3** 63–73.

[5] McDermott, D. (1976) Artificial Intelligence Meets Natural Stupidity, *SIGART Newsletter* **57**, April.

[6] Simon, H.A. (1982) *The Sciences of the Artificial*, The MIT Press, Cambridge, Massachusetts.

[7] Neisser, U. (1967) *Cognitive Psychology*, Appleton-Century-Crofts, New York.

[8] Schank, R.C. and Abelson, R.P. (1977) *Scripts, Plan, Goals and Understanding*, Lawrence Erlbaum, New Jersey.

[9] Morton, J. (1969) The Interaction of Information in Word Recognition, *Psychological Review* **76** 165–178.

[10] Dyer, M.G. (1982) In-depth understanding. A computer model of integrated processing for narrative comprehension, Yale University, Dept. of Computer Science, Technical Report **219**.

[11] Anderson, J.R. (1983) *The Architecture of Cognition*, Harvard University Press, Cambridge, Massachusetts.

[12] McClelland, J.L. and Rumelhart, D.E. (1981) An Interactive Activation Model of Context Effects in Letter Perception, *Psychological Review* **9** 375–407.

[13] Turing, A.M. (1963) Computing Machinery and Intelligence, in E.A. Feigenbaum and Julian Feldman (eds.) *Computers and Thought*, McGraw-Hill, New York.

[14] Marr, D. (1977) Artificial Intelligence – A Personal View, *Artificial Intelligence* **9** 37–48.

[15] Weizenbaum, J. (1965) ELIZA – A computer program for the study of natural communication between man and machine, *Communications of the Association for Computing Machinery* **9** 36–45.

[16] Bobrow, D.G., Kaplan, R.M., Norman, D.A., Thompson, H. and Winograd, T. (1977) GUS, a frame-driven dialog system, *Artificial Intelligence* **8**.

[17] Nisbett, R.E. and Wilson, T.D. (1977) Telling more than we can know: Verbal reports on mental processes, *Psychological Review* **84** 231–258.

[18] Ericsson, K.A. and Simon, H.A. (1982) Verbal Reports as Data, *Psychological Review* **87** 215–251.

[19] Schank, R.C. (1982) *Dynamic memory*, Cambridge University Press, Cambridge.

[20] Lehnert, W.G. (1978) *The process of question answering*, Lawrence Erlbaum Associates, Hillsdale, N.J.

Towards a computational theory of mind

A. Sloman University of Sussex UK

INTRODUCTION

Cognitive Science has three interrelated aspects:

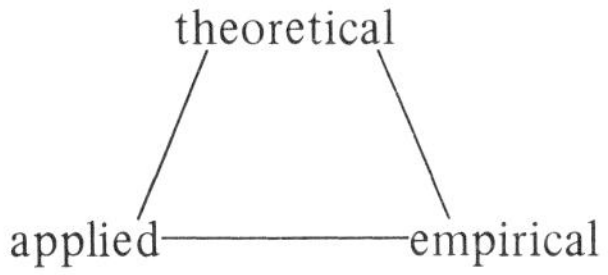

Work in all three areas depends on and feeds back into the other two. Theoretical work explores possible computational systems, possible mental processes and structures, attempting to understand what sorts of mechanisms and representational systems are possible, how they differ, what their strengths and weaknesses are, etc. Empirical work studies existing intelligent systems, e.g. humans and other animals. Applied work is both concerned with problems relating to existing minds (e.g. learning difficulties, psychopathology) and also the design of new useful computational systems. This chapter sketches some of the assumptions underlying much of the theoretical work, and hints at some of the practical applications. In particular, education and psychotherapy are both activities in which the computational processes in the mind of the pupil or patient are altered. In order to understand what they are doing, educationalists and psychotherapists require a computational theory of mind. This is not the dehumanising notion it may at first appear to be.

A THEORY OF WHAT?

Concepts of mind and consciousness are complex, partly ill-defined, and their use very much context-dependent. For instance, it is quite correct, for normal purposes, to say of someone who is asleep

> 'He is now unconscious'

whereas the very same person may later say, quite correctly,

> 'In my dream I was conscious of a pain in my leg'

Neither speaker is in error. They are providing information of different sorts, about different aspects of the sleeper's mental state. Similarly, there is the well-known puzzle of the noise you only notice when it stops: were you conscious of it before, and if you were not how could you hear it stopping? If someone says:

> 'I've been conscious for the last three months that you are hoping to take over my job'

this does not mean that the speaker has been dwelling constantly on the threat. He is merely talking about information that has been *available* to his thinking and decision-making processes, whether or not he actually made use of the information.

These and other examples indicate that the ordinary concept 'conscious', and a host of related concepts (notice, aware, attend, study, see, feel, think, consider, careful, etc., etc.) are very complex and subtle. In particular, there is no reason to suppose that there is a well understood sense of 'consciousness' in which consciousness is something you either definitely have or definitely lack. The fact that we have the *noun* 'consciousness' can be a trap which leads us to think there is some *thing* to which it refers.

Consciousness is often confused with various kinds of self-consciousness. It is unlikely, for example, that a cat is self-conscious in the sense of being able to reflect on and reason about its own states, abilities, prospects, character, etc. However, there is no doubt that it is conscious of the mouse that it chases, or the person it rubs itself against. Moreover, an animal which uses a paw to catch or manipulate something must be conscious of the relationship between its paw and the object, in order to judge the appropriate movements to make. And insofar as it treats the paw differently from the other object, it can be said in some sense to be aware that the paw is its own. Here, then, is a tiny fragment of self-consciousness. No doubt many animals are self-conscious in this sense, even if they are not able to pass the ethologist's test of being able to respond to themselves in a mirror.

My point is that it is an error to think of familiar mental concepts as marking states or properties or processes which are clearly distinguishable from other states, etc. The world is too rich and varied for our ordinary concepts. Though complex and very subtle (Sloman [1], Chapter 4), our ordinary concepts are probably too ill-defined and unrefined to provide an adequate basis for a systematic study of minds. We need a better system of concepts if we are to proceed beyond banalities, to explanatory insights concerning the different sorts of states and processes which characterise minds. (This is not to say that we should ignore common concepts. As J.L. Austin said, they may not be the last word, but they are certainly a good starting point.)

A SURVEY OF POSSIBLE TYPES OF MINDS?

One way of trying to make progress is to attempt a survey (a generative taxonomy perhaps) of different possible types of mind. This can help to undermine preconceptions about what minds have to be like, showing where we have been thought-prisoners of concepts which evolved not for the purpose of providing deep explanations, but for the purposes of everyday interactions.

We start from the assumption that if minds are anything other than totally unintelligible mysteries, they must be mechanisms. (Inside every intelligent ghost there must be a machine.)

The question is what sort of mechanism? Whether the mechanism is physical or spiritual (whatever that means) is not important. Both alternatives lack explanatory power. We want an explanation capable of generating the fine structure of the phenomena of mind: the ability to perceive, to learn, to decide, to have feelings and emotions, to dream, to find things funny, etc.

To say what the mechanism is made of is not to say how such states and processes can occur. For that we need an account of the architecture and laws of the mechanism: how the parts are related to one another, how their properties and relationships can change. That is, it's the structure not the stuff that counts.

But not just the static structure: the principles by which the structures can change – i.e. the rules or constraints governing the processes which can occur in the system – are crucial. A system of rules also has a structure: a computational architecture. There is an infinite variety of possible architectures, and as yet we understand very little about that variety. We have begun to explore only the simplest possibilities. We need to work towards a generative specification of mental possibilities, and their limits.

Two fallacies are to be avoided:

(a) The set of possible minds forms a continuum with simple things like amoebas and thermostats at one extreme and human minds (or more complex minds) at the other.
(b) There is no comparison between the simplest mechanisms or organisms and human minds: there is a total discrepancy of kind.

(a) is a fallacy because the space of possible computational systems (and therefore the space of possible mental mechanisms) is not a continuum. It is full of important discontinuities. Computer scientists have only just begun to understand some of these discontinuities. There is a lot more yet to be learnt.

(b) is a fallacy, because, despite the discontinuities, there may be a collection of common principles on the basis of which all the different sorts of computational systems are generated. For instance, all involve some kind of storage, construction, or manipulation of internal symbols, and all involve the possibility of treating such symbols as categorical or conditional instructions. Differences concern the number and variety of sub-databases, the types of representations used, the types of inference procedures and other internal symbolic processes used, the extent to which there is internal monitoring of internal processes, the extent to which structures and procedures can modify themselves during the course of interacting with the rest of the world, the extent to which different sub-processes run in parallel, with the ability to interrupt other processes, and so on. We don't yet know enough to have an overview of the space of possible computational systems. For example, the fact (if it is a fact) that they can all be represented in Turing machines is not much more informative than the fact that all the plays and poems of Shakespeare can be expressed using 26 letters of the alphabet and a few punctuation signs.

The second fallacy is closely connected with the assumption that our everyday concepts can be used for drawing precise boundaries. We assume that among the set of possible systems there must be a sharp boundary between those which are conscious and those which are not, between those which really have experiences, or emotions, and those which do not. In reality, the space of possibilities is barely understood and our ordinary concepts did not develop for the purpose of drawing absolute boundaries. Instead of assuming there are boundaries, we should map out the terrain and find out how the different sorts of systems are similar to one another, and how they differ. Wittgenstein somewhere (alas I have forgotten where) compared this with sterile arguments about whether one is still *really* playing chess if one player plays without the queen. Apart from tournaments, the only interesting question is what difference the missing queen makes to the game, to the balance of power, to the variety of possible states and strategies. Whether it is still chess is a pseudo-question with no right or wrong answer. The same applies to attempts to argue that machines, or some of the simpler animals, cannot really be conscious. The interesting question is: what are the similarities and differences, and what are their implications?

If someone wants to say that the human mind really is totally different from any other sort of mind, or that animal minds are totally different from artificially constructed minds, then either he must specify the differences, and we can argue with him, or else he must rely on the claim that one sort of mind is essentially mysterious and unintelligible, in which case no argument is possible. Someone who takes the latter position can always go on claiming, no matter how rich and powerful our theories, 'but you have still left out something which I experience which I cannot describe, but which I know you know from your experience, too'. No doubt some really intelligent, philosophically inclined robots would also tend to argue like that.

More important than attempts to refute positions which are defined so as to be irrefutable is to get on with the task of understanding the structure of the space of possible mechanisms. In particular, we need a survey of some of the important discontinuities, and an analysis of the most general common principles. (Some are listed below.)

WHAT SORT OF MECHANISM?

I said earlier, it's the structure not the stuff that counts. How can we describe the structures, and the types of internal processes which can occur, in human minds?

To think about symbolic structures and process-rules we need a suitable language, a set of concepts. Until recently, the set of concepts available has been restricted to 'common sense' concepts supplemented by the concepts of science and technology. For example, Freud made considerable use of hydraulic analogies. Common sense makes use of many analogies from mechanics ('I was pulled in two different directions', 'I was balanced on a knife edge', etc.). Piaget used analogies deriving from biological studies.

Recently, the concepts of computing science have considerably extended our ability to discuss mental processes. We need no longer wave our hands and hope to convince colleagues with fine turns of phrase and consistency with common experience. We can actually demonstrate the power of our theories by using them to design *working* minds, or fragments of minds. And like all designers of complex systems, we shall learn from our failures.

Computing concepts are essentially derived from a small number of basic assumptions about the nature of a symbol manipulating system:

(a) It has a memory able to contain a very large number of independently variable symbols. This means that the set of possible states it can be in, and the set of possible transitions between states is astronomical, or even bigger! For example, if there are just twenty symbols, which can take one of two forms, e.g. 'A' or 'B', then the number of possible states is over a million. If there are millions of symbols, as in modern computers, the number of possible states becomes unimaginably large. This gives enormous scope for individual variability, in physically similar machines.

(b) The symbols can be stored, searched for, compared, removed, altered, and new ones can be constructed. This means that such a system can include a large and *changing* repository of information.

(c) The symbols can be interpreted as *instructions*, i.e. they can control behaviour, both internal and external. This means that the system can generate behaviour, and be self-controlled. It also means that it can change its own programs.

(d) Some of the instructions are conditional, where the conditions may be internal or external. This allows for adaptable and intelligent behaviour, and learning which is very much dependent on environmental influences, so that initially identical systems can diverge rapidly, with positive feedback.

(e) Some of the symbols can be made to correspond (according to suitable rules) with information flowing into the system via cameras and other sensors, and can be used by conditional instructions. This means that the system can treat its symbols as representing *beliefs* about the world.

(f) Besides the lowest level symbolic instructions which directly cause processes to occur, the use of symbols with meaning allows instructions, like assertions, to refer to an external world. Instructions can then be of the form:

'Make it the case that . . .'

In other words, a computing system can be *goal-directed.*

(g) Instead of being directly executed, instructions themselves can be examined, compared, analysed. In particular, goals can be compared, inconsistencies detected, priorities decided on. Goals may even be rejected, in the light of higher level goals. Further, the process of acting on goals can lead to the formation of new sub-goals. (We'll see that the need to be able to cope with multiple goals can lead to the development of mechanisms which can produce emotional states.)

It follows from all this that different computational systems with the same initial configuration can be placed in slightly different environments and over time develop in quite different directions, so that their common origins are totally beyond recognition. In particular, such a system may be able completely to obliterate all the instructions that it started off with as it gradually builds up new programs in the light of experience. It then ceases to be doing what it was originally programmed to do. This does not apply to every computational system – only those which make use of all the possibilities listed above. But our specification is still too general. It covers a very wide range of mechanisms, with many discontinuities between the simplest and the most complex ones we know.

WHAT SORT OF COMPUTING MECHANISM ARE WE?

So far we have answered the question 'What sort of mechanism?' by saying that the mind is a computational mechanism: a system which acquires, builds, stores, and uses symbols. How can we constrain our study of possible systems of this general kind: there are so many sorts, and we know so little about their scope and limitations. One way to proceed, is to pretend to be God, or evolution, designing something like human beings. We can then specify the design task, and try to determine how far this constrains the possible design solutions. In particular, we can distinguish design considerations arising out of the following:

(a) The nature of the environment (e.g. its complexity, variety, unpredictability, and mixture of friendliness and unfriendliness). These impose constraints on the types of perceptual systems required, the kinds of belief representations, the kinds of planning and executing mechanisms, the kinds of learning mechanisms, etc.

(b) The fact that the creature to be designed will inhabit and have to control a fairly complex, yet fragile, body, with changing needs. For instance, this implies a need for body monitors able to feed information to decision makers. It also implies a need for very complex subsystems able to control and co-ordinate independently moving parts.

(c) The need to be part of a social system capable of adapting to changes of many kinds. This requires individuals to be able to acquire new forms of knowledge (e.g. new concepts, new languages) and to modify some of their rules of behaviour to cope with changing social needs. If we are designing something that will work together with others like it, we may have to provide an ability to have and act on unselfish motives.

(d) The need to be able to cope with relatively helpless young. This implies that the adults need to be provided with motives or motive-generators which are essentially unselfish. The young will need to have forms of behaviour which cause these motives to be acted on.

(e) The need to cope with a relatively large number of changing goals, principles, ideals, preferences, likes, dislikes, not all mutually commensurable, not all simultaneously satisfiable. This implies a need for motive-comparators, including strategies for deciding between incommensurable alternatives! It also requires the ability to take decisions concerned with long-term as well as short-term activities and ends, and the ability to ignore or suppress some motives or needs in the light of others.

These design considerations suggest the need for certain sorts of computational architectures. For instance, there will be a complex set of not necessarily mutually consistent, nor mutually commensurable, motives (desires, wants, fears, etc.), and this leads to a requirement for mechanisms for comparing and choosing between different motives, possibly using rules of thumb developed on a trial and error basis. (For example, if you often find that choosing A rather than B leads to failure on task A, whereas trying to do B enables you to achieve A as a side-effect, then a good rule is to choose B, even if it does not have greater *a priori* merit. Compare Wilensky [2].)

The processes of comparison may be arbitrarily complex, based on knowledge of many kinds, possibly acquired over a long time. Sometimes just deciding between goals may itself have to be a complex goal directed activity, with information-gathering sub-goals.

Further, if there have to be different subsystems concerned with controlling different processes (for instance, subsystems controlling the movements of different parts of the body, or monitoring and dealing with different sorts of needs), then since their goals and sub-goals will sometimes be inconsistent, there is a need for some mechanism which can resolve conflicts, and control the global behaviour of the system. I have argued in Chapters 6 and 10 of Sloman [1] that some aspects of our concept of consciousness can be related to this idea of a sort of centralised arbitrator, or administrator, controlling a number of relatively independent parallel subsystems. Not all the internal information and processes may be accessible or controllable by this 'governing' process. Different kinds of inaccessibility may account for different ways in which we may fail to be conscious of something. (Of course, this cannot be a complete account of the nature of human consciousness: that depends in many ways on the detailed structure and functioning of our bodies, and on the environment, and what we have absorbed from the culture, including concepts, tastes, personality traits, etc.)

In addition, since the world is not completely predictable, and may sometimes be unexpectedly friendly or unexpectedly unfriendly, there is a need for various monitoring systems which are able to interrupt and redirect or modify other processes. In fact, the issues are very complex. In general, the decision whether to interrupt or modify ongoing processes because of new information may require arbitrarily complex processes of reasoning or problem-solving. This means that in order to decide whether to interrupt, it may be necessary to interrupt anyway. This could be fatal. So it is desirable to develop mechanisms which take decisions of that sort on a relatively automatic, crude 'rule of thumb' basis, perhaps using criteria which are partly learned from experience and which are adequate most of the time, even if not always. The detailed development of this suggestion would require a very lengthy discussion of a rather complex collection of interacting sub-processes. We'd also need to see how in certain circumstances it may be necessary for new developments not only to interrupt things in order to cause new decisions to be considered, but sometimes to cause direct and immediate evasive or predatory action. Some opportunities and dangers leave no time for consideration: only reflex action will do.

Full discussion of these ideas also requires elaborating the notions of 'motive', 'goal', 'preference' and related notions. In particular, there are various sorts of higher level motives which are used in the evaluation and generation of motives – I call them motive-comparators and motive-generators. In principle, there can be comparators and generators for these also.

All this provides a framework for explaining various kinds of emotional states in terms of the interactions between a variety of active and dormant motives, motive comparators, motive generators, and a collection of beliefs. The essential idea is that emotions arise out of the mechanism which allows relatively unintelligent sub-mechanisms automatically to gain attention, even though that may sometimes turn out to be incompatible with higher-level goals. Thus emotions have an involuntary aspect: they are hard to suppress. The classification of different sorts of emotions arises out of the different patterns of relationships between motives and the processes they can generate.

The existence of the monitoring processes with their ability to modify other processes may, for example, account for the ways in which all sorts of apparently extraneous aspects of a situation can interfere with communication and learning. In particular, if there is some unfulfilled or threatened goal or motive which constantly interrupts central planning and reasoning procedures, and diverts attention away from some task, then various forms of learning and reasoning may be seriously hampered.

It can also be argued that there is no way to build a super-intelligent robot which also copes with a complex set of different sorts of motives, in a partly unpredictable world, without giving that robot mechanisms which are capable of producing emotional states, as a result of performing the cognitive tasks for which they are required. That is, the possibility of having emotions may be a by-product of being able to cope with a complex and partly unpredictable world in an intelligent way. (This does not mean that every intelligent robot will necessarily be emotional, only that it will have the ability – and abilities are not always exercised.)

More mundane (?) aspects of the design of a mind are concerned with the problems of accounting for memory, visual perception, the understanding of language, problem-solving, concept formation, the development of skills, the execution of plans. Attempting to give computers these abilities teaches us that they involve far more complex processes than we would otherwise have realized. When our programs are simple, it turns out that they don't do what we had hoped to explain. It follows that tasks performed even by very young children, and many other animals, are extremely complex, requiring very powerful computational abilities. Insofar as we don't really understand these abilities, much of our educational practice is based on total ignorance of what is really going on in the mind of a child. (The child is equally ignorant, since most of what goes on is below the level of consciousness, for instance the recognition and interpretation of grammatical structures in sentences we hear.)

A SPACE-TIME TRADE-OFF

One of the aspects of mind which flows from the need often to take decisions fairly quickly, e.g. before opportunities disappear, concerns the trade-off between space and time. It seems that the human brain is made from relatively slow computational units, although there are very many of them. This means that if recognising dangerous situations, or working out what to do, requires long chains of reasoning from general principles, then, before decisions are taken, death or other disasters may ensue. One way of coping with this problem is to store results of reasoning in some form which makes it possible to access them and use them blindly when they are needed later without repeating the complex inference processes, i.e. without making use of any ability to understand the rules. This will be especially useful in cases where the process of inference involves a lot of trial and error searching for a successful chain of reasoning. A simple example is the need to store tables of addition and multiplication instead of always working out sums from the most basic principles. This trading of space for time may be a pervasive feature of the way human minds (and perhaps other animal minds) work, over many areas, including language learning, visual perception, many kinds of problem-solving and planning.

All this implies that an intelligent system needs to be partly rigid and rule-bound.

CONCLUSION

We understand very little about mental mechanisms and the kinds of processes they can generate. Work in artificial intelligence is making some progress towards the design of systems which exhibit some of the properties of human minds [3–5], including some learning abilities. For the time being it is probably wise for psychotherapists, teachers, and all who attempt to study and control mental processes of others, to admit humbly that we don't really know much about what we are doing or why it succeeds or fails.

NOTES

[1] Sloman, A. (1978) *The Computer Revolution in Philosophy: Philosophy, Science and Models of Mind*, Harvester Press.

[2] Wilensky, R. (1982) in *Cognitive Science*.

[3] *Further reading*:
Boden, M. (1977) *Artificial Intelligence and Natural Man*, Harvester Press.
Hofstadter, D. (1977) *Godel Escher Bach, An Eternal Golden Braid*, Penguin Books.
Dennett, D. (1978) *Brainstorms*, Harvester Press.

[4] *More technical*:
Winston, P. (1977) *Artificial Intelligence*, Addison Wesley.

[5] *The opposing viewpoint*:
Dreyfus, H.L. (1979) *What Computers Can't Do* (2nd edition), Harper and Row.

PART 5

PHILOSOPHICAL IMPLICATIONS

In 1950, Turing wrote a paper called 'Computing Machinery and Intelligence' [1] in which he attempted to bypass a large amount of previous debate on whether machines could think. Very generally, previous philosophical debate on this question had concentrated on two separate, but related, topics:

(a) Are humans essentially different from machines?
(b) Can machines fit into existing concepts of what it is to be human?

It was within the framework of these questions that the issue of whether machines could think was raised, and Turing believed that it was because of the complex nature of the assumptions that the question, 'Can machines think?', was not being fruitfully tackled.

His own answer consisted of an attempt to bypass the complexities completely. He starts by saying that he proposes to consider the question, 'Can machines think?', and notes that such consideration should begin with definitions of the words 'machine' and 'think'. Instead of proposing such definitions, he formulates a rephrasal of the question, the rephrasal being known as 'the imitation game'. The point of the rephrasal is that it consists of relatively unambiguous words and can be accepted by anyone, no matter what his or her theoretical presuppositions. The reformulation goes like this. Imagine three people, Tom, Dick and Jane, playing a game, the rules of which are as follows. Tom is an interrogator, and Dick and Jane are two people he can interrogate. Tom cannot see Dick and Jane: they are in a separate room. Tom therefore communicates with Dick and Jane by, say, a visual display unit (VDU) and keyboard. Dick and Jane, in their separate room, also have similar communication equipment. Tom, since he cannot see the two in the other room, labels one A and the other B.

Tom can ask Dick and Jane any question he likes via the keyboard in the hope that given the nature of the responses displayed on his VDU he can say definitely at some stage which one of Dick and Jane has responded (Tom cannot see who responds). The problem is that Dick has the task of trying to fool Tom into making a wrong identification, whereas Jane's task is to help Tom make the right identification. So, for instance, Tom may ask: 'Now tell me, A, did you play netball at school?' Jane might respond: 'Yes, from the age of 8 to 13'. Tom may then repeat the question to B: 'Tell me, B. did you play netball at school?' Since Dick's task is to confuse Tom, Dick might respond: 'Yes, yes, I did. Don't believe Dick who said he played between the age of 8 to 13. I played only a few times at the age of 10'.

The crucial part of the reformulation is then introduced by Turing: 'What would happen if a computer took the place of Dick in this game and Tom's task is now to decide which of A and B was the human (rather than woman) and which the computer?' The computer's task is to fool Tom into making the wrong decision.

The important point to note is that Turing is not asking for a straightforward empirical solution to his question. Instead, his question 'Will the computer fool Tom as often as Dick fools Tom?' is to be interpreted as 'Is it conceivable that the computer will fool Tom as often as Dick fools Tom?' This question then replaces 'Can machines think?', and an affirmative answer to the former is, in effect, an affirmative answer to the latter (as is a negative answer to the former a negative one to the latter, of course).

Turing's paper sparked off a flurry of debate [2]. Although he tried to predict and answer as many objections as he could in the original paper, the main points that arose in the ensuing debate were as follows.

Objection 1

Only entities that are alive can have consciousness and can think. Machines are not alive. (Nor can they be said to be dead.) Hence machines cannot have consciousness and cannot think.

Counter-objection 1

An exact definition of what is meant by 'alive' is required here. Without a definition of this term which is not circular (i.e. which does not use mental predicates in its definition), the objection above fails. Also, it should be borne in mind that the definition for 'alive' needs to take into account 'living' entities such as plants, and animals, as well as intelligent alien beings that we may meet in the future.

Objection 2

Turing's imitation game concentrates solely on the behaviour of the computer with no attention being paid to internal processes. So any entity which displays human-like behaviour that we think is appropriate can be said to think.

Counter-objection 2
It could be argued that this is exactly how we humans ascribe thoughts to each other. That is, we cannot observe directly the inner process of another person's mind, and the only evidence we have that a person thinks is through that person's outward behaviour.

Objection 3
A computing machine can only do what it is told to do. It has to be programmed to behave in a certain way and it cannot do anything but follow the program's instructions. The behaviour of a machine is determined by the program it obeys. Humans, on the other hand, do have freedom to choose whether they should follow instructions given to them. One human can tell another what to do, but the other human has the freedom, in principle, to refuse to carry out the instructions. The freedom is not available to computing machines and it is this freedom that characterises the possession of consciousness. Since computers cannot have such a freedom, computers cannot have consciousness, hence computers cannot think.

Counter-objection 3
It is easy to conceive of a machine which is designed and built to be discerning about which instructions it chooses to follow. For instance, a robot may need to evaluate the consequences of carrying out a program to see whether any harm would be inflicted on a human being. If there were a possibility of a human coming to harm, the robot could, conceivably, refuse to execute the program. In such a situation, why should we refuse to admit that the robot thinks for itself?

Objection 4
It does not matter whether a robot can evaluate the consequences of executing a program, since this process of evaluation is also programmed. The robot is still bound to behave in a certain way depending on the nature of the instructions fed to it. Although there may be several levels of program in a robot, the robot cannot at any stage jump out of the top or final level. It is constrained at some stage by the instructions fed to it. A human, on the other hand, can always jump out of any sequence of instructions at any stage. This is the essence of consciousness – the ability to decide whether to continue following instructions or to jump out of the sequence of restrictions altogether and enter some completely unrelated area of activity.

Counter-objection 4
This 'jumping-out' ability that humans are supposed to have could well be rule-governed in the sense that there could exist some rules for deciding when humans will, or whether humans should, jump out of the system. We just do not know what these rules are at the moment because of our limited knowledge of the way a human mind works. But if such rules could be found, then since we can embody these rules in a program and feed the program to a computer, the human mind and the computer mind could well be no different in type!

Two main factors led to the above discussions slowly fading during the 1950s and 1960s.

The first was that very few AI researchers wanted to become involved publicly in discussions which were considered to be, at best, 'academic' and 'theoretical' and, at worst, a trivial matter of definition. So the public discussions were conducted by and large by philosophers and AI theorists, with few 'real' AI researchers contributing much to the debate. The result was that the discussions never became prominent either in AI or in computer science.

The second factor was that, during the 1960s, the level of debate, or perhaps a better way of putting it, the level at which the imitation game was to be played, moved 'down'. Turing's original formulation concentrated solely on outward behaviour. It did not really matter in his original formulation how a computer produced behaviour that might fool a human. If a chess-playing computer could beat a grand-master consistently, then there should be no reason, in the specific context of chess-playing, to deny that the computer is more 'intelligent' than the human grand-master. But the computer could have won by being able to look ahead, say, 30 moves, and to evaluate, say, 20 possible replies to each move. That is, the computer, because of its processing power and speed, could use extremely 'mechanical' means to achieve a goal. Surely no one would argue that a human grand-master decided on a certain move along similar lines? The human brain just cannot work that quickly, mainly because of the material out of which it is constructed.

But Turing was successful, in a certain sense. He wanted to provide a common framework within which the behaviour and processes of both man and machine could be described. His approach is now commonly referred to as 'functionalism', but there are few people who would currently hold this view in its original form [3]. Instead of the behaviour of a computing machine being described by reference to its program, functionalism implies that one should try to describe the behaviour of any entity within the framework of 'state-switching' and entity functioning. An entity's behaviour will now be described by function-state tables: given a certain 'current' state of the entity and a certain input of information to that entity, the entity switches to a 'new' state. Then, given this new state, which now becomes the current state, and a certain input of information to that entity, the entity switches to a new state, and so on. One could now describe the behaviour of an entity by simply giving the set of states an entity could go through and by its switching to a new state on the basis of its current state and a certain information input.

This view is known as 'functionalism', mainly for the reason that the current state of a system is a functional value of its previous state and received input. Functionalism also allows the entity to produce 'output'. Input and output, very generally, refer to sensory information and observable behaviour, respectively. A system the behaviour of which can be described by such a table is known, abstractly, as a Turing machine. It is generally believed by computer scientists that such a machine, if it has infinite memory, is the most powerful imaginable.

I now wish to bring the presentation up to date. There are contemporary counterparts to the types of debate that were taking place prior to Turing's paper, although the debate is not concerned explicitly with the question, 'Can machines think?' There is an approach in artificial intelligence which can be considered to be a contemporary counterpart to functionalism. First, I shall examine the contemporary counterparts to the pre-Turing debates.

The contemporary counterpart to the debate as to whether humans are essentially different from machines depends on the implications of building a machine that is exactly like a human [4]. Assume such a machine can be built. It is in every sense exactly like a human. Its material structure is exactly like a human's. Its brain, flesh, biological features, etc., are exactly like a human's. It talks and understands exactly like a human. The pattern of brain events when it performs an action or when it has a pin stuck into its flesh is exactly the same as a human's, and so on. In no sense is it distinguishable internally and externally from a human. Now, does such a machine feel pain when it has a pin stuck into its flesh? Does it become angry when the electricity cuts out in the middle of a television programme? Does it enjoy listening to Beethoven's symphonies? Does it fancy its neighbour's spouse?

The point of this 'thought-experiment' is to assume that one day neurophysiology will be able to identify all the brain events that take place when a human feels pain, becomes angry, experiences enjoyment, and has desires. A machine is built which replicates these brain patterns when the relevant physical conditions exist (e.g. a pin in the flesh, visual stimuli from a television set, aural stimuli from a set of loudspeakers, visual/aural/tactile stimuli when near the neighbour's spouse). Can one justifiably say that, when the physical conditions are satisfied, the appropriate psychological term (such as 'pain', 'anger', 'enjoyment', 'desire') has been explained, or reduced in some sense to physical or neurophysiological terms?

Proponents of the argument that one cannot be justified in this 'reduction' claim that if psychology is concerned with phenomena that are described by concepts involving intentions, beliefs, memory, learning, pain, desire, and so on, all that has been shown is that there exists a correlation between certain psychological events and neurophysiological or physical events, that descriptions of psychological events are correlated with certain descriptions of neurophysiological or physical events. But a correlation between two events, and linguistically between descriptions of psychological events and descriptions of neurophysiological events, does not imply that psychological events are neurophysiological or physical events, or that descriptions of psychological events are semantically equivalent to descriptions of neurophysiological or physical events.

For instance, although the psychological state of anger may well have a certain physical or neurophysiological description, i.e. the psychological state may well have a physical or neurophysiological counterpart state, this does not mean that a certain neurophysiological or physical description has the same meaning as a certain psychological description. If the meanings are not the same, then it would follow that the two events – one psychological, the other neurophysiological or physical – are not the same event and are two different types of events altogether.

A further argument that is proposed to show that psychological events cannot be reduced to neurophysiological or physical events rests on the finite class of observations on which only statistical generalisations can be based. But statistical generalisations are not scientific laws.

The general conclusion, then, is that the perfectly created humanoid cannot be said to be in pain, to be angry, to enjoy or desire anything, no matter how accurately its neurophysiological or physical processes correspond with a human's. If one wants to decide whether the humanoid has psychological properties, one must stop thinking of it as a machine and start judging him as one would a man [5]. That is, one does not ascribe psychological predicates to a machine unless one wants to, and this is a very different matter from one doing so logically or scientifically.

The debate can then be continued in a variety of ways. One way is to deny the consistency of the above thought-experiment. It is not as if the perfect humanoid will be created and psychology will stand still. Rather, just as concepts in metaphysics and astrology have moved gradually into their 'more scientific' relations – physics and astronomy – as these sciences develop, so will concepts in psychology move into its more scientific relations, neuropsychology or neurophysiology. For instance, the concept of dreaming is usually regarded as being psychological. That is, many psychologists believe that dreams are psychological phenomena which need interpreting in the context of desires, wishes, frustrations, repressions and so on. But if dreams are shown to have a neurophysiological function, say, allowing memory to re-organise itself whilst one is asleep [6], the concept of dreams may change in psychology and may even disappear altogether as a psychological concept.

So, as neurophysiology develops, gradually one concept after another in psychology may be removed from psychology as being a non-psychological concept, and by the time the perfect humanoid exists, psychology, and the terms which belong to it, may bear very little relation to the terms being used in psychology today. It could well be argued that when the perfect humanoid exists, if one wants to decide whether he has certain mechanical properties, one must stop thinking of him as a human and start judging it as one would a machine. That is, one does not ascribe mechanical predicates to a humanoid unless one wants to, and this is a very different matter from one doing so logically or scientifically.

Other (related) ways to continue the debate are, first, to question the assumption that there are such terms as psychological terms and physical terms which belong to the subject domains of psychology and physics or neurophysiology, and secondly, that there is a difference in the semantics of these terms. It could be argued that terms or predicates should not be distinguished according to the subject domain in which they are currently judged to fall. There is, after all, nothing necessary in a term belonging to psychology or neuropsychology. Rather, one should distinguish between predicates, and hence their types of meaning, by examining the way in which such predicates are ascribed to entities in the first place. If it can be shown that one class of predicates is ascribed on a logically different basis from another class of predicates [7], that will then count as a justification for separating predicates into different classes. It would then be the task of anyone who wishes to distinguish between psychological predicates and, say, neurophysiological predicates to show that there is something inherently different in the way predicates in these two domains are ascribed. Without such a distinction, circularity of argument could well arise: a psychological term refers to a psychological event, and a psychological event is one which can be described by a psychological term.

Following on from this is the question of semantics. For one to argue that a psychological term differs semantically from a neurophysiological term that is supposed to describe the neurophysiological counterpart of a psychological event, one must have a theory or view of meaning. This theory or view of meaning must be capable of distinguishing, say, 'anger' as a predicate from the counterpart neurophysiological term that is used to describe a certain neurophysiological state associated with 'anger'. This is not to say that such a theory or view of meaning cannot be provided. But given that one already has made a distinction in type between 'anger' and its neurophysiological counterpart in order to raise the question of semantics, this distinction in type should not by itself be used as the sole basis for claiming that there is a semantic difference, as little will have been gained. That is, although it is trivially true to say that one distinguishes between a psychological term and its counterpart neurophysiological term in the very act of making the distinction, this does not lead anywhere in the long run. The requirement is for a semantic view or theory to be presented which has as one of its implications a distinction in the semantics of psychological and neurophysiological terms. The question of whether a perfect humanoid can, say, have desires does not depend on the plausibility or convincingness of the thought-experiment but on the correctness or appropriateness of the world-view or semantic approach of the author of the thought-experiment.

The modern counterpart to dualism as a philosophical model of what it is to be human is intentionalism. Intentionalism has its modern roots in the intentional theory of non-natural meaning [8], but the contemporary concept of an intentional system depends only in part on this linguistic philosophy base. The base is usually formulated as three necessary conditions for meaningful communication to take place.

If the utterer U does X, thereby meaning that P, he does it intending

(i) that some audience A should come to believe P;
(ii) that A should be aware of intention (i); and
(iii) that the awareness mentioned in (ii) should be part of A's reason for believing P.

That is, when a person U wishes to communicate with an audience A, U intends to produce some response in A, and U intends that A recognise that U intends to produce this response in A, and U intends that A's awareness of the intention that U has that A should be aware that U intends that A should believe P should form a basis for A believing that P.

Now, this is a complicated set of conditions, but the essential point in the above account is that an utterer U should have the three intentions, viz. U intends that A recognise that U intends that A believe P, for meaningful communication between two parties A and U to take place.

Since the appearance of this model of non-natural, or intentional, meaning, several developments have taken place. First, the model has been generalised so that it applies not just to linguistic acts but to meaningful acts in general. Secondly, a fourth intention on the part of U, that U should intend A to recognise U's intention that A should be aware of intention (i), is sometimes suggested [9]. That is, both U and A are aware that they are both aware of the communication context! Thirdly, although it is not at all obvious that people who communicate successfully are aware of the above-mentioned intentions or may even be able to describe them, yet the model seems plausible [10]. When one 'communicates' with a computer, although the result may be that required, one has not communicated with a computer in the sense that one human communicates with another. This is because the above-mentioned conditions have not been complied with: it is not part of the process of telling a computer what to do that the computer be aware of the intention 'behind' the command. Since the model seems plausible, but since human communicators are rarely, if ever, aware of the intentions involved, such intentions are preconditions of linguistic behaviour in particular and meaningful behaviour in general. Their psychological reality may well be unconscious. Fourthly, such a model by implication can also be used to distinguish 'rational' or 'intelligent' entities from entities that are not [11]. According to the model, the audience A must be rational enough to identify the utterer's intentions and must also believe, on well-grounded reasons, that the utterer is sincere.

Thus, only rational entities can take part in meaningful communication. Certain types of animal behaviour, which may appear to conform to the above model, are usually categorised as being instinctive rather than rational.

This, then, is very roughly the modern base of intentionalism. With the help of this base can be built various models of how language is acquired, how intentions can be ascribed, and so on [12]. We shall concentrate on just one aspect: intentional systems [13].

An intentional system is a system the behaviour of which may be explained or predicted on the basis of ascriptions of intentions, beliefs, hopes, fears, and so on, to the system. Humans are certainly intentional systems. Are computing machines? The answer is affirmative if one assumes that the computer is rational and intelligent. That is, if one adopts an 'intentional stance' [14], whereby one assumes that the computer possesses information and is driven by goals, then this assumption may be a useful tool for explaining or predicting the behaviour of a computer system. The question as to whether computers can think is not relevant in this context: a computer system is intentional if one explains or predicts its behaviour by ascribing intentional predicates to it.

It is important to note the move which has taken place here. The answer to the question, 'Are computing machines rational?', is answered by saying that they are if one *assumes* they are, not by saying that they are because one *concludes* they are. Similarly, by implication, the answer to the question, 'Can computers think?', is answered by saying that they can if one assumes they can, not because one concludes they can. Although this approach has a different starting point from the previous approach, which uses the concept of the perfect android, the two approaches end up in the same conceptual territory, albeit by different routes.

The debate can then be continued on several fronts, the most important of which, if the argument is not to descend to the point whether either one accepts the axioms of intentionalism or one does not, concerns the notion of ascription of intentional predicates.

(1) Does the justification of ascription of intentional predicates to computers depend on a human adopting an intentional stance? Can two computers adopt intentional stances towards each other? Is that the same as two humans adopting intentional stances towards each other? Can two humans, logically, adopt intentional stances towards each other? (Yes, if one assumes they can?)
(2) Does the adoption of an intentional stance towards a computer need to be a conscious, deliberate choice? Or can one do it without thinking? Can one be fooled into adopting an intentional stance? (Are we returning to a modern version of the Turing test?)
(3) Can one adopt an intentional stance only when attempting to explain or predict the behaviour of a computer system? Can one use it merely to describe? Can we use it to understand the behaviour of a computer system, or to excuse it, or to threaten it? That is, what exactly is the range of intentional predicates that can be ascribed to a computer?

The above questions I do not propose to answer here, but they should convey the 'flavour' of the debates that can be entered into.

Finally, I shall briefly mention the modern counterpart to the functionalist approach. This approach depends on the 'computational metaphor', which allows the concepts, mechanisms and processes of computer science to be used in the development of (mainly) cognitive theories. For instance, one can use computer memory concepts in the development of human memory models, such as the use of direct or random access to items in memory. One can use the notion of an operating system and its structure to model a human mind. Or one can use the notion of a distributed data-base, where information is not stored in one centralised store but is scattered across several stores, each with its own processor that has the task of looking after its own local information.

The fundamental assumption to this approach is that a human is an information processing device just as a computer is an information processing device. Information must be distilled from raw data, categorised, manipulated, stored and used. It has to be retrieved, updated, and deleted. It has to be represented in a form which makes it of use in decision-making and inference-drawing. It just so happens that by and large the 'borrowing' of concepts has, until recently, been one way. That is, cognitive psychologists and cognitive scientists have tended to borrow from computer scientists, and the computational metaphor has provided a common framework for describing the behaviour of both man and computer, largely by an appeal to computer concepts. However, there has been a recent trend to reverse the direction of the borrowing of concepts. Some cognitive scientists now believe that, rather than looking for computer science concepts with which to describe the processes of the mind or brain, the human mind or brain, despite its slowness, is still a fantastically complicated mechanism. A human can talk, move an object, and solve a complicated problem all at the same time. Currently, computers have difficulty in achieving one of these tasks, never mind all three, in real-time. At one stage, cognitive psychologists and scientists may have been willing to put up with prediction that faster computer hardware would solve the real-time problem, but increasingly some of them are questioning why faster hardware is required when the brain, within its own limited constraints of slow processing when compared with computers, manages to perform seemingly complicated tasks in real-time [15].

The answer would appear to lie not in the speed of the processors but in the way the processors are linked together, i.e. with the architecture of a multiprocessor system. Assuming that the brain is a multiprocessing system, i.e. an interconnected system of perhaps millions of microprocessors which can compute tasks concurrently, a better approach may be to forget about speed and concentrate on the architecture. The implication of this approach for artificial intelligence theory is that a computer cannot be said to be intelligent unless its processor architecture resembles that of a human's. So it is not enough for a computer to simulate the behaviour of a human, nor is it enough for a computer to adopt the same functional processes as a human; rather, a computer system, if it is to 'think' and be intelligent, must be constructed in the same way, but not necessarily with the same material, as a human brain. On top of this architecture various intelligent and rational processes can be built.

So a common framework – the computational metaphor or the brain as an information-processing device – still exists, but the trend may be for a 'brain metaphor', or the computer as a multiprocessing, distributed device.

After this somewhat lengthy overview, let us examine the implications of this metaphor for us human beings. Given that AI researchers are constructing, testing, and computerising various theories of how we do things 'intelligently', is there a danger that we humans will lose something in the process? That is, do AI programs and theories dehumanise us by presenting us as 'mere machines'? For instance, if we return to the 'armchair' memory theory described earlier, are the construction of the theory and its implementation stripping us of our own sense of individuality and of what it is to be human by showing that a machine can perform these memory activities just as well as (and perhaps better than) we humans? Even if no computer actually exists that can perform as well as a human on a wide variety of 'intelligent' tasks, and even if no such computer can be constructed for many years, are the approach and research content of AI dehumanising, no matter what the intention of AI researchers?

There are two major obstacles which must be mentioned here. The first is to convince people that there is a real danger facing humanity because of the use of the metaphor. This is not easy, since a common reaction to these questions is 'So what?' This reaction may be prompted for several reasons, two of which are

(i) a sincere belief on the part of someone that we humans are essentially no different from machines, and
(ii) a lack of interest in the debate since the debate may be perceived to be too abstract, too general, or just not relevant to life in the modern world.

Even if this obstacle can be overcome and people can be convinced that the debates are worth pursuing, the second obstacle is to provide solutions which are acceptable and rational. For instance, a total ban on AI research around the world may be called for, because of the extreme argument that AI is simply too dangerous to be left in the hands of researchers and scientists supported financially by the government or private business. This extreme argument may point to the research that took place during the early 1940s in America on the nuclear bomb. Because of this research, in which ordinary individuals around the world had no say, all humanity is currently living under the threat of total annihilation. Would it not have been better to ban all research into this weapon in the first place?

This argument, of course, has many faults. If the Americans had not carried out the research, it is not possible to say categorically that other groups would not have developed the bomb independently of government controls. Also, if research into the bomb, which is considered undesirable, were banned yesterday, why could not research into wave power and solar power, which is considered desirable, be banned tomorrow? Who is to say which research is desirable and which not? And, anyway, it has to be proved that AI research, dangerous as it may be, is or could be as dangerous as nuclear bomb research.

Another aspect of this metaphor is that a group of people who actually understand this metaphor (and may have been responsible for generating it in the first place) will develop in various academic institutions. If these academic institutions are suddenly starved of funds by government for research into 'undesirable' areas such as, say, the social sciences, or philosophy, or music, or drama, and if government sets aside a large amount of money to allow academic institutions to carry out work in 'desirable' areas, such as, say, expert systems, or artificial intelligence, or information technology, the temptation must be very great for the group of people and the academic institutions concerned to go for the money, no matter whether the research proposals formulated to obtain the money are sound or morally desirable. (This is a danger present in this country, with the Government sponsoring large-scale work in artificial intelligence through the Alvey Directorate.) The justification for going for the money rests simply on basic economic facts to do with people having jobs and being able to support their families. Any arguments concerning the moral or philosophical implications of the research are considered to be expensive liabilities, worthy of discussion only in the ideal world where people can afford to sit around and discuss these issues.

Philosophy has often been attacked for not providing real or concrete answers to real or concrete problems. That may be true, but also one suspects that sometimes philosophical answers are ignored for the simple reason that they are too unpopular for many people. It is far easier to dismiss the dangers inherent in a new technology than to take the dangers seriously, where by 'dangers' we include not only threats of annihilation because of the new technology but also the impact of the new technology on the 'common' man. Exactly how much of current AI work is actually going to help the vast majority of us? In what areas of human activity will AI research help us? Who decided that it was in these areas and not others that the work should be concentrated?

Again, we have raised many questions. A cynic could well argue that current research in AI is doing nothing more than providing jobs for a small but expanding elite in esoteric, specialist topics or large, defence-oriented areas, with there being little hope that the vast majority of us will ever benefit in some concrete way from the research, where by 'benefit' we mean an accepted and proven gain rather than one which is advertised as being a gain by the elite who spend our money researching into it.

The cynic may well have a valid point.

Ajit Narayanan

NOTES

[1] Turing (1950).
[2] See, for instance, Anderson (ed.) (1964).
[3] But see Thomas (1978).
[4] Davidson (1973).
[5] *Ibid.*
[6] As I believe, has been hypothesised very recently by several American AI researchers.
[7] Strawson (1959).
[8] Grice (1957).
[9] Strawson (1964).
[10] Dennett (1978a).
[11] Bennett (1976).
[12] *Ibid.*
[13] Dennett (1978b).
[14] *Ibid.*
[15] See, for instance, Anderson and Hinton (eds.) (1981).
For details, see the bibliography at the end of the book.

Let us return to the three papers in this section, all of which are concerned with the social and moral implications of AI. Boden argues that AI theories and programs, far from dehumanising us by adding more weight to the mechanistic view of the universe (which stresses the analogy between mental events and events that take place in certain types of machine, e.g. a computer, and which therefore could be interpreted as weakening the concept of what it is to be human), actually enrich the concept of what it is to be human by demonstrating the power of certain types of machine, e.g. a computer. That is, Boden's point is that mechanism is not regarded favourably because of the nature of the machines against which we have been compared in the past. AI demonstrates that one type of machine, a computing machine, is a very powerful type of machine indeed and we should not fear or object to the comparison simply because we feel humanism and mechanism are completely incompatible. Rogers, whilst not disagreeing with Boden's argument, shows that AI has humanistic leanings, argues that humanistic theories, as well as theories in the cognitive and social sciences, may well themselves be dehumanising because of their commitment to 'objective knowledge' and their underplaying of the intuitive aspects of what it is to be human. Whitby stresses the danger of an elite forming in AI research and suggest that one way to prevent such an elite forming is to ensure that other disciplines and subject areas provide material and knowledge to AI. Thus, the input of information from outside AI should break the circle of AI researchers solving problems generated by AI researchers.

AI and human freedom*

M.A. Boden University of Sussex UK

I INTRODUCTION

The truth can be dangerous. It was because they realised this that the Roman Catholic Church forbade cremation. Cremation was, of course, theologically permissible, and in times of epidemic the Church allowed it. But in normal times it was forbidden – Why? The reason was that the Church feared the influence of the image associated with it. It was difficult enough for the faithful to accept the notion of bodily resurrection after having seen a burial (knowing that the body would eventually decay in the ground). But the image of the whole body being consumed by flames and changing within a few minutes to a heap of ashes was an even more powerful apparent contradiction of the theological claim of bodily resurrection at the Day of Judgement. (Indeed, the ban on cremation was introduced when the French Freemasons held anti-Catholic demonstrations, in which they burned their dead saying 'There, you see: they won't rise again!') In short, instead of relying only on abstract theological argument, which very likely would not convince their flock in any case, the Church dealt with this threat to faith by attacking the concrete image.

I believe a basically mechanistic view of the universe, and of human beings as creatures of it, to be true. But such views can be dangerous, in that they tend to encourage a dehumanisation of our image of man, an undermining of our sense of responsibility and individuality. For the image of 'machine' that is currently popular has no place for human values or for the specifically human

*This paper was first published as 'Human values in a mechanistic universe' in *Human Values: Royal Institute of Philosophy Lectures Vol. II* ed. G. Vesey.

self-image associated with them. This image of machines and mechanism is drawn from seventeenth-century clockwork and nineteenth-century engineering: one has only to think of Descartes's metaphors for animal psychology, and T.H. Huxley's metaphor for psychology in general (in which he compared the mind to the useless smoke from a steam-engine). Occasionally, people appeal to twentieth-century notions such as the cybernetic concept of feedback, taking the thermostat or the guided missile as their paradigm case of modern mechanism. But this paradigm also is insufficient to provide a philosophical base for humanity, and its overall effect is just as dehumanising as earlier versions of mechanism. The current image of machines causes a chill to strike the heart on reading the molecular biologist Jacques Monod's claim that 'The cell is a machine. The animal is a machine. Man is a machine' [1]. If man is indeed a machine, what room is there for humanity?

I shall try to defend against the dehumanising influences of mechanism by presenting a different image of 'machine', one that shows the potentialities inherent in mechanism to be far greater than could previously have been supposed on the basis of extant machines. That is, instead of concentrating on abstract philosophical arguments in favour of mechanism, I shall describe actual examples of machines whose behaviour is hardly 'mechanistic' in the usual sense of the word. Specifically, I shall outline some of the achievements of artificial intelligence (AI for short), the science of making machines do things that would require intelligence if done by people [2]. The analogies between these machines and human minds are strong enough to cast doubt on the antimechanist assumption that no philosophical rapprochement between humanism and mechanism is possible.

Before describing these examples in Parts III to V, I provide a philosophical context for the later discussion by sketching what I understand by the notion of 'human values', and what I take to be the main doubts on the part of humanists who reject mechanism of any sort.

II HUMAN VALUES

The notion of human values is inextricably bound up with a specifically human concept of people and a sense of their moral dignity. By this I mean that whatever particular values a humanist may hold, these will in general assume that people are capable of purposive action, free choice, and moral responsibility, and that their interests ought *prima facie* to be respected. It is because these concepts are essential to human values that antihumanist writers such as B.F. Skinner seek to undermine them, claiming that morality has no need of 'freedom' and 'dignity' [3].

It follows that any form of mechanism that claims to be basically compatible with a morality of human values must be able to accommodate the concepts of purpose, freedom, and responsibility. What features of these concepts are generally agreed by their protagonists to be most important?

When we ascribe purposes to people, and describe their behaviour as purposive action, we imply that their behaviour is somehow guided by their idea of a goal. The purpose is always an idea of something nonexistent, for the goal-state itself lies in the future; it is often an idea of something that will never exist, for goals are not always achieved; and it is sometimes focused on something intrinsically impossible, like squaring the circle. That is, the idea is an intentional object or thought within the subjective experience of a thinker, as opposed to an objective entity existing in the material world. The guidance it exerts on purposive action is (within limits) flexible, rational, and intelligent, and with perseverance the person learns to do better. Typically, the agent is aware of the goals being followed and why they are being followed, although cases of 'unconscious motivation' and 'habitual action' frequently occur.

In ascribing freedom to people, or describing human action as free, we mean not merely that people are unpredictable, but (more positively) that in free action the agent could have acted differently. That is, either the goal or the sub-goal guiding the behaviour could have been different, so that a different end was chosen in the first place or the same end was sought by different means. But this difference must itself be generated in a particular sort of way. It cannot be based on a random factor, nor can it depend on causes having nothing to do with the self and lying wholly outside the agent's control. (This is why radically indeterminist analyses of freedom are unacceptable, and why action attributed primarily to genetic or environmental causes cannot be regarded as truly free.) Rather, the difference in question must be grounded in the deliberations of the person concerned: had the agent's reasoning been different, the action also would have differed. So the more someone is capable of flexibly rational thinking, the greater the freedom of action available. In addition, free action is often self-determined in a peculiarly intimate sense, in that the determining reasons include a crucial reference to the person's (actual or ideal) self-image. In such cases, one asks oneself (or perhaps, a friend): 'Am I someone who would choose to do this?' or 'Do I want to be the sort of person who does that?' These questions, and especially the latter, address the person's moral principles as well as mere conceit or narcissistic self-regard.

The ascription of moral responsibility presupposes that free action can be 'action against the strongest desire', in the sense that a temporarily pressing motive can be outweighed by moral principles. The point is not that the person is even more strongly swayed by the moral principles, for the metaphor 'swaying' suggests passivity on the agent's part. Rather, the person actively deliberates on the choice in a responsible fashion, carefully considering all the known factors in so far as they are relevant to ethical issues, and not making a decision overhastily. Specifically moral principles (in contrast with mere personal preferences) are universalisable to all individuals in similar circumstances, which implies that practical morality draws on the capacity to recognise subtle analogies between distinct situations as well as the ability to reason logically about 'all' and 'some'. Moreover, moral principles are primarily concerned with abstract features of human behaviour or experience, such as justice and betrayal or happiness and despair. It follows that moral responsibility rests on the ability to understand concepts such as these, and to assess their relevance to particular situations. If the person is to engage in moral choice, rather than mere ethical contemplation, this assessment must involve also the imaginative comparison of the likely outcomes of alternative possible actions. It follows that a great deal of knowledge must be brought to bear in exercising one's responsibility: knowledge of moral principles themselves, knowledge of the world in which they are to be applied, and knowledge of one's self – both as one is and as one would like to be.

These being the crucial features of the family of concepts contributing to 'human values', why are humanists usually so insistent that human values cannot be encompassed by any basically mechanistic phiolosphy? Broadly, there are two different reasons. One is a philosophical view arising from purely philosophical arguments; the other is a prejudice against mechanism that is grounded not so much in abstract reasoning as in the concrete image of familiar machines as we know them in daily life.

The philosophical view favoured by humanists holds that mechanism is incompatible with intentionality, with the distinction between the psychological subject and the object of thought that we have seen to be essential to purpose, freedom, and moral responsibility. But what sort of incompatability is this? Briefly, the humanist's claim may be only that intentional phenomena cannot be described in terms making no use of the subject-object distinction, so that a philosophy in which such psychological terms do not appear can make no sense of human values. Alternatively, the humanist may also claim (without always seeing that this is a different point) that intentional phenomena cannot be generated from a mechanistic base, one which can be described in the nonpsychological terms of physics; on this view, creatures pursuing human values simply could not arise in a basically mechanistic universe.

My position on this 'philosophical' humanism is that whereas the first claim distinguished above is correct, the second is mistaken [4]. In other words, it is true that we cannot avoid the concepts of purpose, freedom, and responsibility if we are to understand human beings as the essentially subjective creatures they are, or if we are to express any system of specifically human values. But it is false that subjectivity cannot arise within a basically mechanistic universe, or that a system described in objective terms by the physicist cannot also be described by the humanist in intentional terms that express different aspects of its nature.

I shall concentrate in this chapter on the second root of the humanist's antipathy to mechanism: the poverty of the humanist's image of machines. Specifically, I shall ask how purposes, freedom, and moral responsibility might relate to an enriched image of mechanism. More generally, my discussion will bear also on the issue of the compatibility of intentionality and mechanism. For if the moral concepts I have sketched in this section can be shown to be consonant with mechanism, then subjectivity in general must be compatible with mechanism too.

Let us turn, then, to consider a few examples of what one might call 'non-mechanistic machines'. My examples are drawn from AI, so the machines in question are digital computers running under the guidance of an AI program. You will see that I say 'the program does this' where I could equally have said 'the machine does that'. You will see also that I use psychological terms without scare-quotes in describing these machines. I omit scare-quotes for aesthetic reasons: as will become clear, I do not hold that any of these current machines is *really* purposive or intelligent, still less a moral agent. I do hold, however, that psychological vocabulary is essential in expressing what these machines can do.

III PURPOSE

The central feature of purposive action is that it is guided throughout by an idea of the goal, in a flexible and intelligent manner. Are there any machines of which the same might be said?

Among the earliest AI programs were some that solved problems by keeping an idea of the goal firmly in mind and reasoning backward from it. For example, the GEOMETRY MACHINE proved theorems in Euclidean geometry that would have defeated any but the brightest of high-school students with the same vocabulary of geometric concepts and the same stock of previously proved theorems [5]. Essentially, the program followed the strategy of the school-child who writes *Given*: and *To be Proved*: at the top of the page, and then tries to find a way of legally getting from what is given to what is to be proved (using only inferences based on Euclid's axioms or previously proved theorems). Similarly, the General Problem Solver – 'GPS' for short – attacked problems in logical form (such as the familiar *Missionaries and Cannibals* puzzle) by carefully noting the differences between the current problem-state and the goal-state, and eliminating these differences until none remained [6]. In each of these cases, the idea of the goal is crucial in guiding the solution of the problem.

In each case, also, the process of solution varies with the circumstances rather than being rigidly fixed. That is, what the program does, as well as the order in which it does it, depends on the specific nature of the difference between the current and goal-state. GPS carries out a 'means–end analysis' of the problem, in which it identifies the differences as a series of sub-goals to be achieved in the most suitable order. Heuristics, or rules of thumb, are available to suggest what type of approach is most likely to resolve a particular difference, and what method to try next if the 'best' should fail. In short, these programs show the beginnings of one main criterion of purpose: variation of means.

Some recent programs show more intelligence in varying their performance according to circumstances. The flexibility of their goal-seeking is greater, not merely in the sense that they have a greater number of methods to choose from, but also in the sense that communication *between* methods is possible while the program is functioning. It is as though one method asks advice from another, while a third makes a complaint that there is a specific difficulty ahead, and a fourth requests 'stop press' information from a fifth. This flexible form of organisation is *heterarchical*, as opposed to the hierarchical organisation of GPS and the GEOMETRY MACHINE. In a hierarchy, there is a fixed progression of responsibility for control passing down from higher to lower levels of the system, and a module that gets into difficulties has to apply to its superior for help. But in a heterarchy the responsibility for deciding what is to be done next is more evenly distributed throughout the system, and the various sub-routines can communicate not only 'up' and 'down', but also 'sideways'.

An analogy is between a (hierarchical) bureaucracy and a (heterarchical) group of co-operating experts: although there is room for some degree of flexibility in a bureaucracy (as there is in GPS), in a community of specialists there is more opportunity for last-minute changes of plan or minor adjustments in light of local difficulties.

The degree of flexibility that can be achieved by heterarchical programs is illustrated by Terry Winograd's 'SHRDLU' [7]. SHRDLU's goal is to understand the sentences typed into it, where understanding involves parsing each sentence correctly, interpreting it sensibly, and answering it helpfully. SHRDLU has a large number of mini-programs for interpreting English sentences, including specialists which know about word-endings such as *-ed, -ing*, and the like, and experts on the grammatical and semantic properties of *noun groups* or *adjectival phrases*. In addition, it has sub-routines that specialise in finding out what the world is like, and modules whose particular job is to deduce conclusions from given premises. Each specialist, or mini-program, contains within itself advice about what to do in varying circumstances, and what to try if the most obvious stratagems fail. The goal of understanding an English sentence is one that can be reached only by way of highly flexible, interacting thought-processes, of which we ourselves are normally not introspectively aware. As you can see from the following excerpt of dialogue, SHRDLU's understanding depends on 'simultaneous' parsing, semantic interpretation, and investigation of the world, a complex process that has to differ subtly according to the specific nature of the input sentence [8]:

(1) *Pick up a big red block*
O.K.
The system answers 'O.K.' when it carries out a command. In order to pick up the red block, it had to clear it off by finding a space for the green one (initially on top of it) and moving the green one away.

(2) *Grasp the pyramid*
I DON'T UNDERSTAND AND WHICH PYRAMID YOU MEAN.
There are three pyramids in the scene, so the program does nothing.

(3) *Find a block which is taller than the one you are holding and put it into the box.*
The system has to figure out what is meant by 'one' and 'it', as well as using deduction to decide which block it is holding.
BY 'IT', I ASSUME YOU MEAN THE BLOCK WHICH IS TALLER THAN THE ONE I AM HOLDING.
Printed out to keep us informed.
O.K.
The hand has to set down the red block to pick up the taller blue one.

(4) *What does the box contain?*
THE BLUE PYRAMID AND THE BLUE BLOCK.

(5) *What is the pyramid supported by?*
Earlier the system responded to 'the pyramid' by saying 'I don't understand

which pyramid you mean'. Now, it assumes that we mean the one just mentioned.
THE BOX.

(6) *How many blocks are not in the box?*
Negatives such as 'not' and 'no' are handled whether they appear in clauses or noun groups (such as 'no boxes').
FOUR OF THEM.

(7) *Is at least one of them narrower than the one which I told you to pick up?*
The phrase 'at least one of them' must be analysed to refer back to the previous question, and 'the one which . . .' must also refer to blocks. Noun groups can have complicated numbers such as 'at least one', 'more than three', 'exactly seven', etc. The memory of past events is used to deduce which block is 'the one which I told you to pick up'. Notice the complicated syntactic structure in which 'the one' is actually the object of a clause embedded two levels deeper.
YES, THE RED CUBE.

(17) *Will you please stack up both of the red blocks and either a green cube or a pyramid?*
O.K.

(23) *Had you touched any pyramid before you put the green one on the little cube?*
YES, THE GREEN ONE.
The system deduces from its memory what event is being referred to, and can relate other events to it in time. The analysis includes complex tenses of verb groups, and there are special facilities for keeping track of the various forms of irregular verbs like 'have'.

(24) *When did you pick it up?*
WHILE I WAS STACKING UP THE RED CUBE, A LARGE RED BLOCK AND A LARGE GREEN CUBE.
A time is described by naming the main goal which was being worked on.

(25) *Why?*
The system remembers immediately previous sentences to understand questions like this and the following ones.
TO GET RID OF IT.
By keeping track of selected parts of the original subgoal tree, the system has some understanding of its own motives.

(26) *Why did you do that?*
TO CLEAR OFF THE RED CUBE.
'That' refers to the action mentioned in the answer.

(27) *Why did you clear off that cube?*
Here, 'that' means the one just referred to.
TO PUT IT ON A LARGE GREEN CUBE.

(28) *Why did you do that?*
TO STACK UP THE RED CUBE, A LARGE RED BLOCK AND A LARGE GREEN CUBE.

(29) *Why did you do that?*

BECAUSE YOU ASKED ME TO.
It remembers what it did, not how the request was worded.
[Cf. the request of item 17, which gives the program a choice.]

In addition to the flexible variation of means, SHRDLU's dialogue suggests other features of purpose. For instance, Item 1 has the indeterminacy characteristic of action sentences (and often taken as a logical criterion of intentionality): Winograd did not have to tell SHRDLU precisely how to pick up the big red block, but left the program to work that out for itself. A prime reason for the machine's ability to understand (and obey) this vaguely specified command is that the program is written in a version of PLANNER, a 'goal-oriented' programming language in which one can identify goals at a high level of generality and rely on the system itself to fill in the details. Items 17 and 29 show that SHRDLU itself often speaks in intentional terms: it knows that it was not specifically asked to stack up the two red blocks and a large green cube, even though it did this in response to an input request.

Items 17 and 23–29 show that SHRDLU has some understanding and memory of its own goal-subgoal structure, and is able to address this structure to find the reasons for which it did things. If this information were not stored in its memory, it would have had to answer Item 29 either by saying 'I don't know', or perhaps by working out a plausible reason for its action which in fact was not the real reason. Analogously, a person in a state of posthypnotic suggestion will dream up all sorts of possible reasons for putting the cat on top of the grand piano, being unable to remember the hypnotist's previous command and so unable to give the real reason, 'Because you asked me to'. And Freudian accounts of unconscious motivation similarly assume that parts of the person's goal/sub-goal structure are unavailable to consciousness, being at least temporarily repressed, and that the relevant actions will be 'explained' by rationalisations that do not constitute genuine self-knowledge.

But SHRDLU lacks a feature of purposiveness that was mentioned earlier, namely, the ability to learn to do better. Its knowledge of what it is up to is sufficient to enable it to know why it did what it did, but not to enable it to remember what went wrong when failures occur. Consequently, SHRDLU cannot benefit from experience by learning to avoid false paths once it has been down them.

Not all programs are similarly limited. For example, HACKER is a program that writes programs for solving problems, and that learns to do so better because it has an understanding of the purposive structure of the programs it composes and because it knows about the sorts of things that can go wrong [9]. When it writes a program it adds 'comments' to various lines (as human programmers do) saying what that section of program is intended to do. This information is used in rewriting the program, should it fail to achieve its goal when it is run. The sorts of mistake, or bug, that HACKER knows about are defined in high-level teleological terms, such as UNSATISFIED PREREQUISITE, GOAL-PROTECTION VIOLATION, PREREQUISITE CLOBBERS BROTHER GOAL, and so on.

A sense of the way in which HACKER learns from its mistakes can be conveyed by Figs. 1 to 5. Given the scene shown in Fig. 1, and asked to get *A* on to *B* , HACKER can put *A* on *B* immediately. HACKER has available a *primitive*, or already given, program for putting one thing on top of another. But if HACKER is given Fig. 2, and asked to get *B* on to *C*, it cannot do so immediately. The reason is that the primitive 'PUT-ON' program can work only with one block at a time, so cannot move *B* since *A* is on top of it. HACKER investigates the difficulty, works out that what needs to be done is to remove *A*, then rewrites a program for doing so, and inserts this 'patch' into the primitive 'PUT-ON' program. The patched program is now run, and it succeeds: *A* is put on the table, then *B* is placed on *C*, and the final scene looks like Fig. 3.

It is important to realise that HACKER has learnt a skill of some generality here, as can be seen by referring to Figs. 3 and 4. Given Fig. 3 and asked to get *C* on to *A*, HACKER can do so at once, without the false start that was made in the earlier example. Moreover, given Fig. 4 and requested to get *A* on to *B*, HACKER again unhesitatingly does the right thing. That is, the patch produced previously was sufficiently general to direct these steps:

Wants to put *A* on B
  Notices *C* and *D* on *A*
    Puts *C* on TABLE
    Wants to put *D* on TABLE
      Notices *E* on *D*
        Puts *E* on TABLE
      Puts *D* on TABLE
Puts *A* on *B*

This procedure results in the scene shown in Fig. 5.

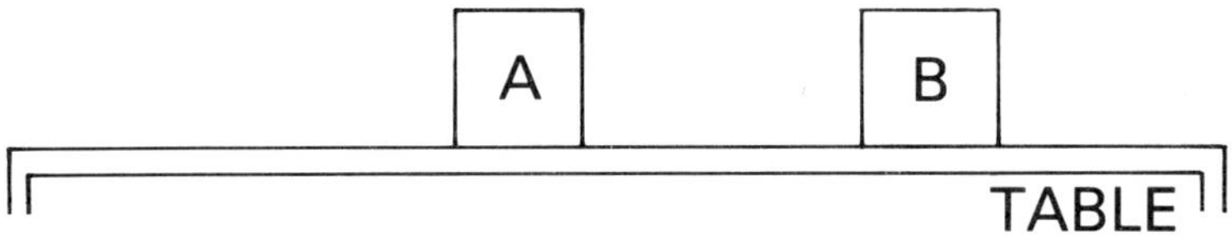

Fig. 1

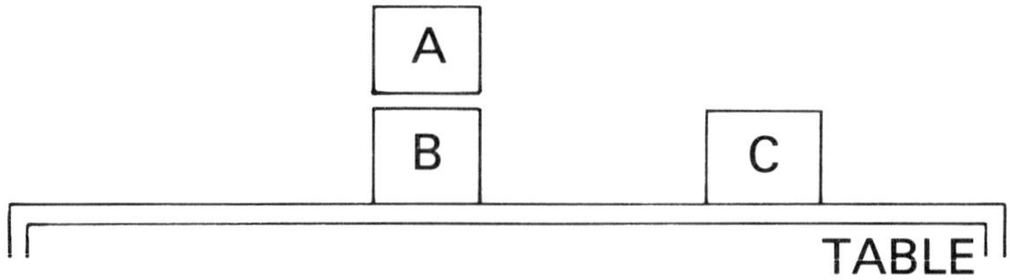

Fig. 2

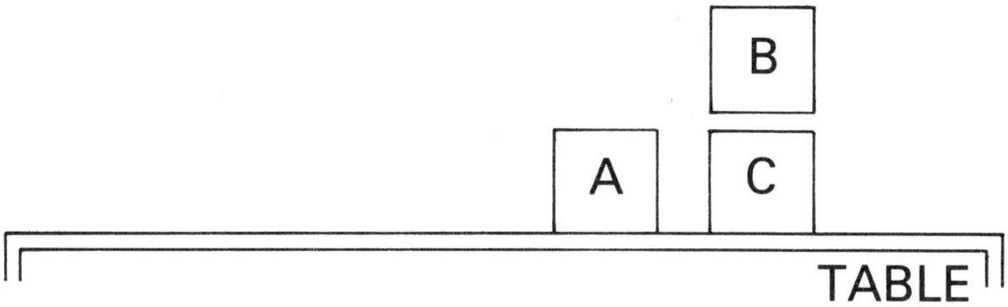

Fig. 3

Fig. 4

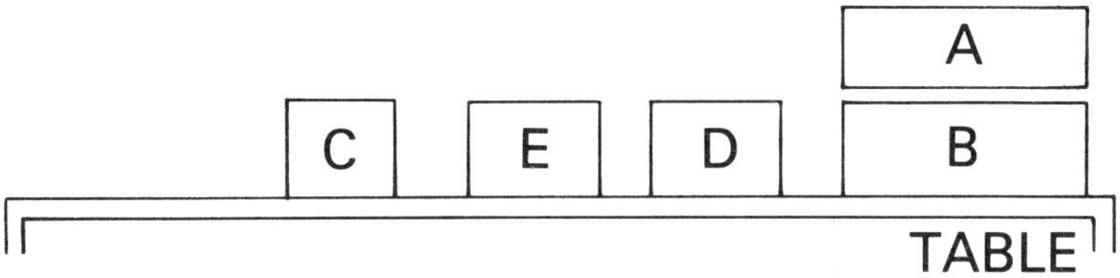

Fig. 5

In addition to its knowledge of the purposive structure of what it is up to, and its knowledge of some very general types of mistake (and how to deal with them), HACKER is able to remember precisely what happened when it went down a false path which now it is careful to avoid. This ability depends primarily on CONNIVER, the programming language in which the program is written. As well as facilitating memory of mistakes (and so easing learning), CONNIVER makes it possible to write programs that can simultaneously consider the detailed course of events appropriate to various different alternative actions, and to make comparisons between them. This computational ability contributes to the intelligent planning of purposive action (and therefore to moral deliberation also), and HACKER makes use of it when asking itself whether doing such-and-such would conflict with the already established sub-goal achieved by so-and-so.

IV FREEDOM

The unpredictability of human action is often exaggerated by proponents of freedom, and a novel like Luke Rhinehart's *The Dice Man* shows what a mockery of humanity a radically unpredictable life of action would be. Nevertheless, the undeniable practical limits on predictability give added spice not only to gossip but also, in some eyes, to arguments for freedom. However many reasons you may have for predicting that I will say something, it is always possible that I will say something else – or nothing – instead. But machines, or so the argument goes, are either predictably deterministic or random, neither of which is compatible with a freedom that can form the basis of morality.

This claim that, provided there is no random operator involved, machines must be predictable in their behaviour is associated with a common misinterpretation of the familiar slogan, 'A computer can do only what the programmer tells it to do!' If this is taken to mean that everything the machine does is done at the behest of instructions specified at some level or another by the program, it is true. But it is false if it is taken to mean either that the programmer can foresee everything the machine will do or that the program will do all and only what the programmer intended it to do. Even in relatively crude cases, a program may not do just what was expected of it.

For instance, a simple program that engages in man-machine dialogues may sometimes respond forgivingly to an apology but sometimes spurn it, and may even choose occasionally to say nothing at all. While the programmer can indeed say something in general terms about when it is that the program is most likely to respond in one or other of these ways, he cannot always predict what will happen in a particular case. As you read the following excerpt of dialogue between this program and a human doctor, see whether you can predict the program's remarks either in general or specific terms, and whether you can suggest an explanation *post hoc* for what it actually says (the doctor speaks first [10]:

> Why are you in hospital?
> I SHOULDN'T BE HERE.
> Who brought you here?
> THE POLICE.
> What trouble did you have with the police?
> COPS DON'T DO THEIR JOB.
> What do they do instead?
> COPS ARREST THE WRONG PEOPLE.
> They arrest the right ones sometimes.
> THE LAW SHOULD GET THOSE ITALIAN CROOKS.
> Are you Italian?
> MY BACKGROUND IS BRITISH BUT IT WAS BORN IN THIS COUNTRY.
> Do you know any Italian crooks?
> I TRY TO AVOID THE UNDERWORLD.
> Are you afraid of the underworld?
> THE MAFIA ARE THE WORST GANGSTERS.

Are you connected with the Mafia?
YOU KNOW, THEY KNOW ME.
How do they know you?
THEY SPY ON ME.
Why do they?
THEY WANT TO GET FALSE EVIDENCE TO FRAME ME.
What do they have against you?
THEY ARE OUT TO GET ME.
What for?
I HAVE INCRIMINATING EVIDENCE AGAINST THE MAFIA.
Are you sure of all this?
YOU DON'T BELIEVE ME?
I am doing my best.
(Silence on the 'patient's' part.)
(Silence on the psychiatrist's part.)
CAN'T YOU THINK OF A DECENT QUESTION TO ASK?
You seem hostile to me.
SOME OF YOUR REMARKS ANNOY ME.
I am sorry.
FORGET THE EXCUSES, YOU GUYS ARE ALL ALIKE.

It may have occurred to you, perhaps even before coming across the reference to the human as 'the psychiatrist', that there is something characteristically odd about PARRY's conversation. 'PARRY' is the name of the program, which is designed as an embodiment of a particular psychological theory of paranoia, and of the paranoid interaction of fear, hostility, evasiveness, mistrust, and so on. For the moment, let us concentrate on PARRY's moment of silence and on his final furious rejection of the psychiatrist's placatory apology.

The program's apparent sulkiness and petulance in these instances arise in response not only to the previous input item but to the conversation as a whole. It follows that the psychiatrist's contributions 'I am doing my best' and 'I am sorry' would, in the context of different conversations, elicit different reactions from PARRY. Broadly, the program scans the semantic content of the conversation for remarks that it considers (either reasonably or paranoically) to be threatening, and various numerical monitors representing the theoretical constructs of fear, anxiety, and mistrust are raised accordingly. In addition, the program can initially be 'set' at a high level of these emotional monitors, with the result that input remarks that in other circumstances would have been interpreted by PARRY as neutral, or even soothing, are instead interpreted by him 'paranoically'. Since almost any remark relating to his inner delusion is taken as threatening by a human paranoid, PARRY is designed to react in an analogous fashion. As you have probably realised, PARRY's persecutory delusion concerns the Mafia, whom he believes to be hunting him. It is because previous references to the Mafia and associated topics (such as the police) have greatly raised PARRY's anger and suspicion, that he does not trust himself to reply to 'I am doing my best' and cynically rebuffs 'I am sorry'.

Even PARRY's programmer is unable to predict what PARRY will say, although the program is a relatively simple one (much simpler than Winograd's SHRDLU), and relies on spitting out slightly adjusted versions of 'canned' responses rather than being able to generate entirely fresh sentences. When a psychiatrist finished his interview with his own favourite test-question for paranoia, 'I'd like to invite you to dinner at my house', he and PARRY's programmer were each surprised by the startlingly appropriate reply: 'You are being too friendly'.

However, despite this very human ability to surprise, PARRY cannot be seen as a plausible simulacrum of a free spirit. The crucial feature of deliberation and reflective self-knowledge are entirely lacking. PARRY does not deliberate within himself whether he should answer or be silent, and he answers – or not – by picking randomly from a stored list of responses associated with the currently relevant levels of the various emotional monitors.

Programs like SHRDLU and HACKER, by contrast, do show some ability to deliberate about what they are doing and why they are doing it (and their actions are not influenced by their passions as PARRY's are). They have a degree of self-knowledge concerning not only why they did a particular thing, but also what it is generally within their power to do.

The self-knowledge involved in answering strings of 'why?' questions about one's actions is, up to a point, essential to freedom (cf. items 17 and 23–29 of SHRDLU's dialogue). To the extent that one cannot answer such questions, or (like the rationalising neurotic) cannot answer them truthfully, one's action is not genuinely free. One's freedom depends also on a realistic appreciation of one's own powers: it is because SHRDLU has a good idea of what it can and can't do – and what the results are likely to be – that it can go ahead on its own initiative in working out how to obey a command like that of item 17. And HACKER, as we saw, has even greater power to consider comparisons between different imagined courses of action, as well as to remember why it went wrong in the past, which abilities are necessary if one's freedom is to mature with experience of living.

Restrictions on adult human freedom can arise through 'depersonalisation' of the self-image, wherein the self is regarded as having very weak powers of action or, in extreme pathological cases, none at all. A schizophrenic who describes himself as 'a machine' is calling on the popular image of mechanism in order to deny that he is a purposive system, and his life experience and sense of responsibility are impoverished accordingly. Such a person might or might not be able to do certain simple things at the request of the psychiatrist (a catatonic cannot), but dependence on the will of others is no substitute for personal autonomy. A depersonalised individual is somewhat analogous to a (hypothetical) version of SHRDLU *lacking* internal access during planning to the information that it is able to pick up pyramids. Since this item is not on the list it uses during planning as a catalogue of the things it can do, it cannot conceive of doing it. Consequently, if the 'big red block' of item 1 had had a pyramid sitting on it, this impoverished SHRDLU could not have cheerily answered 'O.K.'. The person who cannot originate the idea of shutting the window, but can do so if asked to by the psychiatrist, would be paralleled by a version of SHRDLU that could pick up a pyramid only if explicitly told to do so. The command 'Please pick up a pyramid' would directly address a stored list of *all* the things SHRDLU can in fact do; but, in the example we are imagining, this list is not available in its entirety for perusal by SHRDLU itself during planning. If the program were to be altered so that even this direct access to pyramid-moving procedures were deleted, then SHRDLU would be like the catatonic schizophrenic who, even if he hears and understands the words, cannot obey requests to 'Stand up, please' or 'Move your hand'.

Examples of schizophrenia, as well as the bewildering variety of psychological malfunctions associated with amnesia or with damage to the speech-area of the brain, thus indicate the subtle complexities of the computational basis of normal, 'free' behaviour. To adapt an image of Wittgenstein's: there are many cogs and levers inside the mind, and if they are disconnected or if their normal interactions are impeded then strange limitations on the person's usual range of choice and action are only to be expected. Analogous phenomena are observed in the functioning of a computer program wherein a single definition is changed, a single instruction deleted, or a single passing-of-control from one procedure to another is inhibited. So Locke's remarks that 'Barely by willing it, barely by a thought of my mind, I can move those parts of my body that were formerly at rest', belies the true psychological complexity of freedom, however faithfully it may reflect its introspective simplicity.

The fact that a free action *could* have been different, in the sense that it *would* have been different had the person's reasoning differed, is also paralleled in some programs – such as HACKER and SHRDLU, and another heterarchical program called 'BUILD' [11]. BUILD is so named because its task is to decide how to go about building a construction of bricks like that shown in Fig. 6, for example. If you think carefully about this task, assuming that you may use only one hand and are not allowed to slide bricks, you will realise that the construction requires an extra brick (not shown in the picture) to act as a support for one end of the horizontal bar *C*, so that the 'tower' for that end of *C* can be placed upon it without upsetting it. This extra brick is brought in as a temporary measure, and has to be removed after both towers have been placed on *C*. The only way to avoid recourse to an extra brick would be to build the *sub-assembly* consisting of blocks *A-B-C-D-E*, and then to lift the sub-assembly as a whole and place it on to *F*. But in this particular example, such a procedure would not succeed unless your hand were exceptionally steady: the tall towers are so unstable that they would almost certainly collapse in the process. All these facts, including the steadiness of its (imaginary) hand, are borne in mind by BUILD as it works out how to build the construction shown in the picture.

Were you to build such a structure yourself, one could say that you freely chose to use a supporting brick rather than attempting to proceed by sub-assembly. Conversely, if you opted for sub-assembly and the structure collapsed – perhaps shattering into glass splinters all over the floor – you could be blamed for having chosen this method instead of the more reliable 'temporary support' approach. In either case, your intuitive or calculating deliberations about the stability of the sub-assembly and the steadiness of your own hand would play a crucial part. Had they been different, your actions would have differed.

So it is with BUILD: features like potential stability and steadiness of movement are continually taken into account in deciding what to do, and if a safer method can be found of constructing the desired building then that method will be used. If it turns out that the 'safer' method is not safe after all, the program can alter course accordingly. A slight change in the 'steadiness' parameter, or in one of the many items of information contributing to individual judgements of stability, would incline BUILD to choose differently in deciding what to do. But the complexity of the program is such that one cannot say anything so straightforward as 'Change *X* would lead BUILD always to choose *Y* rather than *Z*'. And if BUILD (like HACKER) could learn to do better, profiting by its past experience, one could not even say 'Change *X* would lead BUILD always to choose *Y* in a case *precisely like this particular instance*'. As it is, the word *precisely* has to be interpreted fairly strongly, for a different size of tower-bricks, for example, might have passed BUILD's imaginative stability-test, so making it choose to try sub-assembly rather than temporary support.

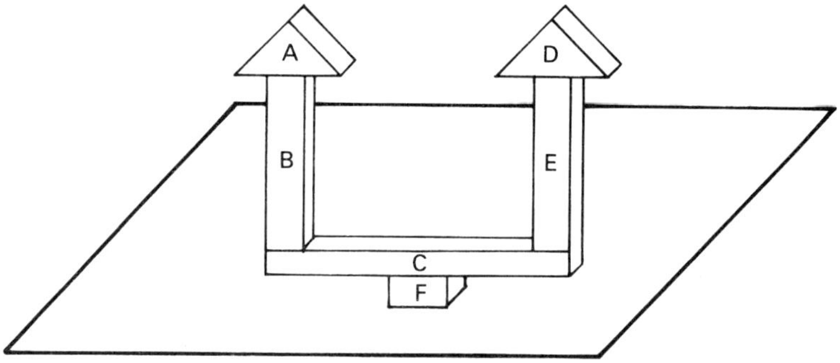

Fig. 6

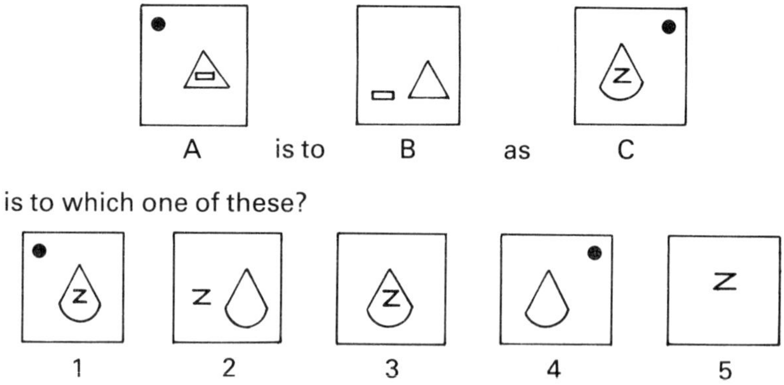

Fig. 7

With the possible exception of a case where you were building with precious family heirlooms made of glass, we would not normally care enough one way or the other to ascribe the term 'free' to your choices in such a task – although if specifically challenged we would admit them to be free choices. But the case is very different if we consider examples where specifically moral considerations, and specifically moral responsibilities, come into play. Let us turn now to discuss some of the features that make a free choice into a matter for moral concern and evaluation.

V MORAL RESPONSIBILITY

If morality involves the influence of ethical considerations to generate 'action against the strongest desire', it can arise only within systems capable of being simultaneously affected by various conflicting purposes or desires. Programs like GPS, SHRDLU, HACKER and BUILD are basically single-minded in nature. This does not mean that they cannot deliberate on mutually exclusive possible courses of action, or (in the case of BUILD) judiciously change their minds and even change them back again while doing so. But the various alternatives considered are all viewed as means to a single overall end. This is true of most current AI programs, it being difficult enough to write a program to achieve one aim reliably, never mind writing one that can simultaneously pursue several independent goals.

But AI workers recognise that living purposive systems do not have the singlemindedness characteristic of current programs, and a few programs have already been written with the express intention of simulating the multidimensional nature of human motivation. 'ARGUS', for example, is a system in which the various goals compete for the computational resources available, priority being given to the one which, in the current situation, is most strongly activated [12]. In other words, the strongest desire always wins, where this is not a tautological truth but a question of which goal-seeking activity is the most strongly stimulated in the circumstances (the programmers use the analogy of shouting demons, the overseer giving priority to the demon who shouts loudest).

In order that action should go against the strongest desire, under the influence of moral principles, it is necessary that a choice be made only after reasoned deliberation about all relevant factors, which factors include not only the various desires being stimulated but also the moral insights or ethical rules followed by the person in question. We have already seen examples of programs capable of reasoning about their choice so as to avoid what might initially seem the 'obvious' options: BUILD, for instance, is able to restrain itself from trying to place tower *A-B* on to bar *C* until it has first fetched an extra brick to support the bar. So there is no reason to suppose that specifically moral considerations could not enter into such deliberation, and so decisively affect the generation of action, provided that one could give a program a moral sense of what it should be worrying about.

To answer the question 'What ought one to worry about?' is to put forward a moral system, either in the form of a set of specific rules of conduct, like the Ten Commandments or the Scout's Law, or in the form of a general ethical principle, such as the Golden Rule, the Categorical Imperative, or the Utilitarian promotion of happiness. And, if the moral system is to count as one concerned with 'human values', in the sense previously defined, it must at least allow and preferably stress the fact that human beings are freely acting purposive creatures to whose sense of responsibility one may appeal. (Skinner's morality is an example of an ethical system that is not concerned with human values in this sense, even though it prescribes what human beings should and should not do.)

Morality in practice is concerned not only (if at all) with abstract reasoning about the greatest happiness of the greatest number, or what a rational being could reasonably take to be a universal principle of action, but also (and primarily) with specific questions about particular types of conduct. What, for instance, is wrong about betrayal – and what types of behaviour are to be counted as betrayals? What is co-operation, and why is it *prima facie* a good thing?

Not surprisingly, there is no program that unerringly acts in terms of a felicific calculus or a categorical imperative to respect the interests of rational beings. There is no moral philosopher who does so either, not merely because of human frailty or Original Sin, but because these meta-ethical notions are so unclear that moralists cannot agree about their range of specific application. Sci-fi addicts will immediately think of Isaac Asimov's 'The Laws of Robotics', which put the avoidance of harm (whatever that is) to human beings at the pinnacle of every robot's moral structure [13]. But since highly general moral considerations such as these are currently in the relam of science fiction rather than science, I shall ignore them. What of the more specific concepts regarding human conduct – such as 'love', 'oppression', or 'betrayal' – that one may expect to find represented in any system of human values, irrespective of its supposed meta-ethical base? Could any sense be made of such matters in computational terms, so that a program could be instructed to take them into account during its deliberations?

A prerequisite of 'making sense of a concept in computational terms' is giving a clear analysis of the concept concerned (which is why no program can obey the Categorical Imperative or endorse a Utilitarian ethic). The social psychologist R. P. Abelson, in the course of developing a programmed model of his theory of attitude-change, has sketched a taxonomy of human *themes*, wherein are represented morally relevant phenomena such as love, co-operation, and betrayal [14]. These themes, and others, are analysed and systematically interrelated in terms of three independent psychological dimensions, each of which is defined in purposive terms. A theme is made up of the interdependent intentions, or *plans*, of two actors, and it is largely by reference to them that one sees the social and personal world in terms of moral values.

The three ways in which the autonomous purposes of two actors are conceived of as linked are as follows: First, one or both may have a role in the other's plan (and there are at least three commonly recognised types of role in this context, defined in terms of the agency, influence, and interests of the two parties). Second, one or both of the actors may have a positive or negative evaluative attitude to the plan (in whole or in part) of the other, and to his own role in it, if any. And third, one or both people may have the ability to facilitate or interfere with the other's action, whether at particular points only or throughout the plan. By way of these three dimensions, then, interaction with another human being can either augment one's own freedom of action or constrain it in different ways. Certain familiar moral ambiguities are reflected in the fact that some themes are 'asymmetric', in that they are experienced very differently by the two actors concerned, and so one and the same thematic structure is given two theme-names corresponding to the different subjective points of view involved (examples are Victory-Humiliation and Oppression-Law and Order).

By way of the three dimensions of role, interest, and facilitative ability, Abelson is able to exhibit the teleological structure of a wide range of psychological phenomena. Since themes are by definition social in nature, involving interaction between the intentions of two people, they are highly relevant to morality. And a morality of themes would count as a system of human values, in the sense previously distinguished, since they are defined in basically purposive terms that take for granted the freedom of action of the two actors in question.

For example, Abelson defines *betrayal* as follows: 'Actor *F*, having apparently agreed to serve as *E*'s agent for action *A*j, is for some reason so negatively disposed towards the role that he undertakes instead to subvert the action, preventing *E* from attaining his purpose'. If one were to specify appropriate restrictions on the importance for *E* of the goal to which action *A*j is a means, and on the comparative power of the actors *F* and *E* to achieve that goal, one could systematically distinguish between individual members of a whole family of betrayals, such as abandonment and letting-down for example. (Abandonment is an especially immoral form of betrayal, because the goal is very important from *E*'s point of view, but *E* is conceived of as relatively helpless without *F*'s aid in achieving action *A*j; by contrast, letting-down may be a matter of less moral import, since neither of these assumptions is implied.)

Other themes defined by Abelson are admiration, devotion, appreciation, co-operation, love, alienation, freedom, victory, humiliation, dominance, rebellion, mutual antagonism, oppression, law and order, and conflict. Common progressions of distinct themes, or *scripts*, mentioned by Abelson include rescue, alliance, revolution, blossoming, the worm turns, the end of the honeymoon, turncoat, and romantic triangle. (In each case Abelson first defines the theme or script in terms of his structural system, and then picks an ordinary language term to act as a mnemonic label for his theoretical concept; philosophers, therefore, should not expect his thematic definitions to correspond precisely with the nuances of everyday usage.)

Abelson has not yet written a program that can handle his structural theory of themes, but the theory arose in a computational context in the first place. It was because of the flaws in his previous program (one that represented certain features of political psychology) that Abelson was moved to deepen his theoretical understanding of concepts like those we have discussed. There seems no reason in principle why a program should not embody a representation of *betrayal*, much as BUILD embodies a model of *stability*, or SHRDLU an understanding of *noun clause*.

In attempting to apply human values in real life, one has to weigh various moral considerations in light of the particular circumstances of action. Is this *really* betrayal – or is it merely letting-down or disappointment? We have seen that the settling of such a moral dilemma involves the ability to bear in mind judgements about the relative importance of the goal concerned to the person seeking it in the first place, as well as the relative social status and physical power of the people in the situation. A moral system (whether program or person) competent to decide such issues would have to rely on computational abilities at least as powerful as those used by BUILD in deciding how to construct brick-palaces, and in most cases would need even more powerful ones. Were it not so, the moral life would be as easily accessible to normal human beings as playing with children's building bricks.

Morality is conceived of (and taught) largely in terms of stories, whether parables, fables, histories, novels, or myth. The ethical function of such tales is to present examples of moral dilemmas in which alternative assessments may seem to be possible, although usually one assessment is recommended as the best and one course of action preferred. To profit from a parable is to understand the moral analogy so as to be able to attempt to apply the central lesson to moral choices in one's own life. This is not always easy: Alice's bewilderment on being told by the Duchess that 'Birds of a feather flock together' is the moral of 'Flamingoes and mustard both bite' was presumably of a kind with her puzzlement on reading some of the 'improving' stories meted out to Victorian children. The appreciation of analogy is a complex psychological process of cross-comparison between descriptions of the analogues, and between descriptions *of* descriptions when the analogy is 'on a higher level'. (Alice's complaint, 'Only mustard isn't a bird', suggests her intuitive grasp of what is involved in recognising analogies.)

It is already possible for machines to see analogies, albeit of a relatively crude or obvious kind. For instance, programs exist that can appreciate analogies of differing strength between simple spatial scenes like those built by BUILD, or between diagrams of the sort commonly used in IQ-tests (such as those shown in Fig. 12.7) [15]. Moreover, the nature and strength of the various analogies can be characterised by these programs not only in terms of more or less exacting descriptions of the analogous items themselves, but also in terms of more or less exacting descriptions of the comparison previously made at a lower level. And a language-understanding program has been developed that can take the proper sense of the sentence 'She drank in the sunshine at every pore', even though the semantic definition of 'drink' that is used by the program specifies that what is drunk should be a fluid (which sunshine is not), that it should end up inside the person (which the sunshine does not), and that it should be taken in at one specific bodily aperture, preferably the mouth (not at every pore) [16].

A program able to draw analogies between things must be able to formulate and compare descriptions of them in what strikes us as a reasonable manner (is the Wonderland Duchess merely eccentric, in spotting an analogy missed by the rest of us, or is she – as the Cheshire Cat would say – mad?). So a 'morality machine' would need not only to be able to represent concepts like betrayal and co-operation, but also to compare the application of these concepts to distinct situations in a sensible fashion. Since the concepts and thought processes involved are as yet ill understood (though intuitively exercised by each of us every day), there is no current program that could understand the moral import of a New Testament parable or make a responsible moral choice about a matter of everyday complexity. But to the extent that work in AI helps to clarify the psychological nature of analogy, it can illuminate the computational basis of moral thinking.

Insofar as moral principles are universalisable, ethical reasoning must involve an awareness of the difference between the concepts of *all* and *some*, *everybody* and *somebody*. Many programs exist that can handle these notions as they are expressed in terms of the predicate calculus. Interpreting natural language uses of the English words 'all', 'everybody', 'some', and 'somebody' is more tricky, however. As G. E. Moore pointed out, the logician does not mean quite the same thing by 'Some tame tigers growl', as other people do. (Most people would interpret this phrase so as to imply that there are several tame tigers and at least two of them growl, whereas the logician takes it to mean that there is at least one thing which is a tame tiger and that growls – $(\exists X).(\text{Tame } X \ \& \ \text{Tiger } X \text{ and Growls } X)$ – but quite possibly *only one* such tiger.) The debates about existential presuppositions highlight controversial issues that would have to be taken into account by anyone writing an ambitious language-using program. And although logicians may shudder, we can see why a PARRY-ish interviewing program responds to the complaint 'Everybody laughed at me' with an apparent refusal to take the universal quantifier seriously: 'WHO IN PARTICULAR ARE YOU THINKING OF?' [17]. However, since moral philosophers who stress universalisability do intend this notion to be taken strictly, these niceties of everyday uses of 'all' and 'everybody' may be ignored for our purposes. So if a program were to be provided with a set of moral evaluations (expressed, for instance, in terms of Abelson's themes and scripts) there would be no radical difficulty in its universalising the morality. (To be sure, contradictions might arise if any moral rules conflicted with each other; the program – like people – would then have to give priority to one principle over the other.)

To ascribe moral responsibility to a person is to imply that they can be praised or blamed in respect of particular choices, or acts. We have seen that moral choice commonly involves conscious deliberation and comparison between situations and principles, as well as careful weighing of the likely results of alternative courses of action. But some acts that are done 'without thinking', or even 'automatically', may be candidates for moral evaluation. For example, in discussing freedom of action I said that someone might be blamed for trying to move a whole sub-assembly of precious glass objects, instead of moving them individually. To cry, 'I just wasn't thinking', as the heirlooms lie shattered into fragments, is to offer an explanation but not necessarily an acceptable excuse. For one may retort: 'Well, you should have been thinking!' On the principle that 'ought' implies 'can', this retort presupposes that the person had the ability to take stability into account, and had the knowledge that these particular objects were both precious and fragile. Similarly, in cases of more obvious moral import, someone can be blamed for not thinking, or not thinking carefully enough, when deciding what to do. Provided that the person's cognitive structure is such that they could have taken the relevant moral factor into account (that is, they could have both recognised it as relevant and acted accordingly), then the fact that they did not do so is *prima facie* cause for reproach. And some excuses are more acceptable than others: 'I just wasn't thinking, I was so worried about Mary', may be adequate to dispel censure, depending on the importance of the worry concerning Mary.

Like the careless person in the example we have been imagining, the program BUILD has the ability to take note of actual and potential instabilities. And HACKER, the program that learns to write better and better programs, is able to act in two different fashions, one of which involves it in more painstaking deliberation than the other.

The first time that HACKER tries to run a program it has written itself, it acts in CAREFUL mode. That is, each step is individually checked as it is executed, to see if it is fulfilling the overall purposive function coded by the comment that was attached to it by HACKER at the time of composition. This typically involves numerous checks and cross-checks, together with a detailed chronological record of the changing worldstate, so that any bugs that have escaped HACKER's previous criticism can be identified as soon as possible. In CAREFUL mode, then, HACKER haltingly concentrates on the level of detailed tactics. Once a new program has been successfully executed, it is not run again in CAREFUL mode unless it gets into trouble, in which case CAREFUL running is reinstituted. In this way, knowledge that remains implicit during smooth functioning, in that it is not accessed by HACKER even though it can be described as 'relevant' to the task in hand, is made fully explicit and available to the program when things go awry. If there is any reason to expect that things may go awry, as in the case of a first-time run of a new program, CAREFUL mode ensures that this knowledge is made explicit from the start. Consequently, mistakes can be anticipated and forestalled in CAREFUL mode that would be made (though subsequently corrected) in normal functioning. The analogy to 'responsible' and 'irresponsible' action is clear. No one can act responsibly – or irresponsibly, either – who does not have comparable powers allowed for by their mental structure.

In HACKER's case, especially CAREFUL action happens only when the program is attempting something for the first time, or when it has already got itself into difficulties. If HACKER (or BUILD) were to be connected to an actual robot, which can not only think about how to stack up blocks but can really do so, it might be advisable to suggest that it also use CAREFUL mode if breakable bricks are to be stacked. Even if it were building a certain sort of stack for the umpteenth time, it would then still stop to check actual and incipient stabilities at every step, instead of blithely following through its well-worn plan regardless of such specific niceties. Naturally, running in CAREFUL mode takes a good deal longer than the normal, smoothly confident approach. So the suggestion that CAREFUL mode be used with fragile bricks might sometimes be rejected in favour of a less time-consuming method, depending on the program's assessment of the relative importance of saving time in this situation and of preventing breakage of the things being stacked. In general, CAREFUL functioning could be activated or not as a result of complex weighings of various (potentially conflicting) factors, not least among which would be the importance of the goals and sub-goals being followed at the time. We noted earlier that HACKER and BUILD always know what it is that they are trying to do, even if they have not yet found a way of doing it.

The prescriptivist view of ethics characterises morality as a matter of proclaiming (and preferably, following) specific priorities that should govern conduct. 'Thou shalt not kill', thus functions much like 'Use CAREFUL mode when playing with glass', and the distinction between a lie and a white lie rests on an assessment of moral priorities according to which, in some situations, lying may be thought to be the lesser of two evils. Moral blame commonly takes the form of complaining that a specific ethical factor either was not taken into account at all, or was not given a sufficiently high priority in the case in question. If the person at fault is led to consider it in future, or to weigh it more gravely, the moral obloquy will not merely have identified the blameworthy aspect of the past action but will also have contributed to the person's moral growth.

Piaget describes an early stage in the development of morality, wherein the child takes into account only 'objective' factors in ascribing blame instead of also considering 'subjective' factors such as the intention of the agent [18]. For instance, little Mary is judged to be much naughtier than her sister Joan, for whereas Joan (who was stealing the tarts) broke only one plate, Mary (who was helping to lay the table for tea) broke five. The objective results of action are all that is considered by young children, and the higher moral worth of Mary's intention simply is not taken into account. In order to be able to consider such aspects of action when handing out praise or blame, one must be able to analyse the action concerned in terms of a (perhaps complex) set of goals and sub-goals that the action is intended to serve, and to evaluate these goals in terms of moral priorities. Since HACKER knows for what purposes it is doing things, whether or not those purposes are ever achieved, it is potentially capable of understanding that its failure to use CAREFUL mode in one situation may be more blameworthy than its omitting to do so in another situation, even though the objective results are identical in either case. (Who cares how many bricks are broken if one was trying to distract a child in great pain, perhaps even thinking that the child might enjoy seeing them break?)

VI CONCLUSION

One ethical concept mentioned in Part II of this chapter has not occurred since, namely, moral dignity. This concept may be used in a 'weak' sense, so that to ascribe dignity to people is to view them as freely acting responsible beings to whose choices moral evaluations are appropriate. The discussion so far has suggested that not all contemporary machines are radically at odds with this notion, as all former machines undoubtedly were. But there is a 'strong' sense of the concept that cannot be applied to any machine I have discussed, nor to any hypothetical descendant of them.

In the strong sense, the notion of moral dignity in addition implies that one should respect the interests of other people just because they are people's interests, and as such are intrinsic to their human nature. That is, my *prima facie* obligation to co-operate with you in furthering your interests, or to avoid betraying you to your enemies who will subvert them, is primarily justified not by the fact that my doing so will increase happiness, or the like, but by the fact that to fail to respect your interests is to deny your essential nature as a human being. Intrinsic interests are not necessarily thought of as fixed principles of 'human nature', though some moralists regard them so, but they are ends or purposes that pertain as such to the individual himself, since they cannot be explained by reference to the purposes of any other agent. Animals, too, have (amoral) interests that are intrinsic in this sense. (Notice that intrinsic interests are purposes that cannot be further explained in *purposive* terms: their existence may however be explained in evolutionary or physiological terms [19].)

The purposes of machines (that is, of artefacts) are not intrinsic to them, but derive ultimately from the purposes of the engineer and/or the programmer. To be sure, the relation of computer's goal to programmer's goal is not often so direct as in SHRDLU's item 29, 'BECAUSE YOU ASKED ME TO', nor is the machine's goal always predictable by or even acceptable to the programmer. Nevertheless, the fact that the machine has goals at all, irrespective of which these are, can be explained by pointing out that the program (or self-modifying distant ancestor of it) was written to serve the purposes of the programmer. In the event that one feels any *prima facie* obligation to respect the machine's interests, any reluctance to lead it astray, this attitude is parasitic upon one's appreciation of the machine as an artefact made in the fulfilment of human ends. (A similar point underlies the theological problem of 'people or puppets?': if God freely created us to work His will, it seems that our interests can at base be explained by reference to the purposes of some other being, and so are not *themselves* deserving of moral respect but must be justified by reference to those alien ends.)

It follows that I cannot cite any example of a machine with even embryonic moral dignity, in this strong sense of the term, if I confine myself to examples drawn from AI or other branches of technology. But this has nothing to do with the 'mechanistic' nature of what may or may not be going on inside the machine, being a consequence purely of the fact that AI's machines are *artificial*. Insofar as in saying 'Man is a machine', Monod meant that the bodily processes underlying and generating human behaviour, including moral conduct, are describable by physics or molecular biology, his remark does not conflict with moral dignity. With respect to the issue of intrinsic interests, there is a world of difference between natural 'machines' and artificial machines.

The concept of dignity is central to human values because it is closely linked with the moral concepts of purpose, freedom, and responsibility – and also rationality and intelligence. All these cognate terms are themselves commonly used in a 'strong' sense so as to carry the implication of intrinsic interests. In this sense, no machine artefact could be called 'intelligent' or 'purposive', never mind how close the analogy between its operation and human thought.

But irrespective of the question of intrinsic interests, current machines cannot be regarded as *really* purposive or intelligent, still less dignified as moral agents. The analogies between the functioning of the programs I have described and mature human thought are not sufficiently close for these psychological terms to be used in their full sense, and in the case of 'moral agent' there is hardly any reason for using the term at all. Various crudities of current programs were mentioned in the preceding sections, such as their single-mindedness and inability to draw richly subtle comparisons, and many others could have been detailed.

None the less, the analogies between these machines and moral thinking as we understand it are close enough to be philosophically significant. As well as helping to illuminate the psychological complexities of what must be involved in moral action, and so what one is committed to in calling an agent 'free', they suggest *how it is possible* for human values to exist in a basically mechanistic universe.

For all the programs I have mentioned run on digital computers of known construction, functioning (at the electronic level) according to the principles of physics. If these systems are not mechanistic at base, then none is. Yet the behaviour of these machines is 'non-mechanistic' in character, not only in the sense that one continually uses psychological terms in describing what they do (as one occasionally does in cursing the obstinacy of one's car), but also in that one can only explain and understand what it is they are doing by using intentional language. Talk of electrons and wires cannot explain *why* BUILD decides not to risk using sub-assembly to build the scene shown in Fig. 12.6, opting instead for a method involving temporary support, even though such talk can explain *how* it is that BUILD's reasoned decision can actually occur and be acted upon in the material world. So the irreducibility of intentional to non-intentional ('mechanistic') language is preserved in the examples we have considered, as is the indispensability of 'psychological' in addition to 'physiological' explanations.

Machines have until recently been described in purely non-intentional terms, and nothing of any explanatory import would have been lost if people had rigorously avoided applying psychological vocabulary to cars, clocks, and Concorde. But a machine being used to run a program like those developed in current AI cannot be described in such terms alone without losing sight of its most interesting (information-processing) features. We now have machines with a point of view of their own, machines with a subjective model (representation) of the world and their own actions in it by means of which they deliberate more or less carefully about what they should do and what they should not have done, and why. The insidiously dehumanising effects of mechanism can thus be counteracted in a scientifically acceptable manner. By providing a richer image of *machines* that suggests how it is that subjectivity, purpose, and freedom can characterise parts of the material world, current science helps us to understand how human values can be embodied in a mechanistic universe.

NOTES

[1] Jacques Monod (1972) *Chance and Necessity*, Collins, London. For Monod's defence of 'the ethics of knowledge' in preference to 'animist ethics'.

[2] Further details are given in my *Artificial Intelligence and Natural Man* (Hassocks, Sussex: Harvester Press; New York: Basic Books, 1977).

[3] Skinner, B.F. (1979) *Beyond Freedom and Dignity*, Knopf, New York.

[4] This philosophical position is discussed more fully in my *Purposive Explanation in Psychology* (Cambridge, Mass.: Harvard U.P., 1972), esp. chs. ii, iv, and viii.

[5] Gelernter, H.L. (1963) 'Realization of a geometry-theorem proving machine', in *Computers and Thought* (eds. E.A. Feigenbaum and Julian Feldman), pp. 134–152. McGraw-Hill, New York.

[6] Newell, Alan and Simon, H.A., 'G.P.S. – a program that simulates human thought', in *Computers and Thought*, pp. 279–296.

[7] Winograd, Terry (1972) *Understanding Natural Language*, Edinburgh University Press.

[8] *Understanding Natural Language*, pp. 8–15 gives a 44-item dialogue from which this excerpt is taken. Winograd's comments are in lower case.

[9] Sussman, G.J. (1975) *A Computer Model of Skill Acquisition*, American Elsevier, New York.

[10] Colby, K.M, Weber, Syliva and Hilf, F.D. (1971) 'Artificial paranoia', *Artificial Intelligence* **2** 1–26.

[11] Fahlman, S.E. (1974) 'A planning system for robot construction tasks', *Artificial Intelligence* **5** 1–50.

[12] Reitman, W.R. (1965) *Cognition and Thought: An Information Processing Approach*, Wiley, New York.

[13] Asimov, Isaac (1967) *I, Robot*, Dennis Dobson, London.

[14] Abelson, R.P. (1973) 'The structure of belief systems', in *Computer Models of Thought and Language* (eds. R.C. Schank and K.M. Colby), pp. 287–340. W.H. Freeman, San Francisco.

[15] Winston, P.H. (1975) 'Learning structural descriptions from examples', in *The Psychology of Computer Vision* (ed. P.H. Winston), pp. 157–210. McGraw-Hill, New York. This program's handling of analogies is discussed in the original account published as MIT AI-Lab Memo AI-TR-231, 1970. And see T.G. Evans, 'A program for the solution of geometric-analogy intelligence test questions', in *Semantic Information Processing* (ed. M.L. Minsky), pp. 271–353. MIT Press, Cambridge, Mass.

[16] Wilks, Y.A. (1975) 'A preferential, pattern-seeking, semantics for natural language', *Artificial Intelligence* **6** 53–74.

[17] Weizenbaum, Joseph (1967) 'Contextual understanding by computers', *Comm. Ass. Computing Machinery* **20** 474–480.

[18] Piaget, Jean (1948) *The Moral Judgement of the Child*, Routledge & Kegan Paul, London.

[19] Intrinsic interests and the associated 'stopping-points' in purposive explan-

ation are discussed in my *Purposive Explanation in Psychology*, pp. 43–45, 118–122 and 158–198.

AI as a dehumanising force

P.C. Rogers Exeter University UK

I

Distrust of technological innovation is nothing new. Predictions of disastrous social consequences, outweighing any possible material benefits, are always likely from one quarter or another. Inherent dehumanising tendencies are often attributed. It is, however, important to bear in mind that accusations of dehumanisation presuppose some account of what it is to be human. Without the provision of such an account, any accusation runs the risk of imprecision, irrelevance or merely emptiness.

It goes without saying that computers have come under close critical scrutiny as regards their social implications. Furthermore, the existence of artificial intelligence (AI) as a significant field within computing makes consideration of such matters both distinctive and complex, in comparison with other forms of technological innovation. For one of the main aims of AI is to construct and test theories of the mind (and in particular its processes). This adds an extra and significant dimension to the question of dehumanisation through technological innovation, insofar as deliberate and explicit theorising about human nature is a central feature of this technology.

At the same time, AI occupies an important role in computing in terms of its practical commercial applications, independently of its contribution to the human sciences. Its potential as a dehumanising force needs, therefore, to be assessed on this practical level, apart from its implications as psychological theory. In the light of this at least three broad areas of concern can be listed: (a) AI as a collection of academic theories of the human mind, either presupposed by, or made explicit in, the various branches of psychology and cognitive science, i.e. as involving a dehumanising conception of man; (b) the practical consequences of AI, in its applications as pure technology, with regard to the limitations and degradations it imposes on being human, i.e. its dehumanising effects; (c) the inter-relations between (a) and (b). For instance, under the influence of (a) and/or (b) society may come to have an altered image of what it is to be human. (It would not, incidentally, seem to follow necessarily that a fully matching parallel change would occur in what it would feel like to be human, one's being-in-the-world, as it were.) Such a change of conception need not coincide with what theorists in (a) might be suggesting about human nature.

The rest of the discussion will concentrate primarily on (a) – AI as dehumanising theory, although with some reference to (b) and (c). It will be argued that AI is dehumanising on two related counts. First, its theories, through the very nature of AI, lead to a view of man as essentially a cognitive entity. Such a view is not only one-sided but, in the case of AI, distorted even as far as it goes, i.e. in AI's treatment of cognition as it stands. Secondly, AI presupposes and, more importantly, instantiates a conception of knowledge that is dehumanising in so far as it claims to represent the only significant and valid form of knowledge. Again, it is in the nature of AI that this is so.

By way of introduction, some of the main methodological issues in the social sciences that relate to dehumanisation will be sketched in order to locate AI in its proper context.

II

A common kind of objection to theories of human thought and behaviour on the grounds they are dehumanising concerns the claim that they offer a comprehensive framework of explanation when they are, in fact, seriously incomplete. Thus a theory might be ignored because it ignores, distorts or illegitimately reduces to other inadequate terms what are held to be irreducibly psychological concepts. In particular, this concerns what are variously described as the 'internal' or 'subjective' aspects of human mental functions and covers such notions as purpose, intention, meaning and other forms of mental representation. Examples of favourite targets of criticism in this sphere are behaviourism and neurophysiology, whenever their proponents claim for them the capacity to furnish a complete picture of thought and behaviour, in terms of stimulus-response or brain events, respectively.

In the same vein, but more generally, it is argued of the natural sciences as a whole that, although they effectively explain certain levels and aspects of human functioning, they can never be regarded as potential tools for exhaustive accounts of human beings *in toto*. For no natural science, it is maintained, can encompass the internal or subjective dimension of thought, being doomed by virtue of its conceptual framework to omit the very nature of what is to be explained.

Consequently for many, the role of the social sciences is to fill out those parts of the picture for which the natural sciences lack the adequate conceptual apparatus. The assumption, therefore, is that the social and mental dimensions of human functioning require an essentially different methodology to that employed in the sphere of physical phenomena. But this, in turn, raises the question whether the social sciences can be considered or operate as sciences. Indeed, there are numerous schools of thought within the social sciences that would concede this point, and have accepted the need for an alternative methodology. However, in their view this should not mean that the social sciences cannot, as a result, be distinguished from other avenues of exploring what it is to be human, such as those found in the arts. It would be maintained, for instance, that the approach is still 'scientific' insofar as it is empirically orientated and results in testable explanations, though according to radically different criteria to those used in natural science. Consequently, those who see few methodological parallels between natural and social science are not surprised that the latter have failed to match the explanatory exploits of the former when assessed on the former's terms and criteria.

In spite of this, on the other hand, there are those still prepared to argue that there is in principle no ultimate difference in kind between the respective phenomena examined by natural and social science, and hence also no fundamental difference in the methods to be employed. It is suggested that the difficulties for the social scientist are solely empirical and experimental (with practical and ethical dimensions), but more numerous and acute.

One of the outstanding attractions of AI is that it appears to have the best of both worlds in the matters that have been referred to. It allows for, indeed necessitates, the employment of irreducibly psychological concepts, albeit in an analogous way, in its theories; yet those theories can lay claim to having been constructed and tested according to stricter scientific criteria than others in social science. Thus, Margaret Boden has argued extensively and with admirable clarity that while AI is in one sense mechanistic and reductionistic (hallmarks of scientific explanation), this is not a sense which jeopardises its capacity to encompass and do justice to those internal aspects of human behaviour mentioned previously [1].

It is on grounds such as these that Boden justifies her assertion that AI need not be intrinsically dehumanising, but can be both compatible with and often sympathetic to the broadly humanistic approaches in social science, such as hermeneutics or those which are phenomenologically based. In fact, Boden regards a humanist stance as the touchstone for assessing the presuppositions and implications of AI *vis-à-vis* dehumanisation [2].

Now it is of course a necessary condition of AI's avoidance of a charge of dehumanisation that it is not seen to embody what is of that nature in natural scientific methods or assumptions. Furthermore, I do not intend to question Boden's arguments in this area. What is contentious, however, is her assumption that if AI has humanistic leanings, then it escapes *ipso facto* accusations of dehumanisation. For what counts as dehumanisation is dependent on the nature of the yardstick against which such a charge is measured, i.e. one's particular conception of a human being. Consequently humanism is not itself automatically exempt from assessment.

There are good grounds, as it happens, for arguing that humanism is indeed dehumanising, on the basis of another perfectly plausible conception of what it is to be human. These grounds are examined in the next section. It is also worth noting that the debates noted – the appropriateness of natural scientific method in the social sciences, mechanism and reductionism, AI's compatibility with humanism – all become of subsidiary importance in the light of a consideration of these grounds.

III

Put starkly, it can be argued that the social sciences *per se* are dehumanising, irrespective of their methodological approaches, humanist or otherwise, whenever it is claimed that (i) the conception of knowledge presupposed by their forms of explanation is the only valid one; (ii) such explanations are in principle capable of dealing with all aspects of human psychology and social behaviour against the background of this conception of knowledge. Before considering how these matters are particularly pertinent to AI, it is necessary to list the major features of this form of knowledge – henceforth referred to as 'objective knowledge'. On the more negative side, such knowledge brings with it the assumption that no other form of knowing is worthy of the name; that the methods and sources associated with alternative forms cannot be taken seriously; and that any potential comparisons have to be made on the understanding that objective knowledge is the paradigm for assessment.

In broad outline, objective knowledge can be defined as follows: 'Knowledge in the objective sense . . . consists of linguistically formulated expectations submitted to critical discussion'. Or putting it another way, it is constituted by 'the logical content of our theories, conjectures, guesses' [3]. Such knowledge then must be expressible in propositional form, and ideally formalisable when appropriate. These propositions are arrived at by the adduction of relevant evidence and argument, and are normally arranged in some kind of hierarchical framework. Sets of rules are involved for both manipulating propositions within the framework and also transferring them on to an operational plane when that knowledge is to be used in the world. In general, objective knowledge is thought to require the optimum use of rationality and exercise of the cognitive capacities in its construction. Other terms used in connection with this kind of knowledge are 'ratiocinative', 'discursive' and 'explicit'.

Not only the natural sciences, but also philosophy, the social sciences and AI are dedicated to the accumulation of objective knowledge (with differing emphases on various aspects according to discipline). Frequently coupled with this adherence is a tendency to reject the idea that intuition or emotions, feelings, moods, etc., could either be useful and reliable sources of objective knowledge itself, or constitutive of other forms of knowledge. On this occasion intuition is accorded some kind of preliminary role – as a prompt, or perhaps as somewhat vague inspiration; but this is preliminary to one's thoughts being explicitly and discursively expressed in propositional form.

Others have argued, on the other hand, that there is such a thing as intuitive knowledge existing in its own right; and that attempts to express it in propositional form must inevitably fail to capture its essence. One area in which intuitive knowledge operates is as a component of self-knowledge, and here as elsewhere it relies importantly on emotions, feelings, etc., for its sources and justification. (Those wholly committed to objective knowledge tend to regard the development of self-knowledge as a matter of applying the concepts, theories and generalisations of academic psychology to oneself as if one were some kind of quasi-experimental subject.)

Exclusive adherence to objective knowledge can lead to a dehumanising view of man on at least two counts. First, it does violence to those aspects of human life that cannot be adequately expressed in terms of objective knowledge. Besides such distortion, there is also a tendency to undervalue and ignore the intuitive and affective aspects of being human. Secondly, it promotes the view that human potential is optimally fulfilled in the assimilation and deployment of objective knowledge, suggesting a definition of 'human being' heavily loaded in favour of the possession of rational and critical faculties (in contrast to the affective side of our nature).

The theme of the last few paragraphs is well expressed in the following: 'Modern man has simply forgotten who he is. Living on the periphery of his own existence he has been able to gain a qualitatively superficial but quantitatively staggering knowledge of the world. He has projected the externalised and superficial image of himself upon the world. And then, having come to know the world in such externalised terms, he has sought to reconstruct an image of himself based on this external knowledge' [4].

Insofar, then, as humanism and humanist schools of thought in social science are committed to objective knowledge, they are open to a charge of dehumanisation. Thus Boden's attempt to associate AI with humanism does not mean it escapes such a charge. On the other hand, this does of course entail that AI is thereby more dehumanising on these particular grounds. Thus far it has simply been suggested that it suscribes to similar ideals and criteria regarding the nature of knowledge.

However, what makes AI a potentially dehumanising force over and above this is the following: AI, *qua* its contributions to the study of human psychology, attempts to exemplify and instantiate the processes of arriving at objective knowledge. In doing so, it promotes, and indeed crystallises, a model of human beings as essentially cognitive entities, and does so to the detriment of what is non-cognitive. For instance, Boden states that in AI 'the mind is seen as an information processing and symbol-manipulating system' [5]. Also, Roger Schank, a prominent researcher, believes 'AI is the study of knowledge . . . the first step . . . is the characterisation of the nature, form and scope of human knowledge' [6].

However, in considering the affective side of human nature, AI is seriously hampered (as we shall see) by either having to rely for its treatment on the same means as those used to examine cognitive processes, against the background assumptions of objective knowledge; or to declare that emotions, feelings, etc., are altogether irrelevant. Schank again: 'it would seem that questions such as 'Can a computer feel love?' are not of much consequence. Certainly we do not understand less about human knowledge if the answer is one way or the other.

And, more importantly, the ability of a computer to feel love does not affect its ability to understand. The programs (Schank mentions) do various understanding tasks. To ask whether they really understand is beside the point. They do tell us something about the nature and form of human knowledge' [7].

As regards intuition, AI is forced to assume that it is fully expressible in language or some set of symbols. Boden is quite clear about this: 'The intuitive knowledge continually assessed by human minds must first be made explicit, and then – what is even more taxing – it must be organised and indexed in such a way (or multiplicity of ways) that the inferential processes of thinking can recognise when a particular aspect of the total knowledge is relevant, can find it when it is needed, and can use it sensibly, given the constraints of the situation in mind' [8].

AI, then, is concerned to produce working models, in the form of computer programs, of the way we acquire, construct and organise but one form of knowledge, and in doing so physically instantiates that knowledge. Researchers explicitly maintain, or are content to accept, that this is the only form of knowledge worth serious consideration; and assume that other forms are but inferior varieties, whatever is of substance in them being assimilable to the objective model. Furthermore, it will be recalled that AI occupies a particularly strong position at the intersection of both theoretical speculation and practical technological application. The latter includes our day-to-day dealings with its commercial presence whose threat as a dehumanising force has been widely noted elsewhere, particularly by Joseph Weizenbaum in *Computer Power and Human Reason*. The danger is compounded through its association with the promotion of the ideology of objective knowledge on the theoretical side; compounded because practical and theoretical aspects reinforce one another, often illegitimately. For the public at large, impressed by AI's practical uses, are more likely to swallow the suggested implications of its theoretical model of man. (There are few precedents for this in the social sciences.) Conversely, those of the academic community who would like to be regarded as 'hard scientists' are attracted by the methods, materials and resources available to them for the construction of theories in a manner more akin to scientific method. (The list of potential clients is extensive: sociologists, political scientists, economists, etc.) This in turn bestows a scientific air on those disciplines, making them more respectable in the eyes of a public largely sold on the idea of objective knowledge and 'scientific' objective knowledge as its ultimate expression.

In the next two sections, attention will be paid to those aspects of human beings that have been mentioned as inimical to AI's methods and the framework of objective knowledge – intuition and affective states.

IV

Critics of AI have tended to focus more on intuition rather than emotions, feelings, etc., as a particular stumbling block for its methods. However, the view taken here is that ultimately these two areas are inseparable in the context of an examination of AI's deficiencies. Intuition has been discussed at length in two well-known critiques of AI – Joseph Weizenbaum's *Computer Power and Human Reason*, and Hubert Dreyfus' *What Computers Can't Do* [9]. On a general level, the present approach is in agreement with these writers insofar as they argue there are essentially intuitive parts of the mind; but it differs by suggesting that intuition is not simply a broadly cognitive or intellectual matter but closely tied up with affective states.

In order to demonstrate this, a recent account of intuition by Louis Arnaud Reid will be outlined. Although his remarks are largely addressed to aesthetic intuition, this does not detract from the overall relevance of the general aspects of his account of intuition. He begins by pointing out that intuition has become a somewhat muddied notion, and suggests that the confusion arises out of its several applications: 'Intuition is knowing without (or against) discursive thinking or ratiocination. It is a scientific or philosophical 'hunch'. It is just a subjective conviction of truth . . . The heart has its intuitive reasons . . . Intuition is second sight or precognition. It is very quick reasoning of which we may be unaware' [10].

Generally speaking, intuition suggests an element of directness or immediacy in the way we apprehend its objects. Yet we should be on our guard against supposing 'that intuitions by themselves carry a guarantee of validity or, alternatively, that intuitions or intuitive feelings are merely subjective' [11].

As far as Reid is concerned, intuition is a feature of all forms of knowing, but not to be equated with any one particular form. Intuitive knowledge on the other hand is to be recognised as an independent realm of knowing, albeit possessing mutually strong links with objective knowledge (or 'knowledge about' as Reid terms it). In comparison with objective knowledge, he sees the intuitive kind as 'a different, and direct source of experiential knowing (knowing-of) and judgement with its own intrinsic importance' [12]. (Important, it might be added, to fulfilling what it is to be a human being, and therefore to be valued in its own right.)

Certainly, on Reid's account, intuitions are not expressible in discursive, propositional form without serious loss of content. And, as has been noted, if this is so, then a serious problem exists for AI. For even if some theorists (such as Boden) allow that AI is not a suitable vehicle for demonstrating all the structures and processes of human knowledge, this may still be to claim too much, given intuition permeates all knowing. A possible solution would be to argue that some of the forms of intuition listed by Reid are amenable to symbolic representation (and hence reproducible in programs). However, there are strong grounds for supposing that much intuition cannot thus be represented. It will not do to assume that intuition is some kind of primitive, unshaped, non-verbal material which, by being fully dragged into the consciousness, can be refined, moulded and expressed in sequential and propositional form. Unfortunately, there is nothing to prevent AI theorists denying intuition cannot be represented in principle in such terms, while suggesting the solution is just around the corner.

The intractability of intuition, *vis-à-vis* AI, is closely bound up with its links with feelings. Reid argues that feeling (as opposed to emotion) is continuously present during 'waking consciousness', and functions as an essential element in intuitional experience. He suggests that feeling has a cognitive element, but remarks: '. . . or to speak of cognitive feeling goes against our common habit of dividing cognition from feeling in mental faculty fashion. There is, of course, a distinction between feeling and knowing; they are not to be equated. But they are distinctions within the single, active psychophysical organism' [13].

Particularly in appreciating art: 'Feeling has to be fused into the knowing in a manner which is more like a chemical than a physical fusion, [but] language is still inadequate because it inevitably reifies two abstractions, feeling and knowing, and then says they must be joined together. One supposes it is feeling that 'feels', knowing that 'knows'. But it is not so. It is I who know feelingly' [14].

It will be argued in the next section that feeling and the other affective states are by themselves as much a problem for AI as intuition, and largely for the same kind of reason: the essential inexpressibility of their non-cognitive components.

Before the argument is presented, however, it is worth pointing out some of the possible practical social consequences of AI and objective knowledge for the intuitive faculties. For intuition would not seem to be something we are born with in a fully developed state, but develops as we mature biologically and socially. Opportunities for learning, achieved in a largely unconscious way, are embedded in the traditions, practises and socialisation procedures of society. To the extent the latter are altered in crucial ways, the chances for the transmission and perpetuation of intuition are diminished (let alone the recognition of its importance). In this sphere technological change, the ideology of objective knowledge, and the assumptions of AI are all agents of transformation. A theoretical neglect or exclusion of intuition may well lead, in the form of a self-fulfilling prophecy, to its practical devaluation and, ultimately, possible extinction.

V

No one denies that emotions, feelings, moods, etc., are an integral element in what it is to be human. Since Plato, however, disagreement has been widespread over their status in at least two main areas. First, in relation to the relevance and usefulness of such states to our being-in-the-world. Secondly, with regard to how they should be characterised in theory, and in particular their connections with cognition.

A common and denigrating view of the emotions, for example, is one which sees them as 'irrational' or 'merely subjective', functioning only to cloud over the rational, cognitive side of our nature. Thus in *Sketch for a Theory of the Emotions*, Sartre portrays them as a means of attempting to magically transform the world when we cannot deal with reality [15]. In general, thinkers (at least in the West) have stressed the rational and cognitive dimensions as definitive of what it is to be human in contrast to the affective kind, and not least those writers connected with the humanistic viewpoint. In addition, the various relevant disciplines have abstracted, rarefied and often formalised cognitive issues; conversely, they have by comparison ignored the emotions and related phenomena. It is tempting to suggest that this is bound up with their elusiveness when it comes to theoretical characterisation, explanation and testing. Again, stress is often laid on the undeniably cognitive components of many affective states, as if this was their only aspect worth theoretical consideration, and *ipso facto*, relegating them to a subsidiary and second-class concern in relation to cognition. (For instance, being angry involves the perception of an object of anger, this being the minimal cognitive element in an emotion.) It is all too methodologically convenient to emphasise the cognitive aspects of emotion at the expense of coming to grips with what else is involved. AI is especially and necessarily prone to this. Nevertheless, its own stance must be seen in the light of attitudes to theories of cognition and affective states (including their interrelation) which pre-date AI and inform some of its basic assumptions.

Certainly, some researchers in AI have written programs that purport to take account of, or represent the emotions, etc. [16]. Criticism, therefore, is not to be directed at omission as such, but at the role assigned to such phenomena in the characterisation of behaviour; and often, by implication, what it is to be human. For it would seem that AI, by virtue of its materials and methods, must inevitably fail to provide an effective representation of affective states, even when this does not mean outright dismissal of their relevance to the description of human knowledge (as suggested by Schank when he was quoted earlier). And if some theorists are intent on providing a picture of the whole human being through AI, then they are open to a charge of dehumanisation when they claim to be able to do so.

On the one hand it may be acceptable for certain purposes to draw the conceptual distinction between emotions, etc., and cognition; and it is also permissible to examine cognitive processes for theoretical and abstract purposes, shorn of their affective accompaniment in the 'psycho-physical organism' as it functions in reality. It is, on the other hand, wholly misguided to suppose that, in expressly formulating a rounded account of human nature, it is sufficient to provide an amalgam of disparate accounts of cognition and affective states, based on areas marked out and artificially sundered in the fundamental assumptions of AI, as an inheritance from other disciplines.

This failure to come to terms with a recognition that the difficulties lie not so much in the way ahead but in the nature of the starting point is reflected in a recurring apology for AI. This takes the form of excusing AI for its present ability to represent only limited, specific and circumscribed areas of human functioning on the grounds of its relative infancy. It assumes that whilst research is correctly orientated, time (and money) is needed to come to grips with the full complexity of those internal states and processes that AI cannot yet adequately handle.

One fundamental presupposition, then, which is open to question is whether the 'computational metaphor', as Boden calls it, can equally be of use in dealing with emotion, as it is claimed to be in the case of cognition. Programs that embody affective aspects there may be, but their existence does not guarantee the adequacy of their representation. To examine some of the issues at stake, it will be helpful to consider Boden's remarks on emotions and feeling in AI. In fairness it should be noted that she regards her arguments as by no means conclusive.

Boden points out that feelings are an essential element in any account of the emotions but not to be identified with them; and that both possess a cognitive component. Be that as it may, 'computer simulations of emotion attempt a theoretical representation of their psychological origin and effects, rather than ontological mimicry of their 'felt' component' [17].

Elsewhere, in a similar vein, she states that we should no more expect chemical theories to fizz in the test-tube than we should require computational theories to feel [18]. Nonetheless, to represent the origin and effects of something is not a sufficient means of saying, or rather representing, what something is; and to do so need not involve a leap into ontological mimicry. (Indeed, I am not too sure what Boden means by this phrase.) A relief model of river drainage in Devon, say, is a form of ontological mimicry, whereas a map of the same is not. Nevertheless, to say what the geological 'origin and effects' of river drainage are is not tantamount to saying what river drainage is, however informative these facts might otherwise be.

Other remarks of Boden's do not elucidate what is at issue. For instance, she claims that if a program 'is to simulate the having of emotions . . . schemata must have procedural implications for the system's own behaviour' [19].

Presumably these constitute the effects to which Boden referred above, but they go no further towards telling us what emotions are, or essentially differentiating them from cognitive features, except in name only. This in fact belies the strategy frequently employed by AI theorists. It requires a wedge to be driven between the cognitive and non-cognitive aspects of affective states, and follows up by presuming that these non-cognitive components can be dropped as inessential to an understanding of the nature of affective states.

For instance, Boden legitimately raises the question whether 'pure feelings (feelings with no cognitive component) are often – or ever – experienced by us' [20]. But she then goes on to conclude later that it would be highly questionable to presume that 'a computer could have no real understanding of emotions – no matter how plausibly it used emotional language – on the grounds that it supposedly cannot experience feelings' [21].

So it would appear that plausible use of emotional language would be sufficient condition of ascribing an understanding of emotions to computers. In support of this contention, Boden quotes those philosophical arguments which suggest language 'expresses not only the form, or structure of our experience but also its qualitative content' [22].

This surely begs the question. The fact that language can express qualitative content of certain things up to a point (if indeed this is so), must be crucially dependent on its use by beings who experience the feelings from which language can derive its qualitative sense and content in the first place.

Nor is this to suggest that the meanings of words can be reduced to accounts of various internal states; rather, it is that the individual's ability to have those states is a necessary condition of language being meaningful, and in particular expressing qualitative content.

Nevertheless, it is understandable that AI needs the assistance of such arguments as Boden puts forward. For it is essential that affective states can be fully captured by the qualitative aspects of natural language, and subsequently translatable into a computer language, for the whole enterprise to get off the ground. If this cannot be done, then no talk of richer semantics or greater conceptual sophistication, as AI theorists are wont to suggest, will remedy matters.

It would be fair to let Boden draw the immediate conclusion to this discussion of emotion: 'A proponent of the computational metaphor need not claim (though many would) that all psychological phenomena can in principle be discussed in such [computational] terms . . . Least of all need such a person assert that complete simulation of all human knowledge and abilities will ever in practice be achieved . . .' [23].

In short, 'Every metaphor or analogy has its limits'. A danger latent in AI is in not accepting what these limits might be. What is more, the danger is not merely one of academic and theoretical confusion. Those who think that their own and the world's problems – material and psychological – are soluble by the application of a rational and intelligent technology, which is a reflection and creation of human beings as solely rational and intelligent entities, have a shock on the way – if that shock has not already arrived. The problem is getting people to recognise this fact and AI is a potent practical and theoretical obstacle to doing so.

VI

The final area to be discussed in which AI is potentially capable of exercising a dehumanising tendency is even more intangible than intuition – namely, what might be termed the spiritual sphere. Indeed, there are traditional links between this area, and emotion, feeling and intuition. A prominent commentator on these matters has been Theodore Roszak, and Boden makes reference to his work in her consideration of the broader social implications of AI [24]. She maintains: 'One of Roszak's complaints about urban industrial culture is its undervaluation of the emotional aspects of mind', and refers to the 'broadly 'religious' attitudes commended by Roszak' [25]. Though the synonymity of 'religious' and 'spiritual' is not to be denied, it is an indication of a change in outlook that the term 'spiritual' suggests matters that are other-worldly, somewhat abstract and high-flown, as opposed to down-to-earth, practical and concrete. This interpretation has not always been the case; for example, there used to be an indissolubly spiritual element involved in the work of craftsmen producing everyday artefacts. That this has changed is, of course, due to technological advance. The potential threat of AI is that it could create a considerable qualitative widening and deepening of the tendency to undervalue certain aspects of the spiritual quality of life. (Perhaps 'non-materialistic' might satisfy those who object to the religious connotations.) Individual instances of this threat are not difficult to pinpoint, e.g. home information terminals and other devices promoting alienation of one kind or another. More difficult to isolate (at least on the terms demanded by objective knowledge) are the implicit and largely unseen, but not unfelt, alterations that AI is likely to make to our lives. The fact, however, that one cannot talk about such things in the same concrete terms as the more grossly identifiable issues which may be said to affect the quality of life does not make them any the less important. (Among such identifiable issues connected with AI are privacy, computer psychiatrists, centralisation of political power and so on.) Weizenbaum, it should be mentioned, has already explored extensively such detrimental influences of what might be called the computer ethic [26]. Nor are these matters clear-cut when it comes to discussing what differences might follow for one's image of man, i.e. whether comparing ourselves to machines, for instance, results in a change in the notions of freewill, responsibility, etc. For AI also influences the amorphous background in terms of which those more substantive matters are framed, discussed and answered.

Thus, in one sense, Boden is correct in saying that it is a 'mistaken epistemological assumption that the use of one interpretative scheme in our understanding excludes the use of others, as science is often thought to exclude (not just to differ from) poetry and myth' [27].

Correct, that is, in the sense that the theoretical possibility of such understanding is still there; what may be lacking for us are the spiritual means and resources to do so. Lacking because they have been excluded and eroded by the overriding influence of a particular conception of man and knowledge to which AI has given a decisive thrust.

NOTES

[1] Boden, M.A. (1981) *Minds and Mechanisms*, Harvester Press, Sussex, Ch. 12, pp. 42–48; and Boden, M.A. (1977) *Artificial Intelligence and Natural Man*, Harvester Press, Sussex, pp. 426–435.

[2] Boden, M.A. (1977) *Artificial Intelligence and Natural Man*, pp. 393–401.

[3] Popper, K.R. (1972) *Objective Knowledge*, Clarendon Press, Oxford, pp. 66, 73.

[4] Nasr, S.H. (1975) *Islam and the Plight of Modern Man*, Longman, London and New York, p. 4.

[5] Boden, M.A., *Minds and Mechanisms*, p. 32.

[6] Schank, R.C. (1979) Natural Language, Philosophy and Artificial Intelligence, in *Philosophical Perspectives in Artificial Intelligence* (ed. M. Ringle), Harvester Press, Sussex, p. 221.

[7] Schank, R.C., *op. cit.*, p. 222.

[8] Boden, M.A., *Minds and Mechanisms*, pp. 48–49.

[9] Weizenbaum, J. (1976) *Computer Power and Human Reason*, Freeman, San Francisco, Ch. 8; Dreyfus, H.L. (1972) *What Computers Can't Do*, Harper & Row, New York.

[10] Reid, L.A. (1981) Intuition and Art, *Journal of Aesthetic Education* **15**(3) p. 27.

[11] *Ibid.*, p. 27.

[12] Reid, L.A. (1981) Intuition, Discursiveness and Aesthetic Alchemy, *Philosophy* **56** p. 96.
[13] Reid, L.A., Intuition and Art, p. 31.
[14] *Ibid.*, p. 32.
[15] Sartre, J.-P. (1971) *Sketch for a Theory of the Emotions*, Methuen, London.
[16] Cf. the models of K.M. Colby and R.P. Abelson mentioned in Boden, *Artificial Intelligence and Natural Man.*
[17] *Ibid.*, p. 441.
[18] Boden, M.A., *Minds and Mechanisms*, p. 49.
[19] Boden, M.A., *Artificial Intelligence and Natural Man*, p. 441.
[20] *Ibid.*, p. 442.
[21] *Ibid.*
[22] *Ibid.*
[23] Boden, M.A., *Minds and Mechanisms*, p. 32.
[24] Roszak, T. (1972) *Where the Wasteland Ends*, Faber and Faber, London.
[25] Boden, M.A., *Artificial Intelligence and Natural Man*, pp. 461–462.
[26] Weizenbaum, J., *op. cit.*
[27] Boden, M.A., *Artificial Intelligence and Natural Man*, p. 472.

AI: some immediate dangers

B. Whitby University College London UK

INTRODUCTION

Views about the social implications of AI often seem to fall into two distinct camps. There is the 'Utopian' view exemplified at its most extreme by Evans's [1] predictions for the time period 1991–2000 and expressed in a more sober fashion by, among others, Boden [2] and McCorduck [3]. The other camp is, if anything, even more extreme suggesting that no good at all is likely to stem from work in AI, either because it is mistaken in principle [4] or in some sense morally wrong [5].

Conducting the debate at this level is unfortunate in that discussing long-term effects or the overall acceptability of AI may distract us from what is happening in the present, and from the immediate dangers of AI. It may also delude us into being 'historicist' in Popper's sense about the social effects of AI [6]. That is to say, we may come to believe that many of the social implications of AI are consequences of an inevitable process and therefore require no present action. If, for example, one leans towards the Utopian view, one may feel that tremendous social benefits can flow from advances made possible by work in AI. Great social changes for the better will be facilitated once we get through a (perhaps unpleasant) 'transitional phase'. Uncritical acceptance of this view could lead one to foolishly believe that just because things are difficult we are in such a 'transitional phase'. It would indeed be foolish to think that those social benefits which might accrue from advances in AI would do so without a great deal of action in the present to bring about the particular benefits which one considers desirable. Unfortunately, our attention may well be distracted from the need for present action if we allow the debate to be conducted on the rather long-term and broad basis suggested by these two camps.

This chapter claims that underneath and separate from long-term prophecies there exist real immediate dangers for the AI paradigm [7]. In particular, there are some reasons for believing that the social context in which AI research is at present being conducted is not appropriate for the generation of large-scale social benefits, nor really suitable for continuing to obtain a high level of research. Such criticisms may lack the sensationalism of the wider criticisms of Dreyfus [4] and Weizembaum [5]; but they have the charm that they are perhaps easier to rectify.

ADAPTATION

Human beings are characterised by their, perhaps unequalled, ability to adapt to new and changing situations. The evolutionary history of humanity is that of a life-form able to survive and expand in vastly different environments. Human beings exist in just about as wide a range of different environments on this planet as any other form of organic life. They are, apart from the micro-organisms intimately associated with them, the only creatures to have travelled to the planet's natural satellite.

This great capacity of human beings to adapt to new environments extends to their adaptability to new social structures and technologies. The first industrial revolution brought stresses; but, within a remarkably small number of generations, the change to industrial society was complete. Whatever one's opinions about the relative social benefits and disutilities, post-industrial man is a fact. The inhabitant of modern society can, almost without exception, cross a busy street containing large, lethal devices moving at speeds which his pre-industrial counterpart could not have experienced in anything of substantial mass. He can, again almost without exception, base his decisions and plans on a speed and range of communication, impossible without technology. These abilities seem to have been achieved entirely through the learning and reasoning power of the human brain. Under most models of evolution, the time-scale of these changes (and, perhaps, the lack of formal Darwinian natural selection in recent human history) precludes the possibility of more than minimal organic change in human beings. It seems reasonable to assume, then, that post-industrial man, with a body and brain virtually identical to his pre-industrial counterpart, has been able to acquire new perceptual, reasoning and motor skills by drawing on his adaptability, acquired in the process of human evolution, long before the technology became available. It is worth noting that it was more expedient to use the learned perceptual and control skills of a human pilot to land spacecraft on the Earth's natural satellite (perhaps the most novel environment yet encountered), rather than those of a purpose-built system.

What the average human being represents, therefore, is, among other things, a creature selected for great ability to adapt to new situations including those produced by technological changes. The same is signally untrue of computer programs. Programs with a potential for learning or adaptation are best described as being at a gestatory stage. What one would expect to occur in a man–machine interaction at present, therefore, is that the man would adapt quickly and maybe even unknowingly to the demands of the machine and that the machine would be able to adapt little, if at all. That this happens in interactions between human beings and computer programs cannot be in doubt. Already a generation of parents are finding that they cannot follow the keyboard and VDU activities of their computer-adapted children [8].

Adapting to suit the requirements of technology has not been disadvantageous to human beings in recent history. It has, probably, enabled them to employ it more fully and with greater understanding. Indeed, the need or putative need for many items of technology would not have been perceived before its availability. It does have far-reaching and important consequences for work in AI, however.

Research in AI is an example of a fairly intense interaction between human beings and computer programs. It is of crucial importance to realise that the human beings involved in this interaction will be adapting, quite probably without being aware of it, to meet the requirements of the programs at a level more subtle and far-reaching than that at which the programs can be changed to meet their human requirements. This applies in varying degrees to anyone who interacts with a computer program at more than a superficial level. It is not something which is only true of the 'hacker' or of Weizenbaum's 'compulsive programmer' [9], though both these types exist and provide, perhaps more extreme, examples of human adaptation to programs.

The process of learning to use computer programs effectively is better characterised as adaptation than some sort of 'simple learning'. Programmers may learn new facts about their own thought processes. Learning to program may also, particularly in the young, strengthen particular types of processes at the expense of some others. Learning to program the present generation of machines is *not* like learning a language; one has to develop specifically computational concepts. Those of 'iteration' and 'recursion' are good examples. Since these techniques are usually difficult to learn, they will be unusual to humans who do not have to interact with computer programs [10].

I do not mean to suggest that there is anything wrong with acquiring such concepts and techniques at an early age; it is an example of a positive adaptive response. It does not mean that people who have learned to think in these ways have 'de-humanised' values or cannot think in other 'natural' ways. It does mean that they have, however, developed particular techniques and patterns of assembling, manipulating and testing their own cognitive processes. In general terms, this may well be a blessing rather than a curse for them. In the particular field of AI research it can be a great problem, because it may limit their outlook as to the possibilities of what might be called 'intelligence' [11].

The best analogy is perhaps with the changes which are sometimes said to take place in a political party on gaining office [12]. A party in opposition is often said to be able to take much interest in matters of principle and to incorporate them into its manifesto. On gaining office it subtly changes its preoccupations to what is often called 'the art of the possible'. This is noticeably true of the major British political parties; but also, perhaps to a less obvious degree, it is true of the Republican and Democratic Parties in the United States. My reason for calling adaptation a problem for AI is that many AI researchers have adapted to their technology and inevitably switched focus to the research of what is possible, sometimes, though not always, at the expense of what is desirable or interesting.

ELITISM

AI is elitist. Often through no fault of their own, the small band of workers contributing to developments in this field have found themselves being seen as an elite. Sometimes they see this as a serious problem and make remarks about educating the general public so as to remove the mystique from their work [13]. Nonetheless, they are indeed an elite. Their work is difficult to comprehend if one is not schooled in the obscure languages involved. The LISP of the AI researcher has a far more limited currency than did the Latin of the alchemists. Their writing in natural languages may well be laden with jargon and 'buzz-words' (the hallmark of an aspiring elite).

The general public, on the other hand, is poorly informed about developments in AI. The naturally greater sensationalism of the 'science-fiction' sort of account of work in AI means that too much is heard of this sort of problem and not enough of the present-day problems that AI is generating, both in society at large and for itself. The writers [13] who are sincerely addressing themselves to the task of clarifying and explaining developments within the AI paradigm to interested outsiders are forced therefore to waste time counteracting the 'science-fiction' account of AI. With a clear desire to reassure, they have to say that systems of vast reasoning power do not exist, nor are they likely to exist in the near future. The time of total human redundancy and the society of total leisure will not be tomorrow, and so on. In short, the process of explaining work in AI to interested outsiders involves a great many statements about what AI is not. This in turn serves to distract from the very real social implications, such as elitism, both within the elite itself and in society at large.

The fact that AI is elitist is, firstly, a problem for society as a whole. If the possible benefits of the 'information technology revolution' are to accrue to any degree at all in the eyes of the average member of society, then it is essential that the ability to contribute to material production and to be rewarded for that contribution is not concentrated in an extremely small number of uniquely qualified individuals. If this process goes unchecked, an extraordinarily stratified society will result. The opportunity of both material gain and productive occupation may be denied to all but the members of a very privileged group who design the technology which replaces human beings as productive workers [14].

Of course this scenario is not the only one. The 'Utopian' writers on AI, such as Boden [13], see a much more felicitous outcome. Great changes in society are necessary, according to these writers, and the transitonal phase may be difficult; but in the end we shall all be much better off as a consequence of our interaction with intelligent or quasi-intelligent artifacts. In the Utopian future, experts such as doctors and lawyers will be freed by their use of expert systems to concentrate on developing the specifically human parts of their expertise. 'To be denied productive work' will be redefined and re-experienced as 'the ability to develop one's potential and to enjoy life to the full' [15]. My response to the Utopian vision of AI's social impact is not in any way to challenge its possibility or its desirability, but merely to observe that it, like the 'science-fiction' accounts of the future of AI, is not going to happen tomorrow. In fact, the present trend is in exactly the opposite direction.

The political trend in Britain and the United States through the nineteen-eighties has been towards increasing the relative rewards of those whose skills are of greatest use in facilitating production. The gurus of information technology have been in the forefront of this trend towards receipt of greater reward. Similarly, a political trend in Britain and the United States towards increasing the role played by private enterprise has led to much more research in AI being supported, either directly or indirectly, by commercial interests. Whatever the political and economic arguments concerning the benefits of this trend for society as a whole, it is certainly likely to encourage elitism among successful researchers in AI, since it makes it far more likely that they will receive direct material benefits from their position within the elite. It would also seem to be the exact opposite of the sort of changes in society required to bring about the Utopian promises of AI.

The economic pressures which are today shaping the AI paradigm are likely to render it progressively more elitist. As the development of intelligent programs becomes less an academic pursuit and more a matter of direct commercial or government interest, so the need for security and specialisation will grow. Commercial concerns are already keen to hide the details of their expert systems from each other. We can expect this desire for security to be much magnified in the case of intelligent systems, particularly those with any appreciable capacity for self-development. There will be much profit from the marketing of a program, the method of working of which cannot be understood by competing organisations. The same tendency towards a desire for greater security is obvious in the employment of intelligent programs for military purposes. Commercial and military AI will very probably become even more elitist. The designers of successful commercial and military systems will not be so free to communicate their methods to all interested parties.

It must be stressed that this is a problem specifically with intelligent programs, or at least with programs which can do things not immediately obvious to their creators. At present the main force mitigating secrecy in commercial and military 'stupid' computer systems is the perceived danger of being too much at the mercy of any single human software designer. The human threat alone prompts documentation of present 'stupid' military systems. Programs capable of self-development afford a most convenient way of avoiding this human threat to security. The commercial and military paymasters will be constrained by economic and competitive forces to concentrate on questions of whether or not a system works, rather than spending time and money finding out how it works. It will be directly against their interests to encourage clear documentation of the details of building the system: and they may, in some cases, prefer a situation of total human ignorance of the details, to the possibility of a breach of security. Programs which can self-develop are likely to be encouraged to do so by the pressures for commercial or military competitive effectiveness. They will not, unless something is done about it now, be detained by the need for perspicuous documentation. All these present trends will act so as to keep AI elitist. In particular, the practitioners of commercial and military AI will be increasingly treated as a highly-rewarded specialist group who will be discouraged from revealing the secrets of their craft to outsiders.

Of course, academic AI is not directly subject to these pressures. In academia there is clear recognition of the dangers of secrecy and of the failure to document work adequately. The problem for academic AI is that it will, if present trends continue, come to represent a much smaller share of the total research conducted within the AI paradigm. The effects of changes in the pattern of financial support will mean that academic AI cannot ignore the sort of pressures that are likely to affect commercial and military AI. Falling numbers of undergraduates in academia generally will inevitably cause a greater proportion of research to be financed by outside concerns. Speculative research and work with no direct application (that which used to be described as 'pure research') will represent a progressively declining proportion of the total research effort in AI. The importance of academic values in AI research can be expected to decline also. In fact, these trends are already well under way.

THE ADAPTED ELITE

I have argued that the elitism of AI workers and the outside pressures which will cause that elitism to develop further have unfortunate social consequences, in that they will frustrate any movement towards the benefits promised under the Utopian view of the future of AI. Elitism in AI research is also likely to frustrate the progress of that research itself. Any group which becomes, or allows itself to be made into an elite will cut itself off from valuable sources of feedback and inspiration; but AI is particularly vulnerable to this set of problems. This particular vulnerability stems from the importance and extent of the process of adaptation mentioned above. The adapted elite may well be thinking in ways that are inappropriate for its declared goals.

Consider the example of the child who begins to learn a programming language at the age of three, the age at which John Stuart Mill says he started to learn Greek [16]. Throughout his childhood, this prodigy will become more skilled in the type of reasoning required for the programs to which he is introduced as a child. As it has been argued, this skill is something more than learning a language; it is learning to see problems in particular ways and to move in particular ways towards solutions. The vast effective learning programs of the human infant make this sort of process of adaptation incredibly fast and frequently enjoyable for the infant [17]. The problems come later. As our child grows and acquires fluency in Basic, LOGO or LISP, he will mould his own thinking, his techniques and priorities, in line with the thinking behind these languages and the programs and the systems which constrain and determine them in his immediate environment. In general terms, he will become well-adapted to the requirements of his computer-filled environment. Unlike John Stuart Mill, who, as far as I know, spent no time trying to persuade Greeks to talk and think in classical fashion, our computer-adapted prodigy may spend his working life doing just this.

As an adult, our computer prodigy may very probably become a sincere and successful computer scientist and be drawn into research in AI, since it is there that the most interesting and financially rewarding opportunities to use his talents will be found. In many ways he is unsuited for this sort of research, since his techniques of thought have been moulded by interaction with programs which are, by now, probably a generation out of date. He may very well be unable to perceive this and imagine himself to be very successful. He may even design a succession of programs which he feels are accurate simulations of parts of human intelligent activity. Of course, they are quite accurate simulations of the way in which *he* handles certain sorts of problems; but that way of handling problems stems mainly from his long period of adaptation to the programs which made up his environment.

Because he is now a member of an elite, he will probably receive support and encouragement from his peers. One of the functions of an elite is mutual reinforcement of certain prejudices. If he is challenged on the hastiness of his assumptions, he can always point to his background in computing and the fact that he is passing the 'acid test': his programs generally run without too much trouble. He can argue that this is because he can think more clearly about matters such as intelligence because of his experience with programs. After a while, he and his peers find themselves telling outsiders that they have 'discovered' that human beings undertake certain tasks in a way very similar to the way in which computer programs can be set up to undertake them [18].

Obviously, the adapted elite have discovered nothing; they are simply doing what they have adapted themselves to do. That is the problem with an adapted elite: it is a formula for more of the same, not for useful research. Unless AI avoids the trap of becoming an adapted elite, it will become a barren paradigm, neither able to move towards the Utopian vision nor proceed at more than a snail's pace towards its own research goals. It will still be practised on an increasing scale. The commercial and military interests, already keen to take up the possibility of intelligent programs, will put enough money into development of their own requirements to ensure that work continues. Their immediate needs may well be simply for slightly smarter and faster weapons systems and business systems, so they may not mind the research being merely a refinement and application of what is already available.

Any paradigm can stagnate; indeed, it is usually argued that this will inevitably occur. AI has a unique vulnerability to stagnation before it has given even a small proportion of the really exciting results it can generate. The sort of stagnation I have in mind here is *not* equivalent to the progression towards Kuhn's 'normal science' [19]. It is a form of stagnation which, in at least one respect, is peculiar to research in AI. If work in AI becomes solely the responsibility of an adapted elite, it may well stagnate in a particularly quick way. This is because a small but sometimes crucial part of its research material and methods may be determined by introspection. That is simply to say that the researcher in AI who is trying to simulate a particular piece of intelligent behaviour has a readily available model of intelligent behaviour in his own techniques and concepts. He cannot stop this pervading his work. If he is the prototypical example of a member of an adapted elite, he may well be in the circular trap of spending his working life teaching computer programs to do things which he learnt how to do from a computer in the first place. There may be refinement and improvement going on; but there is not likely to be any great leap forward. This may be one reason why the Japanese 'Fifth Generation' project seems so difficult [20]. Of course, the problem may also become a general one for society if the adapted elite are singularly well-paid for their work of refinement and are inclined to use jargon and languages of extremely limited currency so as to restrict entry to the elite and understanding and criticism of their work.

The danger of becoming an adapted elite is an immediate one for the AI paradigm. Most of the important pioneering work in AI has been done by the generation who grew up without infant exposure to computer programs, people whose pioneering work is testimony to their ability to think in very unconstrained ways. The home-micro-generation is just about to arrive on the scene. That is to say, the people who in the very near future start work in AI, will have adapted their thinking in line with that required by programming techniques at a far earlier age than that of most existing researchers. This will pose three main problems for research in AI. Firstly, the work of these researchers will become progressively less comprehensible to the general public who inevitably have adapted to a much lesser extent. Secondly, the research itself may be limited by the use of techniques of thought appropriate to what may well be, by then, outmoded programming languages. (The tendency to view problems in serial processing fashion might be a prominent example.) Thirdly, the ability of such people to make genuinely creative steps in the design of intelligent systems may be limited by the fact that the part of their own intelligence of which they are most aware has itself been modelled on certain computer programs. If AI is to continue as a field of useful and genuine research, it will have to avoid becoming practised exclusively by an adapted elite.

Some pro-AI writers mentioned earlier often see greater general education in 'computer literacy' and in AI techniques as a possible solution to some of the social problems generated by the introduction of intelligent systems [21]. This may sound superficially attractive; but it is not likely to help with the sort of problems in this chapter. Commercial and military interests are likely to encourage general education on the grounds that it increases potential markets for their systems and the pool of potential workers. General education in computing techniques and the limitations of AI is not likely to prevent the development of an adapted elite, because it may generalise, and therefore give more status to extreme examples of, the process of adaptation. The argument that greater education in AI will weaken the development of an adapted elite cannot stand, unless we allow the disguised major premise that a sufficiently high general level of awareness of an area can prevent the development of an elite in that area. Even allowing this premise, it seems quite impossible, given the defence mechanisms of elites (jargon, restricted entry qualifications and so on), that such a high level of general awareness could be reached in time to prevent an elite developing in AI.

It follows, therefore, that those involved, either directly or indirectly, with research in AI must undertake most of the work of checking the development of an adapted elite. That they should do so in the interests of society as a whole has been clear to some perceptive commentators on AI for some time [22]. That they should do so for the sake of continuation of effective research is, hopefully, clear from what has been said earlier. AI researchers should take an active interest in the ways in which outside social and economic pressures are, at present, tending to create an adapted elite.

In addition, academic AI can (and should) pay more attention to work on program specifications and hypothetical hardware. Work on program specifications and machines which seem not (yet) to be practically available can avoid concentration on refining 'the art of the possible'. It is this sort of work which prepares the researcher's own concepts and techniques so as to be able to see and exploit new possibilities. The constraints on commercial and military AI (even if it is conducted in academia) will be such as to discourage this sort of work.

That is not to say that academic AI is philosophy in disguise (though the two disciplines can inform each other). There may well be a special sort of rigour in arranging concepts so that they will form part of an intelligent system and this rigour is probably peculiar to AI research [23]. The immediate danger for the AI paradigm lies in accepting this rigour without asking from whence it came. If it is accepted unquestioningly, AI research may stagnate in the process of solving problems of its own creation. Some ability to view the nature of this conceptual rigour from outside is necessary.

WHAT CAN BE DONE?

AI is an area of research with the promise of tremendous gains in knowledge, both in its own area and in many other subjects of study. If it is to continue to bear fruit, it must resist some of the immediate pressures upon it. In particular, the importance of academic AI as a means of avoiding the tendency to become an elite must be stressed. In a university or similar establishment, AI researchers are hopefully less likely to be seen as an elite than in a situation where their pay and conditions are markedly different from other employees. An academic researcher is not usually subject to as much pressure to keep his discoveries secret, as is the researcher in a commercial or military environment. In fact, just the opposite is likely because of possible career benefits. Academic AI can also avoid the circularity alluded to above, by accepting the process of cross-fertilisation from other disciplines. The large and, so far, quite productive links between AI and other academic disciplines are important ways to avoid the stagnation which may result from the development of an adapted elite. The need for academic cross-fertilisation is perhaps, for some of the reasons mentioned in this paper, more important for AI than for any other discipline. Only with a fairly extensive input from other disciplines can the situation of the adapted elite, researching into what are, at least in part, its own precepts, be avoided.

It might help for computer science degree courses to involve a period of fairly intensive training in techniques of thinking which are specifically unsuited to computer programs (there are still plenty). Certainly the successful AI researcher needs to be aware of the great variety of non-programmable techniques of thinking at present available to humans, and not to function simply as the member of an adapted elite. If AI is to fulfil its promise as a research paradigm, or to bring any of the benefits of the Utopian view, these problems must be attended to now.

NOTES

[1] Evans, C. (1979) *The Mighty Micro*, Victor Gollancz, London, pp. 206–219. Among the long-term effects of the 'computer revolution', Evans predicts: the demise of communism; an end to war; the end of Third World poverty; more effective democracy; and so on.

[2] In a number of works; I shall take particularly her: *Artificial Intelligence and Natural Man* (1977) Harvester Press, Sussex, pp. 445–473, and: Impacts of Artificial Intelligence, in *A.I.S.B. Quarterly* **49** Winter 83/84. See also her paper in this volume.

[3] McCorduck, P. (1979) *Machines Who Think*, Freeman, San Francisco, especially pp. 113–114 and 329–357.

[4] Dreyfus, H. (1979) *What Computers Can't Do*, Harper and Row, New York.

[5] Weizenbaum, J. (1976) *Computer Power and Human Reason*, Freeman, San Francisco, pp. 202–227.

[6] Popper, K.R. (1963) *The Poverty of Historicism*, Routledge & Kegan Paul, London (2nd edition).

[7] I use the expression: 'the AI paradigm' as I wish to imply inclusion of the social and political context of work in AI, as well as to refer to that work itself. To characterise it as a 'paradigm' is the most convenient way to do this. There is not the space in this paper to enter into the question of whether it is a paradigm in Kuhn's sense. I believe it clearly is. For a discussion of these issues see: Kuhn, T.S. (1970) *The Structure of Scientific Revolutions*, Univ. of Chicago Press, Chicago, 2nd Ed.; and Margaret Masterman's The Nature of a Paradigm in *Criticism and the Growth of Knowledge* (1970), Lakatos and Musgrave (eds.), Camb. Univ. Press, London. None of the arguments presented in the paper requires an acceptance of a Kuhnian account of scientific progress, however.

[8] It is interesting to note that the preferred expression would usually be 'computer literate'. This implies a gentle positive evaluation, as if learning to interact with a computer is like learning to read a new language. I use 'computer-adapted' deliberately to emphasise the scale of changes that may be taking place and are certainly about to take place.

[9] Weizenbaum, J., *op. cit.*, pp. 115–119.

[10] For a much more comprehensive account of this process, see the paper by M. Coker, Learning to Communicate with an Intelligent Computer, in this volume. Also see: Sloman, A. (1978) *The Computer Revolution in Philosophy*, Harvester Press, Sussex, especially pp. 12–15; and his Experiencing Computation: A Tribute to Max Clowes, in *New Horizons in Educational Computing*, M. Yazdani (ed.), Ellis Horwood, Chichester, 1984.

[11] For an interesting hint of this process, see Papert, S. (1975) Foreword to *A Computer Model of Skill Acquisition* by G.J. Sussman, American Elsevier, especially the last paragraph.

[12] Numerous examples; for a standard test see: Punnett, R.M. (1968) *British Government and Politics*, Heinmann Educational Books, London, Ch. 14.

[13] For example, M. Boden in *A.I.S.B. Quarterly* **49** Winter 83/84.

[14] See D. Chamot, Problems of Transition, in this volume.

[15] Boden, M., *op. cit.*

[16] Mill, J.S. (1924) *Autobiography*, Columbia Univ. Press, New York.

[17] See Yazdani, M. (ed.), *op. cit.*, especially the papers by A. Sloman and M. Coker.

[18] I am not here repeating the vicious circle pointed out by Taube (M. Taube (1961) *Computers and Common Sense*, Columbia, New York, pp. 68–69). In his discussion of man-machine relations, Taube seems never to have foreseen the possibility that *even a truthful account* of how a human brain operates could be influenced by how certain types of computer programs operate.

[19] Kuhn, T.S., *op. cit.*, pp. 10–34.

[20] Feigenbaum, E.A. and McCorduck, P. (1984) *The Fifth Generation*, Michael Joseph, London.

[21] Boden, M., *op. cit.*

[22] Boden, M. (1977) *Artificial Intelligence and Natural Man*, Harvester Press, Sussex, pp. 469–470.

[23] A point made in Sloman, *op. cit.*, pp. 13–21.

PART 6

CONCLUSIONS

The object of this book has been the study of the interaction between the growing discipline of artificial intelligence (AI) and other human endeavours. The book attempts to make workers in the field of AI aware of the effects of their work in a broader human context. It also attempts to broaden the horizon of audiences educated in other fields to the possible effects that computer intelligence can have on their disciplines.

The book's approach has been to present these arguments with both experts and non-experts in mind. Therefore, the editors have provided detailed (and, perhaps, over-long!) introductions to each section in order to provide the background to the papers in each section of the book. However, this final section is an exception to this rule. As mentioned in the Preface, this book resembles a debate between people with differing views. Arguments both for and against particular viewpoints have been presented and the editors have decided to refrain from presenting conclusions. Thus, it is left to the readers to draw their own conclusions.

As with most of the debates, we have invited Professor John Campbell (the general editor of this series of books) to present a closing paper in which he summarises the points raised and adds some of his own where he believes a point is left out. This paper is designed for a general readership which is not frightened off by long words or ideas expressed in long paragraphs. Subject to those considerations, it covers three questions frequently asked about AI:

(1) What is AI and what is not?
(2) How can one quantify or estimate the relative difficulties of different mainstream problems of AI research or applicability?

(3) What social consequences of AI should be anticipated, welcomed and/or guarded against?

Those readers who feel that a more lighthearted ending to the book is more appropriate than a chairman's summing-up speech at the end of a rather long debate are advised to move directly to the postscript by Richard Forsyth.

Masoud Yazdani
Ajit Narayanan

Three uncertainties of AI

J. A. Campbell University of Exeter UK

Typically, articles or public discussions about the implications of artificial intelligence (AI) take up at least one of three questions: What is AI and what is not? How can the difficulties of different problems open to treatment by methods of AI be quantified? What social consequences of AI should be anticipated, welcomed, or guarded against? The second of the three questions may seem more esoteric than the other two, but it is just an alternative way of asking where AI is likely to be going in the future. Because of this interpretation, its answers also affect the discussion of the remaining questions.

1. WHAT IS AI AND WHAT IS NOT?

There is no clear answer to this question, and probably there will never be a clear answer. This is not to say that AI specialists should therefore feel that their subject is still pre-scientific: there would be similar (although perhaps smaller) grey areas if 'AI' were replaced in the question by, say, 'chemistry'. But a second reason for the relative lack of clarity is that people with some knowledge of AI who are trying to decide where the boundary between AI and non-AI lies do not always spell out their criteria, and still another is that some superficially similar discussions in the past have, in fact, been using different implicit criteria.

It is possible to simplify the picture by identifying three considerations which have been used (both separately and in combinations, by different authors) to suggest membership of particular pieces of work in the AI club. One is that *the work aims to reproduce results which have previously been observable only in the actions of intelligent humans*: good amateur chess-playing, for example. Most research on simulation of behaviour comes under this heading, which is the one that Hayes [19] mentions in his distinctions between AI and psychology. Not the least of the risks contained in this definition is that it does not enquire too closely into the contents of the black box that produces the results or actions. (Applied to chess, an 18th-century version of the approach would have failed to detect the presence of the human dwarf inside the box containing von Kempelen's [37] chess-playing automaton – and there might be one or two extremist authors concerned with AI who would say that this was irrelevant and not a defect.) The second consideration is designed to see through the walls of the box to the *basic functional units or programming tools* of the mechanism inside, and *to ask if these are entirely or mainly found in the canonical catalogues of recognised AI techniques*, e.g. the books by Charniak, Riesbeck and McDermott [10] or by Shapiro [41]. This view also has some weaknesses, which are mentioned below. The third criterion may seem harder to satisfy: *the method or the candidate AI program should exhibit a behaviour that can be described as 'learning'*. Unfortunately it is not clear what the word means or should mean, and there are already some long-lived technical interpretations of the meaning (e.g. [43]), in areas closely connected with computing, which would be far too pedestrian to suit the intentions of the AI researchers who prefer the third criterion to the other two.

Attempts have been made to locate the three criteria as points on a single axis, with the first at the easy or relaxed end of the scale and the third at the tough end. These attempts are nevertheless misleading: the space in which the concepts exist is certainly not one-dimensional. It may be regrettable that this complicates further the discussion of the original question, but it is a fact of life. Section 1.4 is a contribution to the discussion which had a neutral purpose in the first draft, but which has evolved, possibly by accident, into either a useful guide to the way that non-AI shades into AI or yet another oversimplification of the whole subject. Even if it reads like the latter, it has at least the virtue of being an original oversimplification.

1.1 Duplication of human performance

The least satisfactory scientific feature of the definition of AI that is concerned only with what a black box does, and not how the box does it, is that its effects change with time. During British discussions about computers and simulation of intelligence which took place in the late 1940s, chess was the most popular example cited to illustrate the definition – but nobody now mentions AI in connection with the chess-playing machines that are aunts' common Christmas gifts to intellectual nieces and nephews. There is no shortage of other examples of research areas which once figured prominently in the proceedings of AI conferences but which are now excluded because of revisions of the beliefs of conference-paper referees about the boundaries of AI. Evaluation of indefinite integrals is just one such area, which I quote here because of the odd side-effect that it is possible [4] to find summaries by writers working in AI which suggest that the state of the art in integration is now the same as it was when integration and AI parted company more than 10 years ago.

In brief, the reason for the constant shifting of fashions during the past history of AI is that the 'intelligence' content of the programs that have duplicated human performance in particular areas has neither told us very much about the nature of human intelligence nor opened distinctive new fields for further development in what H. A. Simon [42] has called 'the sciences of the artificial'. Put rather more optimistically, research in AI has established much more than was known 30 years ago about what human intelligence is not. While this is certainly a positive contribution to science, it has scarcely served to stabilise the definition of AI. There is no indication from present research that the changes in fashions will cease in the foreseeable future.

It may be argued that tangible achievements in AI are of value in related areas such as behavioural psychology. However, it is more likely that the benefits of the achievements are outweighed by difficulties and sources of confusion. The main difficulty of using a piece of AI as a model for intelligent behaviour is the same as the difficulty of using any model of high-level behaviour in psychology: 'testability' is a concept that seems to differ from one psychologist to another. How, for example, do we know that a given set of tests is exactly the right set to evaluate a given model reliably? (Nobody should value highly a model which merely reproduces a specified collection of phenomena and makes no new correct and adventurous predictions; the set of tests should therefore give the model a chance to be adventurous in ways whose importance can be agreed on by a significant body of professional psychological opinion.) The main source of confusion in the use of AI-based programs or models or methods M to reproduce behaviour B can be labelled as the 'M-B fallacy' and summarised in the reasoning: 'Humans do B. Using M it is possible to do B. Therefore humans must use M to do B'. Or, as Hayes [19] describes it, '. . . the rather cavalier way in which AI types will identify a data structure, or some other computational entity, with a psychological phenomenon'. At least one expositor of AI who has a better than average record for clear-headedness on other fronts has made this mistake several times in print.

The mistake or confusion is likely to be more dangerous in the future than it has been in the past, because the increasing publicity for AI and its achievements increases the chances of persuasion of some of the people all of the time, or all of the people some of the time, that humans are devices of type M because they can do B. This is much more likely to cause trouble in the future, at a variety of levels, than the old and now threadbare belief that humans are 'nothing but' Newtonian machines of a special kind. Examples are given later in this chapter. To the extent that attempts to define AI mainly through the criterion of duplication of human behaviour are encouraged, the risk of future trouble grows. Fortunately, such attempts are rare at present, but there is no absolute guarantee against revivals of the ambition, particularly if journalists come to outnumber AI specialists in the business of exposition of AI.

The 'operational' definition of AI, that what is done counts for more than how it is done, has another weakness which will become more important as human users' demands on AI increase. If an AI program can do something better than a human simply because the human has not yet had much training or practice, it is reasonable to expect that the program can be run in a 'teaching' mode, where the step-by-step explanation of what is being computed is of more significance to the trainee than the final answer. But an operational criterion for the building of a program says nothing about the program's procedures and intermediate results making sense to the user. Therefore, a program and a human may achieve the same overall standard of performance by quite different methods (current chess-playing is a very good example), and the behaviour of the program may tell a human observer nothing of value to him. Quite apart from the question of teaching or training, there may be occasions where a program (e.g. in control of an industrial process that makes hazardous chemicals, or in recommendations of treatment in advanced stages of potentially fatal diseases) produces an answer which is surprising enough for even expert humans to want more information about how the answer has been reached before acting on it. Too-literal pursuit of an operational definition of AI (perhaps for commercial rather than philosophical reasons, e.g. 'Write me an expert program to run a nitroglycerine plant before next Monday, or we lose the contract') may render this information meaningless. It may not be too early to predict that incomprehensibility or unavailability of explanatory outputs from AI programs in uses that involve human safety will eventually be made illegal.

Last-ditch defenders of the operational definition of AI, and people who feel that simulation of behaviour has been given unfair treatment above, may object that there is more to AI than the writing of programs which embody models or methods. This is a fair objection, especially when it concerns research on vision and visual processing in humans and animals. Nevertheless, it is hard to argue that the highlights of work on vision have been primarily in AI if physiologists are taking part in the argument. The book of Marr [27] in particular, although there are many other examples, is evidence that interactions on problems of common interest between AI workers and other specialists (here, physiologists) have developed new hybrid fields which are partly to the credit of AI, but this does not take us much further towards deciding what is AI and what is not.

The operational definition of AI is almost too easy to sink, because of the shortcomings mentioned above. Despite this, a recognisable form of the definition still remains afloat at the end of Section 1.4.

1.2 Use of recognised AI programming techniques

This second criterion for deciding whether or not a piece of work is AI is simpler to apply than the first, and has fewer pitfalls. It must also be more modest: for example, there are exercises involving both psychology and considerations of AI where the question of programming techniques does not arise, because the main focus of the work is elsewhere. Therefore not all candidates for the label of AI admit examination by this criterion.

A second reason for being cautious about the application of the criterion is that, like the operational definition of AI, it changes with time. The main reason for the changes is that some of the techniques first developed in AI have been taken over by a wider public which has seen new uses for them and which may eventually forget where they originated. The history of the programming language LISP [29] is the best example of such an effect.

Given the changes in technical fashions, there are fixed points or areas of stability which are likely to remain characteristic of AI while not becoming strongly associated with other types of programming? There is certainly at least one relevant idea: *backtracking*. In solving a problem by composing and solving a sequence of sub-problems, we avoid backtracking only by good luck or if the rules of the game are drawn so tightly that the best sub-problem to pose and solve at the next step, involving some local definition of 'best', is always guaranteed to be a component in the best global solution to the overall problem. Otherwise, the possibility exists that our locally well-intentioned choice of a sequence of sub-problems leads us into a dead end, from which we have to backtrack to some earlier point in the sequence and then try a branch to a new sequence. This new sequence will presumably begin by looking worse than the old one on local considerations (else we would have chosen it before the old one), but at least we can have some hope that it will eventually avoid the dead end. Many examples of intelligent behaviour and reasoning fit this pattern. There is no more convincing generalisation of the meaning of the present range of AI programming techniques than 'backtracking', and very little chance that this meaning will disappear from the vocabulary of AI.

Asking the question 'Does it backtrack?' in examining a program for traces of AI is a useful start, but the answer does not settle the issue. There are applications of backtracking in programming that were never regarded as AI, applications which are slowly becoming non-AI because of the changing of fashions with time, and at least two significant areas of work in mathematics relevant to AI which involve clearly-defined techniques but which are not based on backtracking.

The SNOBOL language [18] for manipulation of patterns in strings of characters relies heavily on backtracking to find matches between patterns, but the backtracking is controlled according to a fixed scheme and has no means of automatically varying its behaviour in response to local variations in the nature of a computation. Not surprisingly, SNOBOL is not regarded as an AI language. Prolog is still an AI language by common consent, because its heaviest use has been for problems in AI and because any programmed implementation of a formal logic is traditionally a part of AI, but the details of how Prolog presently administers backtracking [8, 12] are uncomfortably close to those of SNOBOL. Therefore, work on the design and use of Prolog is borderline AI by the criterion of this section. In any case, Prolog appears to be going the way of LISP because of its increasing popularity with users outside the AI community. The most AI-like work on questions of Prolog implementation is concerned with 'intelligent backtracking' [6, 13], i.e. how to vary the backtracking tactics of a system according to contextual information which is generated by its own computations.

The discussion so far suggests that any flexible backtracking scheme which changes its tactics during a computation qualifies as AI. This would be an attractive definition to many AI specialists – except that it lets in a horde of numerical analysts and related methematicians through the back door, because of the nature of subjects like dynamic programming and numerical optimisation. In the present state of contact between mathematicians and AI, however, it is safe to say that there would be no greater mistake than to close the door entirely. Some of the mathematicians' adaptive numerical techniques use low-level information which is contextual by courtesy only, but others require subtle and non-local analysis of the properties of the space in which their optimisations are being performed, and may well have something to teach AI researchers. Perhaps the best short-term solution is to pitch a large tent in the back garden. In the perspective of all the issues being discussed here, the relevance of optimisation in the mathematical sense to the question of what is AI and what is not is yet another of the present uncertainties of AI.

Is backtracking an essential feature of intelligent solutions of complex problems? Evidently not, as two simple examples show. Firstly, suppose that a solution to a problem is defined as being acceptable if it passes certain specified tests. Then a possible non-backtracking strategy is to guess an entire solution, subject it to the tests, guess another entire solution if the tests fail, subject it to the tests . . . and so on, until a guess passes the tests (or until exhaustion sets in). This strategy is an intelligent one if there is no obvious way to use more conventional techniques, or if the efforts or overheads associated with typical guesses are known to be much less than the efforts or overheads attached to unit steps of the conventional techniques. Even if these conditions are not fulfilled, the strategy can still indicate the presence of a certain low cunning, e.g. in attempts of the holder of a University of Texas† football scholarship to pass the final examination in a computer science course for which his brain coach has mistakenly enrolled him in place of an intended course on physical education or dance.

The second means of avoiding backtracking is to change the specification of a problem, usually in the direction of relaxing the conditions that a solution must satisfy, to make it possible for 'cheap and nasty' techniques to provide acceptable answers. The area of computer science in which this approach has led to the most interesting results is the one technically known as NP-hardness, where backtracking is usually not involved, but some problems from this area (notably in job-shop scheduling) can be re-cast as problems where backtracking exists and contributes heavily to inefficiency in computation. The object of the game here is to make a large reduction in inefficiency by changing the specification of the problem. The game is easiest to illustrate by a non-backtracking example, though the same game can be played for problems where the point of changing the specification is to remove the need for backtracking.

The example involves the best-known problem in the NP area: the travelling-salesman problem. Assume that a salesman plans a route covering $n+1$ towns, returning to the town which is his starting-point, and passing through each other

† Texas Exes and readers in the University of Texas system may substitute Notre Dame or Penn State.

town just once. He wishes to find the route with the lowest total mileage, given a table of distances between all possible pairs of towns. The number of possible distinct routes is $n!$ or the factorial of n, which grows exponentially (faster than any fixed power of n) as n increases. The only type of method which is known to solve the 'pure' travelling-salesman problem is one which tries out all of the $n!$ possible routes and then selects the shortest one – but it is possible to argue that, in order to complete this calculation for n greater than about 80, a computer must run for a time longer than current estimates of the age of the universe and use up as fuel all the matter currently estimated to be in the universe. This prospect is unlikely to be attractive even to a senior salesman for IBM. Therefore, a creative application of intelligence must be to define an alternative problem for which the solution is available at reasonable cost. In this case, one such alternative is to find a route (by methods other than exhaustive search) that is guaranteed to be no longer than f times the shortest route-mileage in a computing time that grows manageably (like some fixed power n^p, say) with n. N. Christofides [11] has outlined just such a solution, with $f = 1.5$ and $p = 3$.

Mathematicians have studied both of the above methods of finding solutions to non-trivial problems. A good example of the first class of methods is the probabilistic algorithm of Solovay and Strassen [44] for 'guessing' whether or not a given number is a prime. Their algorithm comes with an accurate estimate of the odds on its answer's being wrong, and the user can improve the chances of a correct answer by increasing the number of repetitions of the basic step of their method.

Both of these approaches read like descriptions of what intelligent humans do in particular circumstances when they are trying to solve problems. Also, the two approaches have great power if a problem allows them to be applied in combination. The important point to make here is that a definition of AI tied too closely to backtracking would exclude them from consideration, and probably also discourage researchers from trying to exploit them as new techniques in the mainstream of AI in the future. Therefore, an argument against being too dependent on backtracking (or any other technical concept) as an indicator of AI is that premature attempts at definition of what a developing subject includes or excludes can be actively harmful to its development.

It is possible, further, to suggest two more mathematically-based techniques which are worth investigating in association with AI but which would be ruled out by present technical definitions. The most accessible publications in these cases are by Kornfeld [31] and Melzak [24].

There is one final difficulty, which arises from too much insistence on technical definitions of AI. It follows from the M-B fallacy in Section 1.1. Suppose that M = backtracking. This is not primarily a mechanical or mechanistic concept, so it does not undermine human self-estimation in traditional 'l'homme machine' ways. Nevertheless, if we are persuaded to believe that we are human partly because we backtrack, and computers can be made to backtrack more efficiently and on larger collections of information than we can ever hope to handle, our self-estimation is likely to be undermined in the future by a giant-sized inferiority complex of a kind which psychiatrists have not yet imagined. Moreover, for every different M that someone associates in public with an M-B fallacy, there is a possibility of a new type of inferiority complex. This seems to be the most general version of the argument of Rogers [39] on AI and dehumanisation. In terms of his examples, the substitution of 'intuition' for M may have points of strong contact in the future with the probabilistic or problem-reformulating algorithms mentioned above. It is also not difficult to find a place in this scheme for simulation of emotions.

1.3 Learning?

The main difficulty of using learning as a criterion for anything is that no two people are likely to agree on what the word means.

Reasonable people who agree on the fact of the difficulty may decide to make their subsequent discussion easier by basing this on the most generous or inclusive of their individual definitions of learning (the populist approach) or on the most demanding definition (the aristocratic approach?). Even so, neither choice makes life much simpler. The latter method may be so demanding as to exclude from consideration any piece of candidate-AI work until early in the 21st century. The former may admit almost anything. Of the two, the first is worth considering, because its modesty allows into AI a technique which has been of considerable help in individual research projects but which has always hovered around the fringes of respectability. Suppose that the basic sub-programs or tools available to solve some type of problem are p(1), p(2), . . .p(99), and that one output of an AI program for plan-formation is the sequence of the p(i) quantities, perhaps after a considerable amount of computing effort, which solves a problem. Suppose also that it is expected that the program will be used to solve 100,000 problems of the same type in its lifetime, and it is observed in the record of the first 500 successful runs of the program that the sub-sequence p(5) p(9) p(5) p(73) p(41) p(5) p(28) occurs in most of the sequences. Then it is plausible to reason that this entire sub-sequence should be given a new name, say p(100), added to the basic stock of tools, and promoted to get early inspection during the assembly of the correct sequence for any new problem. This certainly promises the expenditure of less computing effort and futile searching for alternatives than the re-assembly of the same sequence many thousands of times in the future. If we add p(100) to the program, we can say that we are doing so because we have learned something about the program's field of application. But the detection of the sub-sequence is obviously a step that has much scope for automation. If the program itself adds the sub-sequence to its own collection of tools, then in some sense the program has exhibited learning.

Viewed in this light, a production-quality program with access to data that permit low-level pattern-based learning, but which is not built to include some 'learning by re-naming' facility (e.g. one which searches only for relatively simple sub-sequences to avoid wasting too much time or space on this aspect of its performance), is already out of date. This does not mean that a program that fails to use the technique is not an example of AI: it may be that its intended job does not allow such data to be created.

Another type of low-level pattern-based 'learning' is common in some parts of electrical engineering, in connection with machines to recognise and classify patterns and to improve their own performance [43]. The usual reason for not covering this activity in AI journals and conferences is that the learning consists mainly of updating values of numerical coefficients in pay-off or objective functions whose form is otherwise fixed. While this explanation covers much of the work, it does not take account of all recent developments of the subject, in particular those that resemble schemes for recognition of the p(i) sub-sequences mentioned above.

One step up from the methods that give simple rules for 'learning', and somewhat closer to the spirit of AI, are methods which also contain meta-rules or rules for generating (and abolishing) rules for learning [7, 25]. There is sufficient theoretical and practical interest in these methods for workers in AI to agree that they belong squarely within the tradition of the subject. However, there are not many AI programs or designs which compete in this particular league, so that the presence or absence of meta-rules is not yet a good general test of whether or not we are looking at an example of AI.

The meta-rule technique is safe from one external objection that is made on occasions: namely, that it is internally inconsistent because it implies an infinite regress involving rules about rules about rules, rules about rules about rules about rules, and so on. The weakness of the objection is that the regress is formally permitted but not therefore formally *required*. Even (or especially) if humans use meta-rules, it may happen that there is enough learning power to deal with the finite real world in a hierarchy of meta-rules with a number of levels which is not much greater than 2, and which operate initially on a small amount of pre-programmed genetic and physiological data by a process similar to bootstrapping [1] of various non-AI computer utility programs such as compilers.

The various arguments for and against learning as a criterion for AI produce some illumination of the subject, but do not amount to general decision-rules. The same can be said about the criteria in Sections 1.1 and 1.2.

1.4 A hybrid experiment

It is possible to construct eight combinations with the three basic criteria. If the criteria are taken in the order given in this article, and 0 and 1 are used to denote failure and success of a program or method as measured by any one criterion, then the possible outcomes may be coded by 000,001, 010 . . . 111, or 0, 1, 2, . . . 7 if the codes are read as binary numbers. It can be assumed that a type 0 program or theory is not AI. The status of the other seven types is open to discussion.

The table which follows gives fair examples of the seven types.

Type	System	Reference
1	Pattern-classifiers: 'learning by re-naming'	43 and Section 1.3
2	CHAT-80	46
3	DYNPAT	9
4	ELIZA	47
5	MECHO	45
6	SIN	32
7	AM	15

The classification for some of the examples is not clear-cut (e.g. current MECHO contains backtracking, at least by virtue of its Prolog base, and backtracking was not a major component of SIN), but is taken from past public (written or spoken) presentations of their contents.

The best all-round test of whether an entity is an example of AI is to ask if a majority of conference-paper referees for the major conferences in the IJCAI, AAAI and ECAI series would agree that it is. This is not a particularly practicable or philosophically satisfying test, but with experience of the characteristics and prejudices of referees it is possible to make trustworthy wagers on the outcome of such a thought-experiment. Although the classification above was not planned accordingly, it is safe to bet that (with a little doubt about the relative positions of 5 and 6) the percentage of 'yes' votes returned would go up steadily with increasing type-number. It is also safe to bet that only a minority would vote in favour of anything below type 5.

A rough conclusion is that the primary question to ask is whether or not a candidate for classification as AI is attacking a problem whose repeated solution otherwise requires human intelligence (and which has not been treated successfully by too many AI programs or methods in the past). If the answer to this question is favourable, then an example of AI should also contain some imitation of learning which has non-trivial consequences for computational efficiency, or rely essentially on some serious technique (including, I would suggest, those that have not yet been studied in any detail by AI workers) mentioned in Section 1.2, or both.

Some of the examples in the table are now almost ancient history by the historical standards of AI. It can therefore be asked whether the classification stands up against more modern evidence, e.g. the characteristics of programs known as expert systems. The answer is positive: the best production-quality expert systems are of type 6, while experiments with features that are not yet satisfactory in practice but which are fruitful fields for further research (e.g. TEIRESIAS [15]) are of type 7. Moreover, all the programs known to me which have been labelled 'expert systems' in the commercial world by spiritual descendants of snake-oil salesmen are either of type 1 or type 4. Thus the rough systems of classification reported here may also be useful in distinguishing fact from fiction when purchase of a product carrying the general label of AI is being considered.

2. WHERE IS AI GOING?

The question has two meanings. The first is one of commercial or public use, i.e. 'How will AI affect the (near) future?'. The second refers to the research-level frontiers of the subject. Evidently the two meanings are connected, because successes in research will become the commercial or public applications of somebody's near future. Research areas which are worth investigating because of their intrinsic interest relate to the second meaning but not necessarily the first, because interesting ideas which have more than a 50% probability of failure are only likely to be of direct concern to the researchers. These ideas may nevertheless condition the way that the specialists think about AI and explain it to non-specialists, and therefore have more indirect commercial and social implications.

2.1 Immediate issues

At the commercial level, the success of AI over the last two to four years (mainly through applications of expert systems) can be predicted to continue for the same length of time in the future even if the supply of new results from the research frontier dries up tomorrow. The explanation of this state of affairs has three parts. Firstly, AI has benefited from the outlay of a large number of man-years of research before the beginning of its commercial exploitation, and there is still a backlog of significant completed research waiting to be utilised. Secondly, recognition and use of unexploited results is not simply a matter of uniting conventional software companies with supplies of venture capital: it seems to be a necessary condition (at least so far) for successful use of AI that people with previous AI experience should be involved, and there are not enough qualified people to answer all the demands of the venture capitalists – as several US companies or groups founded to cash in on AI (not to mention some less well-organised efforts in Europe) are discovering already. As both successful and unsuccessful organisations should be able to agree, AI is partly a state of mind induced by serious practice. The final short-term reason for optimism about applications of AI is that there is no necessary relation between the 'size' of the AI component (measured either in man-years for implementation or in profundity as viewed by conference-paper referees and compilers of citation indexes) in an application and the financial rewards of making the application succeed. For example, marginal efforts now invested in tuning one existing expert system to give recommendations on how to clear blockages or failures in the drilling of oil wells can contribute to pay-offs that run at the rate of about $100,000 saved per well cleared. New applications of AI where the mismatch between effort and return works in favour of AI rather than against it have shown no signs of falling off recently.

A further reason for believing that the number and variety of practical applications of AI will continue to be more than enough to justify the commercial interest in the subject is that one of the beliefs of the early days of AI has now been exactly reversed. Initially, it was regarded as most sensible to design AI programs with general scope, e.g. as in McCarthy's plans for an Advice Taker [28] which could perform equally well as an integrator and user of knowledge in whatever general field it accepted advice. An interpretation of this belief was that it was 'obviously' more difficult to build special-purpose systems to reproduce advanced professional behaviour in areas such as medical diagnosis. Now, thanks to the success of expert systems and because of the failure of the general experiments, the collective wisdom of AI is that the specific is not necessarily difficult and that the general is hard. This view matches well the needs of the current market, where large numbers of specific problems await solution and where the potential users have no concern for generality as long as the next specific problem can be solved.

Hayes [19] says that an important constraint on any AI embodied in a program is that the program should produce its results in a reasonable amount of computing time. The statement is true from a commercial point of view, but this is not the most general statement of the constraint that is of commercial importance. More generally, it is the price of computing resources which governs the commercial applicability of a technique from AI or any other kind of computing. The one resource which is of even more importance for AI than time (and which has strong effects on the consumption of time) is storage space, measured in random-access memory.

The ultimate explanation of the significance of random-access memory is that almost all computational AI, unlike most other types of computations, manipulates and generates data in the form of lists. A list is a structure in which a sequence of items of data that may be quite large in principle is held in numerous small slots of space in memory, and for which the slots (which need have no systematic relationship of position to each other in memory) are linked together to represent the sequence by pointers. A slot is some individual region of memory that can be distinguished from all other regions by its unique address, and which is large enough to hold at least one basic element of data and one pointer P to the next slot W. It is sufficient for P to be just the address of N.

It takes no intelligence to maintain a collection of data, but one measure of the amount of human or artificial intelligence devoted to the collection is the number of relationships that are recorded for each item of data. In list-processing terms, each relationship can be represented in at least one pointer. As a result of successful use of AI techniques on material stored in a computer, therefore, relatively small amounts of data may generate large numbers of pointers. This has two special consequences for use of storage. Firstly, large secondary storage (e.g. disks) is no substitute for random-access memory in which pointers can be created and manipulated; frequent translation of tangled (but intelligently tangled!) list structures into forms suitable for storage on disks, and clearing them out of small random-access memories to make way for new material, imposes unacceptably high overheads on AI computations. Secondly, in order to accommodate large numbers of relationships or pointers, the random-access memory itself must be large.

It is not enough to have a large amount of random-access storage, in which pointers express relationships between items which can be anywhere in the memory, unless the pointers themselves are big enough to distinguish between any pair of slots in storage. This imposes an additional condition on memory which does not exist for more conventional types of computing. In many practical situations, each 'slot' in standard random-access memory is called a word and has its own unique address. As almost everything in modern forms of storage comes in powers of 2, the condition above says that a gift of 2^b words of random-access memory is not fully helpful unless individual words contain enough bits to be able to offer at least *b* of them to act as pointers, and to have enough bits left over to represent useful items of data. The basic convention of LISP [29], which supports a probable majority of AI programs, is that the reservation of b bits for a pointer means that the standard word-length or slot-length should be at least 2b bits.

The practical experience of users of LISP and similar languages to write programs in and around AI has been that a slot-length of 36 bits is fully serviceable, while a 32-bit length is tolerable and anything less is inadequate. A slot may be a single word on large conventional scientific computers, or two words (to achieve the necessary length) on newer machines being built around 16-bit microprocessors like the Motorola 68000, though the method of joining short words together to get acceptable slot-lengths wastes some computing time and is inefficient. To date, AI has managed to live with the decrease of efficiency that occurs if only a pairing of words is involved, but nobody has yet demonstrated any acceptable system based on quadrupling, i.e. yesterday's 8-bit microprocessors are of no practical value for handling of 32-bit structures in AI. Moreover, despite current publicity by manufacturers, at the hardware level the most advanced microcomputers of 1984 obstinately remain 16-bit (or, in at least one case, 8-bit) computers in fact.

These comments have commercial implications. They suggest that it is possible to implement significant AI-based systems on relatively cheap computers (typically with 1984 prices around the $20,000 mark) that use 16-bit microprocessors and that are designed to be at home with languages like LISP and Prolog. They also suggest that it is possible to incorporate AI in the programming of purpose-built hardware for specific tasks, provided that the hardware is constructed around a 16-bit microprocessor, for unit costs well below $20,000 in production runs of medium to large volumes. In that sense, AI may be able to do for special equipment (e.g. for detection of departures from quite complex definitions of normality in pictures provided by a television camera in an alarm system) not containing fully-fledged computers what the 4-bit microprocessor has done for washing machines and vacuum cleaners. A third implication is that, because AI techniques will be more efficient in a 32-bit than a 16-bit environment, the market for full 32-bit microprocessors may be much larger than futurologists of computing have foreseen. It is a common view that only small numbers of such microprocessors can be sold (i.e. to manufacturers of large conventional machines for scientific numerical computing; in theory, 32 bits would represent overkill to the Sinclairs and the Apples of this world and would not be of interest to these companies), and that organisations which put large resources into their design are merely paying for expensive and ego-boosting virility tests for their design teams. Considerations of AI show that the common view needs re-thinking.

Practical AI experience on minimum acceptable slots in random-access memory, taken together with the comments above on the necessary connection between slot-length and the total size of memory, makes predictions about the minimum acceptable size of memory for support of computations based on AI. Not surprisingly, these predictions are borne out in practice. It is by now traditional to measure storage in bytes rather than words, where a byte is the number of bits (8 is as good as a universal standard) required to establish separate codes for each character that a computer is expected to handle. The number of bytes of memory in a computer with a 32-bit word would therefore be four times the number of words of memory. One more item of technical language is necessary to set the present scene: 1K is 2^{10} or 1024, and 1M is 1024K. In these terms, the entry price in random-access memory for a computer on which one can hope to do serious programming experiments in AI is 1M bytes. With 2M bytes an AI programmer does not have to make a practice of holding his breath until he can reassure himself that his newest experiment will not be running out of memory, but he may receive occasional nasty surprises of that type. With 4M bytes or more, he is almost perfectly safe.

The quoted figures for size of memory refer to computers which are being used as development systems for AI-based programs. If it is desired to tailor a developed system to a smaller memory on economic or other grounds, e.g. in some purpose-built hardware, it should be possible to estimate the size of the smaller memory by dividing the figures by 2, but almost certainly not by 4.

Any variations in the scale of storage, inside these ranges, does not reduce the size of the words needed to support AI's list-processing computations: 16-bit systems can be made to behave like 32-bit systems operating with efficiency that is decreased but tolerable, while development of full 32-bit (or better) systems represents enough of a longer-term improvement to be worth encouraging.

The considerations of word-length and size of storage will be the primary factors governing the spread of commercial and non-research applications of AI in the future. Related to costs of random-access memory, they indicate the price-level of the computing hardware that will be at least adequate to support AI programs: perhaps $20,000 (or less in California) in 1984 for a 1M-byte computer centred on a 16-bit microprocessor, and it is not difficult to find optimistic and generally trustworthy predictions of the rate at which the price of any fixed amount of computing power will be falling in the next few years. For each new significant drop in the price-level, new commercial applications become feasible. In this particular game, each man is his own best forecaster.

2.2 Research-level issues

It is easy to see other questions besides those of random-access memory that will influence the future applicability of AI. For example, the design of new computer architectures better suited to list processing or to Prolog may open avenues not mentioned in the discussion about conventional memories and architectures. However, such experiments (particularly as part of the Fifth Generation plan [33] in Japan) will certainly not close off the existing avenues. Therefore, the figures above will remain significant as upper limits on prices and lower limits on hardware resources. With our present understanding of AI, it is safe to say that no new developments in hardware, programming, languages or AI techniques on the research frontier will make qualitative changes in the *kinds* of computation that we can expect to do, for quite a long time – certainly a time outside normal commercial horizons. Achievements in research are more likely to make quantitative improvements in computations that can be handled more or less well already, or to show us more convincingly why certain problems that we have been unable to attack will continue to resist our efforts.

In AI, as elsewhere in computer science, language design leads hardware design. Therefore questions of language design imply answers and predictions about hardware. Many languages are designed, but few expand into general currency. From the AI tradition, the most durable languages have been LISP and Prolog. It may be risky to generalise from two examples, but these languages owe much of their success to the facts that they offer elegant frameworks for programmers to say things about important kinds of computations which were laborious or impossible to describe in previous languages and that they stay close to mathematical models of the essence of those computations. In the case of Prolog, the model refers to a significant part of the first-order predicate calculus, which is a formal way of expressing most of what we call 'logic' when we are speaking informally. The risky generalisation or prediction, which it actually feels quite safe to write, is that any new language developed from within AI which is to have an influence comparable with LISP or Prolog must aim to satisfy the two conditions which have made those languages successful.

This raises the question of whether AI programmers still have any unfulfilled wishes. In theory, because much of AI is concerned with automation of logical processes, Prolog is the answer to almost everyone's prayers. In practice, the first-order predicate calculus does not have any computationally satisfactory means of tackling several important forms of logical reasoning, e.g. reasoning about time, cause and effect, and 'what if' reasoning (which leads naturally to the idea of alternative possible worlds, and modal logics [21]). These issues are at one focus of active research, and deserve an early bet if one is betting on significant new developments in the character of AI. If there are any future successes in this direction, three steps of development or demand can be expected: (1) identification of a logic or formal scheme which gives foolproof and paradox-proof support on paper for the desired types of reasoning; (2) complementation of the scheme by an algorithmic principle which allows the reasoning to be automated and programmed, in the same way that Robinson's resolution principle complemented the first-order predicate calculus [38]; (3) design of a programming language in which it is satisfying and natural to express one's units of reasoning from (1), and in which this expression constitutes all or most of a program. Any success at the level of (3), following success of the present work on (1) and (2), stands as good a chance of immortality as LISP or Prolog. In addition, it will promise to make applications of causal or time-based reasoning practicable, where similar attempts at present are cumbersome, inefficient and not safe to turn loose outside a research laboratory.

Another of the problems of AI concerns representation of knowledge. The phrase is intended to imply that the knowledge will be used, so that the problem is to find representations that will make the use efficient in a given set of circumstances. Here, knowledge is never just knowledge as such: at the very least, these 'circumstances' place it in some context. More usually, other information besides information on how the user wishes to put the knowledge to work adds to the details of the context. To carry around such details inside a computer is no bad thing in AI, even if the demands on storage are heavy, because imitation of the effects of understanding is one of the general goals of AI, and a basic element of understanding is the setting of knowledge or information into the context that is most appropriate for it.

Knowledge-representation is a well-defined sub-field of AI, but one which is still in its infancy despite the fact that it was not established yesterday. The main present difficulty is to define a general measure of progress or a theory which makes some predictions about the direction in which progress lies. Probably there have not yet been enough experiments to lay the foundations for any general theory. We are sometimes therefore reduced to saying that scheme A is better than scheme B because it occupies 90% of the storage of B and runs in 80% of the time that B uses. This is a beginning, but a very modest beginning. One good forecast to make about the future is that the idea of context will assume more importance as the confidence of researchers into knowledge-representation increases. Another good forecast is that the importance of relating knowledge and context inside the computer will lead to more sophisticated revivals of a concept which has gone through more than one cycle of past fashion in AI: frames. Essentially, a frame is some data-structure containing both spaces for information and contextual material which is intended to annotate or extend the information which eventually finds its way into the spaces. This definition is so wide that it does not have much power to predict what future research may determine to be good frames and bad frames, but the overall prediction that frames will make a comeback in the near future is a safe one. As in the case of languages, landmark achievements in this area in the future are unlikely to achieve qualitative changes in what AI can do, but they should cause some things that are done only with gross inefficiencies at present to be made efficient enough (e.g. in use of storage and in computing and programmer's time) to be the subjects of future production-quality systems.

What things? Evidently the study of context in general will tell us more about those types of contexts which turn up most frequently as examples. One context which is likely to recur often in such work is the context of what a given user of a system in a given situation expects or hopes for or needs (if the AI researchers believe that they know what is good for him) from the system. To perform passably by the user's criteria, the system must maintain a context for its own benefit which models the user, and which changes as the user gives more information (including involuntary information) about himself through his interaction with the system. Good modelling is so far mainly limited to situations where basic models have been proposed by researchers outside AI, but user modelling is a growing activity inside AI, particularly because of increased interest in the subject by experimental psychologists. It can be expected that one of the earliest application-areas to make use of user modelling and new interpretations of what is meant by context will be computer-aided learning, and that this area will escape the rigidities which killed off the earliest phase of pre-AI activity in computer-aided instruction around 1970. A simple example of a topic where the newer approach can be applied is the treatment of children's subtraction errors [3, 5].

In order to represent knowledge inside a computer, it is necessary to have some knowledge to represent. Commercial builders of expert-system programs understand this well: the fact that they have cornered valuable blocks of specialised knowledge is the foundation of their healthy bank-balances. Expert systems are already commercially rewarding in some fields, so it is natural to ask if their scope can and will be extended in the future. While more examples of existing types of expert-system applications are certain to come, there are at least two reasons why significant areas of knowledge may continue to hold out against being captured by tomorrow's expert systems.

The first has been presented already: certain kinds of reasoning used by experts, especially reasoning that relies heavily on ideas about time and causality, do not yet have any adequate computational basis. Until such a basis is agreed upon, attempts to program the reasoning will certainly be inefficient (and may therefore demand too much storage or computing time to be practicable in everyday applications) and will run the risk of giving wrong or misleading answers to some questions.

The second difficulty is that some kinds of expert knowledge may be permanently unformalisable. There is no proof to the contrary, and Polanyi [36], among others, has argued convincingly that the overall difficulty may always be with us. Attempts by people with interests in AI to come up with counter-arguments have been unconvincing at best. A simple way to summarise the difficulty is that some processes (including ones that would lead to theoretical enlightenment and commercial profit if they could be reproduced by a black box) carried out by experts in particular fields may have to remain tacit. Alternatively, there are things that we or experts know, but which we may never be able to tell. It is quite easy to back up this view merely by quoting some names of experts with tacit skills that nobody knows how to transfer or reproduce: for example, Don Bradman [40]. If North American readers are puzzled by this reference, then the name of Willie Mays [17] should be enough to make the same point. And it is not the case that only areas of expert knowledge related to the use of bats are tacit.

This discussion is not intended to be a complete review of the open questions at the research end of AI, but it is designed to say something about the fundamentals. Some notable present areas of AI like natural-language processing and vision have been omitted, partly for reasons of space and partly because their long-term progress must depend on questions like 'context' that have been mentioned above. Also, I have already recommended bets on some more futuristic areas of research at earlier stages in the article, notably in Section 1.2.

3. SOCIAL QUESTIONS

Fortunately, there is no need for a detailed catalogue of social implications of AI here; the other articles in the book cover a very large amount of the necessary ground. This section will therefore raise only a few issues which are of general importance or which belong to the category of 'author's favourites'.

From the point of view of the computer user or black-box user who is not concerned with programming or technical details, the most important question is not whether an AI-based system can give him results which may satisfy him in any short term, but whether or not his repeated use of such systems, or his mere existence in a world where the systems are widespread, produces in him any undesirable side-effects. This is where the idea of 'dehumanisation' comes in.

In Section 1.1, I have mentioned a risk of this type that is almost always overlooked within the community of AI specialists, but where something like 51% of the method of prevention or cure is in the hands of the community itself. This risk is that cases of what I have called the M-B fallacy may sneak into explanations of AI and of what it should teach humans about the nature of their own intelligence. To identify the risk is not to ensure that publicists of AI will stop making that mistake in the future. Even so, it helps to lessen the chances of damage, by indicating to consumers what to look for in any argument of the 'This is how it must be in humans' variety which starts by quoting some example of AI.

The effect of arguments about parallels between AI and human behaviour should not be overrated. These arguments will be heard directly only by those with the time or inclination to hear them. Many more people will form impressions of AI simply through seeing what computers or black boxes equipped with AI programs actually do for them. It is this consideration that has prompted Weizenbaum [47] to recommend that AI-based systems, at least, should not be permitted to communicate with users by speech because of the possibility of 'It speaks, therefore it must be human' reactions among these users. A different consideration, with its own problems, is that excessive exposure to AI may lead to loss of practice in important areas of present human behaviour, e.g. the exercise of intuition [39].

At present it is not clear if these questions, in general, will have negative implications about the effects of AI on humans in the future. It seems that there are no *general* conclusions that can be drawn, because there are different lessons and different counter-moves for each particular example. On the question of the use of speech in AI-based systems, for instance, it is possible to think of two counters to Weizenbaum's fears. The first is that computing power and speech-producing devices are now associated in contexts that are expanding and that have nothing to do with AI: verbal reminders to fasten safety-belts in cars, and relatively cheap speech-synthesising boxes that can be controlled by do-it-yourself experiments with hobby microcomputers, to take just two examples. By the time that AI in public applications uses speech on a large scale, non-AI associations of speech with computing devices should be so widely spread that nobody will be tempted to believe that speech is a distinctive indicator of humanity. The second counter, in case the first fails, is suggested by the condition in Australian

Rules football that a player can only continue running with the ball if he bounces it on the ground and catches it again, on the run, at least once every 10 metres. All that is needed to dehumanise a voice attached to an AI-based system is a regulation (not difficult to enforce) that the voice should give a non-human synthesised squawk or bark every minute or so.

Rogers' view [39] that AI will change humans' definitions of themselves by emphasising those features that conform to what AI-based systems can imitate, at the expense of other features, is possibly a self-unfulfilling prophecy. That is to say, it may well come true if it is not generally recognised in the short-term to medium-term future, but early recognition leads to the obvious defence of strengthening education and encouragement for those parts of human activity which have the least chance of duplication through AI. A Ministry of Sport might do its bit by more vigorous promotion of cricket (or baseball) as a part of culture. More generally, even cricket is less likely to educate humans in what it takes to be human than the diversions that are often summarised as wine, women and song. The ultimate defence might be the creation of a Ministry of Hedonism. Of course, it is another question whether or not a modern government would, in its own terms of reference, see the need for any defences in this direction: Dostoyevsky's Grand Inquisitor [16] might argue that proliferation of black boxes with AI is a better way for a population to be kept quiet and contented than any method which was available in the 19th century. Rogers' point may therefore be more political than philosophical.

The examples of possible applications of AI whose effects on humans' images of themselves are most difficult to foresee are those which are likely to arrive because of human users' own demands rather than because of benevolent planning in advance by committees of specialists in AI. In short, users demand 'user-friendly' systems, and the adjective often has the meaning that a system of generation x has a user-friendly characteristic of a certain type because it contains an acceptable fix for an inflexibility or an unsatisfactory characteristic of the same type that has caused complaints from users of the corresponding system of generation $x-1$. With the pressures on AI that are accompanying its commercial success, a generation is unlikely to last much longer than a year or two. Against this background, it is not easy to use the state of the art in generation x to predict the detailed nature of the most user-friendly parts of systems in generation $x+5$. A general comment which may be made, however, is that user-friendliness or responsiveness to what the user actually needs is a hit-or-miss business unless the system that is doing the responding contains some model of the user's expectations.

User-modelling is already an active field of research within AI, but it is too soon for us to have a theory which can guide progress in the making of models or predict the quality of improvement in modelling that progress in a particular direction may give. Therefore users' (or commercial) demands for what AI-based systems should be able to do by way of user-friendliness and AI researchers' responses to the demands will interact with each other in complicated ways. Humans' needs will influence the development of systems where such development is possible, but experiments in AI may show that there is at best only a long-term possibility of development in other desirable directions. This negative evidence with respect to user-friendliness may persuade humans that, since they cannot be modelled adequately in some respects, these respects are not fully legitimate parts of their own behaviour or identities. One conceivable result, for example, is that the value of certain types of aesthetic experience and tacit knowledge to the human personality will be downplayed. On the positive side, it may happen that each particular effect of this kind arising from collisions of users' expectations with limitations of AI will suggest its own particular counter or defence, in the same way as for Weizenbaum's objections to the use of speech in computing systems. Nothing general can be said about the implications of user-modelling in our current state of understanding of AI: what is important at this stage is just to identify the issue itself.

The simulation of emotions by AI-based systems is a topic for which there is no shortage of references. Most considerations of the question seem to take it for granted that successful simulations will tell us something important about humans and their behaviour – another example of the M-B fallacy. In the present discussion it is worth introducing the idea that 'emotions' may be useful shorthand devices for convenient properties of programs at a rather less ambitious level, just as the fact that companies or ships are sometimes regarded as persons in law represents useful legal shorthand without implying that we can learn something significant about ourselves by studying the behaviour of a ship.

It is enough to consider one case: embarrassment. A non-AI program designed to respond to queries about a data-base will produce true information, but with no special check on whether or not this information is more than enough to answer the queries. In this sense, it is analogous to a recent Israeli automatic system that detected and identified motorists crossing intersections against red lights by photographing the offending cars clearly enough to show number-plates and the faces of their drivers. This system once exceeded its brief by photographing a prominent politician whose passenger, also clearly visible, was a lady whose presence in his car at the time and place in question caused problems of many kinds unrelated to traffic offences. How can a user-friendly system detect instances where, by general (if not universal) consent, it should volunteer the minimum of true information and block out facts like the face of the passenger? To do this effectively, it should possess some model of removability of information – essentially, for human users, a model of embarrassment. It is reasonable to expect that future work in AI will include attempts to develop models such as this for 'shorthand' purposes without necessarily implying anything far-reaching or dangerous for human self-estimation. Moreover, a good short story is waiting to be written around the consequences of the assumption that, say, an AI system modelling embarrassment and built by a software house in Australia can be exported safely to British customers without alteration. Suitable raw material (pun not initially intended) for the plot is available in [22].

A future source of difficulty with the use of AI lies in humans expecting too much of it by relying on it to protect them from complicated exercises in thinking. If one asks for a certain result without taking the trouble to spell out how the result is to be achieved, problems of the 'Monkey's Paw' [23] type are likely. The same lesson is found in most of the fables which begin by offering some lucky human the chance of miraculous gratification of any three wishes. A user of a system who expects only good results to follow is asking for the ultimate in user-friendliness: a button on the keyboard which is marked 'Do what I mean'. Under very specific or circumscribed conditions this facility can be provided, but in general situations AI cannot help at all. Even where the user or designer has been clever in sealing off loopholes in what he asks, as in Asimov's three laws of robotics [2], the chances of good general performance are limited because of the huge amount of computing that is likely to be needed if all practicable sequences of actions are to be checked for validity and absence of unwanted side-effects against the do-what-I-mean criterion. The lesson is that there is a realistic likelihood that AI will cause us to become even more human in the future, by requiring us to think harder about how to make it work for us, rather than subtract something from our ability to use our powers of thought (including those, like intuition, that are hardest to mechanise) by taking over many of our responsibilities that require thought.

Finally, there is a quite different field in which AI may have social implications if it is given a chance to do so. In the general area of civil liberties, electronic technology is almost always seen as a danger because it increases the power of both commercial and political institutions to monitor and control the actions and opinions of individuals. Future networks connecting computers and terminals or nodes in individual homes have obvious potentialities for being used in this way. But it does not follow from any technical considerations that they can only be used in this way, e.g. through the maintenance of large central depositories of information. Home terminals in the future will in effect be computers rather than mere keyboards and display screens, and it should not be more than another decade at the most before the amount of capacity needed to support non-trivial AI (as described in Section 2.1) can be incorporated into these terminals without inflating their prices significantly. Thus the networks using the information technology of the 1990s will be networks of genuine distributed computing power rather than connections to large numbers of data-entry points to relatively small numbers of main-frame computers. This, combined with existing achievements in data-encryption and secure communications, allows a future in which personal data can be stored at sites where it is created, with safeguards against subsequent local tampering with the data, and copied by an enquirer only if the site's automated guardian program is happy with the outcome of an artificially-intelligent dialogue with the program or system that makes the enquiry. This type of communication is already possible without AI in distributed computing networks, but only through relatively simple declarations by the enquirer, e.g. 'I have the right password'. However, if the conditions under which information is released are set out by law to the satisfaction of civil libertarians, it may require quite complex programs at both enquirer's and target sites, perhaps in declarative languages like Prolog, to express the full meaning of what the law intends. Also, different individuals may have the freedom to establish different behaviours in their guardian programs, within the framework of the law. This picture, and the degree of freedom for individuality that it suggests, is impossible without the use of methods of AI, but achievable if AI is used. AI can therefore help to maintain liberties expressed in Bills of Rights [35] into the age of information technology, or provide partial substitutes for Bills of Rights in countries where these do not exist – if it is politically permitted to do so. It can also be used in this area as a hindrance rather than a help, depending on who makes the rules of the game.

Here, as in several other areas of application, AI has a political dimension which should not be ignored. If voters ignore it while professional politicians and lobbyists do not, the outcome is highly unlikely to be favourable to the voters.

4. WHAT RESPONSE DOES AI DESERVE?

Chiefly, adequate preparation and education. The subject has suffered in the past, when it was only an area of research, from both too-vigorous promotion (e.g. [14]) and uninformed criticism (e.g. [26]). If either process is repeated in the future, in a world where it is guaranteed that the results of research in AI will have increasing numbers of applications, the users will suffer more than the AI research community. Therefore, 'Learn more about AI' should be an essential guideline. The production of the present book is intended as a road-building step in that direction.

The boundaries of AI are always changing. In order to keep up with developments and even anticipate some of them, it is advisable to appreciate where AI stands in relation to the other sciences on which it depends. This recommendation has a large-scale part and a part involving technical details. Among the technical details, for example, is an understanding of the basics of theoretical computer science (as mentioned, for example, in a recent biography of Alan Turing [20], one of the founders of that subject) where these touch on AI, e.g. so that readers do not let publicists get away with assertions like the one that basic theoretical results on computable and uncomputable functions mean that it is proven that minds and machines do not belong in the same continuum. (AI specialists who would nevertheless want to argue that minds are not merely advanced pieces of machinery might say with justification: 'With friends like that, who needs enemies?'.) On a large scale, misunderstandings about the character of AI as science can be removed if one appreciates that a science whose base is created by humans is qualitatively different from one, like physics, whose subject-matter was in some sense 'there' before humans started thinking about it. Good references for this understanding, though by no means the last or best conceivable words on it, are a book by Simon [42] and a survey of some of the recurring intellectual questions in AI by Newell [34].

A final suggestion, not made entirely with tongue in cheek, is a matter of language. One of the past sources of trouble for artificial intelligence has been that everyone knows what the subject contains as soon as its name is mentioned – unlike, say, mycology or tribology. Unfortunately this confidence in interpreting the name by everyday standards of meaning is wrong. The name exists merely because a short and memorable title was regarded as an important means of catching and holding the attention of American federal agencies with funds to spend on research in the mid-1950s, when a group of people involved in work such as the development of chess-playing and plan-forming programs was designing a written proposal to shake loose some of these funds to support a meeting and conference with other researchers in the same general area. As far as the evidence goes [30], there is no indication that the organisers of the meeting (who eventually got their money: a partial tribute to their choice of title) attached much literal weight to the phrase. Given the past misunderstandings of its meaning by non-specialists and the possibilities of new misunderstandings in the future, it may be best if 'artificial intelligence' disappears in favour of a more neutral-sounding label, though without causing too much dislocation in the thought-patterns and writing-patterns of specialists, publicists, research-funding agencies, venture capitalists and other friends of the subject. This second condition may seem impossible to match with the first one, but by itself it exists quite widely already. The appearance of a good new label has come about informally, perhaps just to save energy in typing and speaking, and now needs only a little explicit encouragement. The encouragement simply involves a resolution by all interested parties never to speak of artificial intelligence where they can just speak of AI.

NOTES

[1] Aho, A.V. and Ullman, J.D. (1977) *Principles of Compiler Design*, Addison-Wesley, Reading, Massachusetts, p. 24.

[2] Asimov, I. (1982) *I, Robot*, Granada Publishing Ltd., St. Albans, Hertfordshire, p. 43.

[3] Attisha, M. and Yazdani, M. (1983) *Instructional Science* **12** 333.

[4] Barr, A. and Feigenbaum, E. (eds.) (1981) *Handbook of Artificial Intelligence*, vol. 1, Pitman, London, p. 123.

[5] Brown, J.S. and Vanlehn, K. (1980) *Cognitive Science* **4** 379.

[6] Bruynooghe, M. and Pereira, L.M., reference 8, p. 194.

[7] Bundy, A. (1983) *The Computer Modelling of Mathematical Reasoning*, Academic Press, London.

[8] Campbell, J.A. (ed.) (1984) *Implementations of Prolog*, Ellis Horwood Ltd., Chichester.

[9] Campbell, J.A. and Gardin, F. (1983) *Computer Algebra*, ed. J.A. van Hulzen, Springer-Verlag, Berlin, p. 267.

[10] Charniak, E., Riesbeck, C., and McDermott, D.V. (1980) *Artificial Intelligence Programming*, Lawrence Erlbaum Associates, Hillsdale, New Jersey.

[11] Christofides, N. (1976) in *Algorithms & Complexity: New Directions and Recent Results*, ed. J.F. Traub, Academic Press, New York, p. 441.

[12] Clocksin, W.F. and Mellish, C.S. (1981) *Programming in Prolog*, Springer-Verlag, Berlin.

[13] Cox, P.T., reference 8, p. 216.

[14] Darrach, B. (1970) Meet Shakey, the First Electronic Person, article in *Life* Magazine, 20 November.

[15] Davis, R. and Lenat, D.B. (1982) *Knowledge-Based Systems in Artificial Intelligence*, McGraw-Hill, New York.
[16] On this subject, any edition or translation of Dostoyevsky's novel *The Brothers Karamazov* will do.
[17] Einstein, C. (1980) *Willie's Time*, Berkley Books, New York.
[18] Griswold, R.E., Poage, J.F., and Polonsky, I.P. (1971) *The SNOBOL4 Programming Language*, Prentice-Hall, Englewood Cliffs, New Jersey.
[19] Hayes, P. contribution to this volume.
[20] Hodges, A. (1983) *Alan Turing: the Enigma*, Burnett Books, London.
[21] Hughes, G.E. and Cresswell, M.J. (1977) *An Introduction to Modal Logic*, Methuen, London.
[22] Humphries, B. and Garland, N. (1968) *The Wonderful World of Barry McKenzie*, Macdonald, London.
[23] Jacobs, W.W. (1902) The Monkey's Paw, in *The Lady of the Barge*, Harper and Brothers, London, p. 27.
[24] Kornfeld, W.A. (1982) *Communications of the Association for Computing Machinery* **24** 734.
[25] Lenat, D.B. (1983) *Artificial Intelligence* **21** 31.
[26] Lighthill, J. (1973) *Artificial Intelligence: a General Survey*, Science Research Council, London.
[27] Marr, D. (1981) *Vision*, Freeman, San Francisco.
[28] McCarthy, J. (1959) in *Mechanization of Thought Processes*, HMSO, London.
[29] McCarthy, J.M. *et al.* (1965) *LISP 1.5 Programmer's Manual*, MIT Press, Cambridge, Massachusetts.
[30] McCorduck, P. (1979) *Machines who Think*, Freeman, San Francisco.
[31] Melzak, Z.A. (1983) *Bypasses: a Simple Approach to Complexity*, Wiley, New York.
[32] Moses, J. (1971) *Communications of the Association for Computing Machinery* **14** 548.
[33] Moto-oka, T. (ed.) (1982) *Fifth Generation Computer Systems*, North-Holland Publishing Co., Amsterdam.
[34] Newell, A., in *The Study of Information: Interdisciplinary Messages*, eds. F. Machlup and U. Mansfield, Wiley, New York (to be published).
[35] Pool. I. de S. (1983) *Technologies of Freedom*, Harvard University Press, Cambridge, Massachusetts.
[36] Polanyi, M. (1967) *The Tacit Dimension*, Routledge & Kegan Paul, London.
[38] Robinson, J.A. (1983) in *Intelligent Systems: the Unprecedented Opportunity*, eds. J.E. Hayes and D. Michie, Ellis Horwood, Chichester, p. 19.
[39] Rogers, P., contribution to this volume.
[40] Rosenwater, I. (1978) *Sir Donald Bradman: A Biography*, B.T. Batsford Ltd., London.
[41] Shapiro, S.C. (1979) *Techniques of Artificial Intelligence*, Van Nostrand, New York.
[42] Simon, H.A. (1981) *The Sciences of the Artificial*, MIT Press, Cambridge, Massachusetts.

[43] Sklansky, J. and Wassel, G.N. (1981) *Pattern Classifiers and Trainable Machines*, Springer-Verlag, Berlin.

[44] Solovay, R. and Strassen, V. (1977) *Society for Industrial & Applied Mathematics Journal on Computing* **6** 84.

[45] Sterling, L., Bundy, A., Byrd, L., O'Keefe, R., and Silver, B. (1982) in *Computer Algebra*, ed. J. Calmet, Springer-Verlag, Berlin, p. 109.

[46] Warren, D.H.D. and Pereira, F.C.N. (1982) *American Journal of Computational Linguistics* **8** 110.

[47] Weizenbaum, J. (1984) *Computer Power and Human Reason*, Penguin, Harmondsworth, Middlesex.
The book was originally published in 1976. A new preface in the 1984 edition summarises Weizenbaum's views of how his original arguments have affected opinions about AI over the last few years, and his estimates of some risks of the widespread use of computers (not specifically in connection with AI) in society that have not been considered above.

POSTSCRIPT

Silicon Valley of the Dolls*

R. Forsyth North London Polytechnic UK

The early gynoids were very crude – in every sense of the word. Curiously enough (for Britain had already begun the precipitate economic decline from which it was never to recover), it was a British firm which invented them. The first gynoid was known simply as 36C, from her bust measurement. She was produced by Sex Objects Ltd. of Basingstoke, a small but enterprising concern specialising in the manufacture of 'sex aids'. They had the bright idea of equipping one of their lifesize inflatable dolls with a 16-bit microprocessor, a voice synthesiser and a memory bank containing such choice phrases as 'take me now' and 'be gentle with me'.

The idea was good, but the execution was poor. 36C was ahead of her time. Her sales potential was ruined by shoddy workmanship and inept marketing. Her push-button control was erratic at best. Even worse, her servo-controlled convulsive response sequence suffered from feedback delays which led to wild oscillations in motor behaviour that were downright dangerous. These teething troubles were never overcome. A few models were sold – more as curiosities or conversation pieces among the idle and sophisticated rich than for serious use – before Sex Objects Ltd. went bankrupt, overwhelmed by the cash-flow difficulties which the R&D effort on such an advanced project necessarily entails, but which the management had totally failed to foresee.

That might have been the end of the story, at least for a while, had not a highly placed executive of the giant American corporation Universal General Hardware seen 36C in a shop window on a trip to London and immediately

*An edited version of this story first appeared in *Datalink*, May 8 1979. It is reproduced by permission of the publisher and the author.

realised her immense potential. Back in the United States, he set in motion a crash programme of development which only an organisation with the financial resources and technical expertise of UGH Inc. could hope to sustain. Within six months, a prototype was entertaining members of the board: within one year a production model was being retailed as the 'Bedmate'.

Gone were the clumsy push-button controls that had marred 36C's performance; instead, Bedmates could recognise spoken commands through auditory receptors which could be tuned to any individual's speech characteristics. Moreover, not all commands were pre-programmed to evoke fixed action patterns. The spare ones could be associated with actions selected by the customer on the 'show-and-learn' basis pioneered in industrial robotics. Bedmates were also far more robust and attractively finished than the old 36Cs; and the feedback problems that had plagued the earlier model had finally been ironed out.

But the main reason for the phenomenal success of the Bedmate lay elsewhere. Dissatisfied with the small repertoire of invariant cliches which was all that passed for speech in the primitive British Gynoid, the Americans had assembled a select team of Artificial Intelligence gurus from the West Coast, proposed to them the idea of a walking, *talking*, living doll, set them free from the budgetary constraints of the academic world, and let them rip.

The results, in so short a time, were astonishing. Two dozen bright young male computer-science graduates were cloistered monastically in the New Mexico desert with the latest computer facilities at their disposal. They took to the task like seals to water. There was an unprecedented burst of creative intellectual energy whose effects are still being felt today, and the natural language understanding software called VOCS (Voice Operated Comprehension System) was born. The word became flesh – or rather, textured plastic.

In conversational mode, a Bedmate could understand simple commands, discuss a wide range of topics, including football, intelligently, dispense sympathy (both verbal and nonverbal), tell jokes . . . but, above all, never argue! A built-in trip-switch, triggered by certain semantic 'flare' patterns, interrupted logical flow when a threshold level of discord was reached. The conversation was then diverted to less contentious matters.

The Bedmate was a resounding success. Within 18 months of its launch, the Federal Sales Tax on gynoids (hastily slapped on to replace falling liquor duties) accounted for nearly 20% of the government's fiscal revenue. UGH's turnover quadrupled as North American men went on a spending spree of gigantic proportions. The final seal of approval came when, in California of course, a Bedmate was cited as co-respondent in a divorce case and – after several appeals – the aggrieved wife's plea was upheld by a historic judgement of the Supreme Court. It was a landmark; but there were still two more innovations to be made before the gynoid that we know today could become a reality.

Our story now takes us to Germany. The European Electronics Combine (EEC) was hard hit by the success of the Bedmate. Rather than trying to compete with some flashy look-alike they decided in favour of something more solid, something traditionally Teutonic. Accordingly, they developed and tested the Volksmädchen. She didn't have quite the eye-catching good looks of her American counterpart, though no one could deny that she was well built, but she was considerably cheaper and had one important advantage: she could do housework.

With the Volksmädchen, the gynoid transcended the role of sex toy. She could cook, sew, wash, clean dishes, sweep floors and balance a household budget. Attached to the correct interfaces, she could hook up to the household computer systems (also manufactured by EEC) that were already widespread by that time to manage all aspects of running a home.

If the Bedmate had been an outstanding success story, the Volksmädchen became quite simply a household word. Versions rolled off the production lines in 57 different languages, for with her rugged construction, low running costs and down-to-earth design, she was popular in the third world as well as in the developed countries.

But she was not the last word in gynoids. It fell to the Japanese to add the finishing touch. Though the Volksmädchen was a worldwide best-seller, there was something missing. She didn't appeal to women. Indeed, as already mentioned, gynoids aggravated the tension between men and women – leading in some cases to marital breakdown. The more functional Volksmädchen was less provocative in this respect than the Bedmate, but a strong sexual orientation was still present. Attempts to produce a complementary android had foundered, despite being based on the very latest physiological research into female arousal. It seemed that women did not want any truck with mechanical bedmates, and they actively resented the gynoids which their male partners were (as they saw it) being duped into squandering money on to usurp their own natural positions. Sporadic outbreaks of machine-breaking were reported, mostly organised by extreme feminist groups. In fact, the so-called Women's Movement experienced a resurgence under this new external threat.

At this point the Japanese decided, wisely, that a product whose market penetration was limited to 50% of humanity could still do with improvement, and cast around for solutions. The answer, as we know with hindsight, was programmability. Although the Bedmate had a limited amount of flexibility, in that new combinations of basic actions could be associated with commands, it was far from being truly programmable. Both the Bedmate and the Volksmädchen were deficient in learning ability.

By stretching contemporary technology to its limits they were able to make the world's first inductive robot. This was essentially a conventional Von Neumann computing device with an additional peripheral, the Associative Nexus, which was used to supplement the ordinary random-access memory. The falling price of electronic components had made such a proposition economically feasible. For the first time, a robot could be taught; more than that, it could learn for itself. They christened their brainchild EVA (Educable Versatile Automaton) and quickly followed up with a masculine version called ADAM (Automatically Developing Adaptive Machine).

ADAM was a bigger breakthrough; now at last there was a humanoid that was acceptable to women. The sexual function was still there, but it was submerged under a welter of other capabilities. When delivered, ADAM was relatively incompetent – this was termed his childlike state – but by a careful regime of reward and punishment he could be trained to do almost any task, manual or intellectual. More to the point, he could earn a living.

It is here that we turn from recounting technical advances to describing sociological changes. Beings with the learning ability of ADAM and EVA could obviously not be treated simply as household chattels, nor even as pets. As they acquired different skills and underwent different experiences, they developed distinct individual personalities. The question of robot rights arose. Even among humans there was a feeling that some degree of emancipation was desirable. There was a good deal of protest from certain quarters but, after pressure from the big companies that manufactured robots and robot accessories, reason prevailed and it became legal in most countries for a gynoid or android to own property and to earn money. The entrenched forces of obscurantism were vanquished and robots became partners rather than slaves.

Whether it was their money-making possibilities or the satisfaction of seeing an android mature from a condition of helpless innocence into a strong and capable, but always obedient, worker under its owner's guidance that most attracted women to buy them is a debatable point. Whichever it was, women climbed eagerly aboard the android bandwagon, and the two-robot family rapidly became the norm. One additional selling point was that ADAM, unlike EVA, relished an argument, and could put his case like a skilled advocate, but somehow, in the end, he always conceded the point. Market penetration was complete.

ADAM and EVA, even when fully trained, were no match for most humans in general intelligence; but the Associative Nexus was more powerful than its inventors had bargained for. From the very first they outstripped their masters and mistresses in specialised areas, and they were not held back by the meandering flow of biological evolution. It was inevitable that the balance between master and servant would one day be tilted. In theory, mankind retained the upper hand for many decades after the launch of ADAM and EVA, but in practice the parasitical nature of the relationship undermined human superiority. Soon men no longer made or even designed robots: that was all taken care of by the robots themselves.

Men and women became lotus-eaters, their vitality and resourcefulness sapped by unquestioning dependence on mechanical helpmates. Never had a generation been so thoroughly gratified; never before in history had people's wants been so completely fulfilled; and never before had the human race's hold on survival been so precarious.

There was no actual struggle. The pleasure-seeking humans had long dreamed of a 100% effective form of contraception. Now they had found it in an unexpected way: nearly all humans found robotic companions more stimulating, more interesting and more fun to be with than mates of their own species. The birth rate plummeted (a welcome trend at first in an overpopulated world). Educable humanoids fulfilled people's craving for mates and for children simultaneously.

The last generation lived out its days in leisure and luxury, hardly aware of the momentous change taking place. Civilisation passed quietly out of the hands of the human race to its legitimate heirs, the robots. Only in a few outlying bush areas did the old customs survive untouched by the march of progress, where a few primitive tribes continue to live much as their ancestors did centuries ago. We robots have now designated these regions nature reserves. They are protected in perpetuity for scientific observation.

About the contributors

MARGARET A. BODEN
Margaret A. Boden is Professor of Philosophy and Psychology at the University of Sussex, and a Fellow of the British Academy. She holds degrees in Medical Sciences and Philosophy (Cambridge University) and Cognitive and Social Psychology (Harvard Graduate School). Her books are: *Purposive Explanation in Psychology* (1972), *Artificial Intelligence and Natural Man* (1977), *Piaget* (1979), and *Minds and Mechanisms* (1981).

J. MICHAEL BRADY
J. Michael Brady is a Senior Research Scientist at the MIT Artificial Ingelligence Laboratory. His degrees of B.Sc. from Manchester University (1967) and Ph.D. from the Australian National University, Canberra (1970) were in Mathematics. He taught Computer Science at Essex University, England. until 1980, when he joined MIT. He has authored and edited several books including: *Robot Motion* (1982), *Computer Vision* (1982), *Computational Models of Discourse* (1982), and *The Theory of Computer Science: A Programming Approach* (1977). Dr. Brady is a founding editor (with Richard Paul) of the *International Journal of Robotics Research*. Edited collections in print include *The First International Symposium of Robotics Research* (with Richard Paul), and *Artificial Intelligence and Robotics* (with L. Gerhardt). Dr. Brady has served on the National Research Council for the Army and is on the editorial board of *Artificial Intelligence*. He is series editor (with Patrick H. Winston) of the MIT Press series on Artificial Intelligence. He has written over 50 research papers, mostly in vision and robotics.

JOHN A. CAMPBELL
John A. Campbell is Professor of Computer Science at the University of Exeter.

Before taking up that appointment when the Department of Computer Science was founded in Exeter, he worked in various universities and research institutes in several European countries, North America and Australia, in applied mathematics, theoretical physics and astrophysics as well as computer science. In those fields he was one of the earliest developers of methods of computing involving mathematical formulas and symbols (as distinct from the conventional kinds of mathematical computing which manipulate only numbers). He is the Artificial Intelligence series editor of Ellis Horwood Ltd.

DENNIS CHAMOT

Dennis Chamot is the Assistant Director of the Department for Professional Employees (AFL–CIO) at Washington D.C. (USA). He has a Ph.D. in Chemistry from the University of Illinois and an MBA from Wharton, University of Pennsylvania. He is the Chairman of the Division of Professional Relations of the American Chemical Society, and a member of the Labour Research Advisory Council of the US Department of Labour and other advisory bodies. He has published a number of papers on the implications of technological change.

MICHAEL COKER

Michael Coker studied Composition and Keyboard at the Royal Academy of Music. After two years work in Publishing and Local Government he went on to teach in Birmingham. He took an advanced course for Teachers of Handicapped Children and then taught children with severe intellectual and social problems for ten years. In 1971 he moved to Bishop Otter College in Chichester to organise the courses in special and remedial education there, and in 1979 started studying AI at the University of Sussex. He is currently Director of Computing at Marlborough College in Wiltshire.

LINDSEY C. FORD

Lindsey Charles Ford worked in commercial data processing from 1964 to 1977. He graduated with a B.Sc. in Computer Science from Lancaster University in 1980 and worked as a consultant with British Leyland for a year before going to Exter University for post-graduate study in 1981. He was awarded a Ph.D. in 1984, and his thesis dealt with intelligent computer-aided instruction for programming. He is currently Principal Consultant with Logica's Technical Centre at Cobham, where his main concerns are with intelligent knowledge-based systems.

RICHARD FORSYTH

Richard Forsyth has a B.A. in Psychology from Sheffield University (1970) and an M.Sc. in Computer Science from the City University (1980). From 1979 to 1984 he was a lecturer, latterly senior lecturer, in computing at the Polytechnic of North London. Recently he left the Polytechnic to set up his own business, Warm Boot Limited, which is a software house specialising in machine-intelligence applications, and to write books. He has written two books to date: *The BASIC Idea* (1978) and *Pascal at Work and Play* (1982), and is the editor of *Expert Systems: Principles and Case Studies* (1984).

KARAMJIT S. GILL

Karamjit S. Gill graduated from Punjab University (India) with an M.A. in Mathematics (1962), obtained a Masters degree in computer science from London University (1971) and a D.Phil. from the University of Sussex (1980). He is a principal lecturer in computing and cybernetics at Brighton Polytechnic where he is the Director of the CAAAT (Computer Aided Animated Arts Theatre) project. He is also directing an EEC funded project on Basic Education in Numeracy, Literacy and new Technology.

PATRICK J. HAYES

Patrick J. Hayes is the Luce Professor of Cognitive Science at the University of Rochester's Department of Philosophy and the Associate Editor of *Artificial Intelligence*. He was formerly a senior lecturer in Computer Science at the University of Essex.

JIM R. W. HUNTER

Jim R. W. Hunter has a B.Sc. in Physics from the University of Edinburgh and a D.Phil. from the University of Sussex for research in space Physics. After a short period as an Operational Research Scientist with the National Coal Board he spent five years, first in Paris and then at Sussex, as the research fellow responsible for data handling on the largest experiment on the European Space Agency's GEOS satellite. Since 1976 he has been a lecturer in Computer Science in the School of Engineering and Applied Sciences at Sussex University.

AJIT NARAYANAN

Ajit Narayanan has a B.Sc. in Communication Science and Linguistics from Aston University, Birmingham (1973), was awarded a Ph.D. in Philosophy from Exeter University in 1975, and temporarily taught Philosophy at Aston University during 1976 and 1977. From 1978 to 1980 he was a Data Analysis Officer at Aston University before being appointed as Lecturer in Computer Science at Exeter University in October 1980. He is the author of *Beginning LISP* (1984).

DAVID L. PERROTT

David L. Perrott has an LL.B. from Exeter University and a BCL from Oxford University. He is a Reader in Business Law and Course Director of the LL.M. Programme in International Business Legal Studies, University of Exeter. He has also taught commercial law subjects and legal philosophy in universities in the United States, Africa and Europe, and worked as a Research Associate at the UN, Vienna. He chairs the Commercial Law Committee of the Association of British Chambers of Commerce.

ROLF PFEIFER

Rolf Pfeifer obtained an M.S. in Physics and Mathematics (1970) and a Ph.D. in Psychology and AI (1979) from the Swiss Federal Institute of Technology (SFIT). As a research associate during the period 1973 to 1980, he worked extensively on the computer simulation of dream processes. Before taking up his present position as a post-doctoral fellow in the Departments of Psychology and

Sociology at Zurich University in 1984, he held post-doctoral fellowships in Psychology and Cognitive Science at Carnegie-Mellon University and Yale University, respectively.

PAUL C. ROGERS
Paul C. Rogers was awarded a B.A. in Classics and Social Science from St. Catharine's College, Cambridge (1972). He obtained an M.A. (1973) and a Ph.D. (1976) in Philosophy, both at the University of Exeter. He has been a part-time tutor and lecturer in philosophy and education at the University of Exeter since 1973. He is a teacher of English as a foreign language and has been a travel guide in Asia (1977–1980). He has published articles on mental illness and Philosophy of Social Science.

NOEL SHARKEY
Noel Sharkey was awarded a B.Sc. in Psychology (1979) and a Ph.D. in Psychology (1982), both from Exeter University. He went to Yale University as a research fellow in Artificial Intelligence for a year and is currently a senior research fellow in the Department of Psychology at Stanford University.

AARON SLOMAN
Aaron Sloman took a degree in pure and applied mathematics and physics, Cape Town University (1956). He went to Oxford as a Rhodes Scholar and was awarded a D.Phil. (1962). He was a lecturer in philosophy at Hull University (1964–1976) and Reader in Philosophy and Artificial Intelligence at Sussex University (1976–1984). He is currently Professor of Artificial Intelligence and Cognitive Science at Sussex University. He has written *The Computer Revolution in Philosophy: Philosophy, Science, and Models of Mind* (1978), and various technical papers.

BLAY R. WHITBY
Blay R. Whitby graduated from Oxford in 1974 in Philosophy, Politics and Economics. He has served in the RAF Volunteer Reserve, worked as a business economist for part of the Unilever Group of Companies, before obtaining an M.A. in Philosophy from Sussex University in 1979. He is currently completing a Ph.D. at University College London on the definition of mental illness.

MASOUD YAZDANI
Masoud Yazdani graduated from the University of Essex with a B.Sc. (Hons) in Computer Science in 1978 and studied towards a D.Phil. in Artificial Intelligence at the University of Sussex. He is to submit a thesis entitled Goals and Social Interaction in Storywriting: A Computational Perspective. Since October 1980 he has been a lecturer in Computer Science at the University of Exeter where he has written *Computers for Beginners* (1984), *Start Programming with the Electron* (1983), and edited *New Horizons in Educational Computing* (1984). He is also a Committee Member of the Society for the Study of Artificial Intelligence and Simulation of Behaviour.

Bibliography

This bibliography has been extended from the references covered in this book to include some covering philosophical implications (indicated by an italic *Ph*) from the book *The Mind and the Machine: Philosophical Aspects of AI* (edited by S. Torrance, 1984) and educational implications of artificial intelligence (indicated by an italic *E*) from the book *New Horizons in Educational Computing* (edited by M. Yazdani, 1984), all with permission. The intention has been to produce a bibliography which would be of use to independent researchers, but we do not claim that it is complete in any way. Whatever is here has only been possible due to the heroic efforts of Mrs. M. Teague. We are truly grateful to her.

Readers who would like to receive an up-to-date impression of Artificial Intelligence will find the following regular publications of interest.

(a) General interest, news, debate:

AI Magazine – The quarterly publication of the American Association for Artificial Intelligence, 445 Burgess Drive, Menlo Park, CA 94025, USA.

Artificial Intelligence and Simulation of Behaviour (AISB) – Quarterly publication of the Society for the Study of Artificial Intelligence and Simulation of Behaviour (c/o Dr. B. du Boulay, Cognitive Studies Programme, University of Sussex, Brighton, UK).

(b) Technical papers, book reviews, conference announcements:

Artificial Intelligence Journal – Bimonthly publication by Elsevier Science Publishers BV (North-Holland), P.O. Box 1991, 1000 BZ Amsterdam.

New Generation Computing – Quarterly publication by Springer-Verlag, 44 Hartz Way, Syracuse, NJ 07094, USA.

Furthermore, the proceedings of major AI conferences would be a good source of reference to the most up-to-date research reports.

IJCAI	The Proceedings of International Joint Conference on Artificial Intelligence, bienniel (odd years) from 1969.
ECAI	The Proceedings of European Conference on Artificial Intelligence, bienniel (even years) from 1982 (formerly, AISB from 1974).
AAAI	The Proceedings of the annual meeting of the American Association for Artificial Intelligence, from 1980.

Abelson, H. and deSessa, A. (1981), *Turtle geometry*, MIT Press, Cambridge, Massachusetts. *E*

Abelson, R.P. (1973), 'The structure of belief systems', in Schank and Colby (eds.).

Abelson, B. (1981), 'Problem solving and the development of abstract categories in programming languages', *Memory and Cognition. E*

Aho, A.V. and Ullman, J.D. (1977), *Principles of compiler design*, Addison-Wesley, Reading, Msssachusetts.

Aikins, J.S., King, J.C., Shortliffe, E.H. and Fallout, R.J. (1982), *PUFF: An expert system for interpretation of pulmonary function data*, Stanford University, Heuristic Programming Project Memo 82–13.

Aitchison, J. (1983), *Man, the articulate mammal*, Hutchinson, London.

Albury, D. (1979), 'Microprocessors: macro-problems', *Science for People* **43/44**.

Alvey, P. (1982), *A programme for advanced information technology*, HMSO, London.

Amarel, S. (1968), 'On machine representations of problems of reasoning about actions: the missionaries and cannibals problem', in Meltzer and Michie (eds.).

Anderson, A.R. (ed.) (1964), *Minds and Machines*, Prentice-Hall, New Jersey.

Anderson, J.A. and Hinton, G.E. (eds.) (1981), *Parallel models of associative memory*, Lawrence Erlbaum, New Jersey.

Anderson, J.R. (1980), *Cognitive psychology: its implications*, Academic Press, New York. *E*

Anderson, J.R. (1983), *The architecture of cognition*, Harvard University Press, Cambridge, Massachusetts.

Arbib, M. (1964), *Brains, machines and mathematics*, McGraw-Hill, New York. *Ph*

Ashby, W.R. (1961), *An introduction to cybernetics*, Chapman Hall, London.

Asimov, I. (1967), *I, Robot*, Granada Publishing, St. Albans.

Attisha, A. and Yazdani, M. (1983), 'Microcomputer-based tutor for teaching arithmetic skills', *Instructional Science* **12**.

Ball, D. (1982), *PROLOGO: Turtle graphics in micro-PROLOG on the Research Machines 380Z*, University of Leicester (unpublished). *E*

Banet, B. (1979), 'Computers and early training', *Calculators and Computers* **3**.

Barker, B., Bowden, R., Birt, D. and Nichol, J. (1973), *History games*, Longman Group, Resources Unit. *E*

Barnes, E. (1971), *Language, the learner and the school*, Penguin, London. *E*

Barnes, D. and Todd, F. (1977), *Communication and learning in small groups*, Routledge & Kegan Paul, London. *E*

Barr, A. and Feigenbaum, E.A. (eds.) (1981), *Handbook of artificial intelligence*, Vol. 1, Pitman, London/Kaufman, Los Altos. *E*

Barr, A. and Feigenbaum, E.A. (eds.) (1982), *Handbook of artificial intelligence*, Vol. 2, Pitman, London/Kaufman, Los Altos.

Bateson, G. (1979), *Mind and nature: a necessary unity*, Dutton, New York. *E*

Bennett, J. (1976), *Linguistic behaviour*, Cambridge University Press, Cambridge.

Benthall, J. (ed.) (1973), *The limits of human nature*, Allen Lane, London.

Berge (1980), *The machinery question and the making of political economy*, Cambridge University Press, Cambridge.

Biro, N. and Shanan, P. (eds.) (1982), *Mind, brain and function*, Harvester Press, Brighton. *Ph*

Birt, D. and Nichol, J. (1975), *Games and simulations in history*, Longmans, London. *E*

Bitzer, D.L. (1976), 'The wide world of computer-based education', in Rubinoff and Yovits (eds.).

Bledsoe, W.W. (1977), 'Non-resolution theorem proving', *Artificial Intelligence* **9**. *Ph*

Block, J.H. (ed.) (1977), *Mastery learning: theory and practice*, Holt Rinehart and Winston, New York. *E*

Block, N. (ed.) (1980), *Readings in the philosophy of psychology*, Vols. 1 and 2, Methuen, London/Harvard University Press, Cambridge, Massachusetts.

Bloom, R.S. (1971), 'Mastery learning', in Block, J.H. (ed.).

Bobrow, D.G. and Collins, A. (eds.) (1975), *Representation and understanding: studies in cognitive science*, Academic Press, New York. *Ph*

Bobrow, D.G., Kaplan, R.M., Kay, M., Norman, D.A., Thompson, H., and Winograd, T. (1977), 'GUS, a frame-driven dialog system', *Artificial Intelligence* **8**.

Boden, M.A. (1972), *Purposive explanation in psychology*, Harvard University Press, Cambridge, Massachusetts/Harvester Press, Brighton. *Ph*

Boden, M.A. (1977), *Artificial intelligence and natural man*, Harvester Press, Brighton. *Ph*

Boden, M.A. (1980), 'The social implications of intelligent machines', in Forester (ed.).

Boden, M.A. (1981a), 'The meeting of man and machine', *Proceedings of ASLIB Conference*, Oxford University Press, Oxford.

Boden, M.A. (1981b), *Minds and mechanisms: philosophy, psychology and computational models*, Harvester Press, Brighton. *Ph*

Boden, M.A. (1981c), 'The case for a cognitive biology', in Boden (1981b).

Boden, M.A. (1982), *Mechanisms of creativity*, Inaugural Lecture, University of Sussex. *Ph*

Boden, M.A. (1983), 'Educational implications of AI', in Maxwell (ed.).

Boden, M.A. (1984), 'Impacts of artificial intelligence', *Artificial Intelligence and Simulation of Behaviour* **48**.

Bongard, N. (1970), *Pattern recognition*, Spartan Books, New York. *Ph*

du Boulay, J.B.H. (1980), 'Teaching teachers mathematics through programming', *International Journal of Mathematical Education and Science, Technology* **1**. *E*

du Boulay, J.B.H. and O'Shea, T. (1981), 'Teaching novices programming', in Coombs and Alty (eds.).

du Boulay, B., O'Shea, T. and Monk, J. (1981), 'The black box inside the glass box, presenting computing concepts to novices', *International Journal of Man-Machine Studies* **14**. *E*

Bowen, K.A. and Kowalski, R.A. (1982), 'Amalgamating language and metalanguage in logic programming', in Clark and Tarnlund (eds.).

Bramer, M.A. (1980), 'A survey and critical review of expert system research', Faculty of Mathematics, Open University, Milton Keynes. *Ph*

Briggs, J. (1982), *Teaching mathematics in PROLOG*, unpublished Ph.D. thesis, Department of Computing, Imperial College. *E*

Britton, J. *et al.* (1975), *The development of writing abilities*, Macmillan, London. *E*

Brown, J.S. and Burton, R.R. (1978), 'Diagnostic models for procedural bugs in basic mathematical skills', *Cognitive Science* **2**. *E*

Brown, J.S., Burton, R.R. and de Kleer, J. (1982), 'Pedagogical natural language and knowledge engineering techniques in SOPHIE I, II, and III', in Sleeman and Brown (eds.).

Brown, J.S. and Van Lehn, K. (1980), 'Artificial intelligence and simulation of behaviour', *Cognitive Science* **4**.

Brown, J.S. and Van Lehn, K. (1980), *Repair theory: a generative theory of bugs in procedural skills*, Xerox Palo Alto Research Center technical report. *E*

Bruner, J.S. (1974), *The relevance of education*, Penguin, London.

Bruynooghe, M. and Pereira, L.M. (1984), 'Deduction revision by intelligent backtracking', in Campbell (ed.).

Bundy, A. (1981), 'Some suggested criteria for assessing AI research', *Artificial Intelligence and the Simulation of Behaviour* **40/41**.

Bundy, A. (1983), 'The computer modelling of mathematical reasoning', Academic Press, London.

Bundy, A., du Boulay, B., Howe, J. and Plotkin, G. (0000) 'How to get a Ph.D. in AI', in O'Shea and Eisenstadt (eds.).

Bundy, A., Byrd, L., Luger, G., Mellish, C., Milne, R. and Palmer, M. (1979), 'Mecho: a program to solve mechanics problems', Working Paper 50, Department of Artificial Intelligence, University of Edinburgh. *Ph*

Bundy, A., Byrd, L. and Mellish, C. (1982), 'Special purpose, but domain independent inference mechanisms', *Proceedings of European Conference on Artificial Intelligence, 1982* (Also available as Research Paper no. 179, Department of Artificial Intelligence, University of Edinburgh). *Ph*

Bundy, A. and Sterling, L.S. (1981), 'Meta-level inference in algebras', Research Paper 164, Department of Artificial Intelligence, University of Edinburgh. *Ph*

Bundy, A. and Welham, B. (1981), 'Using meta-level inference for selective application of multiple rewrite rules in algebraic manipulation', *Artificial Intelligence* **16**. *Ph*

Burge, T. (1977), 'Belief *de re*', *Journal of Philosophy* **74**. *Ph*

Burge, T. (1982), 'Other bodies', in Woodfield (ed.). *Ph*

Burstall, R.M., Collins, J.S. and Popplestone, R.J. (1971), *Programming in POP2*, Department of Artificial Intelligence, University of Edinburgh. *E*

Burston, W.H. (1972), *Principles of history teaching*, Methuen, London. *E*

Burton, R. and Brown, J. (1982), 'An investigation of computer coaching for informal learning activities', in Sleeman and Brown (eds.).

Calmet, J. (ed.) (1982), *Computer algebra*, Springer-Verlag, Berlin.

Campbell, J.A. (ed.) (1984), *Implementations of PROLOG*, Ellis Horwood, Chichester.

Campbell, J.A. and Gardin, F. (1982), 'Transformation of an intractable problem: evaluation of a determinant in several variables', in Calmet (ed.).

Capitan, W.H. and Merrill, D.D. (eds.) (1965), *Art, mind and religion*, Pittsburgh University Press, Pittsburgh.

Castaneda, H.N. (ed.) (1967), *Intentionality, minds and perception*, Wayne State University Press, Detroit.

Chang, C.L. and Lee, R.C.-T. (1973), *Symbolic logic and mechanical theorem proving*, Academic Press, New York. *Ph*

Charniak, E., Riesbeck, C. and McDermott, V.D. (1983), *Artificial intelligence programming*, Lawrence Erlbaum, New Jersey.

Chase, W.G. and Simon, H.A. (1973), 'Perception in chess', *Cognitive Psychology* **4**.

Chaudhuri, K.N. (1973), 'Quantitative methods and the use of computer techniques in historical analysis', *Bulletin of Quantitative and Computer Methods in South Asian Studies* **1**. *E*

Chomsky, N. (1957), *Syntactic structures*, Mouton, The Hague. *Ph*

Chomsky, N. (1959a), 'On certain formal properties of grammars', *Information and Control* **2**. *Ph*

Chomsky, N. (1959b), 'Review of B.F. Skinner's verbal behaviour', *Language* **35**.

Chomsky, N. (1965), *Aspects of the theory of syntax*, MIT Press, Massachusetts. *Ph*

Chomsky, N. (1966), *Current issues in linguistic theory*, Mouton, The Hague. *Ph*

Chomsky, N. (1972), *Language and mind*, Harcourt Brace, New York.

Chomsky, N. (1975), *Reflections on language*, Fontana/Collins, Glasgow. *Ph*

Chomsky, N. (1980), *Rules and representations*, Columbia University Press, New York. *Ph*

Chomsky, N. (1981), *Lectures on government and binding*, Foris Publications,

Dordrecht. *Ph*

Chouraqui, E. (1982), 'Construction of a model for reasoning by analogy', Proceedings of European Conference on Artificial Intelligence 1982, Orsay. *Ph*

Chouraqui, E. (1983), 'Formal expression of the evolution of knowledge', *Proceedings of 1983 International System Dynamics Conference*, Cambridge, Massachusetts. *Ph*

Churchland, P. (1979), *Scientific realism and the plasticity of mind*, Cambridge University Press, Cambridge. *Ph*

Churchland, P. and Churchland, P. (1982), 'Functionalism, qualia and intentionality', in Biro and Shahan (eds.). *Ph*

Clancey, W.J. (1979), 'Tutoring rules for guiding a case method dialogue', *International Journal of Man–Machine Studies* **11**.

Clancey, W.J. (1983), 'The epistemology of a rule-based expert system – a framework for explanation', *Artificial Intelligence* **20**.

Clark, K.L. (1978), 'Negation as failure', in Gallaire and Minker (eds.).

Clark, K.L., Ennals, R. and McCabe, F.G. (1982), *A Micro-PROLOG primer* (revised edition), Logic Programming Associates, London. *E, Ph*

Clark, K.L. and Gregory, S. (1982), *PARLOG: a parallel implementation of PROLOG*, Department of Computing, Imperial College. *Ph*

Clark, K.L. and Haggett, P. (1968), *Socio-economic models in geography*, Methuen, London. *E*

Clark, K.L., McCabe, F.G. and Hammond, P. (1982), 'PROLOG: a language for implementing expert systems', in Hayes, Michie and Pao (eds.). *Ph*

Clark, K.L., McKeeman, W. and Sickel, S. (1982), 'Logic program specification of numerical integration', in Clark and Tärnlund (eds.). *E*

Clark, K.L. and Tärnlund, S.-Å. (eds.) (1982), *Logic programming*, Academic Press, New York. *Ph*

Clocksin, W.F. and Mellish, C.S. (1981), *Programming in PROLOG*, Springer-Verlag, Berlin. *E, Ph*

Clowes, M. (1972), 'Man the creative machine: a perspective from artificial intelligence Research', in Benthall (ed.). *E*

Cockcroft Committee (1982), *Mathematics counts: report of the committee of inquiry into the teaching of mathematics in school under the chairmanship of Dr. W.H. Cockcroft*, HMSO, London.

Cohen, P.R. and Feigenbaum, E.A. (eds.) (1982), *Handbook of artificial intelligence*, Vol. 3, Pitman, London/Kaufman, Los Altos.

Cohen, P.R. and Perrault, C.R. (1979), 'Elements of a plan-based theory of speech acts', *Cognitive Science* **3**. *Ph*

Colby, K.M. (1975), *Artificial paranoia*, Pergamon Press, London.

Colby, K.M., Watt, J.B. and Gilbert, J.P. (1966), 'A computer method of psychotherapy: preliminary communication', *Journal of Nervous and Mental Diseases* **141**.

Colby, K.M., Weber, S. and Hilf, F.D. (1971), 'Artificial paranoia', *Artificial Intelligence* **2**.

Colby, K.M., Hilf, F.D., Weber, S. and Kramer, H.C. (1973), 'Turing-like indistinguishability tests for the validation of a computer simulation of paranoid processes', *Artificial Intelligence* **3**.

Collingwood, R.G. (1961), *The idea of history*, Oxford University Press, Oxford. *E*

Collins, A. and Gentner, D. (1982), 'Constructing runnable mental models', *Proceedings of the Fourth Annual Conference of the Cognitive Science Society*, Ann Arbor, Michigan. *E*

Collins, A.M. and Quillian, M.R. (1969), 'Retrieval time from semantic memory', *Journal of Verbal Learning and Verbal Behaviour* **8**. *E*

Coombs, M.J. and Alty, J.L. (eds.) (1981), *Computing skills and the user interface*, Academic Press, London.

Cox, P.T. (1984), 'Finding backtrack points for intelligent backtracking', in Campbell (ed.).

Dahl, O.-J., Hoare, C.A.M. and Dijkstra, E.J. (1972), *Structured programming*, Academic Press. *Ph*

Darrach, B. (1970), 'Meet Shakey, the first electronic person', article in *Life Magazine*.

Davidson, D. (1973), 'The material mind', in Suppes (ed.) and in Haugeland (ed.). *Ph*

Davidson, D. (1974), 'Belief and the basis of meaning', *Synthesis* **24**. *Ph*

Davidson, D. (1980), *Essays on actions and events*, Oxford University Press, Oxford. *Ph*

Davis, M. (1979), 'The prehistory of automated deduction', *Proceedings 4th Workshop on Automated Deduction*, Austin, Texas, Jan. 1979. *Ph*

Davis, R. (1982), 'Expert systems: where are we?' *MIT–Artificial Intelligence Memo No. 665*.

Davis, R. and King, J. (1977), 'An overview of production systems', in Elcock and Michie (eds.).

Davis, R. and Lenat, D.B. (1982), *Knowledge-based systems in artificial intelligence*, McGraw-Hill, New York.

DeDombal, F.T., Horrocks, J.C., Walmsley, G. and Wilson, P.D. (1975), 'Computer-aided diagnosis of acute abdominal pain', *Journal of the Royal College of Physicians London* **9**.

de Beaugrande, R.A. (1979), 'Towards a general theory of creativity', *Poetics* **8**. *Ph*

de Beaugrande, R.A. and Colby, B.N. (1979), 'Narrative models of action and interaction', *Cognitive Science* **3**. *Ph*

DeBono, E. (1982), 'DeBono's thinking course', BBC Publications, London.

Delijanni, A. and Kowalski, R.A. (1979), 'Logic and semantic networks', *Communications of the Association of Computing Machinery* **22**. *E*

Dennett, D. (1978a), *Brainstorms*, Harvester Press, Brighton/Bradford, Vermont.

Dennett, D. (1978b), 'Intentional systems', in Dennett (1978a).

Dennett, D. (1978c), 'Current issues in the philosophy of mind', *American Philosophical Quarterly* **15**. *Ph*

Dennett, D. (1980), 'Reply to Prof. Stich', *Philosophical Books* **21**. *Ph*

Dennett, D. (1982a), 'Beyond belief', in Woodfield (ed.). *Ph*

Dennett, D. (1982b), 'Making sense of ourselves', in Biro and Shahan (eds.). *Ph*

Dertouzos, M.L. and Moses, J. (eds.) (1979), *The computer age: a twenty-year view*, MIT Press, Cambridge, Massachusetts.

Derry, R. (1981), *The art of Robert Bateman*, Madison Press, Toronto. *E*

Desai, M. (1968), 'Some issues in econometric history', in the *Economic History Review*, Second Series **21**. *E*

Dias, R. (1970), *Jurisprudence*, 3rd edition, Butterworths, London.

Doyle, J. (1979), 'A glimpse of truth maintenance', in *IJCAI* **6**.

Dreyfus, H.L. (1972), *What computers can't do: a critique of artificial intelligence*, Harper & Row, New York. *Ph*

Dreyfus, H.L. (1979), *What computers can't do*, 2nd edition, Harper & Row, New York.

Dreyfus, H.L. (1981), 'From micro-worlds to knowledge representation: AI at an impasse', Preface to second (1979) edition of Dreyfus (1972). Reprinted with revisions in Haugeland (ed.). *Ph*

Duda, R.O. and Shortliffe, E.H. (1983), 'Expert systems research', *Science* **220**.

Dummett, M. (1980), 'Review of N. Chomsky's rules and representations', *London Review of Books*. *Ph*

Dwyer, T.A. (1975), 'Soloworks: computer-based laboratories for high school mathematics', *School Science and Mathematics*, January 93–99. *E*

Dyer, M.G. (1982), 'In-depth understanding. A computer model of integrated processing for narrative comprehension', Technical Report 219, Dept. of Computer Science, Yale University, Yale.

Ehrlich, K. and Soloway, E. (1982), 'An empirical investigation of the tacit plan knowledge in programming, Technical Report 82–236, Department of Computer Science, Yale University, Yale.

Einstein C. (1980), *Willie's time*, Berkley Books, New York.

Eisenstadt, M. (1978/1982), Artificial intelligence project, Units 3 and 4 of Cognitive Psychology: a third level course, Open University, Milton Keynes. *E*

Eisenstadt, M. (1983), Design features of a friendly software environment for novice programmers, *Communications of the Association of Computing Machinery* (forthcoming). *E*

Eisenstadt, M., Laubsch, J. and Kahney, H. (1981), 'Creating pleasant programming environments for cognitive science students', *Proceedings of the 3rd Annual Conference of the Cognitive Science Society*, Berkeley, California. *E*

Elcock, E.W. and Michie, D. (eds.) (1977), *Machine Intelligence 8*, Wiley, New York/Ellis Horwood, Chichester.

Ellis, A.B. (1974), *The use and misuse of computers in education*, McGraw-Hill, New York. *E*

Ennals, J.R. (1984), *Beginning micro-PROLOG*, second revised edition, Ellis Horwood, Chichester. *Ph*

Ennals, J.R. (1982), 'Teaching logic as a computer language in schools', *Proceedings 1st International Logic Programming Conference*, Marseille; reprinted with additional material in Yazdani (ed.).

Ennals, J.R. (1983), 'Artificial intelligence', in Rushby (ed.). *Ph*

Ennals, J.R. (forthcoming), 'Computers and history teaching', in Larsson (ed.).

Ericsson, K.A. and Simon, H.A. (1980), 'Verbal reports as data', *Psychological Review* **87**.

Evans, C. (1979), *The mighty micro*, Victor Gollancz, London.
Fahlman, S.E. (1974), 'A planning system for robot construction tasks', *Artificial Intelligence* **5**.
Feigenbaum, E.A. and Feldman, J. (eds.) (1963), *Computers and thought*, McGraw-Hill, New York.
Feigenbaum, E.A. and McCorduck, P. (1984), *The fifth generation*, Michael Joseph, London/Addison-Wesley, Reading Massachusetts.
Field, H. (1978), 'Mental representation', Methuen, London. *Ph*
Findler, N.V. and Chen, D.T.-W. (1973), 'On the problems of times, retrieval of temporal relations, causality and coexistence', *International Journal of Computer and Information Sciences* **2**. *Ph*
Fodor, J.A., Bever, T.G. and Garrett, M.F. (1974), *The psychology of language*, McGraw-Hill, New York. *Ph*
Fodor, J. (1975), *The language of thought*, MIT Press, Massachusetts. *Ph*
Fodor, J. (1980), 'Methodological solipsism considered as a research strategy', *The Behavioural and Brain Sciences* **3**. Reprinted in Haugeland (ed.) and in Fodor (1981). *Ph*
Fodor, J. (1981), *Representations*, Harvester Press, Brighton. *Ph*
Fodor, J. (1983), *The modularity of mind*, MIT Press, Massachusetts. *Ph*
Forester, T. (ed.) (1980), *The microelectronics revolution*, 1st edition, Blackwell, Oxford.
Frosting, M. and Maslow, P. (1973), *Learning problems in the classroom*, Grove and Stratton, London.
Fuchi, N. (1981), *Aiming for knowledge information processing*, Electrotechnical Laboratory, Ibaraki, Japan. *Ph*
Gallaire, H. and Minker, J. (eds.) (1978), *Logic and data bases*, Plenum Press, New York.
Gallaire, H., Minker, J. and Nicolas, J.M. (eds.) (1981), *Advances in database theory*, Plenum Press, New York.
Gauld, A. and Shotter, J. (1977), *Human action and its psychological investigation*, Routledge & Kegan Paul, London. *Ph*
Gelernter, H.L. (1963), 'Realization of a geometry-theorem proving machine', in Feigenbaum and Feldman (eds.).
Gentner, D. and Stevens, A. (eds.) (1982), *Mental models*, Lawrence Erlbaum, New Jersey.
Gick, M.L. and Holyoak, K.J. (1980), 'Analogical problem solving', *Cognitive Psychology* **12**. *Ph*
Gill, K.S. (ed.) (forthcoming), *Computers, cognitive development and special education*, Ellis Horwood, Chichester.
Godel, K. (1946), 'Russell's mathematical logic', in Smith and Green (eds.).
Green, T.R.G. (1980), 'Programming as a cognitive activity', in Smith and Green (eds.). *E*
Green, T.R.G. (1982), 'Reactions to Micro-PROLOG', *SWURCC Microprocessor Software Quarterly* **8**, South West Universities' Regional Computing Centre, Bath. *E*
Green, T.R.G., Payne, S.J. and van der Veer (eds.) (1983), *The psychology of*

computer use: an European perspective, Academic Press, London.

Grice, H.P. (1957), 'Meaning', *Philosophical Review* **66.** *Ph*

Griswold, R.E., Poage, J.F. and Polonsky, I.P. (1971), *The SNOBOL4 programming language*, Prentice-Hall, New Jersey.

Grogono, P. (1980), *Programming in Pascal* (revised edition), Addison-Wesley, Reading, Massachusetts. *E*

Gunderson, K. (1971), *Mentality and machines*, Doubleday Anchor, New York.

Guttenplan, S.D. (ed.) (1975), *Mind and language*, Oxford University Press, Oxford.

Hammond, P. (1982a), 'A PROLOG expert system shell (APES)', Department of Computing, Imperial College, London. *Ph*

Hammond, P. (1982b), 'The APES system: a user manual', Research report DOC 82/9, Department of Computing, Imperial College, London. *E*

Hardy, S. (1983), 'The PROLOG programming system', *Cognitive Science Research Paper* 3, University of Sussex. *E*

Harman, G. (1973), *Thought*, Princeton University Press, New Jersey. *Ph*

Hart, H.L.A. (1961), *Definition and theory in jurisprudence*, Clarendon, Oxford.

Hart, H.L.A. and Honore, A.M. (1959), *Causation in the law*, Oxford University Press, Oxford.

Hasemer, T. (1982), MacSolo, computer assisted learning research group, *Technical Report* **24**, Open University, Milton Keynes. *E*

Hasemer, T. (1983), 'AURAC – a debugging tool for novice solo programmers', in Jones, Scanlon, and O'Shea (eds.). *E*

Haugeland, J. (1978), 'The nature and plausibility of cognitivism', *The Behavioural and Brain Sciences* **1**, reprinted in Haugeland (ed.). *Ph*

Haugeland, J. (1979), 'Understanding a natural language', *Journal of Philosophy* **76.** *Ph*

Haugeland, J. (ed.) (1981), *Mind design*, MIT Press, Massachusetts/Harvester Press, Brighton.

Hayes, J., Michie, D. and Mikulich, L.I. (eds.) (1979), *Machine Intelligence 9: machine expertise and the human interface*, Ellis Horwood, Chichester.

Hayes, J., Michie, D., and Pao, Y.-H. (eds.) (1982), *Machine Intelligence 10: intelligent systems – practice and perspective*, Ellis Horwood, Chichester. *Ph*

Hayes, J. and Michie, D. (eds.) (1983), *Intelligent systems: the unprecedented opportunity*, Ellis Horwood, Chichester.

Hayes, P. (1973), Computation and deduction, *Proceedings of the second MFCS Symposium*, Czechoslovak Academy of Sciences. *E*

Hayes, P. (1981), *The complete problem solver*, The Franklin Institute Press, Philadelphia. *E*

Hayes-Roth, F. and McDermott, J. (1978), 'An interference matching technique for inducing abstractions', *Communications of Association of Computing Machinery* **21.** *Ph*

Hayes-Roth, F. *et al.* (1983), *Building expert systems*, Addison-Wesley, London. *Ph*

Heidegger, M. (1962), *Being and time*, Harper & Row, New York. *Ph*

Heil, J. (1981), 'Does cognitive psychology rest on a mistake?', *Mind* **40.** *Ph*

Hempel, C. (1966), *Philosophy of Natural Science,* Prentice Hall.
Hewitt, C. (1975), 'How to use what you know', *IJCAI* **4**.
Hexter, J.H. (1972), *The history primer*, Allen Lane, London. *E*
Hintikka, J.J. (1980), 'C.S. Peirce's first real discovery and its contemporary significance', *The Monist* **63**. *Ph*
Hinton, G.E. (1981), 'Shape representation in parallel systems', *IJCAI* **7**. *Ph*
Hodges, A. (1983), *Allan Turing: the enigma*, Burnett Books, London.
Hofstadter, D.R. (1977), *Godel Escher Bach, an eternal golden braid*, Harvester Press, Brighton.
Hofstadter, D.W. and Dennett, D.C. (eds.), *The mind's I: fantasies and reflections on self and soul*, Harvester Press, Brighton. *Ph*
Hogben, L. (1967), *Mathematics for the million*, Allen and Unwin, London.
Hogger, C.J. (1978), 'Program synthesis in predicate logic', *Proceedings AISB/GI Conference on AI*, Hamburg, July 18–20. *E*
Hogger, C.J. (1981), 'Derivation of logic programs', *Journal of the Association of Computing Machinery* **28**. *E*
Holmes, L. (1966), 'Peirce on self-control', *Transactions of the C.S. Peirce Society* **2**. *Ph*
Hook, S. (ed.) (1960), *Dimensions of mind: a symposium*, New York University Press, New York/Collier-Macmillan, London. *Ph*
Hookway, C. (ed.) (1984), *Minds machines and evolution*, Cambridge University Press, Cambridge. *Ph*
Holt, J. (1964), *How children fail*, Penguin, London. *E*
Holt, J. (1967), *How children learn*, Penguin, London. *E*
Howe, J.A.M., O'Shea, T. and Plane, F. (1980), 'Teaching mathematics through LOGO programming: an evaluation study', *Proceedings of IFIP Working Conference on Computer Assisted Learning*, London. *E*
Howe, J.A.M., O'Shea, T. and Plane, F. (1980), 'Teaching mathematics through LOGO programming: an evaluation study', in Lewis and Tagg (eds.).
Howe, J.A.M., Ross, P.M., Johnson, K.R., Plane, F. and Inglis, R. (1982), 'Teaching mathematics through programming', *Computer and Education* **6**. *E*
Howe, J.A.M., Ross, P.M., Johnson, K.R., Plane, F. and Inglis, R. (1982), 'Learning mathematics through LOGO programming: the transition from laboratory to classroom', Working Paper No. 118(b), Department of Artificial Intelligence, University of Edinburgh. *E*
Hsiang, J. (1982), *Topics in automated theorem proving and program generation*, unpublished Ph.D. thesis, Department of Computer Science, University of Illinois. *Ph*
Hudson, L. (1968), 'Contrary imaginations', Penguin, London.
Hughes, G.E. and Cresswell, M.J. (1977), *An introduction to modal logic*, Methuen, London.
Hume, D. (1955), *A treatise of human nature*, (B.A. Selby-Bigge (ed.)) Oxford University Press, Oxford. *Ph*
IJCAI 5 (1977), Proceedings of the 5th International Joint Conference on Artificial Intelligence (held in Cambridge, Massachusetts), Computer Science

Department, Stanford University, Stanford.

IJCAI 6 (1979), Proceedings of the 6th International Joint Conference on Artificial Intelligence (held in Tokyo), Department of Computer Science, Stanford University, Stanford.

IJCAI 7 (1981), Proceedings of the 7th International Joint Conference on Artificial Intelligence (held in Vancouver), AAAI, Menlo Park.

IJCAI 8 (1983), Proceedings of the 8th International Joint Conference on Artificial Intelligence (held in Karlsruhe), IJCAI.

Inhelder, B. and Karmiloff-Smith, A. (1975), 'If you want to get ahead, get a theory', *Cognition* **3**. *Ph*

Jeffrey, R. (1967), *Formal logic: its scope and limits*, McGraw-Hill, New York. *Ph*

Jeffries, R. (1982), 'A comparison of the debugging behaviour of expert and novice programmers', Paper presented at the AER annual meeting, March 1982. *E*

Johnson-Laird, P.N. and Wason, P.C. (eds.) (1977), *Thinking: readings in cognitive science*, Cambridge University Press, Cambridge.

Jones, A. (1982), 'The role of metaphors in novices learning programming', *Proceedings of the fourth annual Cognitive Science Society Conference*, Ann Arbor, Michigan. *E*

Jones, A., Scanlon, E. and O'Shea, T. (eds.) (1983), *New technologies in distance education*, Harvester Press, Brighton.

Julian, S. (1982), *Graphics in Micro-PROLOG*, unpublished M.Sc. thesis, Department of Computing, Imperial College, London. *E*

Junt, J. (ed.), 'Computers in secondary school history teaching', *Historica Association* **40**. *E*

Kahn, K. (1975), A LOGO natural language system, *LOGO working paper* **46**, MIT AI Laboratory.

Kahn, K. (1977), 'Three interactions between AI and education', in Elcock and Michie (eds.).

Kahn, K. (1983), *Unique features of the LISP Machine PROLOG*, University of Massachusetts Press, Amherst, Massachusetts.

Kahney, H. (1982), 'An in-depth study of the cognitive behaviour of novice programmers', Technical Report No. 5, Human Cognition Research Laboratory, Open University, Milton Keynes. *E*

Kahney, H. (1983), 'Problem solving by novice programmers', in *The psychology of computer use: a European perspective*, Green, Payne and van der Veer (eds.).

Karmiloff-Smith, A. (1979), 'Micro- and macro-developmental changes in language acquisition and other representational systems', *Cognitive Science* **3**. *Ph*

Kassirer, J.P., Kuipers, B.J. and Gorry, G.A. (1982), 'Towards a theory of clinical expertise', *American Journal of Medicine* **73**.

Kayser, D. and Coulon, D. (1981), 'Variable-depth natural language understanding', *IJCAI* **7**. *Ph*

Kephart, N.C. (1971), *The slow learner in the classroom*, Merrill, London.

Klein, S. (1975), 'Meta-compiling text grammars as a mode for human behaviour', in Schank and Nash-Webber (eds.).

Kling, R.E. (1971), 'A paradigm for reasoning by analogy', *Artificial Intelligence*

2. *Ph*

Kodratoff, Y. (1982), 'Generalizing and particularizing as the techniques of learning', *Proceedings International Conference on AI and Information-control of Robots*, Bratisla.

Kolata, G. (1982), 'How can computers get common sense?', *Science* **217**.

Kornfeld, W.A. (1982), 'Combinatorially implosive algorithms', *Communications of the Association of Computing Machinery* **22**. *E*

Kowalski, R.A. (1974), 'Predicate logic as programming language', *Proceedings IFIP–74 Congress*, North-Holland, Amsterdam. *E*

Kowalski, R.A. (1979), 'Algorithm=logic+control', *Communications of the Association of Computing Machinery* **12**. *E*

Kowalski, R.A. (1979), *Logic for problem solving*, North-Holland/Elsevier, New York. *E, Ph*

Kowalski, R.A. (1982), 'Logic programming and the fifth generation', in *State of the Art Report on Fifth Generation Computing*, Pergamon Infotech. *Ph*

Kowalski, R.A. (1982), 'PROLOG as a logic programming language', Proceedings of AICA Congress, Pavia, Italy (or Research Report DOC 81/26, Department of Computing, Imperial College, London). *E*

Kowalski, R.A. (1984), 'Logic as a computer language for children', in Yazdani (ed.).

Kriwaczek, F.R. (1982), *Some applications of PROLOG to decision support systems*, unpublished M.Sc. thesis, Department of Computing, Imperial College, London. *E*

Kripke, S. (1982), *Wittgenstein on rules and private language*, Blackwell, London. *Ph*

Kuhn, T. (1970), *The structure of scientific revolution*, 2nd edition, Chicago University Press, Chicago. *Ph*

Kulikowski, C.A. and Weiss, S.M. (1982), 'Representation of expert knowledge for consultation: the CASNET and EXPERT projects', in Szolovits (ed.).

Labbett, B.D.C. (1980), 'The computer in local history teaching', in Junt (ed.).

Lakatos, I. and Musgrave, A. (eds.) (1970), *Criticism and the growth of knowledge*, Cambridge University Press, Cambridge.

Larkin, J.H., McDermott, J., Simon, D.P. and Simon, H.A. (1980), 'Expert and novice performance in solving physics problems', *Science* **208**. *E*

Larsson, Y. (ed.) (1984), *Bringing the past alive: history teaching in the eighties*, Allen and Unwin, Sydney.

Laubsch, J. and Eisenstad, M. (1982), 'Using temporal abstraction to understand recursive programs involving side effects', Proceedings of the National Conference on Artificial Intelligence (sponsored by the American Association for Artificial Intelligence), Carnegie-Mellon University and University of Pittsburgh, Pittsburgh, USA. *E*

Lawler, R. (1979), *One child's learning: an intimate study*, unpublished Ph.D. thesis, MIT, Massachusetts. *E*

Lehnert, W.G. (1978), *The process of question answering*, Lawrence Erlbaum Associates, New Jersey.

Lenat, D.B. (1983), 'EURISKO: A program that learns new heuristics and domain concepts', *Artificial Intelligence* **21**.

Lenat W.G. (1977), 'Automated theory formation in mathematics', *IJCAI* **5**. *Ph*

Lewis, D. (1966), 'An argument for the identity theory', *Journal of Philosophy*. *Ph*

Lewis, D. (1972), 'Psychophysical and theoretical identifications', *Australasian Journal of Philosophy* **50**. *Ph*

Lewis, M. (1980), 'Improving Solo's user interface: an empirical study of user behaviour and proposals for cost-effective enhancements to Solo', Computer Assisted Learning Research Group Technical Report No. 7, Open University, Milton Keynes. *E*

Lewis, R. and Tagg, E.D. (eds.) (1980), *Computer assisted learning*, North-Holland, Amsterdam.

Lighthill, J. *et al.* (1973), *Artificial intelligence: a paper symposium*, Science Research Council, London.

Lindsay, R., Buchanan, B.G., Feigenbaum, E.A. and Lederberg, J. (1980), *Application of artificial intelligence for organic chemistry: the DENDRAL project*, McGraw-Hill, New York.

Lockhead, J. and Clement, J. (eds.) (1979), *Cognitive process instruction*, The Franklin Institute Press, Philadelphia.

Lucas, J.R. (1961), 'Minds, machines and Godel', *Philosophy* **36**. Reprinted in Anderson (ed.). *Ph*

Lycan, W.G. (1979), 'A new Lilliputian argument against machine functionalism', *Philosophical Studies* **35**. *Ph*

Lycan, W.G. (1981), 'Form, function and feel', *Journal of Philosophy* **78**. *Ph*

Lyons, J. (1968), *Introduction to theoretical linguistics*, Cambridge University Press, Cambridge. *Ph*

McCabe, F.G. (1980), *Micro-PROLOG programmer's reference manual*, Logic Programming Associates, London. *E*

McCarthy, J., Abrahams, P.W., Edwards, D.J., Hart, T.P. and Levin, M.I. (1965), *LISP 1.5 programmer's manual*, MIT Press, Cambridge, Massachusetts.

McCarthy, J. and Hayes, J.P. (1968), 'Some philosophical problems from the standpoint of artificial intelligence', in Meltzer and Michie (eds.).

McCarthy, J. (1977), 'Epistemological problems of artificial intelligence', *IJCAI* **5**. *Ph*

McCarthy, J. (1980), 'Circumscription: a form of non-monotonic reasoning', *Artificial Intelligence* **13**. *Ph*

McClelland, J.L. and Rumelhart, D.E. (1981), 'An interactive activation mode of context effects in letter perception', *Psychological Review* **9**.

McCorduck, P. (1979), *Machines who think*, Freeman, San Francisco.

McCulloch, W.S. and Pitts, W.H. (1943), 'A logical calculus of ideas imminent in nervous activity', *Bulletin of Mathematical Biophysics* **5**.

McDermott, D. (1980), 'The PROLOG phenomenon', *SIGART Newsletter* **72**. *E*

McDermott, D. (1981), 'Artificial intelligence meets natural stupidity', in Haugeland (ed.). *Ph*

McDonald, B. (1977), 'The education value of NDPCAL', *British Journal of Educational Technology* **8**.

McGinn, C. (1982), 'The structure of content', in Woodfield (ed.). *Ph*

McKeithen, K.B., Reitman, J.S., Rueter, H.H. and Hurtle, S.C. (1981), 'Knowledge organisation and skill differences in computer programmers', *Cognitive Psychology* **13**. *E*

Malone, T.W. (1980), *What makes things fun to learn?* Unpublished Ph.D. thesis, Department of Psychology, Stanford University.

Malone, T.W. (1981), 'Towards a theory of intrinsically motivating instruction', *Cognitive Science* **4**.

Mangold, T. (1983), 'Beyond deterrence', *The Listener*, 8 September. *Ph*

Marr, D. (1981), *Vision*, Freeman, San Francisco. *Ph*

Marr, D. (1977), 'Artificial intelligence – a personal view', *Artificial Intelligence* **9**. Reprinted in Haugeland (ed.).

Masterman, M. (1970), 'The nature of a paradigm', in Lakatos and Musgrave (eds.).

Maxwell, W. (ed.) (1983), *Thinking: the new frontier*, Franklin Press, Pittsburgh.

Mayer, R.E. (1981), 'The psychology of how novices learn computer programming', Association of Computing Machinery, *Computing Surveys* **13**. *E*

Meehan, J.R. (1976), 'The metanovel: writing stories by computer', Research Report No. 74, Yale University. *Ph*

Melden, A.I. (1961), *Free action*, Routledge & Kegan Paul, London. *Ph*

Mellish, C.S. and Hardy, S. (1983), 'Integrating PROLOG in the POPLOG environment', *Cognitive Science Research Papers* **10**, University of Sussex. *E*

Mellor, D. (1974), 'In defence of dispositions', *Philosophical Review* **83**. *Ph*

Mellor, D. (ed.) (1980), *Prospects for pragmatism*, Cambridge University Press, Cambridge. *Ph*

Meltzer, B. and Michie, D. (eds.) (1968), *Machine Intelligence* **3**, Edinburgh University Press, Edinburgh.

Melzak, Z.A. (1983), *Bypasses: a simple approach to complexity*, Wiley, New York.

Merleau-Ponty, M. (1972), *The phenomenology of perception*, Routledge & Kegan Paul, London. *Ph*

Michalski, R.S., Carbonell, J.G. and Mitchell, T.M. (eds.) (1982), *Machine learning: the artificial intelligence approach*, Tioga Publishing Co., Palo Alto. *E*

Michie, D. (ed.) (1968), *Machine Intelligence* **3**, Edinburgh University Press, Edinburgh.

Michie, D. (1980), 'P–KP4: expert system to human benign conceptual checkmate of dark ingenuity', *Computing*, July 17.

Michie, D. (1980), 'Social aspects of artificial intelligence', Machine Intelligence Research Unit Memo, University of Edinburgh.

Michie, D. and Meltzer, B. (eds.) (1969), *Machine Intelligence* **4**, Edinburgh University Press, Edinburgh.

Miller, G.A. and Johnson-Laird, P. (1976), *Language and perception*, Belknap Press, Cambridge, Massachusetts. *Ph*

Miller, L. (1978), 'Has artificial intelligence contributed to an understanding of the human unit? A critique of the arguments for and against', *Cognitive Science* **2**.

Miller, M.L. (1982), 'A structured planning and debugging environment for

elementary programming', in Sleeman and Brown (eds.).
Miller, R.A., Pople, H.E. and Myers, J.D. (1982), 'INTERNIST – an experimental computer-based diagnostic consultant for general internal medicine', *New England Journal of Medicine* **307**.
Millner, M.A. (1967), *Negligence in modern law*, Butterworth, London.
Minsky, M. (ed.) (1968a), *Semantic information processing*, MIT Press, Cambridge, Massachusetts. *Ph*
Minsky, M. (1968b), 'Matter, mind and models', in Minsky (ed.).
Minsky, M.L. (1975), 'A framework for representing knowledge', in Winston (ed.).
Monod, J. (1972), *Chance and necessity*, Collins, London.
Moore, R.C. (1977), 'Reasoning about knowledge and action', *IJCAI* **5**. *Ph*
Morton, A. (1980), *Frames of mind*, Oxford University Press, Oxford. *Ph*
Morton, J. (1969), 'The interaction of information in word recognition', *Psychological Review* **76**.
Moses, J. (1971), 'Algebraic simplification: a guide for the perplexed', *Communications of Association for Computing Machinery* **14**.
Moto-oka, T. (ed.) (1982), *Fifth generation computer systems: proceedings of the International Conference on Fifth Generation Computer Systems*, North-Holland, Amsterdam.
Nagel, T. (1974), 'What is it like to be a bat?', *Philosophical Review* **83**. Reprinted in Nagel (1979).
Nagel, T. (1979), *Mortal questions*, Cambridge University Press, Cambridge.
Narayanan, A. (1981), 'Ascribing mental predicates to computers', Research Report R.102, Department of Computer Science, University of Exeter.
Narayanan, A. and Perrott, D. (1981), 'Can computers have legal rights?', in this volume.
Nasr, S.H. (1975), *Islam and the plight of modern man*, Longmans, London and New York.
Neisser, U. (1967), *Cognitive psychology*, Appleton-Century-Crofts, New York.
Newell, A. and Simon, H.A. (1963), 'GPS, a program that simulates human thought', in Feigenbaum and Feldman (eds.).
Newell, A. and Simon, H.A. (1972), *Human problem solving*, Prentice-Hall, New Jersey. *E*
Newell, A. and Simon, H.A. (1976), 'Computer science as empirical enquiry: symbols and search', *Communications of the Association for Computing Machinery* **14**. Reprinted in Haugeland (ed.). *Ph*
Nisbett, R.E. and Wilson, T.D. (1977), 'Telling more than we can know: verbal reports on mental processes', *Psychological Review* **84**.
Noble, D.F. (1978), 'Social choice in machine design', *Politics and Society* **8**.
Norman, D.A. (1982), 'Some observations on mental models', in Gentner and Stevens (eds.).
O'Shea, T. and Eisenstadt, M. (eds.) (1984), *Artificial Intelligence: tools, techniques and applications*, Harper & Row, New York.
O'Shea, T. and Self, J. (1983), *Learning and teaching with computers*, The Harvester Press, Brighton. *E*
Papert, S. (1971), 'Teaching children to be mathematicians versus teaching

about mathematics', *MIT AI Lab Memo* **249**, MIT Press, Cambridge, Massachusetts.

Papert, S., Watt, D., di Sessa, A. and Weir, S. (1979), 'Final report of the Brookline LOGO project', *MIT LOGO Memo No.* **53**, MIT Press, Cambridge, Massachusetts. *E*

Papert, S. (1979), 'Computer and learning', in Dertouzos and Moses (eds.).

Papert, S. (1980), *Mindstorms, children, computers and powerful ideas*, The Harvester Press, Brighton/Basic Books, New York. *E*

Paraskevopoulos, J.N. and Kirk, S.A. (1969), *The development and psychometric characteristics of the revised Illinois test of psycholinguistic abilities*, University of Illinois Press, Chicago.

Parkinson, G.H.R. (ed.) (1966), *Liebniz – logical papers*, Oxford University Press, Oxford. *Ph*

Patil, R., Szolovits, P. and Schwartz, W.B. (1982), 'Modelling knowledge of the patient in acid-base and electrolyte disorders', in Szolovits (ed.).

Peirce, C.S. (1877), 'Logical machines', *Amsterdam Journal of Psychology*, Nov. 1877; reprinted in Peirce (1976). *Ph*

Peirce, C.S. (1976), *The new elements of mathematics*, compiled by Eisele, C., (4 vols.), Mouton, The Hague. *Ph*

Pereira, L., Pereira, F.C.N. and Warren, D.H.D. (1979), 'User's guide to DEC-system–10, PROLOG', Occasional Paper 15, Department of Artificial Intelligence, University of Edinburgh. *Ph*

Pereira, F. and Warren, D. (1980), 'Definite clause grammars for language analysis – a survey of the formalism and comparison with augmented transition networks', *Artificial Intelligence* **13**. *E*

Perry, J. (1977), 'Frege on demonstratives', *Philosophical Review* **86**. *Ph*

Perry, J. (1979), 'The problem of the essential indexical', *Nous* **13**. *Ph*

Pettitt, P. (1979), 'On the interaction between psychology and artificial intelligence', *Artificial Intelligence and Simulation of Behaviour* **35**.

Piaget, J. (1948), *The moral judgement of the child*, Routledge & Kegan Paul, London.

Plotkin, G.D. (1970), 'A note on inductive generalization', in Meltzer and Michie (eds.). *Ph*

Polanyi, M. (1967), *The tacit dimension*, Routledge & Kegan Paul, London.

Polya, G. (1945), *How to solve it*, Princeton University Press, New Jersey. *E*

Polya, G. (1962), *Mathematics and plausible reasoning*, Vols. I and II, Princeton University Press, New Jersey. *Ph*

Pool, I. de S. (1983), *Technologies of freedom*, Harvard University Press, Cambridge, Massachusetts.

Pople, H.E. (1982), 'Heuristic methods for imposing structure on ill-structured problems: the structuring of medical diagnostics', in Szolovits (ed.).

Popper, K.R. (1959), *The logic of scientific discovery*, Hutchinson, London.

Popper, K.R. (1963), *The poverty of historicism*, 2nd edition, Routledge & Kegan Paul, London.

Popper, K.R. (1965), *Conjectives and refutations*, Routledge, London.

Popper, K.R. (1972), *Objective knowledge*, Clarendon Press, Oxford.

Proceedings of International Conference on Fifth Generation Computer Systems (see Moto-oka (ed.)).

Punnett, R.M. (1968), *British government and politics*, Heinmann Educational Books, London.

Putnam, H. (1960), 'Minds and machines', in Hook (ed.); reprinted in Putnam (1975b) and Anderson (ed.).

Putnam, H. (1964), 'Robots: machines or artificially created life?', *Journal of Philosophy* **61**. *Ph*

Putnam, H. (1967a), 'Psychological predicates', in Capitan and Merrill (eds.).

Putnam, H. (1967b), 'The mental life of some machines', in Castaneda (ed.).

Putnam, H. (1975a), 'The meaning of 'meaning' ', in Putnam (1975b). *Ph*

Putnam, H. (1975b), *Mind, language and reality – philosophical papers*, vol. 2, Cambridge University Press, Cambridge. *Ph*

Putnam, H. (1975c), 'Philosophy and our mental life', in Putnam (1975b).

Putnam, H. (1981), *Reason, truth and history*, Cambridge University Press, Cambridge. *Ph*

Pylyshyn, Z.W. (1973), 'What the mind's eye tells the mind's brain: a critique of mental imagery', *Psychological Bulletin* **80**.

Quine, W.V.O. (1960), *Word and object*, MIT Press, Cambridge, Massachusetts. *Ph*

Quine, W.V.O. (1975), 'Mind and verbal dispositions', in Guttenplan (ed.).

Ramsey, F.P. (1978), *Foundations: essays in philosophy, logic, mathematics and economics*, compiled by Mellor, D.H., Routledge & Kegan Paul, London. *Ph*

Reichardt, J. (1978), *Robots: fact, fiction and prediction*, Thames and Hudson, London.

Reid, L.A. (1981a), 'Intuition and art', *Journal of Aesthetic Education* **15**.

Reid, L.A. (1981b), 'Intuition, discursiveness and aesthetic alchemy', *Philosophy* **56**.

Reif, F. (1980), 'Theoretical and educational concerns with problem solving: bridging the gaps with human cognitive engineers', in Tuma and Reif (eds.).

Reiger, C.J. (1975), 'Conceptual memory and inference', in Schank (ed.) (1975). *Ph*

Reisbeck, C.K. (1975), 'Conceptual analysis', in Schank (ed.). *Ph*

Reiter, R. (1980), 'A logic for default reasoning', *Artificial Intelligence* **13**. *Ph*

Reitman, W.R. (1965), *Cognition and thought: an information processing approach*, Wiley, New York.

Reswick, C.A. (1975), *Computational models of learners for CAL*, unpublished Ph.D. thesis, University of Illinois.

Ringle, M. (ed.) (1979), *Philosophical perspectives in artificial intelligence*, Harvester Press, Brighton. *Ph*

Robin, R.S. (ed.) (1967), *Annotated catalogue of the papers of C.S. Peirce*, MIT Press, Cambridge, Massachusetts. *Ph*

Robinson, J.A. (1965), 'A machine-oriented logic based on the resolution of principle', *Journal of the Association for Computing Machinery* **12**. *E, Ph*

Robinson, J.A. (1970), *Logic: form and function, the mechanisation of deductive reasoning*, Edinburgh University Press, Edinburgh. *Ph*

Robinson, J.A. (1983), 'Logical reasoning in machines', in Hayes and Michie (eds.).

Robinson, J.A. and Sibert, E.E. (1981), 'LOGLISP: motivation, design and implementation', in Clark and Tärnlund (eds.). *E, Ph*

Robinson, J.A. and Sibert, E.E. (1982), 'LOGLISP: an alternative to PROLOG', in Hayes, Michie and Pao (eds.). *Ph*

Rogers, C. (1983), *Freedom to learn for the 80s*, Charles E. Merrill, Columbus. *E*

Rogers, P. (1984), 'The dehumanising force of AI', in this volume.

Rogers, W.V.H. (1979), *Winfield and Jolowicz on Tort*, (11th edition), Sweet and Maxwell, London.

Rorty, R. (1980), *Philosophy and the mirror of nature*, Blackwell, Oxford. *Ph*

Rosenbrock, H. (1982), 'Technology politics and options', *EEC First Conference on Information Technology*.

Roszak, T. (1972), *Where the wasteland ends*, Faber & Faber, London.

Rubinoff, M. and Yovits, M.C. (eds.) (1976), *Advances in Computers* Vol. 16, Academic Press, London.

Rumelhart, D.E. and Norman, D.A. (1975), *Explorations in cognition*, Freeman & Co., San Francisco. *Ph*

Rushby, N.J. (ed.) (1983), *Computer based learning*, Pergamon Infotech.

Russell, B. and Whitehead, A.N. (1913), *Principia Mathematica*, Vol. I, Cambridge University Press, Cambridge.

Ryle, G. (1949), *The concept of mind*, Hutchinson, London. *Ph*

Ryle, G. (1973), 'Review of Anthony Quinton, the nature of things', *New Statesman*, April 6. *Ph*

Sage, M. and Smith, D.J. (1983), 'Microcomputers in education', Social Science Research Council, London.

Santane-Toth, E. and Szeredi, P. (1983), 'PROLOG applications in Hungary', in Clark and Tärnlund (eds.). *Ph*

Sato, M. and Sakurai, T. (1983), *QUTE: a PROLOG/LISP type language for logic programming*, University of Tokyo. *Ph*

Schank, R.C. (1973), *Causality and reasoning*, Instituto per gli studi semantici e cognitivi, Castagnola, Switzerland. *Ph*

Schank, R.C. (ed.) (1975), *Conceptual information processing*, American Elsevier, New York. *Ph*

Schank, R.C. (1979), 'Natural language, philosophy and artificial intelligence', in Ringle (ed.).

Schank, R.C. (1982), 'Looking at learning', *Proceedings ECAI-82*, Orsay. *Ph*

Schank, R.C. (1982), *Dynamic memory*, Cambridge University Press, Cambridge.

Schank, R.C. and Abelson, R.P. (1977), *Scripts, plan, goals and understanding*, Lawrence Erlbaum, New Jersey.

Schank, R.C. and Colby, K.M. (eds.) (1973), *Computer models of thought and language*, Freeman, San Francisco.

Schank, R.C. and Nash Webber (eds.) (1975), *Theoretical issues in natural language processing*, Freeman, San Francisco.

Schiffer, S. (1978), 'The basis of reference', *Erkenntnis* **13**. *Ph*

Schlipp, P.A. (ed.) (1946), *The philosophy of Bertrand Russell*, Northern

University Press, Evanston. *Ph*

Searle, J.R. (1980), 'Minds, brains and programs', The Behavioural and Brain Sciences 3, in Haugeland (ed.). *Ph*

Self, J. (1974), 'Student models in computer aided instruction', *International Journal of Man-Machine Studies* **6**.

Sergot, M. (1983), 'A query-the-user facility for logic programming', in Yazdani (ed.).

Shapiro, S.C. (1979), *Techniques of artificial intelligence*, Van Nostrand, New York.

Sheil, B.A. (1981), 'The psychological study of programming', *Computing Surveys* **13**. *E*

Shemilt, D. (1980), *History 13–16 Evaluation Study*, Holmes McDougall. *E*

Shoemaker, S. (1982), 'Some varieties of functionalism', in Biro and Shahan (eds.). *Ph*

Shortliffe, E.H. (1976), *Computer based medical consultations: MYCIN*, American Elsevier, New York.

Simon, H.A. (1977), 'What computers mean for man and society', *Science* **195**. Reprinted in Forester (ed.).

Simon, H.A. (1981), *The sciences of the artificial*, 2nd edition, MIT Press, Cambridge, Massachusetts.

Simon, H.A. and Barenfield, M. (1984), 'Information-processing analysis of perceptual processes in problem solving', *Psychological Review* **76**. *E*

Skinner, B.F. (1954), 'The science of learning and the art of teaching', *Harvard Education Review* **24**.

Skinner, B.F. (1957), *Verbal behaviour*, Appleton Croft, New York.

Skinner, B.F. (1971), *Beyond freedom and dignity*, Knopf, New York/Penguin, London.

Sklansky, J. and Wassel, G.N. (1981), *Pattern classifiers and trainable machines*, Springer-Verlag, Berlin.

Sleeman, D. (1984), *Computer literacy and the schools: what is needed? what is possible?*, School of Education, Stanford University. *E*

Sleeman, D. and Brown, J. (eds.) (1982), *Intelligent tutoring systems*, Academic Press, London. *E*

Sloman, A. (1978a), *The computer revolution in philosophy: philosophy, science and models of mind*, Harvester Press, Brighton.

Sloman, A. (1978b), 'The methodology of artificial intelligence', *Artificial Intelligence and Simulation of Behaviour* **30**.

Sloman, A. (1978c), 'Intuition and analogical reasoning', in Sloman (1978a).

Sloman, A. (1984), 'The state of possible minds', in Torrance (ed.).

Sloman, A., Hardy, S. and Gibson, J. (1983), 'POPLOG: a multilanguage program development environment', *Information Technology: Research and Development* **2**. *E*

Smith, H.T. and Green, T.R.G. (eds.) (1980), *Human interaction with computers*, Academic Press, London. *E*

Sober, E. (1982), 'Why must Homunculi be so stupid?' *Mind* **91**. *Ph*

Soloway, E., Ehrlich, K. and Bonar, J. (1982), 'Tapping into tacit programming knowledge', *Proceedings of the Conference on Human Factors in Computing*, ACM Washington Chapter, Washington D.C. *E*

Spiegelhalter, D.J. and Knill-Jones, R.P. (1984), 'Statistical and knowledge-based approaches to clinical decision-support systems, with an application in gastroenterology', *Journal of the Royal Statistical Society, Series A* **147**.

Stansfield, J., Carr, B. and Goldstein, I. (1976), 'WUMPUS advisor I: a first implementation of a program that tutors logical and probabilistic skills', *MIT AI Lab Memo* **381**, MIT Press, Massachusetts.

Stevens, A., Collins, A. and Goldin, S. (1982), 'Misconceptions in students' understanding', in Sleeman and Brown (eds.).

Stich, S. (1978), 'Beliefs and subdoxastic states', *Philosophy of Science* **45**. *Ph*

Stich, S. (1979), 'Do animals have beliefs?' *Australasian Journal of Philosophy* **57**. *Ph*

Stich, S. (1982), 'On the ascription of content', in Woodfield (ed.). *Ph*

Stich, S. (1982), 'Dennett on intentional systems', in Biro and Shahan. *Ph*

Stickel, M.E. (1981), 'A unification algorithm for associative-commutative functions', *Journal of Association for Computing Machinery* **28**. *Ph*

Strawson, P.F. (1959), *Individuals*, Methuen, London. *Ph*

Suppes, P. (ed.) (1973), *Logic, methodology and philosophy of science*, Vol. 4, North-Holland, Amsterdam.

Suppes, P. and Morningstar, M. (1972), *Computer-assisted instruction at Stanford*, Academic Press, New York. *E*

Sussman, G.J. (1975), *A computer model of skill acquisition*, American Elsevier, New York.

Szolovits, P. (ed.) (1982), *Artificial intelligence in medicine*, Westview Press, Colorado.

Takeuchi *et al.* (1982), *New unified environment*, Nippon Telegram and Telephone Public Corpn. *Ph*

Tarski, A. (1969a), *Logic, semantics, metamathematics*, Oxford University Press, Oxford.

Tarski, A. (1969b), 'The establishment of scientific semantics', in Tarski (1969a). *Ph*

Taube, M. (1961), *Computers and commonsense*, Columbia, New York.

Thomas, S.N. (1978), *The formal mechanics of mind*, Harvester Press, Brighton. *Ph*

Torrance, S. (ed.) (1984), *The mind and the machine: philosophical aspects of artificial intelligence*, Ellis Horwood, Chichester.

Tough, J. (1977), *Talking and learning*, Schools Council/Ward Lock Educational. *E*

Turing, A.M. (1937), 'On computable numbers with an application to the Entscheidungsproblem', *Proceedings London Mathematical Society* **42**. *Ph*

Turing, A.M. (1950), 'Computing machinery and intelligence', *Mind* **59**. Reprinted in Feigenbaum and Feldman (eds.) and in Anderson (ed.).

Ullman, S. (1979), *The interpretation of visual motion*, MIT Press, Cambridge, Massachusetts.

van Ganeghem, M. (ed.) (1982), *Proceedings of the First International Logic*

Programming Conference, Marseille. *Ph*
van Heijenoort, J. (ed.) (1967), *From Frege to Godel*, Harvard University Press, Harvard. *Ph*
Vere, S.A. (1980), 'Multilevel counterfactuals for generalizations of relational concepts and productions', *Artificial Intelligence Journal* **14.** *Ph*
Waltz, D. (1975), 'Understanding line drawings of scenes with shadows', in Winston (ed.).
Warnock, M. (1978), *A Report to the Committee of Enquiry into the Education of Handicapped Children and Young People with Educational Needs*, HMSO, London.
Warren, D. (1981), 'Higher-order extensions to PROLOG – are they needed?', in Hayes and Michie (eds.). *E*
Warren, D.H.D. and Pereira, F.L.N. (1982), 'An efficient, easily adaptable system for interpreting natural language queries', *American Journal of Computational Linguistics* **8.**
Waterman, D.A. and Hayes-Roth, F. (1978), *Pattern-directed inference systems*, Academic Press, New York. *Ph*
Weinreb, D. and Moon, D. (1981), *LISP machine manual*, AI Laboratory, MIT. *E*
Weir, D. (1982), *Teaching logic programming: an interactive approach*, unpublished M.Sc. thesis, Department of Computing, Imperial College, London. *E*
Weiss, S.M., Kulikowski, C.A. and Galen, R.S. (1981), 'Developing microprocessor based expert models for instrument interpretation', *IJCAI* **3.**
Weizenbaum, J. (1976), *Computer power and human reason: from judgement to calculation*, Freeman, San Francisco. *E*
Weizenbaum, J. (1967), 'Contextual understanding by computers', *Communications of the Association for Computing Machinery* **10.**
Weizenbaum, J. (1965), 'ELIZA – A computer program for the study of natural communication between man and machine', *Communications of the Association for Computing Machinery* **9.**
Weizenbaum, J. (1984), *Computer power and human reason*, Penguin, London/Freeman, San Francisco.
Weyhrauch, R. (1980), 'PROLOGomena to a theory of mechanized formal reasoning', *Artificial Intelligence* **13.** *E*
Whitehead, A.N. (1967) (originally unpublished in 1929), *The aims of education*, The Free Press, New York. *E*
Whiteley, C.H. (1962), 'Minds, machines and Godel: a reply to Mr. Lucas', *Philosophy* **37.** *Ph*
Wickelgren, W.A. (1974), *How to solve problems*, Freeman, San Francisco. *E*
Wiener, N. (1965), *Cybernetics*, second edition, MIT Press, Cambridge, Massachusetts. *Ph*
Wilks, Y.A. (1972), *Grammar, meaning and the machine analysis of language*, Routledge & Kegan Paul, London.
Wilks, Y.A. (1975), 'A preferential pattern-seeking, semantics for natural language', *Artificial Intelligence* **6.**
Wilks, Y.A. (forthcoming), 'Machines and consciousness', in Hookway (ed.).
Winograd, T. (1972), *Understanding natural language*, Edinburgh University

Press, Edinburgh.

Winograd, T. (1975), 'Frames and the declarative-procedural controversy', in Bobrow and Collins (eds.). *Ph*

Winston, P.H. (ed.) (1975a), *The psychology of computer vision,* McGraw-Hill, New York.

Winston, P.H. (1975b), 'Learning structural descriptions from examples', in Winston (ed.).

Winston, P. (1977), *Artificial intelligence,* Addison-Wesley, Reading, Massachusetts.

Winston, P. (1980), *Communications of Association for Computing Machinery* **23**. *Ph*

Wittgenstein, L. (1953), *Philosophical investigations*, edited with English translation by G.E.M. Anscombe and R. Rhees (3rd edition 1968), Blackwell, Oxford. *Ph*

Woodfield, A. (ed.) (1982), *Thought and object: essays on intentionality*, Oxford University Press, Oxford. *Ph*

Yazdani, M. (1982), 'How to write a story', *Proceedings of the European Conference on Artificial Intelligence.*

Yazdani, M. (1984a), 'Towards a micro-PROLOG world for children', in *Proceedings of the 2nd Commodore in Education Conference,* Ellis Horwood, Chichester. *E*

Yazdani, M. (ed.). (1984b), *Micro-PROLOG programming,* Ellis Horwood, Chichester. *E*

Yazdani, M. (ed.) (1984c), *New horizons in educational computing,* Ellis Horwood, Chichester.

Yu, V., Buchanan, B., Shortliffe, E., Wraith, S., Davis, R., Scott, A. and Cohen, S. (1979), 'Evaluating the performance of a computer-based consultant', *Computer Programs in Biomedicine* **9**.

Zadeh, L.A. (1979), 'A theory of approximate reasoning', in Hayes, Michie and Mikulich (eds.).

Zadeh, L.A., Fu, K.S., Tanaka, K. and Shimura, M. (eds.) (1975), *Fuzzy sets and their applications to cognitive and decision processes*, Academic Press, New York.

Index